ETHNICITY AND DEVELOPMENT

ETHNICITY AND DEVELOPMENT
Geographical Perspectives

Edited by
Denis Dwyer
University of Keele, UK

and

David Drakakis-Smith
University of Liverpool, UK

JOHN WILEY & SONS
Chichester · New York · Brisbane · Toronto · Singapore

National 01243 779777
International (+44) 1243 779777

Other Wiley Editorial Offices

John Wiley & Sons, Inc., 605 Third Avenue,
New York, NY 10158-0012, USA

Jacaranda Wiley Ltd, 33 Park Road, Milton,
Queensland 4064, Australia

John Wiley & Sons (Canada) Ltd, 22 Worcester Road,
Rexdale, Ontario M9W IL1, Canada

John Wiley & Sons (SEA) Pte Ltd, 2 Clementi Loop #02-01,
Jing Xing Distripark, Singapore 0512

Library of Congress Cataloging-in-Publication Data

Ethnicity and development / edited by Denis Dwyer & David Drakakis
Smith.
p. cm.
Includes bibliographical references and index.
ISBN 0-471-96354-2
1. Ethnicity—Developing countries. 2. Pluralism (Social
sciences)—Developing countries. 3. Economic development—Political
aspects. I. Dwyer, D. J. (Denis John) II. Drakakis-Smith, D. W.
GN495.6.E878 1996
305.8'009172'4—dc20 95-47705
CIP

British Library Cataloguing in Publication Data

A catalogue record for this book is available from the British Library

ISBN 0-471-96354-2

Typeset in 10/12pt Palatino by Acorn Bookwork, Salisbury
Printed and bound in Great Britain by Biddles Ltd, Guildford and King's Lynn

This book is printed on acid-free paper responsibly manufactured from sustainable forestation, for which at least two trees are planted for each one used for paper production.

Contents

List of Contributors

Mr Dawit Abate is an Ethiopian writer

Dr Colin Clarke, Department of Geography, Oxford University, Mansfield Road, Oxford, OX1 3TB

Professor David Drakakis-Smith, Department of Geography, University of Liverpool, Liverpool, L69 3BX

Professor Denis Dwyer, Department of Geography, Keele University, Keele, Staffordshire, ST5 5BG

Ms Jill Eyre, Department of Geography, University of Derby, Derby, DE22 1GB

Professor Björn Hettne, Centre for Peace and Development Studies, University of Gothenburg, Brogatan 4, Gothenburg, 541301, Sweden

Mr Jayum A. Jawan, Department of Geography, University of Hull, Cottingham Road, Hull, HU6 7RX

Professor Terry King, Department of Geography, University of Hull, Cottingham Road, Hull, HU6 7RX

Dr Anthony Lemon, Department of Geography, Oxford University, Mansfield Road, Oxford, OX1 3TB

Dr Ooi Geok Ling, Institute of Policy Studies, National University of Singapore, Kent Ridge, Singapore

Dr Anders Närman, Department of Human and Economic Geography, Gothenburg University, Gothenburg, 541180, Sweden

Dr Michael Parnwell, Centre for Asian Studies, University of Hull, Cottingham Road, Hull, HU6 7RX

Dr Jonathan Rigg, Department of Geography, University of Durham, South Road, Durham, DH1 3LE

Dr Peggy Teo, Department of Geography, National University of Singapore, Kent Ridge, Singapore

Professor Colin Williams, Department of Welsh, University of Wales, Cardiff, CF1 3XW

Dr Abede Zegeye, Visiting Professor, Department of Black Studies, University of California, Santa Barbara, USA.

Part I

Introduction

1 Ethnodevelopment or ethnochaos?

Denis Dwyer

The increase in the number and intensity of ethnic conflicts has been a conspicuous contemporary phenomenon, to the extent that it has been estimated that of the 37 major armed conflicts in the world in 1991 25 were internal conflicts and that most of these could plausibly described as ethnic conflicts (Eriksen 1993, pp.2–3). Yet it is only since the late 1960s, in anthropology, and since the 1980s in the other social sciences, that the study of ethnicity has become a major preoccupation, a development that has paralleled, and undoubtedly reflected, the decline of the idea of the nation state as the principal territorial answer to the problem of human political, social and economic organization

During the first four-fifths of the present century, and particularly at the end of the First World War, the actual and anticipated break up of empires was met by the world's statesmen, initially under the leadership of President Woodrow Wilson, with a general endorsement of the principle of national self-determination and the creation of a succession of nation states. As Bogdanor (1994, p.7) has observed, in August 1914, with war inevitable, the Kaiser received the German Social Democrats with the words, 'I no longer recognize parties, I only recognize Germans'; and everywhere the masses found, contrary to Marx's prediction of international class-based revolution, that during the conflict they had much more in common with the ruling classes of their own country than with the workers of another. At the end of the war, not only had new nation states been established in Europe, but popular nationalism had come to prevail to such an extent that in some cases it even produced extreme anti-democratic forms such as National Socialism in Germany and Fascism in Italy.

A more lasting problem that resulted from the nationalist tide and the modern creation of nation states, however, was that there were virtually no homogeneous national populations to underpin them. As Gellner (1964, p.169) wrote, 'Nationalism is not the awakening of nations to self-

Ethnicity and Development: Geographical Perspectives. Edited by Denis Dwyer and David Drakakis-Smith.

consciousness: it invents nations where they did not exist.' Almost everywhere in Europe – and later in the tropical colonies too, as they came to independence and became nation states themselves – majorities were mingled with various numbers of minorities in the course of nation building. The 20th-century nation state thus contained *ab initio* the seeds of ethnic problems powerful enough in some cases to bring about its own dissolution, or near-dissolution.

What prevented this problem from emerging in full force before the late 1980s, however, was a further consequence of the First World War and its immediate aftermath: the victory of communism in Russia. Wherever it gained power, international communism suppressed popular nationalism, and as the world's nations split into two camps – a polarization that reached its zenith in the years after the Second World War – so the system of nation states became increasingly fossilized. The end came in 1989 with the collapse of communism in the Soviet Union, its fractioning into a number of ethnically based states and the conclusion of the Cold War. Within the New World Order which has followed, ethnicity has become a highly visible international issue.

Ethnicity is one aspect – now often a vital aspect – of relationships among groups. It is essentially concerned with the idea of distinctiveness, the Them and Us dichotomy, and distinctiveness on a claimed basis of shared origins and common cultural characteristics. Ethnicity is a product of contact, not isolation; indeed as Eriksen (1993, p.3) has put it, to consider ethnicity in terms of a totally isolated group would be as ridiculous as the idea of one hand clapping. If there are no distinctions between insiders and outsiders, there can be no ethnicity. Equally, it is easy to appreciate how in situations of political flux, migrational change and resource competition – to identify but a few major global trends – ethnic identities tend to attain their greatest significance. In addition, both contact and the pace of change of all kinds have increased very markedly as the present century has progressed. These are additional reasons for the emergence of the present situation of prevalent ethnic discontent, agitation and even violence in the world today.

Yet another reason is the persistence of global poverty, since it is by no means unusual to find particular ethnic groups associated with, and protesting against, poverty within specific national settings. It can be, and frequently has been, plausibly claimed that the failure both of the international community and of the nation state to deal effectively with problems of mass poverty following the Second World War has been a major contributor to the rise in ethnic tensions (Dwyer, in press). In what, in all too many cases, are euphemistically called the 'developing' countries, development programmes frequently are controlled and administered at the higher levels by members of the politically dominant ethnic group; and most of the fruits of such development flow into the pockets of a tiny ethnic elite or, at best, are distributed in a limited manner within the same ethnic group. An outstanding example is Nigeria where at present a small coterie of army generals from the poverty-stricken Muslim north controls both the political life and the wealth of the oil-rich non-Muslim south, which contains a variety of ethnic groups and a legacy of Christian missionary work. The south-east tried to break away from an earlier version of this situation in the Biafran war of the late 1960s, and while it is not likely that this disastrous experience will be repeated in the near future, secession is on the agenda as it is on the agenda of many other ethnic groups in Africa and elsewhere. The challenge in terms of the avoidance of future conflict based on ethnic secession is how to devise and implement equitable political and economic arrangements within states which contain an often bewildering variety of ethnic groups. With two thousand or so language groups and countless subdivisions of tribes and clans, Africa as a whole presents a seemingly intractable problem in this respect but one which is mirrored in varying degrees the world over.

The present book has been developed from papers originally presented at the Fifth Keele Geographical Symposium held in March 1993. It examines various aspects of this central problem, largely through detailed case studies focusing on the political and economic aspects of specific problem situations and of the difficulties involved in formulating comprehensive and innovative approaches that would be applicable within a context of what might be termed 'ethnodevelopment'.

As Hettne points out (Chapter 2), the ethnic struggles going on in all parts of the world present a major challenge to mainstream conceptions of development, both political and socio-economic, and raise the question of how material improvement can be made compatible with the maintenance of fundamental cultural identities which, in some senses, can even be considered a human right. To meet the problems of south Asia, which he discusses in detail and which, he asserts, currently exhibit strong evidence of tendencies towards ethnocidal development, further indigenization both of the social sciences in general and of development theory in particular will be necessary; and the logical goal of such a process must be the evolution of valid theories and workable local processes of ethnodevelopment. This is a radical concept since it turns the conventional conception of ethnicity as an obstacle to modernization on its head and in the process reverses the prevalent bias favouring national, as against ethnic, identification.

For Hettne, ethnodevelopment is a variety of the Another Development tradition (Hettne, 1995), not an alternative form of development but rather an essential precondition for harmonious development. Its essential principles are: (1) the acceptance of cultural pluralism in place of the prevailing hegemonic concept of culture which views it as diffusing downwards and producing an allegedly shared national culture; (2) internal self-determination but within a situation of compromise with state power; (3) territorialism, which would mean the devolution of power to local communities, with the centre taking the role of mediator; and (4) sustainability, or the conscious avoidance of ecocide becoming ethnocide. As was contended earlier in this Introduction, the emergence in recent decades of the 'ethnic question' has been the fundamental contradiction of 20th-century nationalism and the mass movement towards the nation state. For Hettne, this contradiction cannot be resolved unless the whole idea of the nation state is redefined for the 21st century. From this follows the need to redefine the concept of development as well.

This theme is taken up by Williams (Chapter 3) who argues that ethnicity, group identity and language are all too frequently subjected to cultural homogenization in the search for what, in essence, is an incorrectly identified development. Movements which seek to identify and promote specific elements of ethnic identity are characterized as reactive and as obstacles to be overcome in pursuit of the nation state and development objectives. His chapter focuses on the ways in which political choices identify language planning as a critical element in identity formation, and he stresses the communication aspect of development, especially in terms of the empowerment of some groups at the expense of others by means of the official sanctioning of specific languages. In Williams's view, because institutional means of dissent are denied to them subject peoples almost invariably focus on such issues as language and religion as means of asserting their own separateness and resistance to the external state. Such issues therefore constitute the very essence of a subordinated group's relationship with the state and are not merely supplementary. A conscious language policy thus becomes a crucial ingredient in development. Yet to accept this proposition is also to admit to a considerable dilemma in development policy since the promotion of a national language, and/or regionally-(ethnically-based) languages, involves the danger of marginalization from international scientific and technological developments. In this sense, the ongoing debate over ethnicity and language becomes part of the wider debate over the global division of labour, the continuing technological lead of the industrialized countries and the steady movement towards world dominance by English language mass media.

As Lemon points out (Chapter 4), a further dilemma facing national politicians in the newly independent countries of the post-colonial era has been the conflation of ethnicity with backwardness, especially spatial backwardness. As a result, such politicians spurned political structures such as federation, which might have provided legitimate outlets for the force of ethnicity, and expanded their political energies in the building of unified nation states within what were all too often highly artificial boundaries established during the colonial period. Within such boundaries, however, within the new nation states, other politicians quickly discovered the idea of ethnicity as a focus for political mobilization and the building of a power base. The result, frequently, has been nation states that are expressions of majority ethnic nationalism in predominant and sometimes repressive fashion; and where the ethnonationalist politics of the majority ethnic group have become too exclusionary, the scene has been set for ethnic conflict. After some decades of relative stability, in that pressures were contained without changes to state boundaries, disintegration is now becoming more the norm, Lemon contends.

Against this broader scenario, he examines the emerging ethnic situation in post-apartheid South Africa and, in particular, analyses the ethnic geography of the country in relation to the various proposals for its regionalization that were presented by the leading political parties to the regional demarcation commission as part of the formation of the new constitution. Lemon draws particular attention to the current position regarding the Zulu, who, he says, exhibit the signs of ethnonationalism more strongly that any other group at present. Although less than half of the Zulus have been politicized within the Inkatha Freedom Party led by Chief Buthelezi, it is their group which poses by far the greatest challenge to the currently widely accepted concept of South Africa as a nonethnic unitary state. Lemon makes particular reference to the geography of this situation in that the territorial position of the Zulu is relatively strong. This arises from the fact that while their 'homeland' Kwa Zulu is territorially more fragmented than any other, it abuts several towns and cities such as Durban, Pietermaritzburg, Newcastle and Richards Bay which make 'frontier commuting', and thus Zulu economic strengthening, possible. Whether this internal position of strength will lead to some form of partition involving the Zulu remains to be seen, however.

The contributions by Narman (Chapter 5) and Zegeye and Abate (Chapter 6), on Kenya and Ethiopia respectively, are indicative of the ubiquitousness of the problem of majority ethnic nationalism and the growing possibilities of fractionalization. In Kenya, the lengthy political domination of the country by one ethnic group, the decline into mass corruption and the constantly descending spiral of the economy have led to recent attempts to form a multi-ethnic opposition party around a white man, though third-generation Kenyan, Richard Leakey, the world-famous anthropologist. In Ethiopia, in contrast, events have been taking place which could lead to the abandonment of a basic principle of the Organization for African Unity: that the sovereignty and territorial integrity of the states carved out of the continent by the colonial powers must be safeguarded. This is ironic since Addis Ababa was chosen as the headquarters for the Organization for African Unity in 1963 precisely because Ethiopia was the only African country that could claim never to have been colonized. Yet as Zegeye and Abate describe, in recent years the country has been beset by regional warfare arising from ethnic difference. Eritrea broke away in 1993, but this left other considerable problems unsolved, notably that involving Tigray. In what is perhaps the most significant revolution in thinking on the territorial issue involving the question of ethnicity since the close of the colonial period, the framers of Ethiopia's new constitution (accepted in December 1994) abandoned the concept of the highly centralized authoritarian state in favour of a federal republic, in which sweeping powers would be devolved to ethnically defined regions. Ethiopians went to the polls on this basis in May 1995, implicitly endorsing a region's right, as laid down in the new constitution, to secede from their country, thus challenging for the first time in the modern era, what has been a basic political and developmental notion, that of the nation state. 'The theory is', according to one diplomat quoted in the *Financial Times*, 'that if you don't give the regions the right to secede they will fight for it. If you do, they will look over the brink and draw back' (Wrong 1995, p.6).

As Wrong states, however, the success of Ethiopia's experiment will probably depend less upon ideology than its ability to feed the inhabitants of what is the world's second-poorest country. When poverty beckons, ethnicity looms; thus the second major section of this book is devoted to an examination of the issues surrounding the relationship of ethnicity to economic development. In his analysis of the situation in Mexico and the Caribbean (Chapter 7), Clarke examines in depth the concept of pluralism and especially the work of Gamio in Mexico and M.G. Smith in Jamaica. Whereas in Mexico pluralism in its cultural aspect is now expressed only in 'islands' of indigenous non-Spanish speakers who constitute less than 10 per cent of the national population, in the former British, French and Dutch colonies of the Caribbean plural features are particularly marked, with, Clarke claims, majority populations characterized by cultures that are substantially at variance with European norms. His thesis is that neglect of the implications of cultural pluralism for economic development has been mirrored in government policy throughout the Commonwealth Caribbean. The result, as in Mexico in respect of the minority Indians, has been a development that corresponds closely to the internal colonialism model on which a structure of social relations is produced that is based upon domination and exploitation among heterogeneous groups. In Jamaica, to which he draws particular attention, the sorry state of the national economy has been paralleled by a succession of development plans that have rarely taken the socio-cultural characteristics of the population into account. While in Mexico Clarke sees some signs that in the most recent phase there has been a tendency for Indians to seek to regain control of their resources and to emphasize ethnodevelopment, in the Caribbean internal distinctiveness continues to be neglected in favour of copying economic models created elsewhere. Yet, in the end, Clarke argues, it is only self-empowerment that can set a new agenda with better prospects of success, particularly in the vital area of rural development.

In contrast to the situation in Mexico, in what is now Malaysia the achievement of independence was accompanied by a politically successful assertion of rights by those who considered themselves to be original inhabitants, the Malays. In the process, the idea of positive discrimination on an ethnic basis, introduced by Britain as the colonial power largely in respect of certain land rights and access to jobs in government service for Malays, has been progressively widened throughout the nation's economic sphere. After serious ethnic rioting in Kuala Lumpur in 1969, it was formalized into a specific national programme known as the New Economic Policy to cover the 20-year period 1970-90. The country's two other major ethnic groupings, the Chinese and the Indians, officially but not entirely accurately regarded as later immigrants, were given political rights and their wealthier members incorporated into a ruling alliance government.

Malaysia thus presents a significant opportunity to examine some aspects of the concept of ethnodevelopment as it might work in terms of practical politics and the realities of development if applied more widely to the solution of ethnic problems in the contemporary world. Basing their study on field work carried out in Penang, in Chapter 8 Eyre and Dwyer examine the advancement of Malays in Malaysia's industrial sector and also provide an overall assessment of the New Economic Policy. In industry, the principal objectives were to increase the employment of Malays at all levels to a position corresponding to that of their share of the national population and also to increase their proportion of industrial equity holding to 30 per cent. Erye and Dwyer show, however, that whereas a substantial intake of Malays into manufacturing industry as unskilled workers was achieved, the skilled and managerial levels of the industrial workforce remain dominated by Chinese and, to a lesser extent, Indians.

In addition, the comparative poverty of the Malays has prevented any significant widening of their industrial equity holding; rather equity has had to purchased by government organizations to be held 'in trust' until such time as its wider distribution becomes possible. Not unexpectedly, the New Economic Policy as a whole, now extended into the post-1990 period in modified form, has generated considerable controversy both within Malaysia and internationally, and a critique has been mounted from many directions. While the eradication of poverty among rural Malays has remained high on the list of the government's goals, it has emerged that it would be most unwise to take official claims of considerable success in this area at face value. Positive discrimination in education, particularly in higher education, is widely considered to have led to the institutionalization of mediocrity. Further, the period has seen a marked rise in personal corruption, even at the highest levels of government; the blatant use of economic opportunities under the New Economic Policy and its successor by UMNO, the dominant Malay political party, as a means of consolidating its power; the obvious emergence of a *rentier* class of Malays; and indeed a widening rather than a narrowing of income differentials, though not so much between the major ethnic groups as within each group.

The essentials of this assessment are confirmed in the analysis of the situation in Sarawak, East Malaysia, by King and Jayum in Chapter 9. Here the focus is on the position of the Iban, who constitute almost 30 per cent of the population but have remained economically subordinate not only to the immigrant Chinese who form a similar percentage but also, since the incorporation of Sarawak into Malaysia in 1960, to the proportionately smaller Malay population. King and Jaym stress the significance of the physical and economic geography of Sarawak as elements in Iban disunity and consequent weakness. As in the case of those areas of the Caribbean discussed by Clarke, they show how imported economic solutions, in this case transferred by the Malay elites from West to East Malaysia, have consistently failed to work, particularly in the area of land development, and so have perpetuated general poverty. Perhaps most significantly of all, they also draw attention to the recent history of rapid depletion of forest resources in Sarawak through logging, in order to benefit, partly again through high-level corruption, not the indigenous inhabitants, of whom the Iban are largest in number, but local Malays and Chinese, national politicians and powerful overseas interests, principally Japanese. Overall, although Malaysia has developed rapidly in recent years in the economic sense, ethnic divisions and tensions still run deep and the country remains more a case study of ethnodominance than ethnodevelopment, albeit with a change in the dominant group from a combination of colonial British and immigrant Chinese to the Malays.

The level of ethnic differentiation considered in the contributions on Malaysia, and in particular in the chapter by Eyre and Dwyer which uses only a tripartite distinction between Malays, Chinese and Indians, contrasts markedly with that adopted by Parnwell and Rigg in their consideration of the ethnic and regional problem of north-east Thailand (Chapter 10) and calls attention to the important question of fineness of scale in the consideration of ethnic/developmental problems in general. Although the people of the north-east, the region of Isan, belong to the same broad T'ai ethnic group as the vast majority of the national population, and can hardly be called a minority since they constitute about one-third of the country's population, Parnwell and Rigg argue that there are a number of more subtle factors, many of which have ethnicity, ethnic identity or ethnic differentials at their heart, which explain the relative economic disadvantage of the Isan people. As they point out in their careful, detailed analysis, there are in fact real differences, particularly in language and culture, which point to the validity of a subdivision between the 'Thai-Lao', of which the people of Isan are part, and the 'Siamese' or 'Central Thai'. They also contend that it is not the numerical status of the Isan people that is most significant in the consideration of their possible minority status but rather their position relative to, and the nature of their relationship with, other groups within the national society, particularly the more economically advantaged groups of central Thailand. Parnwell and Rigg trace the origins of the regional disadvantage of the north-east well back into the 19th century and point out that, although the region is widely seen to be one of the clearest examples of 'lagging' regions within the currently booming Pacific Rim, in many ways economic conditions are improving, though at a markedly slower pace than in the central region of the country. They emphasize the significance of migration from the region to Bangkok, and consequent financial remittances, as one of the significant factors enabling the people of Isan to participate in Thailand's economic growth; in so doing they call attention to another geographical factor of significance in the more general relationship between ethnicity and development.

Finally, Teo and Ooi (Chapter 11) turn attention to the workings of the ethnicity and development relationship within an almost purely urban setting and, moreover, one characterized for a relatively lengthy period by high levels of economic growth. Upon independence, the government of Singapore, as in Malaysia, inherited a deeply entrenched plural society but one dominated even more than in Malaysia by immigrants, many of whom saw themselves much more as sojourners than as potential citizens. The official response, within what in effect has become a one-party state, has been what Teo and Ooi describe as the 'strict enforcement of racial harmony' in the search for 'a multiracial, multicultural, multireligious and multilinguistic society which is inherently equal in its treatment of the various ethnic groups'. In terms of the language dilemmas discussed by Williams in Chapter 3, for example, in Singapore English has been encouraged as the language of science, technology and business, while Malay has been adopted as the official national language. In schools, pupils can opt for two first languages (English with Malay or English with Mandarin), the intention being to preserve as far as possible the island's diverse cultural heritage.

Teo and Ooi examine in particular population and housing in relation to ethnicity in Singapore. Much of the perceived problem of population revolves around the relatively low fertility rate of the Chinese, but there is also another aspect that is extremely controversial because it is clearly eugenic: the government has laid stress since 1983 on the quality of population in terms of the relatively low reproductive rates of the more highly educated. Sterilization for the lesser educated has been encouraged, while efforts, sometimes bordering on farce, have been made to encourage more university-educated women to marry and have children. Implicit in population policy has been the official desire for the Chinese to have more children than the Malays for, despite Singapore's rapid economic progress, the fruits of which have reached all ethnic groups, the Malays in general continue to be the most disadvantaged in terms of the incidence of poverty and its attributes such as level of educational attainment. Singapore houses about 85 per cent of its population in publicly built housing estates with a high level of home ownership as opposed to renting. Apart from solving the housing crisis of the early years of independence, the public housing programme has been used as a major tool for the integration of the different ethnic groups through the use of allocation policy to break down ethnic spatial separateness by deliberate mixing; indeed specific legislation has been introduced to prevent ethnic regrouping occurring as a consequence of owner - occupiers selling flats. Though the extent to which this spatial integration has promoted social integration between the ethnic groups seems questionable, like its close neighbour Malaysia, because of several decades of active official involvement in the problems of ethnicity and development, the experience of Singapore merits much more widespread study and assessment.

In seeking to draw the various threads in this book together, Drakakis-Smith's concluding chapter emphasizes the centrality to the discussions of the spatial dimension or, in other words, the importance of the geography of ethnicity. He also points out that so far in few development strategies or theories has ethnicity been designated a specific role. This neglect in a sense echoes that of an earlier period when the colonial powers not only ignored ethnic geography in the drawing of boundaries but also collapsed specific ethnic identities into larger more convenient categories for the purposes of easier administration, leaving a legacy of problems that is only now becoming fully apparent. The concluding chapter repeats and emphasizes one of the central themes of the present volume, enunciated by Hettne in Chapter 2: the necessity for a fundamental reconsideration of both the goals and the means of political and economic development in a world where ethnic issues are coming to take precedence over the relationships among nation states, hitherto the predominant issues for most of the present century.

References

Bogdanor, Vernon (1994) 'Exorcising the Ghosts of 1914', *The Independent*, 1 August 1994.

Dwyer, Denis (in press) 'Ethnicity, Self-Determination and Development in South East Asia', in B.J. Craige, Clifton W. Pannell and S. Elliott-Gower (eds), *Ethnicity and Nationalism in the Pacific Rim*, University of Georgia Press, Athens, Georgia.

Eriksen, Thomas Hylland (1993) *Ethnicity and Nationalism*, Pluto Press, London.

Gellner, Ernest (1964) *Thought and Change*, Weidenfeld and Nicholson, London.

Hettne, Bjorn (1995) *Development Theory and the Three Worlds*, Longman, Harlow.

Wrong, Michela (1995) 'Ethiopia Buries the African Nation State', *Financial Times*, 5 May 1995.

Part II

Concepts of ethnicity and development

2 Ethnicity and development: an elusive relationship

Björn Hettne

Introduction

There can be no doubt about the serious consequences of ethnic conflict for economic development. Lebanon, Sri Lanka, Liberia, Guyana and Ethiopia are some particularly severe cases (not to speak of the former Soviet Union and the former Yugoslavia). However, the causal relationship between ethnic revival and different patterns of development is at present not very clear. Ethnicity has been a neglected dimension in development theory. It is this blindness which in retrospect seems remarkable, hard to explain and important to correct.

In modernization theory, ethnic identity belonged to the traditional obstacles to development which, however, were ultimately supposed to disappear, in the course of development. Claims to ethnic identity were thus seen as anti-development. The recent revival of liberal orthodoxy, what John Toye (1987) has termed 'the counterrevolution' in development economics, only underlines the economistic bias. Although the older modernization theory gave a comprehensive macro view of the function of ethnicity in society, it did not focus on ethnic conflict as such, since this was more or less seen as a 'pre-modern' epiphenomenon.

For Marxists concerned with development issues, the ethnic issue has traditionally been discussed in terms of 'the national question' which, typically, has been outside and beyond Marxist theorizing. This is precisely what made it a 'question'. Ethnicity is, as in modernization theory, associated with pre-modern values and ethnic mobilization is usually described in terms of class, as a class struggle in disguise. Nationalism was good when it promoted social revolution; otherwise it was bad.

Dependency theory and neomarxism emphasized external factors, and therefore had little to say about ethnic conflicts *per se*, although they

Ethnicity and Development: Geographical Perspectives. Edited by Denis Dwyer and David Drakakis-Smith.

usefully introduced an international context to the analysis. In world system theory, for instance, ethnicity was associated with the distribution of production roles in an international division of labour. This relation between economic function and ethnic identity is undeniable but, as an explanation of the ethnic phenomenon, somewhat simplistic. More relevant to the analysis of ethnic conflict is the idea that ethnicity is activated in centre – periphery exploitative relations, for instance in situations of 'internal colonialism'. The *dependentistas* analysed contemporary relations of exploitation as essentially 'colonial', implying that one ethnic group (Ladinos) exploited another (Indios). This type of relationship coincided with but should be distinguished from class or urban – rural relations. As was the case between rich and poor countries, the solution did not lie in catching up but in liberation and in autonomous development (Gonzalez Casanova 1969). The model was later used to study the Celtic fringe in British development (Hechter 1975, 1983).

The overall impression, after reviewing what the major theoretical traditions have to say, is that ethnicity and development belong to different worlds. One obvious reason for this neglect is that development theory is concerned with 'states' and 'national economies' as basic units which precludes a serious treatment of the ethnic factor. Consequently, the sudden rise of this factor in the empirical world took the social sciences by surprise, at least as far as systematic explanations are concerned.

In what follows we shall discuss how ethnic conflicts may relate to various patterns of development and spell out the principles and preconditions for 'ethnodevelopment', i.e. a model of development that releases the potential inherent in different ethnic groups, rather than bringing them into feuds. We shall take a closer look at one particular region in so far as ethnopolitics and the potential of ethnodevelopment are concerned, namely South Asia. But first of all, some conceptual remarks on the two concepts under consideration: ethnicity and development and how they relate to the process of nation-building. Only then can we start to think about, and rethink, their relationship.

A reality in search of a theory

The argument of this chapter is not that there is an economic cause behind every single ethnic conflict. On the contrary, many ethnic conflicts defy 'economic rationality'. Nevertheless, numerous ethnic struggles all over the world clearly indicate that economic development has an ethnically differential impact and that in order to be compatible with ethnic peace development strategies must take this impact on ethnic identities and mobilization seriously. As a first step, it is necessary to look into the various meanings of ethnic identity and development.

What is ethnicity?

Ethnicity is necessarily an elusive concept, since the type of identity usually referred to as 'ethnic' can be manipulated for political purposes and thereby transformed. Ethnicity has a primordial or ascribed quality, but it is also true that ethnic identity is shaped by historical experiences. It is thus at the same time objective, given, and subjective, a creation. It is the many possibilities of shaping ethnic identity, the combinations of different primordial criteria and their interrelations with a changing historical context, which make the concept both difficult and indispensible. As stressed by Stavenhagen (1990), objective as well as subjective factors are necessary elements for the existence of an ethnic group. The (more or less) 'objective' factors can be listed: language, religion, territory, social organization, culture, race, common origin. The 'subjective' factor is any particular combination (out of countless possibilities) of the factors chosen by a group to assert its identity which is then used as a common resource to achieve a certain goal. Depending on the goal and the historical context, the set, or 'package', of factors may differ, thus producing different levels of ethnic identities. Furthermore ethnic identity changes in intensity over time (ethnicization, de-ethnicization, re-ethnicization). It is a variable rather than a constant. This is why ethnic identity is, and has to be, a fluid concept: contextual, situational and relational.

One problem which suggests itself, however, is that if ethnicity by itself does not exist, how many of the constituent criteria must form part of the package? If only one is present, then it makes more sense to describe a particular movement as territorial, or religious or whatever the main characteristic may be. One could perhaps venture the hypothesis that localized survival issues give rise to the typical ethnic movements where the ethnic package is varied and comprehensive, whereas, for instance, regional, religious and national issues involve alliances of groups where the shared characteristics and common reference points, even if basically cultural, are fewer and the ethnicity *diluted,* as it were. If some criteria are to be singled out as more 'ethnic' than others, I would favour those which imply *a shared history* and a *problematic future* of a particular group.

Ethnicity may overlap with class, in which case the result will be an enforcement of class consciousness. Ethnicity may also cut across class, in which case the effect on class consciousness may be the opposite. Thus ethnic identity should be studied as interacting with class consciousness rather than postulating any incompatibility between the two or subsuming one under the other. Normally, class analysis is needed to understand the internal tensions and factions building within ethnic groups. What is now being realized, however, is that ethnicity must be treated as a distinct and independent phenomenon, as a primary object for study.

There are two rather different approaches which deal with ethnicity, not as an epiphenomenon but as something to be studied in its own right. First, there is the *plural society approach*, which takes ethnicity as the basic organizational principle in multiethnic societies, which thereby become 'plural'. Second, there is the *interest group approach*, which in contrast, analyses ethnicity as a rather voluntary phenomenon, something which can be chosen for instrumental purposes. The interest group approach is of importance in emphasizing the flexibility of ethnic identity as a mode of organization for the purpose of achieving a specific goal, e.g. to force the state to change the pattern of resource allocation in favour of the mobilized group. However, the deeper cultural and psychological needs associated with ethnicity are neglected. The plural society approach, on the other hand, overstates the primordial dimensions of ethnicity and fails to understand the flexibility and instrumentality of ethnic identity.

Here we treat ethnicity as a *composite* term. Ethnic identity may be derived from different sources, often in different combinations. In each ethnic group there are usually more or less distinct subgroups. Fiercely competing groups may, nevertheless, have surprisingly many characteristics in common. The dividing line may in fact be drawn by little else than the manifest hostility between them, indicating that it is not the degree of 'objective' difference that matters. There are thus several levels of identity on which the ultimate boundaries defining the mobilized group may be drawn. Thus politicized ethnicity, ethnic identity mobilized for a political purpose, must be understood in its historical context. It is very often shaped by a conflict inherent in the process of nation-building.

To a large extent the contemporary phenomenon of ethnicity is the same as what was previously discussed as 'national awakening', which emerged either in declining empires or in the form of pan movements. But today the issue is also ethnonationalism within so called 'new states' in the conflictive process of nation-building. Since it is often conceived of as a threat to this process, the emerging ethnic revivalism is generally considered less legitimate than classical nationalism. The similarities are, in spite of this, strong. 'Nation' is an 'imagined community' (Anderson 1983), but as Urmila Phadnis (1989, p.259) points out, so are the ethnic communities in many ways.

If all ethnic groups had wanted their own state we could have called them 'national groups', but since this is not the case, the distinction is needed. The 'national question' has become the 'ethnic question', or rather the two issues are appearing simultaneously and partly merging, thus presenting social scientists with a demanding task and probably a need to reconsider some conventional wisdoms concerning nation-building.

The nation-state project

Ethnic conflicts are rarely possible to understand unless put in the context of the nation-building process, or what I shall call *the nation-state project* (Hettne 1984). This concept is meant to avoid the deterministic bias in traditional theories of modernization and nation-building. To see the nation-building process as a project to be implemented, implies an acting subject (the nation-building elite), a set of obstacles to overcome, a set of resources to work with and, above all, the possibility of failure. This possibility is today becoming increasingly evident, but not long ago the cases of complete political disintegration were rather few. Another type of failure is when the 'nationness' of the nation-state project is given up and replaced by a purely ethnic project of creating an ethnic or ethnocratic state. This is an unstable 'solution' containing contradictions which ultimately will lead to disintegration.

A nation-state project is universal in terms of its purpose but at the same time unique in the way it is realized. This is because it uses a specific territory and a specific population living within the state territory as 'building materials'. From the perspective of the different cultural groups living in the state territory, nationness must be multiethnic. However, if for a moment we take the perspective of the political elite, all nation-building projects ideally contain common objectives, ranging from more narrow state-formation to more comprehensive nation-building:

- The exclusive political/military control over a certain territory;
- The defence of this territory against possible claims from outside;
- The creation of material welfare within this territory;
- The creation of political legitimacy within this territory;
- The creation of a certain degree of cultural homogeneity within the state territory.

The nation-state project thus has the double objective of increasing 'stateness' (Tilly 1975) and 'nationization' (Phadnis 1989, p.251). In order to succeed with such a project there is a need for an economic surplus which can be created internally (though the domestic economic process) and externally (though participation in the world economy). The means which can be applied (type of development strategy) depends on the room-for-manoeuvre of the state in question, both externally and internally. Whatever the means, the goal of mainstream development is first of all the strengthening of the nation state. Thus a development strategy is also a strategy for nation-building. The two cannot be separated.

What is development?

As should be clear from our brief discussion of the different schools of development theory, there are various conceptions and definitions of development. A major distinction should be made between positive and normative definitions (Hettne 1995). In this context we are primarily concerned with the former, i.e. how the actual process of economic and social change affects the relations between ethnic groups and between ethnic groups and state power. We shall later on explore a possible normative approach to the problem.

In conventional terms, development, or what will be referred to as mainstream development, has typically meant a strengthening of the material base of the state, mainly through industrialization in a form remarkably similar from one country to another. In this sense development is identical with 'modernization'. Modernization, a concept closely related to the concept of nation-building, also had a deterministic bias in the earlier literature (from the 1950s and 1960s). The concept implies an increase in shared characteristics among social groups and an increasing homogenity in the society at large.

To avoid this evolutionist and determinist bias, the concept of modernization should be seen as an externally imposed 'imperative' rather than as a 'natural history' of development. The modernization process is enforced by the security concerns of the ruling elite. It typically implies not only conflicts between competing states within the inter-state system but also between, on the one hand, state power and, on the other, various subnational interests challenging the legitimacy of the state. More often than not, state power is linked with a dominant ethnic group which therefore becomes the carrier of modernization and nation-building. The 'ethnic interest' of the dominant group and the 'national interest' coincide.

A nation-state project is normally based on the territorial principle in its external relations and the functional in its internal relations, i.e. in the former it defends the integrity of the 'nation' against forces of subordination and peripherization; in the latter it seeks to structure production in the most efficient way with little regard for regional justice. Within the state territory all resources are 'national'. In this state-centric perspective, mainstream development is a rationalization of the interests of the nation-building elite which necessarily implies contradictions in a multiethnic society. Mainstream development thinking does therefore not exclude the idea of victims of progress: 'It is generally recognized that tribal peoples are being drastically affected by civilization and that their cultural patterns and, in many cases, the peoples themselves disappear as civilization advances' (Bodley 1982).

This is indeed true but only slowly becoming widely recognized. One of the more unexpected and still not very well understood outcomes of the mainstream development process is an explosion of ethnic violence. The way ethnic movements and ethnic conflicts relate to the development process is highly complex, but the differential outcome of growth, as well as stagnation, on different social groups and regions must obviously have an impact on ethnic relations. The causation going from ethnic conflict to economic decline is, as we already have noted, obvious. If we also could establish the link from economic development to ethnic conflict, we would in fact have a theory of economic decline in multiethnic societies.

Development and ethnic conflict

The reality of ethnic conflicts can no longer be disregarded by theorists and practitioners of development, since the rise of ethnopolitics must be related to economic development one way or the other. The problem is that we do not really know how. I therefore agree with Stavenhagen when he says that the neglect of the ethnic question in development thinking is not an oversight but a paradigmatic blind spot (Stavenhagen 1986, p.77). In order to build a theory of Another Development with special reference to ethnic relations, one must explore the ethnic factor in development within a rather simple framework to start with. The time for generalizing and theorizing will come later.

The basic departure from conventional theory that we shall make here is that people are seen as divided in ways which are different from conventional categories such as consumers and producers, sellers and buyers, employers and employees, etc. We are thus concerned with the impact of development on groups which are distinguished through *cultural* and *racial* criteria rather than by their function in the production process, even if this particular role plays an important part in the development of conflict and thus forms an indispensible part of the analysis.

In what ways can conflicts between specific ethnic groups be related to different patterns of economic development? The range of economic problems that may influence ethnic relations is great indeed: struggle for scarce resources, regional imbalances, infrastructural investments with a great impact on indigenous economic systems, labour-market conflicts, distributional conflicts, etc.

In situations described as 'internal colonialism', there is a strong correspondence between economic structure and ethnic distribution/stratification. Here the main concern is with conflicts which are directly caused by the pattern and content of economic development and where the effects on ethnic relations are sometimes unintentional. The intent may even be to reduce the base for ethnic conflict.

Most problems associated with uneven development affect all societies, but in multiethnic societies they are more severe and tend to become permanent. There may be so called 'spread-effects' within ethnic groups but definitely less so between them. In order to provide the outlines for an analytical framework, I shall try to work with the following tentative distinctions, forming a rough typology of conflict-generating economic processes:

Conflicts stemming from the unevenness of long-term trends such as modernization, proletarianization, demographic change or urbanization The most basic type of conflict has to do with the inherent unevenness of development on the national as well as the world level. This means that certain regions are placed in more advantageous positions than others and consequently attract more investment and skills. Such centres usually become the bases for nation-building, whereas people in the backwash or marginalized regions are the reluctant citizens. Their protests are often expressed in ethnic terms, since this, typically, is the only mode of social organization known to them. The state usually develops common interests with the most commercialized regions since they provide the type of free-floating resources upon which various state functions depend. Furthermore the 'state class' is often recruited from the same ethnic group which again reinforces the bias. This particular factor is sometimes elevated to *the* explanation of the ethnic phenomenon (Hechter 1975; Nairn, 1977). However ethnoregional solidarities are also resurging in the comparatively advanced regions (the Basques, the Croats, the Sikhs).

Conflicts concerning the control of scarce natural resources Scarcity of natural resources creates conflicts when resources shared by several groups are diminished or when these resources are claimed by an external power. Conflicts over water, for example, will be a major source of tensions in the next decade both between and within states (Ohlsson 1995). Conflicts which concern the external control of natural resources can also be exemplified by the way forest wealth is used by indigenous tribes on one hand and urban middle-class populations on the other. For the former a forest represents a way of life; for the latter a forest may represent simply a valuable resource. Urban groups may not even be aware that a forest is inhabited by human beings. The conflicts resulting from such clashes of interest are fundamental. They represent two different paradigms of development: growth and modernization versus ethnodevelopment or, in spatial terms, functional versus territorial development. I shall come back to these concepts. For the moment, suffice it to say that the pattern of resource control is an important criterium for distinguishing development strategies with regard to basic collective human rights.

Increased resource scarcity and competition for scarce resources seems inherent in modern development. Sometimes this competition leads to ethnocide or the exodus of marginalized groups such as indigenes or nomads etc. In any case there will be an enforced change of lifestyle which means a destruction of tribal cultures.

Conflicts associated with major infrastructural and industrial projects affecting local ecological systems The problem of dislocation also applies to infrastructural and industrial projects which affect local eco-systems. This implies the harnessing of resources for functional development but leads to the underdevelopment and environmental deterioration in the region directly concerned. Parts of it may become uninhabitable. Its population will have to adapt to a reduced quality of life and may even be forced to abandon the traditional habitat. In Ethiopia and Sudan irrigation schemes displaced pastoralists and forced them into less favourable and more crowded terrain. Already fragile eco-systemes deteriorated further. The marginalization of pastoralism bred dissidence and ethnic rebellions (Markakis 1991). All over the world millions of tribals have become ecological refugees or, to put it more frankly, 'development refugees'. Ecocide often has ethnocidal consequences, something still to be learnt by the international 'aid' agencies.

Conflicts relating to the differential effect of development strategies Most of the consequences we have referred to so far are more or less implicitly reflected in the development strategy carried out by a particular regime, but in some cases the ethnic issue is part and parcel of the strategy itself and therefore directly intervening in the ethnic struggle. This is for instance the case with the *bumiputra* policy of the Malaysian government (see Chapter 8) which is based on the assumption that 'the causes of ethnic conflict reside in objective disparities between groups that can be eliminated through policies aimed at those disparities' (Horowitz 1985, p.659). More generally, access to the state is the way to influence economic development to the advantage of a particular group. In an ethnically divided society a particular strategy is often seen in purely ethnic terms which implies non-participation from those who define themselves as outsiders (Premdas 1991).

Conflicts related to the distribution of public goods among culturally defined groups Government directly intervenes in the ethnic struggle by the way it distributes public works, education, employment and patronage. This policy can be motivated by an idea of 'protective discrimination', but it can also be a weapon for the dominant group in its efforts to create an 'ethnic state'. The allocation of education and public employment opportunities by quotas even make it necessary to belong to a certain community and remain a loyal member of it. One example is the Malays, who are given a special status in the Malaysian constitution. This is different from the case of correcting a certain imbalance through temporary measures, even if these measures tend to become permanent, as in India.

Some of these processes are inherent in 'modern development' and adaptation is the rational response. Even development strategies are less optional than the concept may indicate, since governments labour under the 'modernization imperative' and with limited room for manoeuvre. Nevertheless, there are different development strategies, and a further step in exploring the links between development and ethnicity is to evaluate the impact of different types of development strategies on ethnic peace.

Principles of ethnodevelopment

It can be argued that mainstream development in many complex ways is causing the present rise in ethnic violence, not necessarily by intention but rather through its inherent nature, as a side effect as it were. Thus, assuming that this analysis is correct, the solution to this increasingly grave problem must be found in another pattern of development, what is sometimes called 'Another Development' (Hettne 1995). This is an explicitly normative definition of development. It is obviously easier to spell out general principles for this alternative pattern, which in this context could be called *'ethnodevelopment'* (Stavenhagen 1986), than to change the actual course of mainstream development. However, one has to start somewhere. The vision must first of all be given some degree of concretization. Thus, four principles for a pattern of development compatible with ethnic peace are tentatively discussed below. The discussion concludes with some general structural preconditions.

Cultural pluralism

Development theorists have always stressed the importance of 'noneconomic' factors, only to forget about them after having made the obligatory reference. The reasons are easy to see as soon as one tries to define 'culture', the common denominator of most available definitions of ethnic identity (Markakis 1991, p.1). A culture can be seen as an unconscious frame of reference which becomes specific in confrontation with other cultures. This conscientization, caused by an external challenge, starts a process of objectification. The reified culture becomes a weapon of defence or a source for political mobilization and sometimes, unfortunately, for aggressive ethnocentrism. Upon deeper probing, 'cultural development' thus turns out to be an ambiguous phenomenon. Its realization may be destructive to other cultures. Cultural pluralism as a principle of development must therefore imply a respect for other cultures – a sort of 'power balance' between cultures. One way to achieve this is through 'positive discrimination', which, as was noted above, may also be a source of conflict.

Sometimes it is asserted that a development strategy must take the culture of a specific country into consideration. The synthetic 'national' culture is, however, often rather artificial compared to regional and local cultures, unless one particular subnational culture is elevated to serve as *the* national culture which, as we now can see, generates a new set of problems with the potential of undermining the nation-stage project.

Thus, ethnodevelopment is a challenge not only to mainstream development but also to the nation state. It implies development within a framework of *cultural pluralism,* based on the premise that different communities in the *same* society have distinctive codes of behaviour and different value systems (Worsley 1984). This pluralistic conception of culture could be contrasted with a *hegemonic* concept of culture, as diffused downwards and resulting in an allegedly shared national culture but in reality implying ethnocide. This is the concept of culture associated with mainstream development thinking, whereas cultural pluralism should be seen as the first and most basic principle of ethnodevelopment. It grants to the subnational cultural groups the right to use their own language, practice their religions and to carry out cultural practices forming part of their identity and socialization process. Thus, due to the predominance of cultural factors in the definition of ethnic identity, cultural pluralism normally amounts to the same as ethnic pluralism. It should be distinguished from structural pluralism, which implies an institutionalized division of ethnic groups.

Internal self-determination

Self-determination is to the ethnic group what self-reliance is to the nation state: the collective capacity to control one's destiny in a situation of interdependence. This means that neither self-determination nor self-reliance, in contradistinction to sovereignty and autarky, can be absolute. What usually is qualified as *internal* self-determination does not necessarily have an impact on the territorial integrity of the nation state. However, the relative degree of self-determination of the constituent cultural groups has a direct bearing on the success or failure of the nation-state project. With a high degree of self-determination for the constituent groups ('micro-nations' or 'quasi-nations'), the role of the central state becomes that of a mediator. Self-determination, just like cultural pluralism, is a *general* principle which implies a balance between the interests of different 'selves'. Cultural pluralism is a precondition for self-determination. The latter concept implies control over resources as an important component.

It is true that the principle of self-determination can be applied to different 'selves'. In this context, the 'self' coincides with a group which in order to maintain its cultural characteristics, i.e. to survive as a cultural group, needs the capacity to *determine* how these characteristics best are preserved. As noted above, this capacity can never be absolute because this would imply national sovereignty. Internal self-determination thus involves situationally specific compromises with statepower, which normally holds a monopoly on the use of force, as well as with other social groups claiming the same right to self-determination. Internal self-determination is distinct from political decentralization since it refers to social groups rather than to administrative units. It is usually very difficult to find even small administrative units which are ethnically homogeneous.

It is important to conceive and further develop internal self-determination as a *relative* concept and clearly to distinguish it from traditional state-orientated conceptions branding it as a road to balkanization. The demand for internal self-determination may ultimately lead to secession (external self-determination), but this is usually not the way the demand is originally articulated. The idea of creating an independent state is often quite farfetched. What self-determination means in concrete cases cannot be decided a priori, and it can only be realized in a meaningful way if supported by the other principles of ethnodevelopment. From the perspective of a particular social group, self-determination can include the right to speak its native language, to maintain traditional religious practices, to participate in the political process, to influence the pattern of development or to exercise control over land and other resources (Steinzor 1991, p.60). It is the refusal of these rights, which go beyond a constitutional right to *self-government*, that normally stimulates secessionist ambitions.

At the same time, the refusal of this 'right' is also normal and sometimes legitimate, since self-determination implies constraints on the use of natural resources of a country. In a nation state all resources are to a degree national, but the *sharing of resources* must be distinguished from *robbery*, even if the distinction is disputable and controversial. Some ethnic minorities (this particularly applies to indigenous peoples) maintain 'extensive' modes of production which unavoidably clash with the industrial 'modern' modes. In this contradiction we can probably find the most important reason behind the rise of ethnic violence. In its resolution we consequently find the solution to the problem of ethnic polarization, but it is no easy solution. It implies a completely new (*nota bene*: not traditional) pattern of development, i.e. ethnodevelopment.

Territorialism

According to the mainstream model, development is an abstract process related to an artificial 'national economy', an aggregate of production data and other indicators of development. Behind this abstraction we can observe the concrete socio-economic 'worlds' that most people identify with and depend upon. Ethnic identity is usually based on a strong territorial link, in fact many definitions of ethnicity include an attachment to a specific habitat or a territory. When this relationship is disturbed and threatened by 'modernization', conflicts occur over the goals and means of development.

The third principle of ethnodevelopment thus asserts that territorialism rather than functionalism must have priority in the development process. According to the latter principle, development is basically a result of specialization and an advanced division of labour among regions; according to the former, it is the regions themselves which are to be developed, not the functional order as a whole.

> A functional order is always hierarchical, accumulating power at the top. Territorial relationships, on the other hand, though they will also be characterized by inequalities of power, are tempered by the mutual rights and obligations which the members of a territorial group claim from each other (Friedman and Weaver 1979, p.17).

The problem is how to reduce the current dominance of function over territory, and how a 'recovery of territorial life' can be brought about. Smaller territorial units lack autonomous power in the functional system, typically life would therefore not be possible without a transfer of power to local communities, while the centre takes the function of mediator and co-ordinator.

The territorial principle was implicit in the theorizing around the concept of ecodevelopment, once defined by Ignacy Sachs as: 'a style of development that, in each ecoregion, calls for specific solutions to the particular problems of the region . . . Accordingly, it operates with criteria of progress that are related to each particular case, and adaption to the environment plays an important role (Sachs 1974, p.9).

From this perspective there are no models to emulate. A 'backward' region should not look for the image of its own future in the 'advanced' region but in its own ecology and culture. Development, as was pointed out above, has no universal meaning but should be contextually defined. There is no development *as such*, only development of *something*, which in this case would be a certain ecoregion. A development strategy informed by this territorial perspective must make efficient use of those resources which happen to exist in that particular area and in a way that both sustains the ecological system (outer limit) and provides the people living there with their basic human needs (inner limit).

Territorial development thus necessitates a development strategy which differs radically from conventional strategies with their *universal* elements: land, capital and labour; investment and growth. In contrast, it consists of *specific* elements: a group of people with certain cultural values living in a region with a certain set of natural resources. The goal of territorial development, then, is to improve *that specific situation,* to realize those values and to maintain the habitat, not to bring about 'development' in terms of GNP or some other abstraction.

It is easy to see the connection between these two sharply contrasting principles, on the one hand, and ethnic conflicts, on the other. Ethnic groups are most commonly locally based and their cultural identity is closely related to the ecological particularities of the region and to a certain mode of exploiting the natural resources. A process of 'development' that threatens the ecological system of a region is therefore also a cultural threat against the ethnic group for which this region is the habitat. Obviously such a process cannot be regarded as development for the ethnic group thus threatened, even if this is considered to be development in the macro-system, or functional system.

When an ethnic group has lost its territorial link, like the Gypsies, the Palestinians and the diaspora Jews, this also becomes part of its cultural identity and its special trauma. Thus, even indirectly, territory forms part of the definition of ethnic identity.

Sustainability

Ethnic conflict is often related to environmental degradation (Timberlake and Tinker 1984). Diminishing natural resources have become an important cause of violent human conflicts both between and within states. The relationship as such is obvious, since the changing environment provides the context in which varying types of conflicts emerge, but the actual cause – effect problem has not been the subject of systematic research. The problem of environmental refugees in Africa, the Indian subcontinent, Central America and the Caribbean shows the undeniable connection between environment, conflict and security.

Until recently the problem of interactions between ecology and society has been conspicuous by its absence from the social sciences, with the exception of social anthropology, where the man/environment relationship and its ramifications have been more difficult to hide than in social sciences dealing mainly with industrial, functionally organized societies and macro-structures. It is well known that anthropologists, generally in vain, have emphasized the local interests of populations in connection with dams or other large-scale constructions. 'Progress' has most often had its way.

Environmental interdependence transcends political borders, thereby increasing the importance of international actors and institutions. Thus, the new scarcity, or the problem of planetary finality, poses new issues in world politics, reminding us of the basic oneness of the world from an ecological point of view. These issues are summarized in the concept of *sustainability*.

Sustainability is a normative concept that has appeared in development theory as a consequence of the environmental concerns from the early 1970s and onwards. It is particularly associated with Lester Brown and the Worldwatch Institute (Brown 1981). It also stands out as a key concept in *Our Common Future, the Brundtland Commission Report*, which was a breakthrough that put sustainability on the international political agenda. The main message it carries is that neither the old nor any new international economic order would be viable unless the natural biological systems that underpin the global economy are preserved. This ecological imperative in turn calls for a redirection of the development process itself (Redclift 1987).

The problem of development in the context of ecological constraints is something the social sciences will have to deal with in spite of their lack of preparedness. The orthodox view of unlimited economic growth as some kind of natural law must be replaced. On the other hand, a general hostility towards growth because it threatens the ecological balance must also be avoided. There is no point in substituting one myth for another. The road forward goes somewhere between growth mania and ecologism.

Preconditions and limitations

Finally, we must consider some global structural preconditions for ethnodevelopment, as well as some obvious limitations of its applicability and relevance. It is rather obvious that the process of global homogenization is a threat to culture pluralism and therefore an obstacle to ethnodevelopment. There are indications that with the ending of the Cold War, a more multipolar world is taking shape, facilitating the development of a new kind of regionalism, with coexisting world regions, as a possible structural pattern of a new world order.

Regionalism seems to be on the rise also in the Third World, although very unevenly and rather embryonically in comparison with Europe (Palmer 1991). However, there is in the post-Cold War order a new freedom to act and no really important external constraints for 'new regionalism' or grouping of states. The problems are rather internal to each region: economic problems, regional hegemonism creating suspicions among states, national conflicts and ethnic rebellions influencing the regional security systems. The regions of the world have not become more peaceful in the post-Cold War era; instead some old problems frozen in the cold war complex are emerging.

On the other hand, 'the new regionalism' may in the context of ethnodevelopment in fact provide solutions to these problems. Self-reliance was never viable on the national level (for most countries) but may be a feasible development strategy on the regional level (collective self-reliance). Moreover, collective bargaining on the level of the region, i.e. a regional grouping of states rather than on the level of the Third World, could improve the economic position of Third World countries in the world system; and collective strength could make it easier to resist political and strategic pressures from the North. Furthermore, certain conflicts between states could be more easily solved within an appropriate regional framework without being distorted by the old Cold War considerations. Ethnic conflicts often spill over into neighbouring countries and are perceived as threats to national security. The way states commonly deal with these issues is the most certain way to perpetrate them. Therefore a regional solution is often the only realistic option. A regional organization can more easily than the state take the role of mediator.

It should be stressed that the principles of ethnodevelopment are mutually supportive, constituting a package. Cultural pluralism is a basic precondition for distinguishing among different needs and conceptions of development which are specific for various groups. Self-determination as a group right (internal self-determination) is the means whereby these specificities are politically articulated and implemented by the groups concerned. Territorialism guarantees those essential rights and needs which are dependent on a particular habitat. Sustainability secures the maintenance of this habitat and the groups living there over time.

Regionalism, finally, is the relevant line of protection, the defensive bulwark, against the anarchy of the world market and the global forces of homogenization and ethnocide. It constitutes the necessary international political framework for implementing the four principles. Even when this structural prerequisite is fulfilled, there are obvious limitations to the ethnodevelopment approach. For instance, ethnodevelopment applies fully to ethnic groups which constitute more or less distinct societies with a relatively autonomous territorial base. In cases where the groups in question are highly integrated in a functional system, ethnodevelopment may benefit the group to the extent that it has ethnically specific needs which normally are sacrificed in the process of mainstream development. In the case of dispersed, i.e. nonterritorial, ethnic minorities, the principles of ethnodevelopment, would not of course, apply except in the form of protection of human rights in the framework of a functional system.

South Asia: ethnocide or ethnodevelopment?

In what follows, we shall apply the above framework to the South Asian region and discuss some of the key issues, in particular the question of ethnic conflicts, some of them potentially ethnocidal, and their relationship to different patterns of development. The ethnic heterogenity of the region makes the nation-building projects exceedingly difficult, and the need for institutional innovations in conflict resolution and in development is great.

Nation-building in South Asia

As was emphasized in our general theoretical discussion, ethnic conflicts are usually part and parcel of the nation-building process, which we analysed in terms of nation-state projects. The current nation-state projects in South Asia were all moulded by complex historical processes in which the formation and dissolution of the British Empire played a major role. It is of great importance to note that the intensity of colonial penetration varied in different parts of the empire (Phadnis 1989). The post-colonial Indian government inherited what can be termed a 'colonial project', which then formed the basis of its own nation-state project. The primary aim of that particular project was initially not to create a nation within a state boundary but rather to hold the empire together in a new form. In this sense, India can be considered to have failed from the start.

The creation of the Indian Union in 1947 can be viewed as a milestone in a longer process, whereby every ethnic group/nation, if capable, attempts to secede from or increase its autonomy within the empire. The first example is the 'Indian' (largely Hindu-Brahmin) elite itself, which created the Indian National Congress and then used it to gain independence. Second, the Muslim elite organized the Muslim League and seceded from the new Indian empire. Third, other nations or ethnic groups, such as the Nagas and the Sikhs, have subsequently tried to do the same. Particularly during the last decade, an increasing number of ethnic groups have begun to question the legitimacy of the Indian state and have formed autonomist or separatist movements over the entire subcontinent.

So far there are not more than seven states. Pakistan was divided into two, but on the other hand Sikkim was absorbed by India. Bhutan is at present semi-absorbed, a fate referred to as 'bhutanization' by the smaller states in the region. Since the traumatic partition of Pakistan, there is a sensitivity about border changes in the region. India's response was secularism, what the Rudolphs have called India's founding myth, strongly associated with the Gandhi family (Rudolph and Rudolph 1988). The more pragmatic ground for secularism was that the Congress party before the second rise of Indira Gandhi (1980) to a large extent relied on the minorities' vote. Pakistan's response was to make Islam the state religion, which could not prevent the secession of an equally Islamic Bangladesh. Sri Lanka originally took the secular route but is now on its way towards a Sinhalese/Buddhist state with a rebellious Tamil/Hindu minority, the latter with a nation-state project of its own (Eelam). Nepal is a Hindu monarchy, previously authoritarian but now in a process towards a more secular, democratic system. Bhutan is a traditional monarchy with a consociational power structure and has until recently experienced little ethnic strife. In order to soften the external impact, Bhutan has adapted a gradualistic approach to economic development (Phadnis 1989, p.80). The Maldives is a comparatively homogenous state in this region, with one religion (Islam) and one language (Divehi). A certain element of authoritarianism has survived the sultanate (which was replaced by a presidential system in 1968) and there are no political parties in this atoll state. The overall trend is towards occasionally crisis-ridden, muddling-through democracies, where the internal heterogenity is more problematic than inter-state conflicts. However, to an increasing degree, internal and external issues become interwoven.

The regional security complex

South Asia has an old civilization with, in spite of innumerable ethnically diverse micro-societies, many shared characteristics. As a security complex (Buzan and Rizvi 1986), it is dominated by one 'regional power', although Pakistan and India had a more balanced relationship before Pakistan, due to an ethnic conflict, split up in 1971. The division of Pakistan further destabilized the region, transforming it into an arena of superpower competition, as a weakened Pakistan received support from both China and the United States, while India entered into a treaty with the Soviet Union.

As a culture and civilization with a special capacity for handling diversities and contradictions, India was and still is a giant, capable of controlling the whole region. The problem of regional hegemonism is thus ever-present. Size is not always a source of power, however. The process of modernization in India as a complex civilization has created as many problems as it has solved. The resulting conflicts are a great strain on India as a centralized nation state, in contradistinction to India as a decentralized civilization. In the former sense, India may not survive, since the internal forces of distintegration are tremendous. The dominant political trend now is Hindu chauvinism, which makes the conflict more threatening to the political order as a whole. Previous conflicts were more localized and could be managed by the centre one by one. The domestic situations in Pakistan and Sri Lanka also reveal similar weaknesses in terms of national integration, while ethnically more homogenous Bangladesh suffers from a general economic and political decay.

The security situation in South Asia cannot, thus, be understood unless the ethnic, regional and religious conflicts within the states – and the way these affect inter-state relations – are carefully considered. Ethnic conflicts constitute the major security concerns and shape the security complex of South Asia (Jørgensen 1991).

In a situation of geopolitical dominance by India, ethnic strife, secession and disintegration could be the main vehicles for changes in the inter-state system. Over the years the security situation has grown more and more complicated. India is strengthening her position in relative terms due to the increasing disorder in the region, but in the emerging 'new world order' this also means a high risk of external penetration, should things go out of control. These ominous trends are bound to have security implications both for regional security and for the political systems concerned (Hettne 1988). Below follows a brief survey of the major subnational conflicts in the countries of the region.

Ethnopolitics in the South Asian states

India India is the largest and most heterogeneous state in the region. The perplexing feature of Indian politics, so far, has in fact been the lack of confessional politics (Rudolph and Rudolph 1988). There are many different types of cultural groups, stretching the concept of ethnicity to the point of being meaningless. Religion, caste and tribe all enter into the picture, creating a great variety of ethnic conflicts. Yet, all efforts to confine the concept to specific types of cultural groups turn out to be artificial and arbitrary. We must try to learn to live with the concept of 'ethnic' as an approximation.

After a period of relative stability under the Congress System the political equilibrium was broken, and a multiparty system began to take shape. Ethnic identities became more and more exploited in the competitive political process, and the ideal of 'Indianness', associated with the Congress party and the name of Gandhi, probably disappeared with the assassination of Rajiv Gandhi. In its place has become a 'subnational' pattern of conflict which almost defies definition and suggests an extremely complex cause/effect relationship.

If we insist on some order and try to classify the conflicts, we could perhaps distinguish between *social* (related to socio-economic structure and status), *cultural* (relating to identity and life style) and *territorial* (an attachment to a certain territory which transcends class and kinship). Thus the conflict map contains conflictive relations such as Hindu – non-Hindu, Brahmin – non-Brahmin, caste Hindu – Harijan, Tribal – non-Tribal, North

– South, 'sons of the soil' – immigrants etc. Of course the criteria overlap to a large degree in concrete conflicts, and categories such as 'Hindu' and 'tribal' are, furthermore, extremely complex in themselves.

The current conflicts take place between tribals and the Hindu population, for instance in Bihar. In Assam the 'sons of the soil' defend their primary right (as they conceive it) to resources and employment against immigrants from Bangladesh, West Bengal and Bihar. 'Sons of the soil' organizations are active in many states, for instance Maharashtra and Karnataka. In Gujarat the higher castes attack lower castes because of the policy of protective discrimination. In Kashmir and Andhra Pradesh, Muslims and Hindus kill each other, as do Hindus and Sikhs in Punjab. All these conflicts largely take place in the name of preserving cultural identity and are to that extent, therefore, 'ethnic'.

It is amazing that no comprehensive change to the federal structure has been made since 1956, in spite of the enormous challenge to Delhi represented by the ethnic and regional rebellion and the growing contradictions of the federal system. Instead, Delhi has been one political actor among others, occasionally even exploiting the ethnic tensions as it suited the interests of the central power. Decentralization can either be planned to increase the coherence of the larger system or unplanned, making the larger system anarchic.

Anarchy would further weaken the secular principle and pave the way for Hindu nationalism and the 'ethnic state'. It is true that universal brotherhood and respect for other religions form part of the Hindu tradition, but should an ethnic state be created, that particular part of the Hindu legacy as a 'non-organized' religion would be eliminated and the nature of Hinduism transformed.

Hinduism, comprising 80 per cent of the population, will remain heterogenous, however, and therefore Hindu domination will mean little change for the majority of the Hindus. The project of building an ethnic state in India would therefore defeat its own purpose, but it could still be a Hindu state with non-Hindus as second-class citizens.

Pakistan Pakistan was created on the principal of religion but (when the Bengali province seceded to form Bangladesh) divided on the principle of ethnicity. The ethnic struggle is still defining the political game and is approaching that pathological level when the nation-state project can be considered a lost cause. The Punjabi dominance is challenged by Sind, Baluchistan and the Pathans of North-West Frontier Province (NWFP). Furthermore, it is challenged by the Mohajirs (immigrants from India), who originally constituted a bureaucratic backbone of the Pakistani state and as such were strongly committed to the nation-state project but now claim status as 'the fifth nation' of Pakistan, with a kind of 'territorial' base in the former capital of Karachi. In this decaying old metropole the

Mohajirs fight with Pathans in the streets, while they compete with the Sindhis for control over the rest of the province.

Ethnic violence and criminalization of politics are inseparable in the Pakistani context and have created a serious law and order problem, particularly in Sind, the stronghold of the PPP under Benazir Bhutto. The Mohajirs are organized in the MQM. When Benazir Bhutto came to power in 1988 the Punjab – Sind cleavage wrecked the emerging but still fragile post-authoritarian political system, and after less than two years the PPP regime was replaced by the (anti-PPP) Islamic Democratic Alliance under Nawaz Sharif which implied a move back to Punjabi and military dominance. The major challenge for the new regime was to solve the inter- and intra-provincial ethnic conflicts and save the nation-state project. First priority was given to the old issue of sharing the waters of Indus, the life-line of Pakistan as well as the major source of regional disputes. The accord between the regions was at least a positive sign of a turning point.

Sri Lanka In Sri Lanka, the Sinhalese – Tamil conflict during the last decades has taken the form of civil war. Since there are two major groups inhabiting different parts of the country, the ethnic conflict early became extremely polarized. The recent process of polarization goes back to the 1950s and the intense competition between the two major parties, the SLFP (Sri Lanka Freedom Party) and the UNP (United National Party), both of them building on Sinhalese votes. As Sri Lanka developed into an 'ethnic state', the Tamils also became radicalized in their response to discrimination. A crucial event was the Colombo massacre in 1984, in which Tamils were killed in a more or less organized and preplanned way. Militant groups competing among themselves opted for secession and for the creation of Eelam. Consequently, the government militarized its mode of crisis management but without much success.

In 1987 India sent peacekeeping forces (the Indian Peace-Keeping Forces) to the island after an accord between Rajiv Gandhi and President Jayawardene which included some degree of self-determination for the Tamils. This intervention turned out to be a great failure and was interrupted in 1990. Not only was it a failure, it led to another traumatic political murder in South Asia. The armed struggle continued and no resolution of the conflict other than a military victory for the government seems possible.

Bangladesh Bangladesh is, in spite of its size, a homogenous country, made up of predominantly Muslim Bengalis who freed themselves from Muslim Punjabis who were in control of the state in undivided Pakistan. Today it experiences ethnic conflicts between Buddhist Chakmas from the Chittagong Hill Tracts (CHT) and Muslim Bengalis from the over-populated plains. History thus ironically repeats itself in the form of new patterns of internal colonialism. In this case, ethnocide is more likely than secession, however. The indigenous population of Bangladesh is quite small (1 per cent) and consists of perhaps 36 distinct groups, one-third of them living in the CHT, the largest being the Chakma.

Smaller states The smaller states have so far showed little ethnic strife. The Maldives is a rather homogeneous state. Bhutan is a traditional kingdom where the signs of ethnic conflict have only recently emerged in the persecution of Nepalese. This is a result of the policy of forced cultural assmilation adopted in 1989. As the case of Nepal shows, the ministates can not remain unaffected by what goes on in the larger region. Nepal's step towards parliamentary democracy was possible after some pressure from India. Without idealizing the old monarchical/panchayati raj system, it is nevertheless obvious that the new order contains new problems in the form of ethnopolitics which may weaken the coherence of the state and increase its dependence on India.

Towards ethnocidal development?

The typology of development and ethnic conflict outlined above can easily be applied to South Asia, where the mainstream pattern of development has been conflict-generating and at times ethnocidal. It is consequently more difficult to find concrete examples of ethnodevelopment in spite of spiritual traditions in support of alternative development. In most ethnic conflicts in the region, there is an economic factor, of varying importance but never wholly absent. However, there is no uniform cause behind them.

The conflicts connected with *uneven development* usually have an ethnic-cum-territorial dimension and may easily develop into separatism, as the division of Pakistan shows. The Bengali resentment against the Pakistan regime was phrased in terms of struggle against 'internal colonialism'. Even in West Pakistan there were similar trends which later have become manifest, for instance in the conflict between Sind and Punjab.

Bangladesh provides a tragic example of an ethnic conflict centred on resource control and resource competition. The CHT (Chittagon Hill Tracts) were integrated in the British colonial empire over the past century, and the subsequent post-colonial governments have claimed the rich resources, such as forest products, energy sources (both oil and river waters) and agricultural land. The indigenous ('tribal') populations have resisted encroachment with increasing militancy. As in other parts of the world, the penetration is legitimized by an ethnocentric ideology which changes from benevolent paternalism to ethnocidal racism as the resistance grows (Bertocci 1989). Illustrations from India can be found in the 29th Report of the Commissioner for Scheduled Castes and Scheduled Tribes (*Economic and Political Weekly*, 20 April, 1991, p.1027).

In India there is also a major controversy about a large scale infrastructural project in Gujarat, the Narmada Valley Project, which threatens to dislocate a large number of tribals in order to provide the peasants with irrigation water. The conflict pattern is repeated in many parts of the world, and, as in so many other cases, the project has been sponsored by the World Bank.

Sri Lanka provides an example of the ethnic impact of development strategies. To what extent was the ethno – political conflict in the country caused by the 1977 change of development strategy from a regulated to an open economy? Even if ethnic rioting is an old phenomenon in Sri Lanka (or Ceylon), there was a marked increase in tensions after 1977 (Gunasinghe 1984). There is a link, obviously, but the actual causality is not easily established without detailed research about how the two types of development strategies affect different classes and sections with varying economic position within different ethnic groups. The point I want to make here is rather the conspicuous lack of that kind of analysis in the field of development studies.

However, it is very likely that a transformation of a regulated, protected non-dynamic economy, where political patronage plays an important role, into a fluent, unpredictive and achievement-orientated economic system easily disturbs a sensitive relationship among ethnic groups, which have become used to exploiting specific niches in the economic system and have come to regard these as a kind of natural right. On the whole, Tamils were better situated to take advantage of the new rules of the game; the Sinhalese reacted violently, and the government, in spite of being the architect behind the economic change, seems to have encouraged the anti-Tamil riots of July 1983. This was the beginning of a civil war-like situation and the end of the economic miracle. The economic costs of the conflict have been enormous (Richardson and Samarasinghe 1991).

Finally, what are the experiences of public goods redistribution in South Asia? In India 'positive discrimination' (reservation system, quota system, affirmative action, reverse discrimination) is a very established and (for scheduled castes and tribes) constitutionally sanctioned but increasingly controversial policy (Galanter 1984). It is discrimination in favour of members of certain groups in order to rectify an inherent inequality of opportunity with regard to seats in legislative bodies, positions in the public services and admission to specialized institutions of education (Maheshwari 1991, p.12). Sometimes the backward groups other than scheduled castes and tribes are referred to as 'other backward classes'

(OBCs), raising rather intricate problems of definition. In the South 'backward classes' is broadly defined, in some states, to include the majority of the population. Reservation is a long-standing policy since the non-Brahmin movement in the early 20th century.

In the North the issue is more controversial. In 1985 Gujarat raised the reserved quota for backward castes which resulted in widespread riots. On the level of the Indian union, a backward classes' commission (the Mandal Commission), reporting in 1980, expended the concept so that it comprised 52 per cent of the population. In 1990 the United Front government announced its acceptance of the recommendations of the commission: 'The percentage of reservation for the socially and educationally backward classes will be 27 per cent. This reservation will be applicable to services under the Government of India and public undertakings.' This political decision led to violent disturbances (including incidents of self-immolation) which shook northern India and forced the V.P. Singh government to resign. The reaction was predictable but not its intense violence. The caste war signalled a new era in Indian politics (*Far Eastern Economic Review* 2 May 1991).

Gandhiism and the 'new regionalism'

It may seem provocative to suggest than an Indian nationalist provides solutions to South Asia's problems, but as a thinker Mahatma Gandhi was essentially a South Asian. He borrowed ideas from all religions of the region and his philosophy was universalist. The 'India' for which Gandhi struggled was really South Asia. That is why he ultimately became marginalized in the Indian nation-state project and was subsequently killed by those who wanted to make this project ethnic, i.e. to make India an 'ethnic state'. It is true that Gandhi mobilized all communities *as communities* into the freedom movement by dramatizing their grievances and appealing to their specific interests. This 'communalistic' Gandhian heritage is looked upon with ambivalence by progressive Indians, but, on the other hand, India's subsequent development as a modern state is in fact marked by the contradiction between the universal rights of citizens and the special rights of communities.

Gandhi was a critic of modernity and the modernization project as applied to India. In fact the Western discussion on alternative development or 'another development' is inspired by Gandhian/Buddhist ideas of Sarvodaya (Kantowsky 1980). The ethnodevelopment concept is compatible with the idea of Indian society as a mosaic of communities, each with its right to realize its inherent 'self'. Both ideas are therefore controversial, but the reality behind them cannot be wished away. To take one example, the resource conflict between south and south-east Asia's hill peoples and the dominant cultural systems based on plough agriculture can not be solved without an appreciation of the hill peoples' mode of subsistence (Bertocci 1989). Thus Another Development, which in the south Asian context means Gandhiism, is the answer to the imperative of ethnodevelopment, the right of various cultural groups to a mode of development which does not deny them their identity as cultural groups. But there are other preconditions.

A regional security system which includes a mechanism for dealing with ethnic conflicts is a precondition for any kind of development, mainstream or otherwise. Any regional co-operation in the south Asian situation would mean a change for the better, although the economic rationale is not overwhelming at present; rather it has to be created (Adiseshiah, 1987). Thus, what I call the 'new regionalism' is above all a political project. If 'Indianness' could work as a myth, there is no reason why 'south Asia' could not become a level of identification.

In 1985 South Asian co-operation after five years of preparations, at last got its own regional organization, the South Asian Association for Regional Co-operation (SAARC). The idea originated from Bangladesh. India was rather lukewarm, while the smaller countries strongly felt the need for it (Mishra 1984; Muni 1985). Thus regional co-operation was initiated as a counterforce to regional hegemonism, but India continued to insist on bilateralism in all controversial matters. The 1987 intervention in Sri Lanka's civil war by the IPKF (Indian Peace-Keeping Forces) was a bilateral affair and received a very mixed regional response (Phadnis 1989, p.227), endorsed by the governments of Maldives and Nepal, reluctantly accepted by Bangladesh and vehemently criticized by Pakistan. A regional intervention would thus have been difficult to organize but would have had made more sense. Obviously, south Asia has a long way to go before a regional approach to ethnic conflict resolution can be found.

It is, however, both a strength and a weakness that SAARC contains all the states of the region. It is a weakness because the regional conflicts will paralyse SAARC for a long time to come, confining its scope to marginal issues like tourism and meteorology. It is a strength precisely because controversial problems, for instance ethnic tensions, can be handled within one organization and that at least a framework for regional conflict resolution has been created. Put differently, the regional organization coincides with the regional security complex and can be seen as at least an embryo to a security community, as political changes within the member states increase the level of homogenity among them.

There is now a trend of political homogenization in the form of democratic openings in Pakistan, Bangladesh and Nepal. India may also opt for a more open economy due to pressures from the IMF, thus reducing the gap in economic policies between the regional power, with its introvert tradition of import substitution, and the more extroverted smaller states.

If, furthermore, the internal power structure becomes more balanced by a weakening of Delhi and a greater political autonomy for the regions of India, the fear of regional bullying would diminish and a more constructive regional climate created. If India can survive as a multiethnic nation, south Asia as a whole would have no problems in developing a stronger regional identity. The 1991 SAARC meeting (Colombo, 1991) indicates that the prehistory of SAARC is over and that the next five years may provide substantive results.

Conclusion: the prevention of ethnocide

The ethnic struggles going on in all parts of the world constitute a major challenge to mainstream development and raise the question of how material improvements (the essential meaning of development) can be made compatible with the maintenance of fundamental cultural identities which by some are even considered a human right. However, it is a complex and highly controversial issue. It negates the basic idea of cultural convergence inherent in the concept of development as modernization.

The debate in the 1970s, particularly in India, on what was called 'indigenization' of the social sciences, and development theory in particular, was undoubtedly a promising start in the problematization of conventional mainstream development and the development of alternatives (Singh and Uberoi, 1968), but before it could be launched, the debate somehow was nipped in the bud. One reason was probably that the project of indigenization was based on the assumed existence of more or less homogenous national cultures. In many cases this proved to be an erroneous assumption. The 'national culture' was a mystification, a Pandora's box of increasingly parochial identities. Indigenous concepts of development were revealed as new formulas for 'development monopolies'.

Ethnodevelopment may be seen as the ultimate consequence of the indigenization process, revealing its contradictions. Put in negative terms, it may imply global balkanization and an apartheid mode of development. It is therefore important to see ethnodevelopment as a corrective to mainstream development, not as a complete reversal of this process. Ethnic solidarities must have their limit, and the borderline goes where they represent a threat to other groups. There are cases – and they seem to be increasing in number – where ethnic solidarity has reached pathological levels, and where the ethnic struggle is incompatible with any kind of development (Premdas 1991). Sri Lanka is a case in point, and in a European context a similar collective madness has been reached in the former Yugoslavia and is repeated on a larger scale in the former Soviet Union.

The relationship between economic development and ethnic conflict is not at all clearcut. This is also true in south Asia. For the forest tribes in different parts of India, their mobilization is a matter of physical survival. For the Assamese the economic interest is mixed with a feeling of political subordination. For the Sikhs in Punjab, the economic interests involved are harder to specify and a class analysis of the community is needed (Brass 1991). The clashes in Karachi have a lot to do with 'lumpendevelopment'. The economic relations between the Sinhalese and the Tamils in Sri Lanka are also complex, but the importance of the economic dimension of the conflict is evident.

Ethnodevelopment means a systematic and consistent voluntary strengthening of those characteristics that make up ethnic identity and, most importantly, which are consistent with cultural pluralism and internal self-determination for all groups. It is a radical concept since it reverses the conventional conception of ethnicity as an obstacle to modernization (Thompson and Ronen 1986, p.7). There is in most social science literature an inbuilt bias against ethnic identification and in favour of national identification, regardless of how unrealistic a particular nation-state project may be. Put in positive terms, the re-emergence of ethnicity may be seen as a 'reaffirmation of a long-existing ethnic identity in the process of positive development – as an integral part of development, where the state (or at least certain aspects of it), not ethnicity, is an obstacle to development' (ibid., p.6).

Ethnodevelopment is a variety of the Another Development tradition (Hettne 1990) where the basic need of a cultural (ethnic) identity is seen as a fundamental right and, being cultural, related to the group. It certainly complicates the whole issue of development. Rather than seeing the principles of Another Development – or Sarvodaya in the south Asian context – as an alternative *form* of development, they should perhaps be seen as basic *preconditions* for development. In the context of ethnicity and development, the principles of ethnodevelopment (cultural pluralism, internal self-determination, territorialism, sustainability) are thus a set of guarantees against ethnocide. These guarantees are needed, since mainstream development has been shown to be inherently ethnocidal. From a human rights' perspective such a consequence is absolutely unacceptable, regardless of how much GNP growth this particular pattern of development may generate. Just as ecodevelopment is a guarantee against ecocide, ethnodevelopment is a guarantee against ethnocide.

The emergence of the 'ethnic question' is the fundamental contradiction in the nation-state project, a contradiction which cannot be resolved unless this project is redefined. From this follows the need to redefine the concept of development as well. The contents of a development strategy enforcing cultural variety and ethnodevelopment are easily spelled out:

decentralization, participation, rural rather than urban bias, territoriality, self-reliance and self-determination, ecological balance, etc. In the South Asian context many of those ideas were articulated by Gandhi.

The ways states are formed and ruled are, however, generally not conducive to cultural pluralism. This is precisely the reason behind the ethnic violence referred to at the beginning of this chapter. Unpleasant as it may seem, the current wave of ethnic violence may have the necessary historical function of modifying the nation-state project and the pattern of development inherent in it.

References

Adiseshiah, M. (1987) 'The Economic Rational of SAARC' *South Asia Journal*, 1(1), 14–27.

Anderson, B. (1983) *Imagined Communities*, Verso, London.

Bendix R. (1964) *Nation-Building and Citizenship: Studies of our Changing Social Order*, John Wiley & Sons, New York, London, Sydney.

Bertocci, P.J. (1989) 'Resource Development and Ethnic Conflict in Bangladesh: The Case of the Chakmas in the Chittagong Hill Tracts', in D. Vajpeyi and Y.K. Malik (eds), *Religious and Ethnic Minority Politics in South Asia*, Manohar, Delhi.

Bodley, J.H. (1982) *Victims of Progress*, Mayfield Publishing Company, Palo Alto.

Brass, P. (ed.) (1985) *Ethnic Groups and the State*, Croom Helm, London.

Brass, P. (1991) 'Socioeconomic Aspects of the Punjab Crisis' in Samarasinghe and Coughlan (1991), 224–39.

Brown, L. (1981) *Building a Sustainable Society*, Norton, London.

Buzan, B. and G. Rizvi (eds) (1986) *South Asian Insecurity and the Great Powers*, Macmillan, Ithaca and London.

Donnelly, J. (1989) *Human Rights in Theory and Practice*, Cornell University Press, Ithaca.

Friedman, J. and C. Weaver (1979) *Territory and Function: The Evolution of Regional Planning*, Edward Arnold, London.

Galanter, M. (1984) *Competing Inequalities: Low and Backward Classes in India*, University of California Press, Berkeley and Los Angeles.

González Casanova, P. (1969) 'Internal Colonialism and National Development', in I.L. Horowitz, I. de Castro and J. Gerassic (eds), *Latin American Radicalism*, Random House, New York.

Goulborne, H. (ed.) (1979) *Politics and the State in the Third World*, Macmillan, London.

Gunasinghe, N. (1984) 'The Open Economy and Its Impact on Ethnic Relations in Sri Lanka' in *Sri Lanka. The Ethnic Conflict*, Committee for Rational Development, Navrang Publishers, New Delhi.

Gupta, D. (1990) 'The Indispensable Centre: Ethnicity and Politics in the Indian Nation State', *Journal of Contemporary Asia*, 20(4), 521–39.

Hechter, M. (1975) *Internal Colonialism: The Celtic Fringe in British National Development, 1536–1966*, Routledge and Kegan Paul, London.

Hechter, M. (1983) 'Internal Colonialism Revisited' in David Drakakis-Smith and Stephen Wyn Williams (eds), *Internal Colonialism: Essays Around a Theme*, Monograph No.3, Developing Areas Research Group of British Geographer, 29–41.

Held, D. (1983) *States and Societies*, Martin Robertson, Oxford.
Hettne, B. (1984) *Approaches to the Study of Peace and Development: A State of the Art Report*, EADI Working Papers, Tilburg.
Hettne, B. (1988) 'India' in J. Carlsson and T.M. Shaw (eds), *Newly Industrializing Countries and the Political Economy of South-South Relations*, Macmillan, London, 147–60.
Hettne, B. (1995) *Development Theory and the Three Worlds*, Longman, London.
Horowitz, D.L. (1985) *Ethnic Groups in Conflict*, University of California Press, Los Angeles.
Hydén, G. (1984) 'Ethnicity and State Coherence in Africa', *Ethnic Studies Report*, 2(1), 147–60.
Jøgensen, B.D. (1991) 'Ethnic Dimensions of Regional Security' in Leif Ohlsson (ed.), *Regional Conflicts and Conflict Resolution; Case Studies II*, Padrigu Papers, Gothenburg, 146–59.
Kantowsky, D. (1980) *Sarvodaya: The Other Development*, Vikas, Delhi.
Lijphart, A. (1977) *Democracy in Plural Societies: A Comparative Exploration*, Yale University Press, New Haven.
Maheshwari, S.R. (1991) *The Maṇḍal Commission and Mandalisation. A Critique*, Concept Publishing, Delhi.
Markakis, J. (1991) *Ethnic Conflict in Ethiopia and Sudan*, UNRISD, Geneva.
Mishra, P.K. (1984) 'South Asia's Quest for an Identity and SARC', *India Quarterly*, July–December.
Muni, S.D. (1985) 'SARC: Building Regions from Below', *Asian Survey*, 25(4).
Nairn, T. (1977) *The Break-Up of Britain: Crisis and New-Nationalism*, New Left Books, London.
Ohlsson, L. (ed.) (1995) *Hydropolitics: Conflicts over Water as a Development Constraint*, Zed Books, London.
Palmer, N.D. (1991) *The New Regionalism in Asia and the Pacific*, Lexington Books, Lexington, Mass.
Phadnis, U. (1989) *Ethnicity and Nation-building in South Asia*, Sage, New Delhi.
Polanyi, K. (1945) 'Universal Capitalism or Regional Planning', *The London Quarterly of World Affairs*, January.
Premdas, R. (1991) *Ethnic Conflict and Development, the Case of Guyana*, UNRISD, Geneva.
Puthucheary, M. (1991) *Ethnic Conflict and Development in Malaysia*, UNRISD, Geneva.
Redclift, M. (1987) *Sustainable Development*, Methuen, London.
Richardson, J.R. and S.W.R. de A. Samarasinghe (1991) 'Measuring the Economic Dimensions of Sri Lanka's Ethnic Conflict' in S. Samaqrasinghe and R. Coughlan (1991), 194–223.
Rothschild, J. (1981) *Ethnopolitics: A Conceptual Framework*, Columbia University Press, New York.
Rudolph, L.I. and Susanne Hoeber Rudolph, (1988) 'Confessional Politics, Secularism and Centrism in India' in James Warner Björkman (ed.), *Fundamentalism, Revivalists and Violence in South Asia*, Manohar, Delhi.
Sachs, I. (1974) 'Ecodevelopment', *Cares*, Nov–Dec, 42–7.
Samarasinghe, S.W.R. de. A. and R. Coughlan (eds) (1991) *Economic Dimensions of Ethnic Conflict*, Pinter, London.
Seers, D. (1983) *The Political Economy of Nationalism*, Oxford University Press, Oxford.
Shiels, F.L. (ed.) (1984) *Ethnic Separatism and World Politics*, University Press of America, London.

Skocpol, T. (1979) *States and Social Revolutions*, Cambridge University Press, Cambridge.
Smith, A.D. (1981) *The Ethnic Revival in the Modern World*, Cambridge University Press, Cambridge.
Stavenhagen, R. (1986) 'Ethnodevelopment: A Neglected Dimension in Development Thinking' in R. Anthorpe and A. Kráhl, *Development Studies: Critique and Renewal*, E.J. Brill, Leiden, 71–94.
Stavenhagen, R. (1990) *The Ethnic Question: Conflicts, Development and Human Rights*, United Nations University Press, Tokyo.
Steinzor, Madia, (1991) *The Web of Self-Determination: The Focus on Native Americans*, Padrigu, Gothenburg.
Stepan, A. (1978) *The State and Society: Peru in Comparative Perspective*, Princeton University Press, Princeton.
Thompson, D.L. and D. Ronen (1986) *Ethnicity, Politics and Development*, Lynn Rienner Publishers, Boulder.
Tilly, C. (1975) *The Formation of National States in Western Europe*, Princeton University Press, Princeton.
Timberlake, L. and J. Tinker (1984) *Environment and Conflict: Links Between Ecological Decay, Environmental Bankruptcy and Political and Military Instability*, Briefing Document No. 40, Earthscan, London.
Toye, J. (1987) *Dilemmas of Development*, Blackwell, Oxford.
Uberoi, S. and Singh, J.P. (1968) 'Science and Swaraj' in *Contributions to Indian Sociology*, New Series, 2, 119–23.
Worsley, P. (1984) *The Three Worlds: Culture and World Development*, Wesdenfeld and Nicholson, London.

3 Ethnic identity and language issues in development

Colin H. Williams

Introduction

Language has a critical influence on development and is intimately related to questions of political, economic and social stability in multiethnic societies. This chapter explores the role of language policy and planning as instruments of development and examines selected dilemmas faced by multilingual states as they seek to formalize language choice through educational, occupational and communication policies.

Accounts of the development process often assume as given the ethnic plurality of contemporary states while presuming that macro-economic theories can be adapted to suit the cultural exigencies of any specific place. In general, development is interpreted as an external process which acts upon a society rather than as an interactive process which simultaneously changes the social order *in situ*. Development involves communication, and in a multilingual environment the official recognition of specific languages empowers some groups and individuals at the expense of others. This chapter's central proposition is that as ethnicity, group identity and language are all interrelated, any structured attempt to reduce a population's ability to express itself in its own tongue must weaken development. This runs counter to the orthodox view that language rationalization is a prerequisite of political development. Attempts to resist such cultural homogenization often lead to communal–state conflict, for movements which seek to promote non-official elements of identity, religion or cultural affiliation are interpreted as reactive rather than as purposive agencies. They are seen as obstacles to be overcome in the 'nation-state project' (Hettne 1984) rather than as resources to be harnessed as part of the fulfilment of human potential.

This chapter is focused on the way in which political choices structure identity formation and language policy as components in development.

Ethnicity and Development: Geographical Perspectives. Edited by Denis Dwyer and David Drakakis-Smith.

This perspective consciously underplays the economic and functional aspects of language learning and cultural transmission in favour of highlighting the political dimensions of language use as embodied in state policy.

The complex process of state development has resulted in the inexorable integration of diverse cultural groups into 'national' populations; such cultural groups become constituent citizens of a modern state within a system of sovereign states. For many subject peoples, state-integration has resulted not only in the conquest of ethnic territory and the denial of popular rights but also in external intrusion in the development of their ethnic homeland. Whether through forced out-migration as a result of land enclosure (such as Scotland in the clearances or South Africa after 1948), of famine (Ireland in the 1840s, Sudan, 1980–94; Ethiopia, 1948–94) or rapid industrialization (the Basque country in the late 19th century), most ethnic–linguistic minority groups perceive their territory as having been under threat in modern history.

Because institutional means of dissent are denied them, subject peoples invariably focus on cultural diacritical markers, such as language or religion, as a means of asserting their own separateness and demonstrating their resistance to external state and commercial incursions into their territory. If we accept that ethnic–linguistic groups comprising subject or subordinate peoples are also relatively underdeveloped economically and politically, it is clear that questions of language, culture and identity are not merely supplementary to the more routinized socio-economic concerns of development. They can constitute the very essence of a subordinated group's relationship with the state in whose name the dominant group exercise power and control. As group identity and power differentials are rooted in their environment and expressed through material acts of construction or change, it is not surprising that any threat to the immediate territory of a subordinated group is interpreted as a challenge to culture and group survival. Place and territory are critical in the process of control and development and their appropriation by external agencies has a long history related to the extension of state hegemony and strategic, capital projects of 'state-building' and 'nation-formation'; which are essentially contestations over space.

The incorporation of ethnically differentiated territories is a necessary precursor to the creation of the territorial–bureaucratic state. Normally incorporation strengthens central rather than local interests and serves to threaten the material and spiritual sustenance which ethnic groups derive from the immediate locale. In consequence, patterns of development are often over-centralized, without a corresponding attention to the needs of the 'periphery', except, of course, the need to integrate it politically and strategically. This has led to charges of core discrimination, peripheral marginalization and the denial of group rights and cultural reproduction.

For some this is a necessary product of global development, but should the price of economic and bureaucratic incorporation into the mainstream involve the denial of distinctiveness? Must we perforce sacrifice cultural autonomy for political–economic advancement?

Language diversity

As one of the chief components of ethnicity and the means by which the ideas and techniques of development are diffused, language has become one of the most sensitive issues of the contemporary world. It is estimated that some 6170 living languages (Mackey 1991, p.51), exclusive of dialects, are contained within the 185 or so sovereign states, and if we admit dependencies and semi-autonomous polities, the number rises to *c*.200. Fewer than a hundred of these 6000 languages are 'official' since 120 states have adopted either English, French, Spanish or Arabic as official languages, and some 50 nation states have their own indigenous official language (15 per cent have two or more). If we add to this 45 regional languages with official status, that still only accounts for about 1.5 per cent of the total spoken languages having formal recognition. The situation is even more complex in that only 1 per cent of the world's languages have more than half a million speakers and only 10 per cent have more than 1000 000. Hundreds of languages have no adolescent speakers (Mackey 1995; Williams 1995).

Clearly there is a lack of congruence between the formal political system and the cultural inheritance of its constituent citizens which suggests that there will be a near-permanent crisis involving attempts to maintain linguistic diversity in the face of increasing linguistic standardization somewhere in the world. In terms of ethnic conflict, language-related tension can indeed exacerbate socio–political strains. Often language issues are an overarching mobilizing factor within which other issues are pursued. Consequently the sovereign state's language policy can be a key determinant of the direction and rate of 'development'. If a language policy is harmonious and effective, it can release collective energies into other more profitable avenues. If, on the other hand, it is authoritarian, divisive and dysfunctional, it can lead to alienation, pressures for regional separatism and ultimately to civil war. David Laitin (1994) has observed that 'rulers have an interest in promoting efficient language outcomes' because the 'failure of the market to overcome the inefficiencies of the Babelian curse adds to the transaction costs of rule, if only because governmental monitoring of compliance to its laws is more costly if the rules themselves must be translated into a number of languages' (p.622). Multilingual societies necessitate choice in communication at all levels from the individual to the state. Choice also implies conflict and tension, for one person's choice is another person's denial of opportunity; such is the competitive nature of languages in contact. The situation is complicated in many developing contexts because colonialism has introduced a new range of intrusive languages of wider communication (LWC) whose adoption both challenges the indigenous languages and has a profound influence on the nature of the development process. Language policy choices are essential because a standardized means of internal and external communication is a prerequisite to large-scale development.

UNESCO has developed a typology of the range of choice available to language planners which has been in use for two generations. It includes the following categories:

1. INDIGENOUS LANGUAGE – the language of the original inhabitants of an area;
2. LINGUA FRANCA – a language used habitually by people who have different first languages so they can communicate for certain specific purposes;
3. MOTHER TONGUE – the language one acquires as a child;
4. NATIONAL LANGUAGE – the language of a political, social and cultural entity;
5. OFFICIAL LANGUAGE – a language used to do government business;
6. PIDGIN – a language (formed by mixing languages) used regularly by people of different language backgrounds;
7. REGIONAL LANGUAGE – a common language used by people of different language backgrounds who live in a particular area;
8. SECOND LANGUAGE – a language acquired in addition to one's first language;
9. VERNACULAR LANGUAGE – the first language of a group socially or politically dominated by a group with a different language;
10. WORLD LANGUAGE – a language used over wide areas of the world (a language 'of wider communication', or LWC) (UNESCO 1951, pp.689–90).

Though useful in a heuristic sense such typologies have been criticized. Kay (1993) argues they are too imprecise to be used in any specific place or context. One may also query how 'original' a language must be to be classified as indigenous and why a vernacular language is associated with subordination in the UNESCO classification, as if a dominant group could not also possess a vernacular language. Such imprecise definitions, however, were commonplace in the initial stages of language planning, which often transferred European or North American models of social and linguistic behaviour to African, Asian or Latin American contexts without due regard. This is a common complaint for the development process was not sufficiently understood and appreciated then. Forty years on we have accepted that the Third World has a very definite context for development, including a marked distinction between indigenous/local and implanted/world technologies and economic/political systems; and a recent 'colonial' history in which the superior power has subjugated 'Third World' peoples and created proto-states as political and economic entities (Kay 1993).

Language Policy

As most African societies have retained the repertoire of language policies they inherited from the colonial past, they are faced with severe difficulties in matching institutional agencies and organizational structures to the reality of serving the legitimate demands of a multilingual population. Conceived as a central feature of post-colonial development, language planning became a crucial tool of 'state-formation' and 'nation-building'. The key question was whether national linguistic communication was to be based upon the use of indigenous or foreign languages. The new state could either promote one exclusive 'national' language, at the expense of all others, the 'one-nation–one language plan', or it could seek to recognize important languages within its boundaries and employ one or more for official functions, the 'one-nation–more than one language plan' (Stewart 1968; Eastman 1983).

The first type of plan was common in the Western European experiences of state formation, as in the French, Spanish and British versions of 'national' development. It is best represented in Africa by post-war Rhodesia and to a lesser extent by Tanzania's political determination to create a 'national' culture by replacing English with Swahili as its 'official' language. Other examples of endoglossic nations would be Somalia (Somali), Sudan (Arabic) and Ethiopia (Amharic).

Such endoglossic policy seeks to institute political and cultural autonomy by giving an indigenous language full opportunity to be developed as the language of government, administration, law, education and commerce. In so doing a number of goals may be met simultaneously, among which are the search for national integrity, the legitimation of the new regime and of its state apparatus, the re-establishment of indigenous social organization, the reduction of dependence upon Western organizations and influence and the incorporation of the citizenry in a wide range of para-public social domains. Foreign languages are reserved for the very specialized functions of higher education, international diplomacy and commerce.

Of those nations which do not practice an active endoglossic policy, Heine (1992, p.24) cites Botswana (Tswana), Burundi (Rundi), Lesotho (Sotho), Malawi (Chewa), Ruanda (Kinyarwanda) and Swaziland (Swati).

They may aim to encourage an indigenous language, but as most are derived from colonial units with centralized political organization and one dominant language, they tend to favour the use of the colonial language for official purposes. In this respect there is a wide gap between the rhetoric of the declared national language policy and the actual experience of daily communication in the colonial lingua franca.

The second type of language planning exists when the 'national' goal is to maintain cultural pluralism. It is best represented in Africa by the commitment of the Bureau of Ghanaian Languages to introduce 11 languages in the education system, including three variants of Akan. A quite different interpretation of such planning was the extension of the apartheid system in the Republic of South Africa from the initial Bantustans to the creation of the putative independent homelands. Under this system language was used to define national citizenship, even if language affiliation was a putative rather than a measurable attribute as in the case of all the people of mixed descent who by being allocated to a homeland were automatically denied South African citizenship. South Africa's over-concern with the fit between language and political boundaries expressed in its homeland policy (language=culture=homeland) derives from the cornerstone of the *Genootskap van Regte Afrikaanders* (Fellowship of True Afrikaners), founded in 1875, 'our language, our nation and our land'. Herbert (1992, p.5) comments that this Trinitarian conception which formed the homelands tribalization policy stems from 'the projection of the Afrikaner's sense of ethnic particularism and linguistic chauvinism onto other people' (Van den Berghe 1968, p.221). A radically different version of the pluralist goal of achieving unity through diversity is currently being established in the New South Africa with the recognition of 11 languages to serve its newly enfranchised citizens.

However, the delicate choice of whether to promote one or many African languages in the educational domain and public agencies of new states is becoming less and less of a 'free choice' as the increasing burdens of economic, social and cultural development crowd in on the limited resources available for language planning policy and its implementation. The dominant trend towards the globilization of economic, political and cultural relationships is a major factor in language choice. But there is also a counter trend which emphasizes the value of cultural diversity and the worth of each specific language. Concern over endangered languages in Africa, no less than in Europe and North America, has lead to a re-examination of the relationship between culture, development and political identity (Williams 1993). Since decolonization, truly endangered languages in Africa are threatened more by endoglossic policies (favouring the strongest African languages over the others) than by exoglossic.

The 'national language question' in Africa has always reflected the triumph of political zeal over the realization of bilingual or multilingual communicative competence. The will has always out paced the reach. In consequence one might argue that language planning is an acute expression of political social engineering. Yet W. Mackey avers that: 'In the development of standard languages, edict has been less effective than example, the ideologies of the practitioners more powerful than the ideas of the planners.' (Mackey 1991, p.56). The Tanzanian example would suggest that edict and example, ideology and plan must be synonymous if such planning is to be truly effective. Yet the replacement of English by Swahili has revealed Tanzania's real need of English. That there are so few examples of effective planning in Africa suggests that there is very little consensus over both means and ends in this domain of language policy.

Language planning, as an attempt at behaviour modification, depends to a large extent on four attributes identified by Stewart (1968, p.533). They are the degree of standardization; the degree of autonomy; the degree of historicity and the degree of vitality. These continua of language freedom are critical in order to help planners evaluate the existing language functions in multilingual societies. As Eastman (1983, p.54) has cautioned, we need to temper the bland perspective offered by the UNESCO classification with Stewart's more useful categorization which has a societal, functional and attitudinal basis rather than being merely political. Echoing Mackey's general reminder above she suggests that 'language choice from the perspective of social roles, has not so much to do with political goals as with what people do and think' (p.54).

The multiplicity of language and the dynamics which characterize many multilingual societies are well illustrated by Stewart's categorization of language function as:

1. official languages;
2. provincial languages (such as regional languages);
3. languages of wider communication (LWCs), which are used within a multilingual nation to cross ethnic boundaries;
4. international languages, which are LWCs used between nations;
5. capital languages (the means of communication near a national capital);
6. group languages (often vernaculars);
7. educational languages (used as the media of education);
8. school-subject languages (those taken as second languages);
9. literary languages (for example, Sanskrit) and
10. religious languages (such as Islamic Arabic in Kenya) (Stewart 1968, pp.540–41).

To this we may add the role of cross-border languages.

Critics argue that such lists lack precision and definition. Kay (1993) comments that Stewart's categories do not explain that any given

Table 3.1 Types of language choice (modified from Fishman 1969, p.192)

Features	a-modal nations (Type A)	uni-modal nations (Type B)	multi modal nations (Type C)
1. Is there a Great Tradition?*	no	yes	many
2. Reason for selection of national language	for political integration	for nationalism	for compromise
3. Reason LWC is used	as a national symbol	for a transition	a unifying force
4. LP activity; modernization to be done	standardization	diglossia	
5. Is bilingualism a goal?	no	yes, but situational	yes
6. Is biculturalism a goal?	no	yes, but situational	yes

*The term Great Tradition refers to a literary tradition of long standing thought to be great by the people who have it and considered a part of their cultural heritage.
Source: Eastman (1983) p.13

language could be simultaneously of type 5/6/7/8/ for the categories are not mutually exclusive. However, Eastman contends that Stewart's language types may be used as a guide for deciding what language choices are best in multilingual settings at either a state or sub-state level. It is clear that these types cross-cut the 10 political situations of choice established by UNESCO as applicable in any 'national' context. But what type of 'national context' we are concerned with is also crucial in this decision-making process. When the question is whether to use a language of wider communication (LWC) as a 'national' and 'official' language, planners should consider the six socio–political variables that characterize three modal types of 'nation.' (Eastman 1983, pp.58–59). Joshua Fishman (1969) argues that whether a 'nation' is modal type A, B or C depends largely on whether *nationism* (instrumental attachment and operational efficiency) or *nationalism* (ethnic authenticity and sentimental-primordial attachment) is the goal.

As is evident from Tables 3.1 and 3.2, a-model (Type A) nations initiate language choices so that they may integrate a linguistically heterogeneous area with a primarily oral rather than written tradition. Eastman (1983, p.13) comments that many developing states are of this type and frequently choose a LWC as an official and national language. Often indigenous language standardization is also initiated so that people can learn to read and write their first regional language as well as the LWCs as is illustrated through the promotion of six regional languages together with English and French in Cameroon.

Table 3.2 Varieties of language situations

Situation of Language CHOICE (National)	Situations of Language FUNCTION (Social)
1. Indigenous	1. Official Language
2. Lingua franca	2. Provincial language
3. Mother tongue/first language	3. School-subject language
4. National language	4. Group language
5. Official language	5. Language of wider communication
6. Pidgin	6. International language
7. Regional language	7. Capital language
8. Second language	8. Literary language
9. Vernacular language	9. Educational language
10. World language	10. Religious language

Variables affecting LANGUAGE TYPE	Variables Affecting MODAL NATION TYPE
1. Standardization	1. Great Tradition
2. Autonomy	2. National language rationale
3. Historicity	3. LWC rationale
4. Vitality	4. Type of LP activity
	5. Bilingualism
	6. Biculturalism

Variables Affecting the LANGUAGE–NATION RELATIONSHIP
1. Type of national language (endo-or exoglossic)
2. Status of languages within the nation
3. Juridical status of speech communities in the nation
4. Numerical strength of speech communities in the nation.

Source: Eastman (1983) pp.59–60

Type B nations are called uni-modal and are characterized by an indigenous language with a literary tradition, plus an LWC usually dominant because of former colonial policy. The intelligentsia and employees of the bureaucratic–territorial state tend to favour the LWC, while the indigenous language with the literary tradition is promoted as both the symbol and the substance of nationalist mobilization. Swahili's challenge to English in Tanzania would exemplify the uni-modal nation's choice of national language.

Type C nations are multimodal and have a range of competing languages with their own literary traditions. The selection of one all-purpose indigenous national language undoubtedly creates tension, especially in the ranks of supporters and speakers of the languages not chosen, but this may be a necessary price to pay for communicative efficiency in the new state. In multimodal nations, bi- or trilingualism is a political goal, and in the case of India, for example, the indigenous national, all-state language

Hindi has been championed at the expense both of other regional Indian languages and, to a lesser extent, at the expense of English, the LWC.

Developing this distinction between 'nationism' and 'nationalism', Ralph Fasold (1988) has distinguished three main functions of national languages (1) nationalist/national, or identificational; (2) nationist/official or administrative and (3) communicative. Brann (1991) has added a fourth element, the territorial or 'son-of-the-soil' function, and suggests that in most former colonial situations new states must take account of all four criteria, namely: territoriality, communality, representation and status when choosing one or several 'national' languages.

Language planning as an instrument of development

Development theory often assumes that language-choice behavior is utilitarian and rational and can be measured through techniques such as cost-benefit analysis of language switching. It also assumes that the broad tenets of modernization theory influence patterns of language maintenance and shift. Eastman (1983, p.148) has summarized the development assumptions of Language Planning which I have modified below:

- People with language skills are favoured over those without; people with linguistic disabilities are held back in economic advancement.
- Population increases via birth rate *or* migration which affects the relative strength of languages or speech varieties.
- A quality increase as well as a quantity increase in per capita growth requires an expansion of linguistic knowledge; that is, people need to know and use more of a language as they acquire more and better goods.
- People need to be aware of, and know how to use, different language features (such as social dialects, special vocabularies, argots, jargons, or special-purpose languages) to adjust to changes in professional and industrial growth.
- International trade requires people to be able to use and have access to LWCs.
- Linguistic homogeneity adds to the ability of people of cross occupational, industrial and status lines.
- Where the spread of modern economic growth is sequential, modern linguistic growth is also sequential. The need for vocabulary development makes it likely that the world languages will be chosen for adoption in preference to attempts to enhance local languages.

Clearly language planning is not a precise instrument and is as capable of manipulation as any other aspect of state policy. Neither does it demonstrate an *a priori* commitment to legitimizing all current indigenous languages. Value recognition is not an essential part of language planning, although one might argue that it should be, for how can planning of any kind be effective without explicit recognition and practice of this principle? Hegemony prevails and will continue to do so until minority people band together and form some kind of common front to have their perspectives incorporated in the development planning process. This will involve a clash of discourses and a conflict over the very definition of what counts as the problem that development is seeking to overcome. From a local, community perspective the problem may be a lack of real power to transform their immediate situation. From the point of view of the central state apparatus it may be that ethno–cultural differences are perceived as an impediment to the creation of a state-wide programme of economic development where institutional agencies can redefine the populus as workers and consumers regardless of ethnic criteria. The commodification of identity is thus an essential feature both of the economic and political restructuring of the state.

Conscious of this ideological struggle, some language planning and development studies theorists have recognized the contextual effects on language maintenance and language loss and have sought to incorporate environmental and politico-economic factors more directly into their analyses. This bodes well for a realistic, holistic assessment of language change in developing societies. The work of Conklin and Lourie (1983), summarized by Baker (1992), offers a very useful framework and balance sheet for the factors influencing language maintenance and loss. Table 3.3 illustrates the complexity of the issues involved, but I would argue that all three sets of factors need to be addressed simultaneously if practical proposals are to be constructed in any particular context. In addition, as with nearly all examples of language planning schema, it also needs to identify the role of language in economic development and modernization.

A staggering range of variables faces the language planner concerned with mobilizing the state's educational system in order to produce functional bilingual or multilingual citizens. There is enough case-study experience in the literature for us to be able to predict weak and strong forms of education for bilingualism and biliteracy. Table 3.4 illustrates the available range, which will be illustrated below by reference to specific examples in East Africa and Malaysia. It is my contention that the construction of an articulate bilingual or multilingual citizenry is an essential prerequisite of a developing state. The key issue is who decides on what basis such bi/multilingualism is to be constructed. Which languages are chosen, and who benefits by this act of state-sponsored social and identity formation? Only when we can anticipate the utilitarian power of a language in particular economic contexts can we begin to talk of the pragmatic links between language processes and development processes.

Table 3.3 Factors encouraging language maintenance and loss. Reproduced by permission from Colin Baker (1993) *Foundations of Bilingual Education and Bilingilism,* Multilingual Matters Ltd, Clevedon, Avon

FACTORS ENCOURAGING LANGUAGE MAINTENANCE	FACTORS ENCOURAGING LANGUAGE LOSS
A. Political, Social and Demographic Factors	
1. Large number of speakers living closely together.	Small number of speakers well dispersed.
2. Recent and/or continuing in-migration.	Long and stable residence.
3. Close proximity to the homeland and ease of travel to homeland.	Homeland remote.
4. Preference to return to homeland with many actually returning.	Low rate of return. to homeland and/or little intention to return.
5. Homeland language community intact.	Homeland language community decaying in vitality.
6. Stability in occupation.	Occupational shift, especially from rural to urban areas.
7. Employment available where home language is spoken daily.	Employment requires use of the majority language.
8. Low social and economic mobility in main occupations.	High social and economic mobility in main occupations.
9. Low level of education to restrict social and economic mobility, but educated and articulate community leaders loyal to their language community.	High levels of education giving social and economic mobility. Potential community leaders are alienated from their language community by education.
10. Ethnic group identity rather than identity with majority language community via nativism, racism and ethnic discrimination.	Ethnic identity is denied to achieve social and vocational mobility; this is forced by nativism, racism and ethnic discrimination.
B. Cultural Factors	
1. Mother-tongue institutions (e.g. schools, community organizations, mass media, leisure activities).	Lack of mother-tongue institutions.
2. Cultural and religious ceremonies in the home language.	Cultural and religious activitiy in the majority language.
3. Ethnic identity strongly tied to home language.	Ethnic identity defined by factors other than language.
4. Nationalistic aspirations as a language group.	Few nationalistic aspirations.
5. Mother tongue the homeland national language.	Mother tongue not the only homeland national language, or mother tongue spans several nations.
6. Emotional attachment to mother tongue giving self-identity and ethnicitiy.	Self-identity derived from factors other than shared home language.

Table 3.3 Continued

FACTORS ENCOURAGING LANGUAGE MAINTENANCE	FACTORS ENCOURAGING LANGUAGE LOSS
7. Emphasis on family ties and community cohesion.	Low emphasis on family and community ties. High emphasis on individual achievement.
8. Emphasis on education to enhance ethnic awareness or controlled by language	Emphasis on education if education in mother tongue community.
9. Low emphasis on education if in majority language.	Acceptance of majority language education.
10. Culture unlike majority language culture.	Culture and religion similar to that of the majority language.
C. Linguistic Factors	
1. Mother tongue is standardized and exists in a written form.	Mother tongue is non-standard and/or not in written form.
2. Use of an alphabet which makes printing and literacy relatively easy.	Use of writinging system which is expensive to reproduce and relatively difficult to learn.
3. Home language has international status.	Home language of little or no international importance.
4. Home language literacy used in community and with homeland.	Illiteracy (or aliteracy) in the home language.
5. Flexibility in the development of the home language (e.g. limited use of new terms from the majority language).	No tolerance of new terms from majority language; or too much tolerance of loan words leading to mixing and eventual language loss.

(Adapted from N. Conklin & M. Lourie, 1983, *A Host of Tongues*, Free Press, New York)

Language choice

A central issue for developing countries, especially in Africa, is what is the relationship to be between colonial languages and indigenous African languages? The question is just as urgent in Tanzania, where Kiswahili, rather than a European language is promoted nationally. Conventionally multilingual approaches to communication are adopted in such societies. How is this promotion of language spread best formalized in policy? What steps would be necessary to ensure that multilingual strategies in, for example, education are not again hijacked by an elite (Robinson, 1993)?

Language spread is an immensely complicated area of analysis and there are many ways in which it may be characterized. Carl Sauer's

Table 3.4 Weak and strong forms of education for bilingualism and biliteracy. Reproduced by permission from Colin Baker (1993) *Foundations of Bilingual Education and Bilingualism* Multilingual Matters Ltd, Clevedon, Avon. (adapted from N. Conklin & M. Lourie, 1983, *A Host of Tongues*, Free Press, New York

WEAK FORMS OF EDUCATION FOR BILINGUALISM

Type of Program	**Typical Type of Child**	**Language of the Classroom**	**Societal and Educational Aim**	**Aim in Language Outcome**
SUBMERSION (Structured Immersion)	Language Minority	Majority Language	Assimilation	Monolingualism
SUBMERSION with Withdrawal Classes/ Sheltered English)	Language Minority	Majority Language with 'Pull-out' L2 Lessons	Assimilation	Monolingualism
SEGREGATIONIST	Language Minority	Minority Language (forced, no choice)	Apartheid	Monolingualism
TRANSITIONAL	Language Minority	Moves from Minority to Majority Language	Assimilation	Relative Monolingualism
MAINSTREAM with Foreign Language Teaching	Language Majority	Majority Language with L2/FL Lessons	Limited Enrichment	Limited Bilingualism
SEPARATIST	Language Minority	Minority Language (out of choice)	Detachment/ Autonomy	Limited Bilingualism

Table 3.4 Continued

STRONG FORMS OF EDUCATION FOR BILINGUALISM AND BILITERACY

Type of Program	**Typical Type of Child**	**Language of the Classroom**	**Societal and Educational Aim**	**Aim in Language Outcome**
IMMERSION	Language Majority	Bilingual with Initial Emphasis on L2	Pluralism and Enrichment	Bilingualism & Biliteracy
MAINTENANCE/ HERITAGE LANGUAGE	Language Minority	Bilingual with Emphasis on L1	Maintenance, Pluralism and Enrichment	Bilingualism & Biliteracy
TWO-WAY/DUAL LANGUAGE	Mixed Language Minority & Majority	Minority and Majority	Maintenance, Pluralism and Enrichment	Bilingualism & Biliteracy
MAINSTREAM BILINGUAL	Language Majority	Two Majority Languages	Maintenance, Pluralism and Enrichment	Bilingualism & Biliteracy

Notes: (1) L2 = Second Language; L1 = First Language; FL = Foreign Language. (2) Formulation of this table owes much to discussions with Professor Ofelia García.

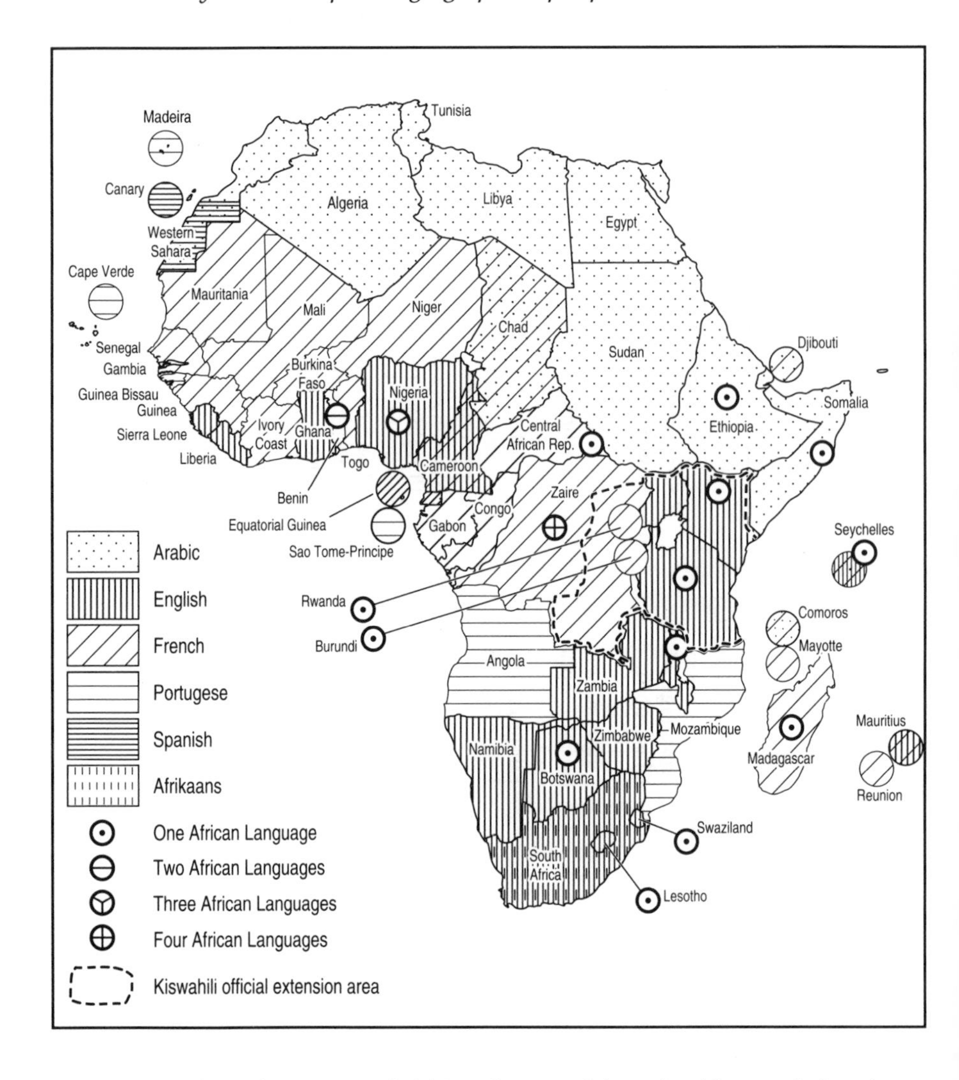

Figure 3.1 State languages of Africa. Source: Adapted with permission from Breton (1991a, p. 173)

dictum was that 'speech, fire and tools' are the tripod of civilization and were independently 'invented' in numerous places in the early histories of humankind. Kay (1993) avers that while speech has divided humankind; fire and tools have served to unite it. Mackey (1995) observes that writing, one of the greatest inventions for civilization, has often united people. A radically different perspective is provided by Ali Mazuri who asserts that 'Africa invented language; Asia sacralised language; and Europe universalised it' (Mazrui and Mazrui 1992, p.96).

In Africa's case, its triple linguistic heritage makes it an acute case of linguistic dependency. Mazrui and Mazrui (1992) have argued that the cultural interplay between indigenous, Islamic and Western legacies promoted a functional complementarity within the continental array of languages. But in the recent period new political, economic and cultural forces have infused a spirit of linguistic competition in social domains and have created different socio-linguistic dynamics and formations. These changes are important because recent strands of development theory are increasingly concerned with the impact of development on groups which are distinguished through cultural criteria rather than by their function in the production process as Hettne states in Chapter 1 of this volume.

How then do cultural complementarity and competition affect the process? The determining factor is, of course, colonial history and pericolonial contemporary reality. Africa, no less than any other part of the world, is differentially integrated into a global division of labour which is mediated through ideology and culture. But the language of this integration is primarily Western, essentially English or French, and Afro-Islamic, particularly Arabic. Thus while Afro-Islamic or Western languages are transnational or national in their communicative range, most Afro-ethnic languages are subnational, limited to specific regions within state boundaries but with a substantial minority of transnational languages which are bisected by former colonial political boundaries.

This logic suggests that in so far as development relates to the global division of labour and international/universal technologies, then transnational languages are essential to development and indigenous languages are a barrier hindering access to the wider world. However, in most culturally plural societies such logic is politically unacceptable, and therefore states must search for a modern version of a 'hybrid' communication system. This should relate both to the heritage of traditional cultures and to the structures and opportunities of the wider world. A language which is capable of embracing both requirements is thus essential and should be the one with the greater versatility, vocabulary and functional utility (Kay 1993).

The difficulty facing politicians and language development managers in Africa is that very few indigenous languages are capable of satisfying the criteria of both preservation and modernization. For as Mazrui and Mazrui (1992, p.89) advise, the proportion of Afro-ethnic languages which have the potential to be truly national or transnational is rather small. They include Amharic (Ethiopia and Eritrea), Bemba (Zambia and Zimbabwe), Kituba (Zaire and Congo), Lingala (Zaire, Congo, Angola, Central African Republic, Sudan and Uganda), Lwena (Angola, Zaire and Zambia), Nyanja or Chewa (Malawi and Zambia), and Sango (Central African Republic, Cameroon, Chad, Congo and Zaire). Such claims are open to question, but what is not in doubt is that many attempts are currently being made to redefine indigenous languages as 'national' languages (which they may become), the common heritage of most or all of the citizens of post-independent states.

It is often argued that speakers of Afro-ethnic languages tend to be mostly rural in terms of their core area of demographic concentration and linguistic value (though this is not true of Amharic, for example). This gives them an authenticity in both time and space, and a certain literary and psychological legitimacy, in that most Afro-ethnic language speakers 'tend to regard the rural homeland as their real home' (Mazrui and Mazrui 1992, p.90). However, functionally it limits their geographical spread and domain usage in an increasingly technological world. Examples of urban African concentrations which are growing quickly tend to weaken this claim, but the principle of low relative utility for Afro-ethnic languages in an increasingly inter-connected world holds true. In contrast most Afro-Islamic languages depend upon the dynamics of urbanization; they prosper as regional lingua francas serving commerce, politics and leisure pursuits. Thus the top three in terms of speakers are all Afro-Islamic languages, namely Arabic, Kiswahili and Hausa.

At the macro-scale, languages tend to specialize according to their utility and function. The trend is that 'Afro-ethnic languages fulfil *intra-ethnic* communicative and social-psychological needs in non-formal, and many formal, domains of discourse. Afro-Islamic and Afro-Western language facilitate *inter-ethnic* communication and horizontal mobility'. (Mazrui and Mazrui 1992, p.91). However, this old divide between vernacular and vehicular languages is no longer so tenable. One cannot simply juxtapose indigenous with exogenous, rural with urban, traditional with modern. Kay's (1993) argument in favour of language and cultural displacement as a means of escaping structural poverty and the open prison of ethnic identity certainly seems like a rational justification for the encouragement of the 'new African'. His 'pragmatic' solution of the adoption of English in multilingual Zambia, as elsewhere, as a language of wider communication appears rational. But is it reasonable? Is the North's globalizing role in reforming African identity through technology, bureaucracy and ideology inevitable and therefore to be incorporated within development strategies and political policies? What are the consequences of adopting a Western language in multiethnic contexts on both the constituent ethno-linguistic groups and upon the universalizing language 'community'?

Let us illustrate by asking whether English should be encouraged as the official co-equal or second language of many African states? Is it better to anticipate the inevitable or to resist the spread of English as the globalizing language? What are the immediate implications of encouraging such global language spread in Africa?

One obvious consequence is the relative functional decline of many African languages, whose communicative power and symbolic purchase is reduced by changing socio-economic circumstances. Another is the loss of creativity and spontaneity mediated through one's own language(s), contributing to a quenching of the human spirit. This argument alone may prove convincing to many. However, systematic exposure to external influences has revealed the limited functional utility of most African languages in a changing context. Need this sound the death-knell of particular ethnic identities? Not necessarily so, for as Edwards (1991, p.270), Kay (1993) and Williams (1991, pp.35–39) have argued, there is no necessary correspondence between linguistic reproduction and ethnic identity. Indeed cultural activities and symbolic manifestations of ethnicity often continue long after a group's language declines. Many of Africa's threatened languages are, in fact, comparable to other European or Asian declining linguistic minorities, and thus generalizations about their plight are useful (Williams 1993). Edwards recognizes that change is inherent in any inter-ethnic relationship and asserts that we should not necessarily interpret the 'abandonment of original or static positions as decay or loss' (Edwards 1985, p.86). His generalizations are derived from European and North American history and would have to be modified to take account of the African experience of the emerging universalization of language and the widening of human communication. But the general thrust of his observations is pertinent: that the strength of the dominant language has less to do with numbers and more to do with its utility and inherent power *vis-à-vis* declining language groups.

Most recognise that change is inherent in any language contact situation whereas Kay argues that language loss is a necessary aspect of the development process involving the 'destruction' of cultures, so as to usher in the full benefits of choice, increased wealth and freedom he sees in the liberating effect of modernization from the narrow confines of ethnicity. 'Diversity within the brotherhood of one world does not require the protection of today's particular pattern of ethnicity' (Kay, 1993).

Displacement is the predominant trend, but one person's definition of protection is another's natural expression of ethnicity. If Kay is right in arguing that ethnicity is inextinguishable (a dubious assumption), it still behoves us to ascertain what is the significance of such identity for the individual and the social group and how development influences structural and social-psychological adjustment.

Roland Breton avers that without energetic language defence policies, most African languages will be submerged within three generations. He recognizes that the old pattern based upon language complementarity is being challenged by the pervasive spread of more functional 'official' and inter-ethnic languages.

> Today Africa is involved in a vertiginous breath-taking process of urbanization which has already lead to cities where all ethnic groups are mixed together, half of the population of many countries; there is the central

> 'melting pot' whose pestle is the state language; there, there is nothing to compare with the old rural complementarity between vernacular and vehicular (Breton 1991a, p.174).

Language dependency

The process of language dependency obtains at all levels of the socio-political and spatial hierarchy. Individuals have to perform daily cost-benefit analyses on the economics of language choice. This situation is not new, as from ancient times traders and travellers throughout Africa have exercised the same diglossic fluency as do modern taxi drivers in Cairo, or government officials in Lagos. But what changes the situation today is that the freedom of possibility of exercising such choice is increasingly determined by state-influenced infrastructural decisions. The individual and the state are conjoined by

> the drastic law of economy which commands language development (for) planning, psychology meets economics, and individual identity joins national design. The options faced by the man in the street are those of the man in power. Masses and governments, in this case at least, are alike – time and money are limited; emergency drives you in one way, the highway of modernity, which is a no return route (Breton 1991a, p.174).

This lack of freedom and creativity is exacerbated when alternative power bases promote different languages for different reasons. Thus Tanzania and the Republic of South Africa are both cases where economic, commercial power required English, but political power promoted a rival tongue, namely Swahili or Afrikaans respectively. This lack of congruence adds a further element to the already difficult process of modernization.

The 'new Africans', the 'men of power', have been in a privileged position, because of their command of a Western or other international language. Military, political and commercial leaders have exercised their multilingual skills to great effect such that the

> credentials for ruling an African country are disproportionately based on a command of the Euro-imperial language. In Africa south of the Sahara it has become impossible to become a member of parliament or President without being fluent in at least one of the relevant European languages (Mazrui and Mazrui 1992, p.84).

The same observation can be made about senior executives in business, senior civil servants and academia. Should the elite's diglossic capacity be extended to the masses? This is one of the biggest questions of social development policy. Kay argues that certain international languages should become available to all forthwith in order to liberate and develop people in Africa (Kay 1993). In similar vein Carol Eastman has recently advocated an institutional diglossia with 'English as a medium of instruction, at all levels, while at the same time encouraging first language in home, neighbourhood and regional activities' (Eastman 1991, p.148). Others may not be so persuaded by the functional necessity of massive language switching from African to European languages; therefore let us demonstrate a series of alternative answers to the key question of whether most Africans should possess, at the least, both one indigenous and one international language.

Pragmatic adjustment to a changed order

Pragmatists have a well-established pedigree in language planning. They urge the adoption of a universal language, such as English, in order to provide a 'passport to the modern world'. This perspective views ethnicity as a dualistic concept, reflecting both its potential for dynamic change and for reactionary conservatism. Because it is essentially a behavioural phenomenon reflecting acquired values, it can be manipulated for good or evil. Given the conviction that a Western language would better serve the developmental needs of sub-Saharan Africa than would an indigenous tongue, Kay has argued that 'plural societies, (in Europe no less than Africa), are better served by pragmatic, 'neutral' *non*-racial and *non*-ethnic policies which are fairly cognizant of the nature and needs of all individuals, groups and peoples whom they serve'. His Zambian case study demonstrates that the people are divided by 72 ethnic and seven regional languages and united by one official language, English. 'Like all human constructs, this language policy evidently is not without either history or ethnic origins; but it is pragmatic and seeks to serve the best interests of 8,000,000 people. English is their passport to the modern world' (Kay 1993).

Such pragmatism, whether by design or default, is also encouraged by technological developments and by the globalization of culture and economy (Williams 1993). There is an acute inevitability surrounding the universalization of English and, to a lesser extent, of French. The question arises as to whether such inevitability should be welcomed and adapted to specific 'national', group and individual needs; or resisted and restricted only to the functional domains of an elite communication network, thereby perpetuating privilege and access to material and intellectual power bases. In the context of the gradual democratization of language use both trends seem increasingly likely to lead to conflict in and over language competition.

Clearly the reasons why this form of pragmatism does not automatically endear itself to all is that both English and French symbolize and realize a colonial inheritance and perpetuate a neo-colonial intellectual and political dependency. Virulent anti-colonial nationalism fed on this obvious manifestation of inequality and forced incorporation into a European imperial system. Post-colonial nationalism was faced with an acute dilemma of either rejecting the colonial instruments of subjugation or somehow incorporating them into the new nation-state project, as described in this volume by Hettne. Kay (1993) counters this observation by arguing that Western languages *per se* were not instruments of subjugation *except* by their policies of exclusion. The stark choice facing educators was either to

> revert to 'tribal obsolescence' or to 'modernise – which included the adoption of a *modern* (Western) language. Here we encounter a major misconception, it is the Tanzanian (Swahili) and RSA (Afrikaans) language policies which are the policies of subjugation (Kay 1993).

This attitude is intricately bound up with the perceived status differentials among constituent groups in the respective states.

The linguistic imperialism of English

Critics of English, as an instrument of imperialism and modernization, claim that the spread of English perpetuates an unequal relationship between 'developed' and 'developing' societies because access to information and power does not depend solely upon language fluency. It also depends upon institutional structures, economic resources and relationships. Tolleson illustrates this need to take account of infrastructural investment when he reminds us that

> in order to gain access to English-language resources, nations must develop the necessary institutions, such as research and development offices, 'think tanks', research universities, and corporations, as well as ties to institutions that control scientific and technological information. From the perspective of 'modernising' countries, the process of modernisation entails opening their institutions to direct influence and control by countries that dominate scientific and technical information . . . the result is an unequal relationship (Tollefson 1991, p.84).

The spread of English is also deeply implicated in the creation of new forms of inequality within societies. Most post-colonial societies are characterized by a dual institutional system, which nevertheless presents different ranges of opportunities to their respective members in the conventional and modernized sectors.

In a powerful critique of the role of ELT, (English Language Teaching) Phillipson (1992, p.270) has demonstrated how arguments used to promote English can be classified into three types based upon the language's:

1. 'capacities: English-intrinsic arguments, what English *is*';
2. 'resources: English-extrinsic arguments, what English *has*'

3. 'uses: English-functional arguments, what English *does*'.

Each element is mediated by the structure of the world order in which English is dominant and each develops its own discourse which locates English *vis-à-vis* competing languages. Thus

> English-intrinsic arguments describe English as rich, varied, noble, well adapted for change, interesting etc. English-extrinsic arguments refer to textbooks, dictionaries, grammar books, a rich literature, trained teachers, experts, etc. English-functional arguments credit English with real or potential access to modernization, science, technology, etc.; with the capacity to unite people within a country and across nations, or with the furthering of international understanding (Phillipson 1992, p.271–2).

The functions of English are nearly always described in positive terms. Whether the argument for its extension is couched in terms of persuasion, promise or threat, they represent various ways of exerting and legitimating power. This was well understood during colonial times and post-colonially in more subtle, sophisticated ways as is demonstrated in the rhetoric of the British Council. When the British 'do not have the power we once had to impose our will ("sticks"), cultural diplomacy must see to it that people see the benefits of English ("carrots") and the drawbacks with their own languages, and then, consequently, want English themselves for their own benefit ("ideas"): the demand is insatiable.' And that means that British influence, British power has not diminished, because Britain has this 'invisible, God-given asset'. Thus 'Britain's influence endures, out of all proportion to her economic or military resources' (*British Council Annual Report, 1983/4,* p.9; quoted in Phillipson 1992, pp.286–7). France's 'mission to civilize' strategy is a variant on this theme.

Language, and the ideology it conveys, is thus part of the legitimization of positions within the global division of labour. Attempts to separate English from its British and North American value system are misguided, for English should not be interpreted as if it were primarily a *tabula rasa*. Any claim that English is now a neutral, pragmatic tool for global development is disingenuous because it involves a 'disconnection between what English *is* ('culture') from its structural basis (from what it *has* and *does*). It disconnects the *means* from *ends* or *purpose*, from what English is being used for. This type of reasoning

> is part of the rationalization process whereby the unequal power relations between English and other languages are explained and legitimated. It fits into the familiar linguistic pattern of the dominant language creating an external image of itself, other languages being devalued and the relationship between the two rationalized in favour of the dominant language. This applies to each type of argument, whether persuasion, bargaining, or threats are used, all of which serve to reproduce English linguistic hegemony' (Phillipson 1992, p.288).

Table 3.5 The labelling of English and other languages

Glorifying English	Devaluing other languages
World language	Localized language
International language	(Intra-) national language
Language of wider communication	Language of narrower communication
Auxiliary language	Unhelpful language
Additional language	Incomplete language
Link language	Confining language
Window on to the world	Closed language
Neutral language	Biased language

Source: Phillipson (1992 p.282)

A summary of the manner in which English linguistic hegemony is 'glorified' in a competitive situation is presented in Table 3.5.

The challenge to colonial linguistic hegemony

There are at least three significant ways in which the former imperial languages have been challenged and, to an extent, replaced by autochthonous tongues. These are the modernization of indigenous languages, the adoption of a national language and the internationalization of a 'colonial' language.

The modernization of indigenous languages

The most common way of reducing the linguistic hegemony of an intrusive language is to modernize an indigenous tongue. This was one of the most virulent aims of the African nationalist intelligentsia in the period prior to independence. After early experimentation with the use of vernacular languages a decade or so after independence, it was all too frequently claimed that such languages were incapable of providing an adequate means of mass communication in a modern, technocratic world. Fishman (1971) suggested that the maintenance of the colonial language was an indication that the independence elite were primarily concerned with 'operational efficiency' rather than with authentic nationhood (Mansour 1993, p.120). Some elements of the post-independence African elite have argued that support for African languages is tantamount to confining them to a dependent, inferior position. Arguing thus, they have come to accept and reproduce the logic of linguistic imperialism.

In a significant collection of papers on this theme Florian Coulmas (1988) has asked a key question. What are national (African-ethnic) languages good for? This question opens up a Pandora's box revealing the contradictions inherent in the search for national congruence. Some of the related questions we may pose are: why have the Asian and African multilingual states opted for the conflict-ridden process of establishing a single, usually foreign or predominant, official language through which they can express state unity and channel development? Why is a common language so often seen as essential to 'nation-building' or state development? If conflict is such a predictable outcome why not opt for linguistic and cultural pluralism as a dominant ideology? Is it merely a post-colonial reaction to a European model of state formation and citizen socialization? Is the faculty of imitation, and the search for legitimacy through national congruence, so strong as to impel political elites on such a conflict-ridden trajectory?

Because language rationalization has so often involved the denial of indigenous identity Coulmas (1988, p.18) asks: 'Why, then, is not the multiplicity of languages of a given country stressed as a matter of pride, while the language for communicating at the national level is restricted to a practical convenience without any sentimental value?' The answer is surely that language is power: power to confer privilege, to deny opportunity, to construct a new social reality and to overturn or radically modify an inherited past which is not conducive to the pursuit of state aims and the growing aspirations of the people. Coulmas's 'sentimental value' is another's essential culture, Kay's 'pragmatism' is another's open prison of neo-colonial practices. Language choice is thus an open battleground for contending discourses, ideologies and interpretations of the multiethnic experience. The spread of English in Africa and Asia can also be interpreted as a recognition of the insufficiency and lack of authority of Afro-ethnic, or Asian-ethnic languages. Yet questions of sufficiency and authority are culturally and politically determined. No wonder that generations of African intellectuals have rejected the European claim that their model of language displacement is a 'rational' response to language functionality. Consider Ngugi wa Thiong's's indictment of English for carrying 'the disease of imperialism' and for having 'wrought destruction on other languages and cultures in its march to the position it now occupies on the world' (Ngugi wa Thiong, 1991, p.32, cited in Mazrui and Mazrui 1992, p.96).

Such criticisms are a two-edged sword. Without the ability to transmit concerns through an international language, African ideas and voices would be even less well represented on the world stage than they are at present. While this is true, virulent opposition to the oppressor in the oppressor's language is a common feature of most inter-lingual conflict situations. This is all the more difficult to sustain in contemporary Africa because there are very few genuine transnational languages that can replace English or French as languages of wider communication.

One exception is the development of Kiswahili, which has passed through a number of stages in response to external, contextual changes. These were the Islamic stage, the ecumenical, the secular and the stage of universalization (Mazrui and Zirimu 1990). In its pre-colonial stage, Kiswahili was 'at the peak of its Afro-Islamic mould', the carrier of Islam and trade, ideas and influence. Precisely because it was a vehicular language British and German missionaries adopted it and successfully transformed the language into an ecumenical tongue. Wider colonial interests of trade and military conquest demonstrated Kiswahili's secular potential for inter-ethnic communication and administration. But it now became a key instrument for social mobilization and for class formation, as anti-colonial nationalists embraced it as the 'language of practical politics'. On independence all three East African states adopted Kiswahili in order to develop the territorial–bureaucratic and military structures of the new order, and it has also become significant beyond its core area as part of the education policy in Tanzania, Kenya and Uganda and to a lesser extent, in the border regions of Zaire.

President Nyerere's policy in establishing Kiswahili as Tanzania's 'national' language produced both an effective state-wide socialization process and created a new form of identity derived from the historical potential of communicative power which Kiswahili as a regional lingua franca bestows on the Tanzanian people. Before independence it was used as the medium of basic education, of communication for supra-ethnic fraternal unions, anti-colonial movements and political association. Kiswahili had thus demonstrated its utility as a language for political organization (Russell 1990).

Kiswahili is an *African* transnational language and ethnically neutral. It is no longer overly associated with either a particular geographical group or with Islam. The speakers of the primary dialects on the coast do not constitute a tribe, their linguistic affiliation is considered cultural rather than ethnic. Further, the speakers of other Bantu languages can mark their ethnicity by use of their vernacular language. By using Kiswahili as their L2(second language), some speakers demonstrate their acquisition of formal education, their experience of the wider East African context and of urban life. Others, who have only a minimal competence in it, can also identify with Kiswahili as a symbol and instrument of national mobilization (Russell 1990, p.366).

Nyerere's great commitment to Kiswahili stemmed in part from his desire to exploit its value as a transnational vehicle of communication and as a symbol of national development. Russell (1990, p.371) argues that the initial thrust of post-colonial development was grounded in local decision-making, improved agricultural amenities and practices, rather than imported technologies. For most people Kiswahili was the language of development and modernity because of its great communicative strength in forging power and solidarity. This was manifested in material acts of improvement such as agricultural reform, piped water, primary education and well-stocked village dispensaries. Such advances offer a useful counter to the tendency in most language planning writing to equate modernity with the widespread adoption of a European language.

However, Kiswahili's dominance also resulted in the relative neglect of many local languages. Breton (1991a, pp.165–6) observes that:

> The implementation of such a strict monopoly, aiming to subsume scores of other ethnolinguistic forces, is quite exceptional in Africa. The fact is, that this policy worked; now all over Tanzania, far from the coast, the home of native Kiswahili speakers, have arisen generations of Tanzanians having Kiswahili as their mother tongue, sometimes called the new Baswahili people, compared to numerous old local ethnicities.

By contrast English is perceived by most people as a foreign language, though in response to several crises and policy reversals a decade ago, its position as the medium of secondary and higher education was strengthened. It is claimed that this is at odds with the socio-linguistic environment nurtured in the post-colonial era. 'The alienating implications of the linguistic gap between primary (Swahili-educated) and secondary (English-educated) school leavers does not seem to have been the subject of open discussion in government circles in recent years' (Russell 1990, p.371). Tanzanian linguists, writing in Rubagumya (1990), question the relevance of English to young people and assert that resistance to Kiswahili as a medium derives from an association between English and elitism which reproduces African dependency on Western resources and power.

Currently Kiswahili is becoming universalized to meet the growing educational, technical, scientific and mass-media needs of East Africa. Language planning policies have encouraged its use as the language of modernization writ large, as with Amharic, its closest indigenous comparison in terms of communicative power and vehicle for the spread of new scientific-based knowledge.

Where Kiswahili is an intrusive, or contested, language as in Kenya, then the impulse of modernization accentuates class fragmentation and ethnic divisions. Domains, which were once the preserve of the colonial language, such as public administration, parliament and the legal system have been the subject of intense debate for, as Harries (1983 p.120) has argued the decision to opt for an African language was 'to make a political declaration in favour of what is African, however unfamiliar Swahili may be to Kenyans, especially in rural areas'. Watson (1992) urges 'that a public declaration for English would have been tantamount to supporting all things foreign' (p.114). Despite considerable opposition from the English-speaking elite, Kiswahili has joined English as a joint national language, an examinable subject in both primary and secondary schools. The long-term implications are that real power is perceived as having been vested in the Kikuyu, at the expense of other ethnic groups, and that English proficiency as a path to upward socio-political mobility is being paralleled by the formation of a Kiswahili educational elite.

But there are deeper implications, for who hears the voice of indigenous development in such circumstances? Is not the power of politicians intent on building their inviolable 'nation state' given priority over 'development'? These questions strike at the very heart of the development process for they involve the renegotiation of internal power relations. We may ask: what is happening to the ethnic languages under such circumstances? Could this not be described as a new round of 'internal colonialism' whereby the elite-backed language is reinforced at the expense of the powerless and marginal groups? Is the colonial legacy of the modern African 'nation' state any the more just than its imperial European legacy in its treatment of subordinated language groups? Tanzanian specialist suggest that 'contemporary political and economic leaders in Africa are likely to be forced by current political and economic necessity to begin to learn from the European Christian missionaries *vis-à-vis* the use of indigenous African languages' (Rubagumya 1990, p.152).

In some ways the attempts by contemporary elites to limit popular access to international languages, and by implication opportunities for self-advancement, are analogous to the manner in which British, Belgian and German colonial elites sought to maintain their power of patronage by refusing to share their 'cultural values and institutions' with others. Before the 1830s, for example, there was a constant struggle between the British Colonial Office and local elites in the colonies over the question of how the colonies should be run. In an attempt to reduce the power of the Elected Councils, locally elected district councils were introduced so as to reduce the oligarchic power of the elite. They in turn favoured the nurturing of local languages so as to maintain the divide and rule principles upon which they operated. The net effect was that a cultural division of labour was established which simultaneously allowed the colonial system to function without threatening the ascendancy of the settler population. The French and Portugese, by contrast, allowed for a more complete assimilation of selected individuals through the granting of citizenship rights in the motherland.

While accepting that elites today can exercise raw power in a more sophisticated fashion, it does not always follow that they exploit their fellow nationals in socio-linguistic matters. Among Cameroon's elite, for example, mastery of English or French is a prerequisite for access to power but does not necessarily imply a denial of other relationships. The elite has many of the hallmarks of political power, high socio-economic status, access to education, links with the North, the capacity for self-perpetuation. But Robinson argues that this type of analysis is simplistic

> since it ignores a basic characteristic of the members of the elite, namely that they are individually also members of one of the 'minority' ethnic groups of the country. What looks like a homogenous ruling elite at a distance is in fact a coalition of members of different ethnic and linguistic groups. For those members of the elite whose personal identity and security are linked more to their ethnic ties than to the elite group, French and English are not so much symbols of identity but tools for pragmatic purposes. Thus the official neglect of Cameroonian languages finds its cause in inertia and pragmatism, rather than in outright hegemonic design on the part of the elite (Robinson 1992b, p.7).

Where the elite did display its hegemonic power was in the imposition of French by the francophone elite, at the expense of English.

Jayakan Bahasa Kebangsaan Malaysia offers another example where the colonial linguistic legacy which favoured the use of English has been challenged in favour of an indigenous language, Bahasa Malaysia. The slogan used as the title above means more than 'glorify the national language'; it implies 'glorify the Malays' (Watson 1992, p.115). One of the first acts on independence in 1957 was to introduce Malay medium secondary education, while during the 1970s and 1980s Bahasa Malaysia gradually displaced English. This reflected the switch away from 'a reasonably successful consociational democracy' (Lijphart 1979, pp.150–61) that was institutionalized in the governing alliance between Malay, Chinese and Indian political parties towards a more strident Malay and pro-Islamic stance which accelerated in the 1980s under Dr Mahathir (Brown 1985, p.991). Because the main tool of ideological and social control is language, the state sought to redefine the parameters of acceptable identities through ethnolinguistic manipulation, relying on the metaphor of a nation under siege. The government's use of 'siege legitimacy' to avoid a repetition of the 13 May 1969 inter-ethnic riots and to deny succour to the opposition parties, especially the DAP (The Democratic Action Party) and PAS (Partai Islam Se Malaysia) was a deliberate strategy designed to define the limits of identity. Thus, 'the government intervenes to define the distinction between the legitimate version of Islam which can be incorporated within notions of Malayness and Bumiputra; and the non-legitimate extremist versions of Islam associated with the PAS and its allies' (Brown 1985, p.1007).

This version of democracy relies on the leaders' ability to convince the populace that internal dissent and criticism of the regime stems from competing ethnic interests in society which have to be checked. Communal disunity is a severe challenge to national unity and it is claimed that only strong, authoritarian leadership can prevent political instability. Ethnicity gives rise to ambiguity in such a context. On the one hand the siege argument stresses the value of national cohesion over and above subordinate ethnic identities. On the other hand, because of the resilience of such ethnic identification, ethnic cleavages are a constant reminder that ethnic ties are potentially stronger than ties to the state and must therefore be contained. Brown (1985, p.1008) stresses that this view of ethnicity 'clearly inhibits attempts both at depluralisation and at ethnic accommodation, and thus induces an element of incoherence into such government policies'.

Watson (1980; 1992) has shown how comprehensive language planning has secured the dominance of the Malay majority in education, administration and politics, through such devices as imposing quotas on non-Malay students for access to higher education and selective employment within the public sector. This was to the advantage of the Malays, at the expense of the Chinese and Indians. Reversing ethnic structural discrimination through social planning is, of course, a well-established political strategy. But observers have recognized that in attempting to defuse the economic time bomb created by colonialism, Malay education and public preference policies may be building up another political time bomb, as the Chinese in particular come to resent and mobilize against their periodic exclusion from the opportunities afforded by the new socio-political structure (Lee Yon Leng 1979; Williams 1985). Speakers of other languages also resent their marginalization in a system which forces their children to pursue secondary education through Bahasa Malaysia. Filtering the five primary media of instruction into the single medium at secondary level is a complex process which has come under sharp attack of late leading Gaudart to warn that 'to be an educational planner in Malaysia is a massive responsibility' (Gaudart 1992, p.222). It is time that Malaysia asked very severe questions of its language-education policies, including what is best for the child. Gaudart argues that for too long planners and ideologues have been using the criteria of majoritarian-influenced economics, social acceptability and national unity to determine education policy. In contrast one should recognize that the value of multiple language skills in an additive bilingual situation can be a real strategic resource for both state and society. The insistence on employing Bahasa Malaysia as the means of creating intercultural understanding and national unity is now suspect. Communal politics, it is claimed, rather than pedagogic conviction, has formed the national educational plan.

Rural opportunities for social advancement and majoritarian political confidence may have been boosted by the Bahasa Malaysia status language programme, but there is evidence that the pendulum may have swung too far in favour of Bahasa Malaysia for, as Watson (1992, p.114) claims, fears are currently expressed about the declining standards of English and the consequential effect this is having on Malaysia's competitive position in the international economic system. Singapore, by contrast, has allowed market forces to operate in the education system and has benefited from the adoption of English in education to carve out a successful niche in international trade, computer technology and advanced electronics. But just as in Malaysia, Singapore, under the pragmatic leadership of Lee Kuan Yew, sought to induce a siege mentality. Brown (1985, p.998) argues that the modification of ethnic identity serves both to exacerbate the sense of insecurity which the government seeks to sustain, and to promote political depluralization.

Originally its fragile stability was explicable by reference to Singapore's geopolitical position. Inter-ethnic rioting in the 1950s and 1960s was put down to Chinese 'extremism' manifested in communist-inspired disturbances such as the 1955 Hock Lee riots. Malay 'extremism' was also manifest in the 1964 communal riots. Singapore dared not discriminate against its Malay minority in an overtly ethnic manner for fear of a political backlash from its Malay-dominated neighbours. Rather, the Chinese elite of Singapore have sought to depluralize daily politics by creating a 'Singaporean national identity' which is distinct from the particular communal identities which constitute the society. Brown suggests that while the government encourages Indian, Malay and Chinese cultural traits, it has effectively depluralized the political arena, 'which is instead depicted as an ethnically blind meritocracy' (p.999).

A second reason for the depluralization policy lies in the internal differentiation of the Chinese community. Political opposition to the People's Action Party leadership has been strongest among the vernacular-speaking Chinese groups, the Hokkien, Teochew, Cantonese and Hainanese. These were also the groups most isolated from the political mobilization activities of the better-educated, English-speaking elite. In consequence the PAP has used the educational system to change the language of the Chinese masses, promoting English as the international language and Mandarin as a common Chinese language so as to neuter, in part, the allegiance to the vernacular tongues. Accompanying these reforms was an active rehousing programme which relocated mono-ethnic communities into multiethnic housing estates dispersed throughout the island. Also Brown claims that the shifts in school language, curriculum and entrance policies, the closure of the Chinese university and Chinese newspapers have been achieved without major discontent. This he attributes to the skill and timing of the moves and to the belief that sensitive issues, like language and religion, are best dealt with by being depoliticized so as not to handicap the economic success of the country. Pragmatic 'common sense' policies prevailed throughout the 1980s and opposition criticism was interpreted as ethnic chauvenism and therefore suspect. Having achieved both stability and prosperity, programmes have recently been implemented to encourage various Chinese dialects to serve the 76 per cent Chinese population, though English remains dominant (Watson 1992). Thus language complementarity rather than language displacement comes to characterize the later stages of economic and political development.

The model of development clearly influences the choice of language in the public sector. Where perceptions of development are locked in only to the macro-level of the international community and the state structure, then local linguistic realities will remain almost invisible and certainly irrelevant. Where development is about helping people initiate, sustain and manage change in their own communities, grassroots communication (and therefore language) will come into view. This is the urgent message of much recent rural development thinking, best represented by Robinson (1992a). However, there is a constant tension between the life of a minority group within itself and its own environment and the linkages which must be formed and maintained with other groups, the state and the wider world. Whose criteria will predominate in language choice and development, and how will the different criteria at each level be integrated into a language and communication policy/practice which serves internal group cohesion and external linkages? Little attention is given to the micro-level, and almost no effort is expended on the ground to give speakers of minority languages the option of a viable choice to use their language in education, for development, for mass entertainment etc. This is as true for Tamil or Iban in Malaysia a it is for the estimated 238 to 275 languages in Cameroon. It is a pressing global problem, for language diversity implies some degree of decentralization of power, while the need to preserve 'national unity' predisposes even sympathetic governments to drag their feet on implementing reforms which favour the local language. Investment in language development responsibility, covering such features as the codification of a writing system, standardization of particular dialects, vocabulary expansion, production of materials, human-resource training and applied linguistic research is an essential aspect of ethnodevelopment (Robinson 1992a).

If we deny such investment in human, creative potential, we will be guilty of having witnessed the decolonization of the land but not of the spirit of the developing world. Language is both a call to liberty and a form of denying the full expression of exercising such liberty if it is stifling indigenous socio-cultural forms.

Internalizing international colonial languages

Displacing a colonial language by an indigenous one is not the only solution to the 'Catch 22' position of most multilingual societies. One consensus position is to internalize the colonial language as part of the indigenous heritage of the multilingual, multiethnic state. Thus English will remain central to India's development 'because it has become part of the Indian heritage' (Pattanayak 1985, p.17; see Coulmas 1988, p.17). Absorbing English as a constituent element of India's history goes some way to

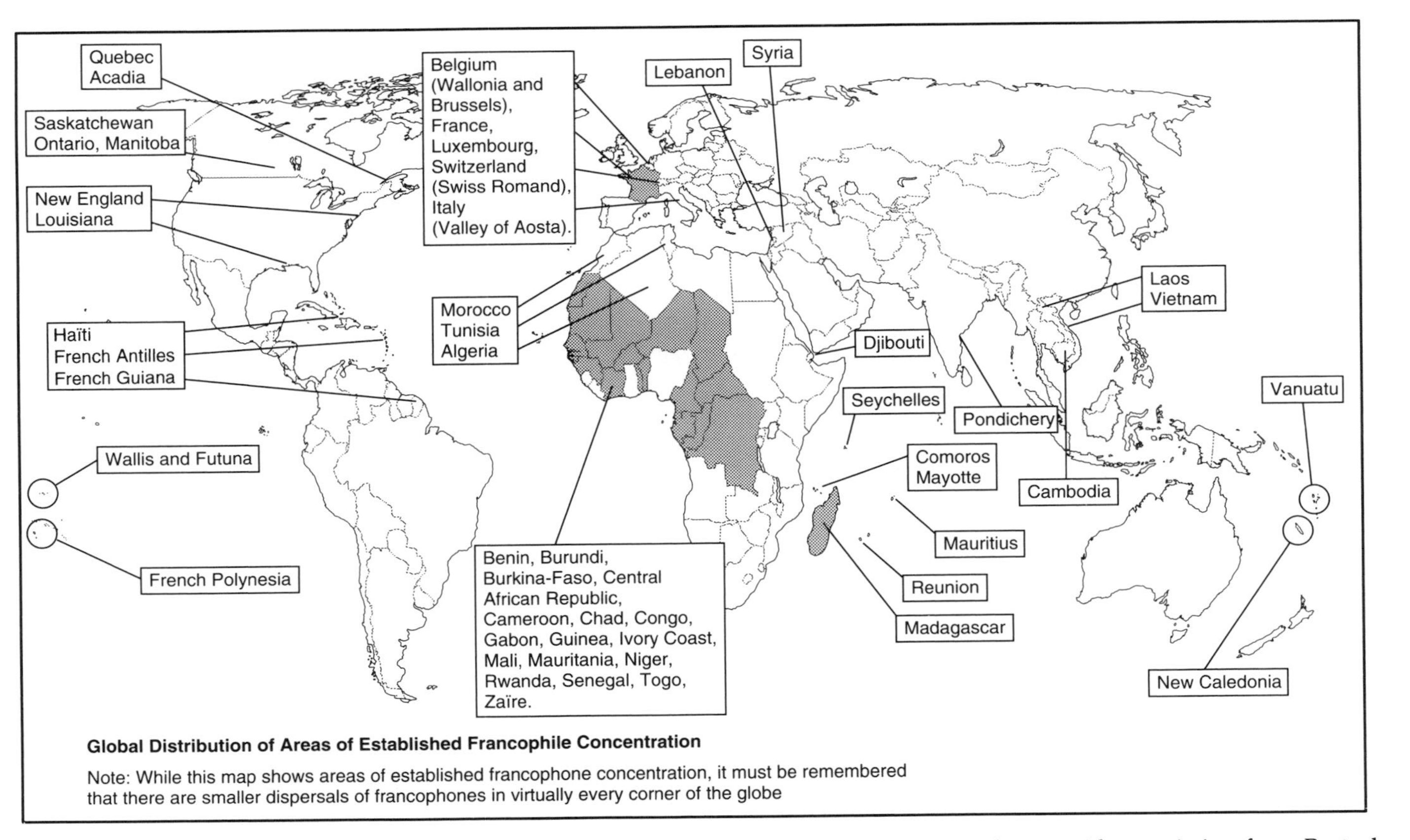

Figure 3.2 Global distribution of areas of established Francophile concentration. Source: redrawn with permission from Bostock (1988, p. 76)

satisfying both the nationalist search for authority and legitimacy and the practical necessity of India's education and development being integrated into the wider world. More recently it may also have served as a useful brake on the increased inter-faith rivalry between Hindu and Muslim. Because it is not related to a single faith, English is an unmistakable bulwark of a secular state. Were Hindu fundamentalism to triumph in an extensive part of the Indian state then the prospects for pluralistic co-existence would be considerably diminished. The recent destruction of three mosques in Uttar Pradesh and the episodic 'ethnic cleansing', whether of Sikhs, Muslims or Hindus, are a forceful reminder of the religious divisions and geo-ethnic complexity of India's constituent peoples. In such a context English can play a functionally integrative role, but in return the huge mass of English-speakers in India also contribute to the development of English as the major world language and not just the inherited tongue of an Anglo–American cultural system. This two-way process of drawing from and contributing to a world language also influences the basis of Indian identity and transforms English into a transnational language but with Indian roots and varieties, conjoined with Jamaican English, Singapore English, Philippine English, Nigerian English and even British English (Coulmas 1988, p.18).

However, this strategy also serves to demonstrate the force of the national language ideology which causes such conflict in inter-ethnic relations. Coulmas (1988, p.18) argues that by interpreting 'localized forms of English' (Strevens 1983) as national characteristics and making them part of a national heritage, the state's ideology justifies the creation of an institutional infrastructure which promotes the widespread adoption of English as both a national and a transnational language.

Transnational languages have been significant elements of imperial rule since Persian, Greek and Roman times and greatly influenced the spread of capitalism and the modern world system. The roles of English and French in particular are crucial to the development of former overseas possessions, not only by relating former colonies to the motherland but also to unite each other through such devices as the Commonwealth and *la francophonie*.

Re-nationalizing the former colonial language of wider communication is especially prominent among former French territories, but it can also serve to unite people in otherwise very disparate regions world-wide. (Figure 3.2). Bostock's (1988) analysis of the authenticity of *la francophonie* as an international movement reveals the widespread influence of transnational agencies who use French and reinforce its power base as a medium for the spread of specific values and ideologies. The role of agencies such a l'Academie Française or the Alliance Française in reinforcing language standardization or in providing the material artefacts to construct the 'identity shield' of modern French for the Lebanon or Louisiana are well documented. But in terms of development planning it is the operation of the leading francophone Agency for Cultural and Technical Co-operation established in 1969 at Niamey in Niger which is more significant. Its 40 full-member states represent a powerful multicultural pressure group. Fears that France would dominate the Agency through neo-colonial practices are considered to be ill-founded both by Bostock, who cites the fact that the Agency's founders were non-French francophones and by Gordon (1978), who argues that many of its leading lights subscribed to the initial Malagasy view that the organization could be used as 'a vehicle of protest against colonialism and as a medium in which to express black identity'. In one of those remarkable transformations where the colonial medium is used to preach anti-colonial messages, French became a language for liberation just as English did in India. It is even more remarkable, given the pillage of Black Africa, that so many of *la francophonie's* most ardent advocates are to be found in the former colonial possessions of French West and Equatorial Africa. The paradox is well illustrated in Gordon's magisterial survey of the French language, particularly in the elites' search for authenticity and national congruence.

> In the case of Black Africa where borders have been among the cruellest cases of the 'rape of geography by history' (Jacques Ancel's phrase), nations, in the legal sense, have been created where no common language other than that, on an elite level, of the coloniser existed to help form a nationality – the vernacular language, rather than being a component of national identity, serves in most of these linguistically heterogeneous countries as a force for disruption and loss of national identity (Gordon 1978:17).

The search for legitimacy and popular involvement through mass socialization has been a major policy goal of many African states, but it is compounded by the conflict between those wishing to integrate a new state via an international language into the world system and of those wishing to play down such dependence in order to construct a stronger, indigenous communication system.

Interpreting French and English as heritage languages can accentuate the marginalization and dependency of most indigenous languages which are thereby deemed to be inadequate in an increasingly interconnected world. If so, the key policy choice is to ask what are the relative costs/benefits of either making good their deficiencies or of replacing them outside of the home and domestic socio-linguistic domains by 'adequate' languages (Kay 1993). It can also lead to the perpetuation of elite–mass differences unless means are found to encourage multilingualism in the formal education system, a daunting enough task in resource-rich states, let alone in the impoverished multicultural societies which constitute the South today.

Elite–mass relations also figure in the meaning of *la francophonie*. Critics have warned against the growth of *francite*, which is the attempt to reserve '*francophonie* for whites only'. Such racist tendencies have not been fully realized and do not threaten the more integrative values attached to the current interpretation of *francophonie* as a global movement (Williams 1988). But a resurgence of racism in France has called into question the openness of *francophonie* as a global phenomenon. The racialization of core–periphery relationships, however, is not just the product of extremist positions, whether of the left or the right. MacLaughlin (1993) and Williams (1993) have demonstrated that there are more pervasive, subtle and pernicious institutionalized barriers to racial and ethnic harmony both within the European Community and in its relationship with the 'developing' world.

The 3+1 way forward

The dynamic of socio-linguistic change in most African countries has reflected the conflict between the rationalization of language repertoires and the emergence of insitutionalized multilingualism. We have seen that European languages are firmly entrenched. Modernized indigenous forms are likely to grow but not displace European languages, especially within the civil service, technological and commercial sectors. Populous regional vernaculars are set to take their place as languages of local administration in clearly demarcated regions. In contrast, the majority of threatened minority languages face a depressing future as they slip further down the ladder of marginality.

David Laitin (1992, 1994) has argued that market forces in many African countries are working toward a '3 + 1' language outcome whereby aspiring citizens in different regions will need to have facility in the vernacular (primary language) through elementary education, an African lingua franca and a colonial language. If the individual's vernacular is the same as the lingua franca, the citizen will need to learn only two (3-1) languages.

If the citizen's vernacular is different from that taught in the region of residence, then he/she must learn four (3+1) languages. This is the Indian solution. Although no African state has yet declared this formula to be its official policy, strong elements of this approach characterize contemporary Nigeria, Zaire, Senegal, Zambia, and Ghana. It is a promising formula for it respects cultural diversity without compromising the need to be integrated into a wider world.

Critics argue that this perpetuates ethnic differences, and because of its presumption of linguistic regionalization could serve to increase discrimination against minorities. Laitin's response is that 'what Africa has produced best in the post colonial era has been refugees' (p.160), and it would be far better to institute a pattern of group political activity based upon tribal identities than to have no political activity at all based upon civil society. His fieldwork suggests that 'as an alternative to the present situation of empty centralization, the recognition of a hegemony of reified tribal boundaries might well be acceptable to many citizens of African states' (p.163). In his detailed analysis of Ghana he demonstrates how, with appropriate political initiative and investment in educational infrastructure, the 3+1 equilibrium would give all Ghanaians the ability to communicate efficiently with each other, while English would continue to serve as an international link language. Of course, he recognizes the dangers of populist leaders manipulating this cultural programme thereby increasing inter-regional division, yet this formula offers a realistic alternative whereby some degree of co-ordination in language planning policy can be achieved without sacrificing societal multilingualism.

Conclusion

Language policy is a crucial ingredient of development. Those who favour a diglossic situation with an international vehicular language being used alongside an indigenous language are in the ascendancy and will prevail in much of the developing world. This will favour certain class fractions and the urban population. It follows that wherever there is linguistic denial there is cultural and inter-cultural weakness, and this suggests that development must be impaired. It is quite a different matter as to how rural sustainable development can encourage functional bilingualism and the promotion of science, technology and indigenous economic development by following such a pattern. Watson (1992, p.117), in summarizing this dilemma, argues that

> many, if not most, developing counties are caught in a 'Catch 22' situation. If they develop a national language there is a danger that they marginalise themselves from international scientific and technological developments. If they develop an international language as the national language this can create scientific and technological dependency because western scientific knowledge is fitted and interpreted for local conditions. Either way, rural children are increasingly marginalised from scientific developments because neither they, nor their teachers, have adequate linguistic skills to be able to truly understand the scientific concepts being taught to them. Marginalisation and dependency, especially in Africa, therefore, result from the use of European languages.

Some would argue that such marginalization and dependency are integral to the West's globalizing role in spreading its languages and technology, especially through the mass media. Others would interpret this as a classic illustration of political correctness applied to the development process. If Africa was to abandon the widespread use of European languages at this stage, it would surely damage its prospects for economic diversification, social development, mass socialization, political involvement and technological transformation. For even, if on occasion, as in Tanzania, such technology can be adapted to promote Kiswahili, at the expense of English (Mazrui and Mazrui 1992), the general trend is towards the globalization of world culture and technology via the univerzalisation of language choice. Choice implies freedom and opportunity for some at the expense of others. It would appear that in linguistic identity, as in all other aspects of the development process, the new world order reinforces the global division of labour, guaranteeing the primacy of dominant languages.

In most of Africa, state-inspired language planning which seeks to resist the penetration of Western languages into new social domains has patently failed. Breton (1991a, p.172) points to the futility of most language planning schemes and the inevitability of language shift. In the shift process features like attitude to international languages, the role of the media and the attraction of mass popular culture all need to be taken into account. Yet very little empirical work has been undertaken on measuring such factors. Nor do we have many accurate accounts of the actual successes and failures of formal language planning schemes in the development literature. As Paulston and McLaughlin (1993, p.327) have argued,

> we have no theory of language planning; there is no evidence of significant cross-disciplinary work, no criteria for evaluation, no greater insight into the process . . . the frequent failure of language planning [would suggest that] a classificatory study of such failures, with an attempt to identify causal factors, might be very useful toward the development of a theory of language planning; at present, failure is mostly ignored.

If state-inspired language planning programmes are often deemed to be failures, then collective, non-state attempts to support threatened minority languages and their respective cultures are even more likely to fail and in the attempt to increase frustration and inter-group conflict.

Given this, it is imperative that the development process should take due account of minority rights and threatened identities without halting the emergence of new forms of ethnic and cultural identification. For only if people and groups are incorporated within the process on equitable terms will the development of society operate at a reasonable political level; otherwise it is the tyranny of the powerful masquerading as progress and social change.

Acknowledgements

I wish to thank Elaine Bjorklund, David Dalby, George Kay, William Mackey, Clinton Robinson and Charles Whebell for making valuable suggestions which have widened the interpretative element of this chapter.

References

Ammon, U. and Kleineidam, H. (Issue eds) (1992), 'Language Spread Policy: Languages of Former Colonial Powers', *International Journal of the Sociology of Language*, 95.

Baker, C. (1993) *Foundations of Bilingual Education and Bilingualism.* Multilingual Matters Ltd, Clevedon, Avon.

Bostock, W.W. (1988) 'Assessing the Authenticity of a Supra-National Language-Based Movement: La Francophonie' in C.H. Williams (ed.), *Language in Geographic Context*, Multilingual Matters Ltd, Clevedon, Avon, 73–92.

Brann, C.M.B. (1991) Review of F. Coulmas, *With Forked Tongues: What are National Languages Good For? History of European Ideas*, (13), 131–5.

Breton, R. (1991a) 'The Handicaps of Language Planning in Africa' in D.F. Marshall (ed.), *Language Planning: Focusschrift in honour of Joshua A. Fishman*, John Benjamins, Amsterdam.

Breton, R. (1991b) *Geolinguistics: Language Dynamics and Ethnolinguistic Geography*, University of Ottawa Press, Ottawa.

British Council (1983/4) *Annual Report*, British Council, London.

Brown, D. (1985) 'Crisis and Ethnicity: 'Legitimacy in Plural Societies', *Third World Quarterly*, (7), 988–1008.

Coulmas, F. (ed.) (1988) *With Forked Tongues: What are National Languages Good For?* Karoma, Ann Arbor.

Dua, H.R. (1991) 'Language Planning in India: Problems, Approaches and Prospects' in D.R. Marshall (ed.), *Language Planning: Focusschrift in honour of Joshua A. Fishman*, John Benjamins, Amsterdam.

Eastman, C.M. (1983) *Language Planning: An Introduction*, Chandler and Sharp, San Francisco.

Eastman, C.M. (1991) 'The Political and Sociolinguistic Status of Planning in Africa' in D.F. Marshall (ed.) *Language Planning: Focusschrift in Honour of Joshua A. Fisman*. John Benjamins, Amsterdam, 135–51.

Edwards, J. (1991) 'Gaelic in Nova Scotia' in C.H. Williams (ed.), *Linguistic Minorities, Society and Territory*, Multilingual Matters, Clevedon, Avon.

Fasold, R. (1988) 'What National Languages are Good For' in F. Coulmas (ed.), *With Forked Tongues*, Koroma, Ann Arbor, 180–5.

Fishman, J.A. (1969) 'National Language and Languages of Wider Communication', *Anthropological Linguistics*, (11), 111–75.

Fishman, J.A. (1971) 'The Sociology of Language' in J.A. Fishman (ed.), *Advances in the Sociology of Language*, Vol. I, Moutan, The Hague, 217–404.

Gaudert, H. (1992) *Bilingual Education in Malaysia*, Centre for Southeastern Asian Studies, James Cook University.

Gordon, D.G. (1978) *The French Language and National Identity*, Mouton, The Hague.

Government of India (1955) *Report of the States Reorganization*, Government Printer, Delhi.

Harries, L. (1983) 'The Nationalisation of Swahili in Kenya' in C. Kennedy (ed.), *Language Planning and Language Education*, George Allen and Unwin, London, 118–28.

Heine, B. (1992) 'Language Policies in Africa' in R.K. Herbert (ed.), *Language and Society in Africa*, Johanesburg, Witwatersrand University Press, 23–35.

Herbert, R.K. (ed.) (1992) *Language and Society in Africa*, Johanesburg, Witwatersrand University Press.

Hettne, B. (1984) *Approaches to the Study of Peace and Development, A State of the Art Report*, EADI Working Papers, Tilburg.

Horowitz, D.L. (1985) *Ethnic Groups in Conflict*, University of California Press, Berkeley.

Horowitz, D.L. (1991) *A Democratic South Africa?* University of California Press, Berkeley.

Kay, G. (1970) *Rhodesia: A Human Geography*, Africana Publishing Company, New York.

Kay, G. (1993) 'Ethnicity, the Cosmos and Plonomic Development, with Special Reference to Central Africa', Mimeo.

Kennedy, C. (ed.) (1983) *Language Planning and Language Education*, George Allen and Unwin, London.

Kelman, H.C. (1971) 'Language as an Aid and Barrier to Involvement in the National System' in J. Rubin and B. Jernudd (eds), *Can Language be Planned?* University of Hawaii Press, Honolulu, 21–51.

Laitin, D.D. (1992) *Language Repertoires and State Construction in Africa*, Cambridge University Press, Cambridge.

Laitin, D.D. (1994) 'The Tower of Babel as a Coordination Game: Political Linguistics in Ghana', *American Political Science Review*, 88, 622–34.

Laponce, J. (1984) 'The French Language in Canada: Tensions between Geography and Politics', *Political Geography Quarterly*, (3) 91–104.

Lee Yong Leng (1979) 'South-east Asia: The Political Geography of Economic Imbalance', *Tijdschrift voor Economische en Sociale Geografie*, (70), 339–49.

Lijphart, A. (1979) *Democracy in Plural Societies*, Yale University Press, New Haven, Conn.

Mackey, W. (1991) 'Language Diversity, Language Policy and the Sovereign State', *History of European Ideas*, (13), 51–61.

Mackey, W. (1995) Personal Communication.

MacLaughlin, J. (1993) 'Defending the Frontiers: the Political Geography of Race and Racism in the European Community' in C.H. Williams (ed.), *The Political Geography of the New World Order*, Belhaven/Wiley, London, 20–45.

Managan, J.A. (ed.) (1993) *The Imperial Curriculum. Racial Images and Education in the British Colonial Experience*, Routledge, London.

Mansour, G. (1993) *Multilingualism and Nation Building*, Multilingual Matters, Clevdon, Avon.

Mazrui, A. and P. Zirimu, (1990) 'The Secularization of an Afro-Islamic language: Church, State and Market-place in the Spread of Kiswahili', *Journal of Islamic Studies*, (1), 24–53.

Mazrui, A.M. and A.A. Mazrui (1992) 'Language in a Multicultural Context: The African Experience', *Language and Education*, (6), 83–9.

Msanjila, Y.P. (1990) 'Problems of Teaching Through the Medium of Kiswahili in Teacher Training Colleges in Tanzania, *Journal of Multilingual and Multicultural Development*, (11), 307–18.

Nelde, P.H., N. Labrie and C.H. Williams (1992) 'The Principles of Territoriality and Personality in the Solution of Linguistic Conflicts', *Journal of Multilingual and Multicultural Development*, (13), 387–406.

Ngugi Wa Thionglo (1991) 'What in a language'. *Africa Events*, July, 30–3.

Pattanayak, D.P. (1985) 'Diversity in Communication and Languages; Predicament of a Multi-lingual National State: India, a Case Study', in N. Wolfson and J. Manes (eds), *Languages of Inequality*, Mouton, Berlin 309–407.

Pattanayak, D.P. and J.M. Bayer (1987) 'Laponce's "The French Language in Canada: Tensions between Geography and Politics", a rejoinder', *Political Geography Quarterly*, (6), 261–3.

Paulston, C.B. and S. McLaughlin, (1993) 'Language in Education Policy and Planning', *Annual Review of Applied Linguistics*, ARAL, New York, 53–81.
Phillipson, R. (1992) *Linguistic Imperialism*, Oxford University Press, Oxford.
Platt, J.T. (1981) 'The Chinese Community in Malaysia: Language Policies and Relationships' in J. Megarry, S. Nisbet and E. Hoyle (eds), *Education of Minorities*, Kogan Page, London. 164–76.
Robinson, C.L.D. (1992a) *Language Choice in Rural Development*, International Museum of Cultures, Dallas.
Robinson, C.L.D. (1992b) *Where Minorities are in the Majority*, paper presented at the International Conference on the Maintenance and Loss of Minority Languages, Noordwijkerhout, The Netherlands, 1–4 September.
Robinson, C.L.D. (1993) Personal communication.
Rubagumya, C.M. (ed.) (1990) *Language in Education in Africa: A Tanzanian Perspective*, Multilingual Matters, Clevedon, Avon.
Russell, J. (1990) 'Success as a Source of Conflict in Language Planning: The Tanzanian Case', *Journal of Multilingual and Multicultural Development*, (11), 363–75.
Stewart, W.A. (1968) 'A Socioloingistic Typology for Describing National Multilingualism' in J. Fishman *et al.* (eds), *Language Problems of Developing Nations*, Wiley, London, 503–53.
Strevens, P. (1983) 'The Localised Forms of English' in Braj B. Kachru (ed.), *The Other Tongue: English across Cultures*. Pergamon, Oxford, 23–30.
Tollefson, J.W. (1991) *Planning Language Planning Inequality*, Longman, London.
UNESCO (1951) *The Use of Vernacular Languages in Education*, UNESCO, Paris.
Van den Berghe, P.L. (1968) 'Language and 'Nationalism' in South Africa' in J. Fishman, C.A. Ferguson and J.das Gupta (eds), *Language Problems of Developing Countries*, Wiley, New York. 215–24.
Van Essen, A. and E.I. Burkart (1992) *Homage to W.R. Lee: Essays in English as a Foreign or Second Language*, Foris Publications, Berlin and New York.
Watson, K. (1980) 'Cultural Pluralism, Nation-building and Educational Policies in Malaysia', *Journal of Multilingual and Multicultural Development*, (1), 155–75.
Watson, K. (1992) 'Language, Education and Political Power: Some Reflections on North–South Relationships', *Language and Education*, (6), 99–123.
Weinstein, B. (ed.) (1991) *Language Policy and Political Development*, Ablex Publishing, Norwood, NJ.
Williams, C.H. (1985) 'Minority Groups in the Modern State' in M. Pacione (ed.), *Progress in Political Geography*, Croom Helm, Beckenham, 111–51.
Williams, C.H. (ed.) (1988) *Language in Geographic Context*, Multilingual Matters, Clevedon, Avon.
Williams, C.H. (ed.) (1991) *Linguistic Minorities, Society and Territory*, Multilingual Matters, Clevedon, Avon.
Williams, C.H. (ed.) (1993) *The Political Geography of the New World Order*, Belhaven/Wiley, London.
Williams, C.H. (1994) *Called Unto Liberty: On Language and Nationalism*, Multilingual Matters, Clevedon, Avon.
Williams, C.H. (1995) 'Global Language Divisions' in T. Unwin (ed.), *Atlas of World Development*, Wiley, London.

PART III

The political context

4 Ethnicity and political development in South Africa

Anthony Lemon

Much of the cultural discord in the world is probably an inevitable consequence of the uncomfortable containment of too many people in too few states (Mikesell and Murphy 1991, p.601).

Ethnicity and ethnonationalism

When European powers partitioned Africa in the last quarter of the 19th century, they paid scant regard to ethnic geography, either through ignorance or because other concerns were accorded higher priority (Prescott 1979). Almost a century later, when decolonization ensued, their behaviour in this respect was curiously similar. Anti-colonial movements seemed to have transcended ethnic differences, and it was widely assumed that such differences were not serious obstacles to 'nation-building'. By the very labelling of ethnic difference as 'tribalism', it was condemned as something backward, doomed to extinction because it was, in Hettne's words in the opening chapter of this volume, 'an obstacle to modernization'. Such views rested on misplaced optimism about the 'plasticity' of human society (Slabbert and Welsh 1979), whether seen through the eyes of liberals emphasizing the salience of the individual or through Marxist class-based analyses.

New African leaders were correspondingly anxious to minimize the significance of ethnicity: to do otherwise would, in the intellectual climate of the 1960s, threaten to confirm African 'backwardness'. In their concern to build nation states within artificial boundaries, they spurned political structures such as federation which sought to protect ethnic groups, fearing that these would give ethnic forces a power-base and fatally weaken their fledgeling states. But in the absence of the external force represented by the colonial power, the very introduction of democratic

Ethnicity and Development: Geographical Perspectives. Edited by Denis Dwyer and David Drakakis-Smith.

politics tended to contribute to the growth of ethnicity. Political leaders seeking power-bases discovered, like the Afrikaners before them, the salience of ethnicity as a focus of political mobilization (Adam and Giliomee 1979).

In part, Western post-war attitudes to ethnicity reflect a tendency to see it as only marginally less deplorable than racism, which was universally condemned in the aftermath of Nazism (Slabbert and Welsh 1979). The nonracial society was also to be nonethnic; as an aspiration, it constituted 'the plural society's analogue to the utopian aspiration for a classless society' (Horowitz 1991, p.28). In consequence, much Western scholarship has ironically followed the example of the colonizers and decolonizers in ignoring, denying or explaining away the significance of ethnicity and failing to recognize positive attributes of community, neighbourliness, mutual assistance both at home and far from home, familiarity and a sense of collective worth (ibid., pp.28, 40). There was even fear that studies of ethnicity might actually serve to foment ethnic divisions: 'when scholars tread close to ethnicity, they deal in euphemisms or walk on eggs' (ibid., p.29).

In recent years ethnicity and ethnonationalism have been the subject of more explicit scholarly reappraisal. Most notable in the context of southern Africa is the historical research of Vail (1989) and his contributors and Horowitz's (1991) attempt to apply political theory to the problems of constitution-making in South Africa. The former demonstrate that ethnic consciousness, far from being an anachronistic cultural artifact, is a relatively new ideological construct, formed in the context of profound social, economic and political change in southern Africa in the 19th and 20th centuries. Horowitz (1991) broadly accepts these findings but rightly warns against making the conceptual leap from ethnicity as a human construct to the conclusion that ethnicity is politically insignificant. Indeed the bulk of his analysis is premised on the actual, or at least the potential, salience of ethnicity in South Africa's political future.

This premise is broadly accepted here. Ethnicity may be a construct, but this does not reduce either its present reality or political significance, actual or potential. Global evidence from the 19th and 20th centuries suggests that ethnic groups, rather than socio-economic class or the regional economic disparities of core and periphery, have been the basic building blocks of nations (Hennayake 1992). But if there is a degree of coincidence between class or regional economic inequality and ethnicity, this certainly has the potential to intensify ethnonationalism.

It is generally recognized that the political role of ethnicity, once created, is a contingent one, arising under certain political conditions (Breuilly 1982 pp.383–4). Ethnicity is well summed up by Harries (1989, p.112) as 'a fluctuating situational expression of group identity aimed at the achievement of specific political ends'. Two recent geographical studies have stressed the interactive nature of ethnonationalism. Mikesell and Murphy (1991, p.582) focus on the 'discourse of demands advanced by minority-group members, together with the shifts that occur in that discourse in response to government policies'. Hennayake (1992) pursues a similar approach but argues that the nation state is itself an expression of majority ethnic nationalism, using the example of Sri Lanka. Where the nation state has successfully pursued hegemonic politics, minority ethnic groups have extended their consent, but where the ethnonationalist politics of the majority ethnic group have become too exclusionary, minority groups have become politicized, thus setting off an interactive process.

Conditions favouring the politicization of minority ethnic groups may transcend national boundaries, as they seemed to do in the 1970s, when simultaneous separatist pressures in a number of countries in Western Europe, as well as Canada, led to a search for theoretical models embracing conditions common to all cases (Williams 1979, 1980). Undoubtedly such pressures have their own diffusive tendency too, as the events of the 1990s in Eastern Europe, the former Soviet Union and the former Yugoslavia seem to demonstrate. After some decades of relative stability (the 1970s pressures were all contained without changes in state boundaries), disintegration has become the norm. Pressure to reunite South Africa goes against this trend, but the historical circumstances of its imposed and artificial fragmentation make any other course difficult to conceive. Ethnic considerations have, however, influenced the demarcation of regional boundaries in what seems likely to be at least a quasi-federal state.

The ethnic composition of South Africa's population

Provisional results of the 1991 census give South Africa a population of 32.17 million, to which must be added a further 6.75 million people in Transkei, Venda, Bophuthatswana and Ciskei, the four nominally independent black 'homelands' or 'TVBC states', which are responsible for their own population counts. The ethnic composition of all 39 million people is shown in Table 4.1.

At this stage five simple observations on these data will suffice. First, the officially enumerated categories correspond to the peoples allocated to 'homelands' or bantustans under apartheid, except that the Xhosa are split between Ciskei and Transkei. This exception is probably explained by the fact that Transkei, as a large contiguous territory, ethnically homogeneous and largely rural, was a ready-made candidate for an autonomous homeland after the passage of the Promotion of Bantu Self-Government Act in 1959 (anonymous 1989, pp.396–7). Ciskei, on the other hand, was a fragmented collection of reserves which, even after consolidation under

Table 4.1 South Africa: ethnic composition of the population (including the TVBC states), 1991

Blacks (1)	No. (m.) Number (m.)	% of blacks	Others	No. (m.)
Zulu	8.7	30.2	Whites (2)	5.5
Xhosa	7.0	24.4		
Tswana	3.5	12.4	'Coloureds'	3.3
Pedi	3.5	12.3		
Sotho	2.7	9.3	Indians	1.0
Shangaan	1.4	4.8		
Swazi	0.8	2.7	Sub-total	9.8
Venda	0.7	2.3		
Ndebele	0.4	1.6		
Sub-total	29.1 3	100.0	Overall total	38.9

Notes:

1 Numbers of Xhosa, Venda and Tswana include the total populations of Transkei and Ciskei, Venda and Bophuthatswana respectively. This probably exaggerates the Tswana population by c. 0.5m., mainly at the expense of Sotho, Shangaan and Venda.

2 The white population includes approximately 550,000 Portuguese speakers, and small minorities speaking other European languages. Among the remainder, the ratio between Afrikaans- and English-speakers is roughtly 60:40.

3 Discrepancy in sub-total reflects rounding of numbers for each ethnic group to first decimal place.

apartheid, has 'absolutely no basis in any ethnic, cultural or linguistic fact whatsoever' (ibid., p.394).

Second, these categories are not perfectly demarcated; boundaries between them are not always sharp, and other subdivisions could easily be made: the Xhosa, for instance, include Pondo, Thembu and Mfengu minorities (Horowitz 1991, p.49). In most cases, however, the association of territorially defined political units with the enumerated groups does not give the latter greater political significance, at least in the short term.

Third, the numerical strength of the Zulu is self-evident and of critical importance given that Inkatha represents by far the strongest current or foreseeable attempt at ethnic political mobilization among blacks. The fourth observation concerns the Zulu and Xhosa together, who comprise just over half the black population; as will be seen these two groups have disproportionate political importance. Both have more or less homogeneous home areas; blacks in the Durban functional region, for instance, are over 90 per cent Zulu, while Eastern Cape blacks are almost exclusively Xhosa.

These two key groups differ markedly in their perceptions of social distance and group identity. Commenting on the results of a 1986 survey of group identity among female Africans in Durban, Pretoria and the Reef, Soweto and the Eastern Cape, Horowitz (1991, pp.51–2) draws attention to the polarity between the Zulu in Durban and the Xhosa in the Eastern Cape. Xhosa responses were more South African, pan-African and less tied to locality. Zulu responses were more parochial, more place-orientated and more ethnically focused. This confirms the results of a much earlier investigation of social distance (Edelstein 1971), which found that intra-ethnic differences were less significant for Xhosa than for Zulu, Sotho and Tswana, whereas racial differences were so important for the Xhosa that they were discontinuous from intra-African ethnic differences on the scale.

Finally, the numerical significance of Afrikaners is worthy of note. To the three million white Afrikaans-speakers may be added the majority – some 2.5 million – of coloured people, making Afrikaans the third-largest home language in South Africa. Apartheid represented a fundamental assault on the identity of coloured people, strongly portrayed in John Western's *Outcast Cape Town* (1981). Surveys of electoral opinion during 1993 nevertheless suggested that for most coloured people fear of the ANC outstrips suspicions of a reformed National Party (NP). This could conceivably provide the base for a reformulated and more inclusive Afrikaner ethnicity, although the author's research on another issue – educational reform – suggests that most coloured parents are likely to choose English-medium education for their children in a new dispensation, despite their own use of Afrikaans as a home language.

Ethnicity and 'modernization' in South Africa

Viewed superficially, ethnicity appears potentially less significant in several respects for political development in South Africa than in most of sub-Saharan Africa. Most obviously, the South African conflict has hitherto been primarily racial rather than ethnic, as a black majority has struggled to overthrow domination by a white minority intent on defending economic privilege, the erstwhile political stability represented by its system and its cultural values. The anti-apartheid struggle has to some extent united oppressed blacks – and in the 1980s also many coloured or mixed-race people and Indians – across both ethnic and racial boundaries. But such alliances often prove fragile, as the experience of post-colonial Africa shows only too clearly. It is encouraging in this respect that existing political divisions within the black population presently follow ideological rather than ethnic lines, with the partial exception of Inkatha and other ethnically based 'homeland' parties (see below).

The relatively developed, industrialized nature of the South African economy, and the high degree of urbanization which accompanies this, constitute another set of factors which have encouraged the hope that ethnicity will be less significant in South African political development than elsewhere in Africa. The black population, while far less urbanized than Indians, whites and 'coloured' or mixed-race people, are nevertheless between 50 and 60 per cent urban in *de facto* terms (i.e., including the eight million or so informal settlers in urban areas, most of them outside the formal boundaries of municipalities). It has long been apparent that the 'influx control' practised under apartheid succeeded only in displacing urbanization across 'homeland' boundaries, rather than preventing it, giving rise to the 'frontier commuting' phenomenon (Lemon 1982). Since the relaxation of influx control from 1986 onwards, not only does the rate of urbanization appear to have increased, but the distribution of those already urbanized and the forms of their settlement have in some cases changed rapidly (Crankshaw 1993).

The debate concerning the 'detribalization' of urban Africans is an old one (Mayer 1961). It has to be remembered that black South Africans experience not one but several urban environments. A fortunate few had been able, in the closing years of urban apartheid and especially since the repeal of the Group Areas Act, to move into white suburbs. In the townships where most blacks live (although they may soon be outnumbered by those in informal settlements), the government tried, with limited success, to minimize ethnic mixing through a policy of urban ethnic apartheid, especially in the southern Transvaal where the number of ethnic groups converging on particular urban areas was greatest (Pirie 1984; Christopher 1989). The mining companies also tended to segregate ethnic groups within the mine compounds, and inter-ethnic violence has long been a feature of these crowded, all-male environments. The mining compound or migrant labour hostel is clearly a distinctive urban environment and one which can foster ethnic divisions.

In the informal settlements a degree of ethnic mixing occurred, as blacks moved from 'homelands' distant from major urban areas to settlements within the 'homelands' of other groups which offer the possibility of access to urban employment. Most notable in this respect is the Winterveld of Bophuthatswana, where non-Tswana people continued to live in increasing numbers despite the harrassment of the Bophuthatswana authorities (Lemon 1987, pp.228–9). Outside the southern Transvaal, however, many informal settlements as well as townships remain dominated by a single ethnic group: thus Zulus are preponderant in the urban areas of Natal, including Durban and Pietermaritzburg, Xhosa in most of the Cape, including East London, Port Elizabeth and Cape Town, and Sotho in Bloemfontein.

Even where urbanization has led to significant ethnic mixing, it cannot be assumed that ethnicity has no actual or potential political significance. Studies of the urban sociology of mining areas in Central Africa long ago suggested that ethnicity was a phenomenon of the urban workplace in which boundaries and distinctions between people had been built up (Epstein 1958; Mitchell 1958). This resulted, *inter alia*, as different groups formed stereotypes of one another, as employers preferred certain groups for certain types of work and as they consciously manipulated ethnic differences to keep the workforce disunited (Vail 1989, p.4), all factors which have been present in South Africa too.

Nor should one look to education to counter the politicization of ethnic groups. Horowitz (1991, p.140) notes that in divided societies generally, the majority of studies actually show that ethnocentrism *increases* with education. Admittedly there are problems with the available South African evidence in this respect, as much of it relates more to racial than ethnic attitudes, and some of the more specifically ethnic studies date from the late 1970s. The hardening of racial attitudes with education may plausibly be associated with increased political awareness, which is perfectly compatible with a lessening of barriers between black ethnic groups. To the extent that such a process does occur, however, it could constitute primarily a process of coming together in the liberation struggle, in which case there can be no guarantee of its permanence.

Historical recollections are frequently a powerful ingredient in ethnic sentiment, and in South Africa these are often heightened by the unusual turbulence of the 18th and 19th centuries. The Zulu clan was originally quite small but grew by absorbing those whom it conquered, subsequently moving out in all directions in the *mfecane*, subjugating Swazi, Sotho, and Pondo, and causing others to flee, notably the Ndebele, most of whom crossed the Limpopo and today occupy western Zimbabwe. Eventually the British occupation of Natal ended Zulu expansion and subsequently dismembered Zululand, an action which underlies the fragmentation of the former KwaZulu ruled by Chief Buthelezi. This relatively recent expansionist history is well remembered by both its victims and by the Zulu themselves, who revive their martial spirit from time to time, and symbolize it – if no more – in the carrying of the spears which they claim to be 'cultural weapons'.

For the Xhosa, memories relate primarily to conflict with whites on what the latter regarded as the 'eastern frontier', where nine wars were fought over the course of a century beginning in 1779. This undoubtedly underlies the Xhosa attitudes to whites described above and their strong identification with militant movements today (see below). Sub-group rivalries can also be traced back to 19th century struggles between whites and blacks. The Mfengu, who fled from Zululand during the time of Shaka (1818–1828), at first took shelter among the Xhosa, but subsequently fought alongside colonial forces in the frontier wars and were rewarded with Rharhabe land. More than a century later, Lennox Sebe took his Ciskeian National Independence Party to victory in 1973 through a combination of South African assistance and 'a narrow, Mfengu-bashing, Rharhabe ethnicity' (anonymous 1989, p.400).

Current divisions in black politics: the ANC, PAC and AZAPO

Sebe's election tactics and Bophuthatswana's harassment of non-Tswana in the Winterveld are but two examples of ethnic conflict in bantustan politics. But such conflict is to be expected in territories which are apartheid creations and supposedly based on principles of ethnic exclusivism. Given that all 10 'homelands' have now disappeared from South Africa's political map, the particular ethnic bases of their politics are likely to disappear with them unless, as in KwaZulu, an ethnic base is large enough to be potentially disruptive at the national scale. Inkatha will be considered further below, but here we shall briefly survey what is known of the support bases of the African National Congress (ANC), Pan Africanist Congress (PAC) and Azanian People's Organization (AZAPO).

All three are formally non-ethnic, nationally based groups of several different organizations. The ANC's position with regard to non-Africans has varied; its 1949 Programme of Action banned co-operation with other groups, but this was reversed after 1952 when the ANC resumed co-operation with the disproportionately white and Indian South African Communist Party, an alliance which continues today. It was only in 1985, however, that the ANC included non-Africans on its National Executive Committee (NEC). Xhosa representation on the NEC has been disproportionately strong, while Zulu have been dramatically under-represented (Horowitz 1991, p.54). Despite some changes since the ANC was unbanned in 1990, this remains the case, and the most prominent ANC leaders are predominantly Xhosa-speakers, strengthening fears of Xhosa domination of the ANC and giving a degree of credibility to perceptions of ANC/Inkatha conflict as ethnically determined.

The PAC was formed in 1959 when 'Africanists' within the ANC – those espousing an 'Africa for the Africans' sentiment – broke away. It has characteristically viewed whites as colonial 'settlers' in 'occupied Azania' but does embrace 'coloured' people and Indians as members and in its leadership structure. Its founder, Robert Sobukwe, was a Xhosa-speaker, and Xhosa again dominate its Central Committee and foreign representation, with nearly a threefold over-representation in 1989 (Horowitz 1991, p.55). Xhosa are also prominent in AZAPO, which was founded in 1978, in the black consciousness tradition, a year after the death in detention of Steve Biko. Like its affiliate, the National Forum, AZAPO incorporates strong elements of class analysis in its thinking (ibid., p.15), but this does not preclude its overtly racial, as distinct from ethnic, approach.

It is difficult to separate ethnic from regional factors in relations to all three organizations. Several historical and present influences combine to make the Eastern Cape a strongly politicized region. The area now occupied by Ciskei and the Queenstown/King William's Town/East London corridor was the territory of the 19th century frontier wars to which reference has already been made: the Rharhabe Xhosa resisted white conquest longer than any other ethnic group in southern Africa. The region also experienced extensive missionary activity, which produced a relatively high level of black education. The rise (and subsequent fall) of an independent commercial peasantry in this region has also been documented by Bundy (1979). To these historical factors may be added both the low levels of rural subsistence and lack of job opportunities which prevail today in what has become South Africa's most economically depressed region.

Such is the region which has produced a disproportionate share of black political leaders. King William's Town was the home of Steve Biko and the spiritual centre of the black consciousness movement during the 1960s and 1970s (anonymous 1989, p.396). Until recently the Eastern Cape was arguably the real organizational heartland of the ANC, continuing a deep-rooted tradition of fierce resistance to 19th-century colonial domination.

After the unbanning of the ANC and PAC in 1990, it seemed initially that the willingness of the ANC to negotiate and compromise could result in a loss of support to the more hard-line PAC. This did not appear to have happened in the early 1990s, but the murder of Chris Hani, the Communist Party Leader who was a particularly influential figure among black youths in the townships, renewed the threat of PAC gains as the ANC leadership faced strong militant criticism from Winnie Mandela and some regional and youth leaders. In the event the damage was contained, and support for both the PAC and AZAPO remained relatively small. Horowitz (1991, p.270) suggests that 'if the PAC or AZAPO could credibly make the accusation of Xhosa dominance against the ANC, that would make the PAC or AZAPO much more dangerous'. Given the strong Xhosa element in both the PAC and AZAPO, this seems an unlikely scenario. It is far more probable that these organizations (or new ones) will find strength in exploiting economic issues, to which we now turn.

The exploitation of unfulfilled expectations

Economic inequality may well prove the Achilles' heel of any purely political settlement in South Africa (Stone 1992). Arguably the greatest political problem for any new government in South Africa will be the unrealistic expectations of its black citizens, especially with regard to employment, housing and education. Such expectations are based on comparison with the privileges which a ruling minority was able to award itself (Smith 1992), but the South African economy is far too small to sustain such standards for the majority of the population. While there is clearly some scope for redistribution of existing wealth, the demographic arithmetic will ensure that the losses suffered by whites produce virtually insignificant gains for most blacks. In education, for example, existing urban–rural disparities in black educational provision are such that an averaging of per capita expenditure for all race groups would scarcely improve levels of current spending on black township schools, themselves the focus of struggle (Lemon 1994a, b)

Economic growth is clearly vital for the success of any redistribution strategy, but even the most optimistic growth scenario will make possible only a modest reduction of inequality in the short term. A massive external aid programme is most unlikely, given the priorities of the principal actors in the new world order. A recent investigation of redistributive possibilities in the South African economy highlights the potential dangers of both macroeconomic populism or 'growth with redistribution' strategies and nationalization (Moll *et al.* 1991, pp.130–3) and instead proposes a set of measures which would lead to steady but gradual improvement.

Now that the ANC and the National Party have effectively agreed to share power for five years after the first elections, the danger is not that such a gradualist approach will not be followed but rather that its dividends will be too small in the short term to satisfy the majority of South Africans. Their frustrations will then be open to exploitation by ethnically based parties or others with a populist platform which attempt to outbid an ANC constrained by the realities of government. To avoid this scenario, the new government has to convince people that they are receiving tangible if limited benefits from the start and that its gradualist approach really does promise greater long-term dividends for all.

Such dangers arise not only from continuing racial inequality but from growing inequalities within the black population. South African capitalism, as it has slowly begun to break down racial barriers since the 1970s, has given rise to increasing inequality within the black population. Intra-black inequality today is comparable with the most unequal societies in the world, with a Gini-coefficient of inequality of 0.62 in 1991, not very different from the overall coefficient for South Africa (Bernstein and Simkins 1992). Such inequalities are not, and are unlikely to become, ethnically based: they will reflect the high incomes of those who acquire marketable skills, the struggles of the informally employed and the unemployed, and the gap between urban and rural incomes and service provision. The latter could even widen if the ANC yields to the temptation to give priority to its more vocal urban constituency. Given the 'homeland' bases of ethnic parties such as Inkatha, and the tendency for such parties to draw most of their support from more rural parts of their territories, increasing urban–rural disparities could have clear ethnic implications.

Ethnicity, regionalism and federation

Regions have played an important part in the current negotiating process in South Africa. Both the ANC and the National Party proposed regional divisions, but the National Party sought constitutionally entrenched regional powers in a federal state, while the ANC preferred a more centralized, unitary state. The interim constitution has clearly federal elements. Nine provincial assemblies of 30–100 members are elected by proportional representation from a party list. During the transitional phase these assemblies may write their own constitutions (consistent with nationally agreed principles) by two-thirds majority. Each elects a premier who heads an executive council, or provisional cabinet, with up to 10 members. Each provincial legislature, regardless of the population it represents, elects 10 members of the Senate, or upper house of parliament, which sits jointly with a 400-member lower house (the National Assembly) as the body responsible for drawing up the country's final constitution.

The constitution provides for significant devolution of power to provincial governments in areas such as education, health, welfare, urban and rural development, and language policy. However the central government retains powers to intervene to impose uniform national standards and where national economic policy or security is affected. These provisions have allowed differing interpretations as to how federal the constitution is; much will clearly depend on the extent to which the new government actually intervenes in practice. Such uncertain provisions were insufficient to satisfy Inkatha and the right-wing white parties, and remained subject to negotiation even after parliamentary approval of the constitution in December 1993. Eventually Inkatha obtained a promise of international mediation as an inducement to participate in the April 1994 election, but this is the subject of disagreement between the ANC and Inkatha at the time of writing.

No one, except perhaps elements of the far right, favoured retention of the current 'homeland' boundaries. Neither the NP nor the ANC overtly advocated ethnically defined regions, and in terms of boundaries the debate began with a considerable measure of agreement, centring on the nine existing development regions which cut across 'homeland' boundaries: Transkei, for instance, is divided between regions D (Eastern Cape) and E (Natal), and parts of Bophuthatswana fall into four regions (Figure 4.1). During 1992, however, both the NP and the ANC modified these regions in ways which suggested that ethnic thinking played some part

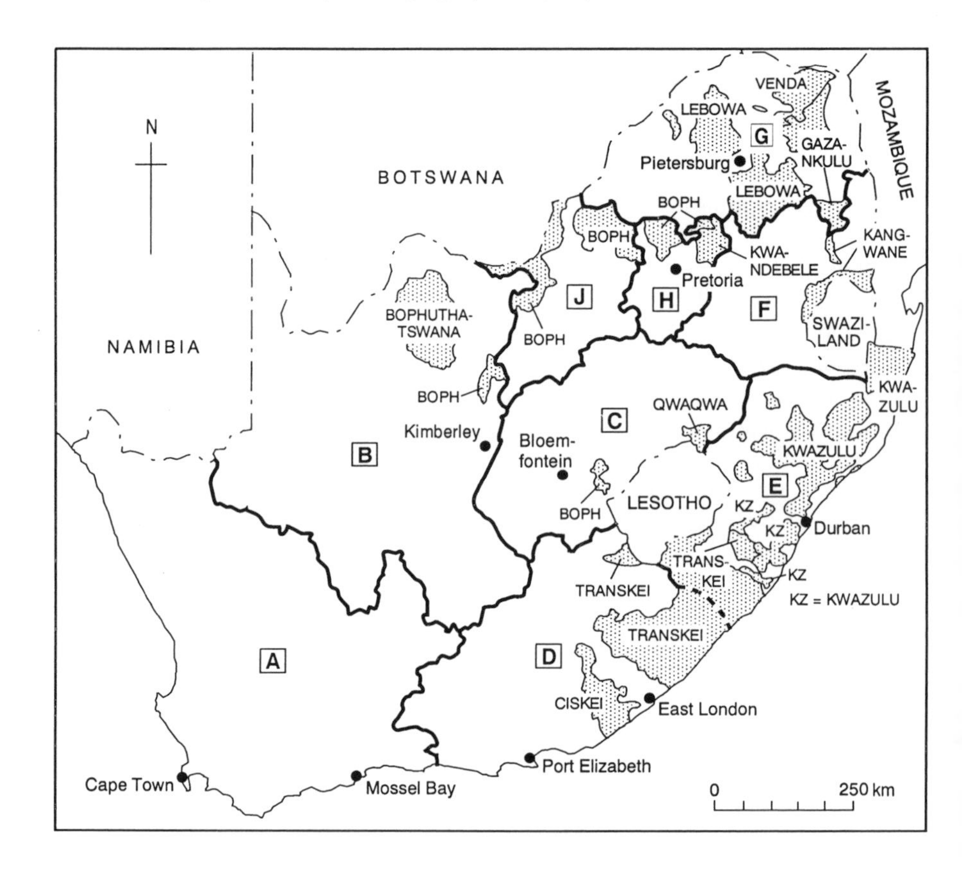

Figure 4.1 South Africa: the nine development regions established in 1982

(Fox 1992). The ANC put forward a 10-region proposal (Figure 4.2) in which the main change was the reunification of Transkei, removing the detached Umzimkulu section and the 'white' district of East Griqualand from Natal to a new Border/Kei region, separate from a new Eastern Cape region which included Ciskei. In making this proposal it seemed likely that the ANC was bowing to the wishes of its ally General Holomisa, the Transkeian leader.

The NP reduced its nine regions to seven in August 1992 (Figure 4.3). Its map accepted the unification of Transkei but included Ciskei as well in its Kei region, perhaps in the hope of diminishing relative support for the ANC by including that for Brigadier Gqozo, the Ciskei leader whose troops massacred ANC demonstrators at Bisho early in 1993. More significantly, the National Party's 1992 proposals envisage an enlarged north west region which re-amalgamated much of Bophuthatswana with the

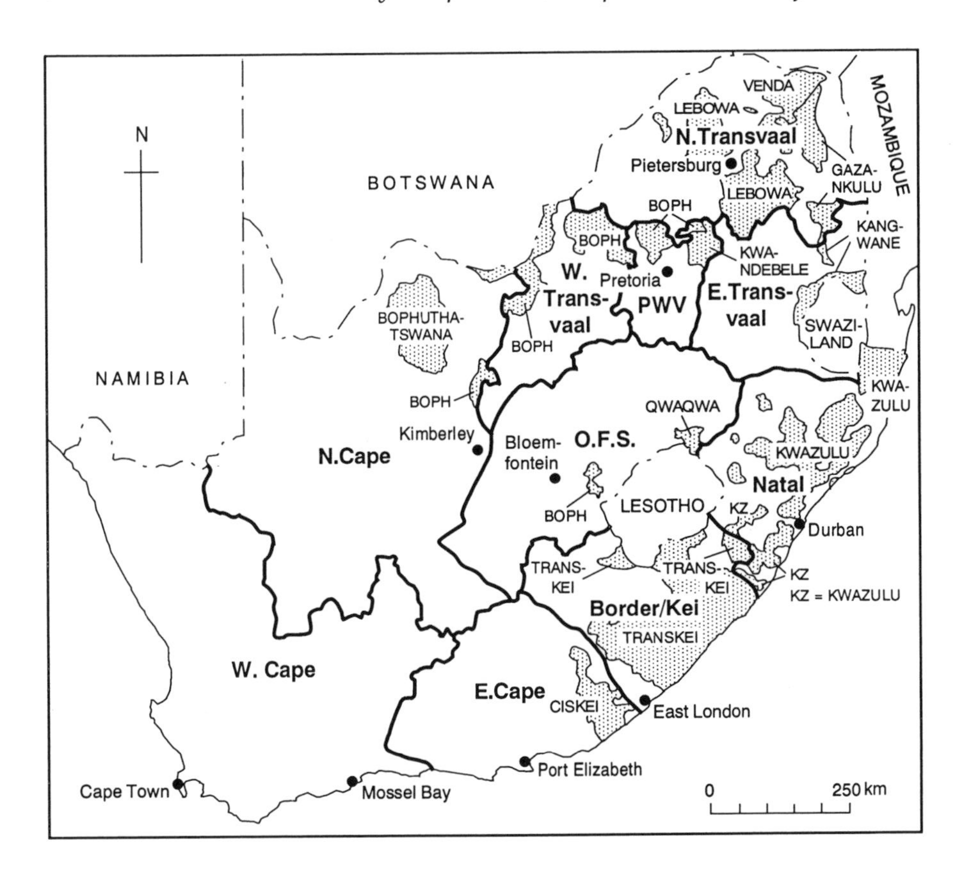

Figure 4.2 South Africa: the ten regions proposed by the ANC in 1992

northern Cape and western Transvaal. An alliance with President Mangope of Bophuthatswana might have enhanced NP prospects in this region, particularly as the Odi and Moretele districts of Bophuthatswana, which include the Winteveld squatter areas where Mangope's support was minimal, were excluded. This seemed to be the NP's *quid pro quo* for accepting the unification of Transkei (Fox 1992).

Both parties changed their plans yet again in their actual submissions to the regional demarcation commission in July 1993. In the eastern half of the country, their plans were virtually identical, even to the inclusion of the Odi and Moretele districts of Bophuthatswana, and parts of KwaNdebele, in the Pretoria–Witwatersrand–Vereeniging (PWV) region: quite apart from its ethnic and potential electoral significance, this makes good sense in terms of the functional urban area. The ANC proposed eight regions in all, including a united Eastern Cape/Border/Kei region (Figure

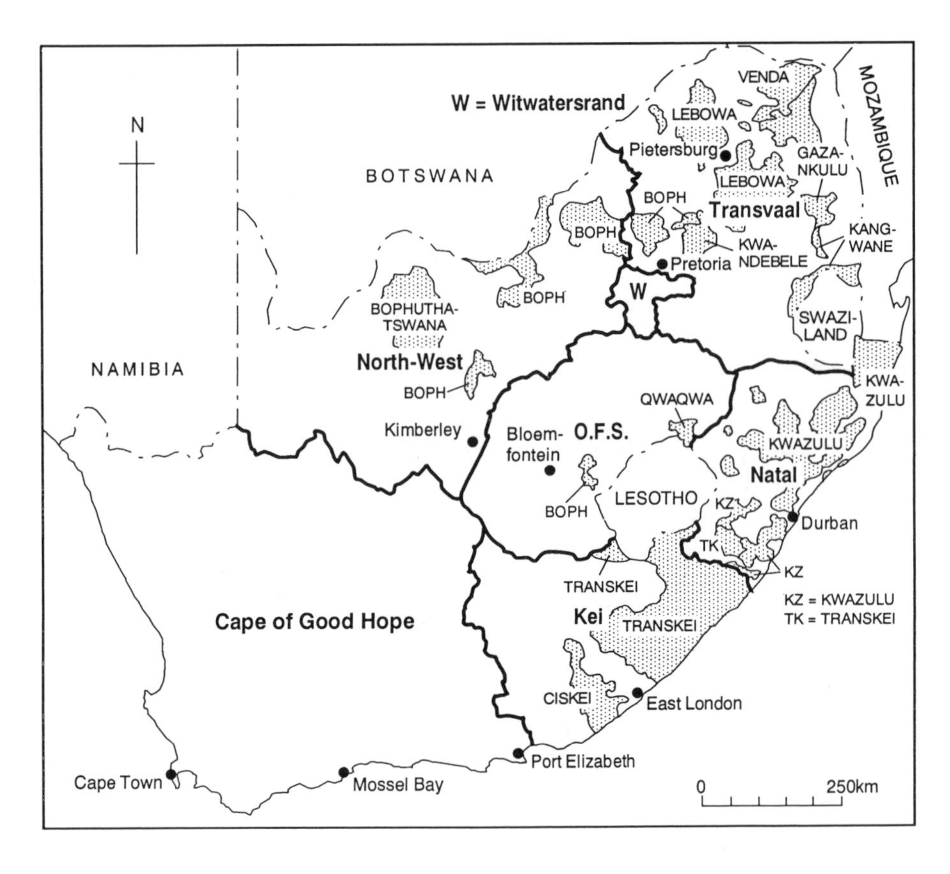

Figure 4.3 South Africa: the seven regions proposed by the National Party in 1992

4.4) but argued the need for a referendum on this issue, given the controversy involved. Eastern Cape opposition to a combined region (especially from the white population in Port Elizabeth) centred on the perceived economic burden of a Border/Kei region even more economically depressed than itself (*Eastern Province Herald* 1993). The ANC rightly observed that the decision on separation would be influenced by the nature of the taxation powers to be exercised by the regions and the degree to which the central government was expected to redistribute tax revenues to the regions.

The NP submitted two proposals, for nine and seven regions (Figures 4.5 and 4.6), while making clear its preference for the former, which divided the Eastern Cape from a Border/Kei region whose boundaries managed to include both Ciskei and Transkei. In both NP plans most of Bophuthatswana, excluding the Odi and Moretele districts, was linked to

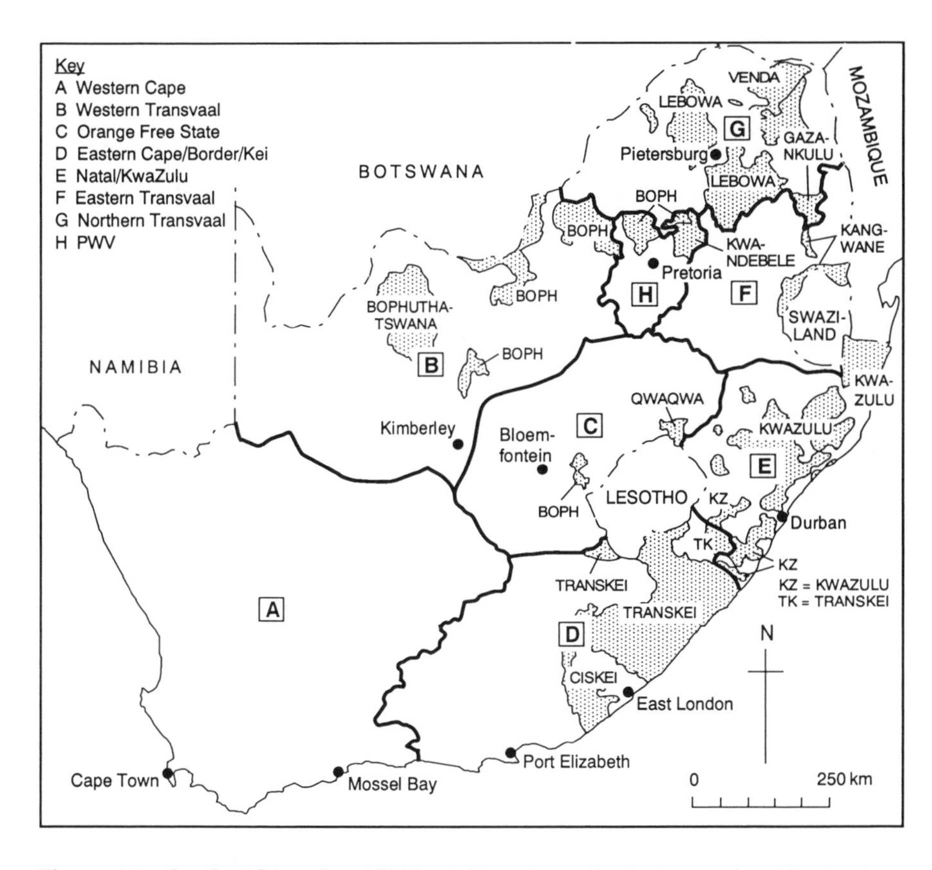

Figure 4.4 South Africa: the ANC's eight-region submission to the delimitation commission in 1993

the Orange Free State: in ethnic terms, a Tswana/Sotho/Afrikaner region. The northern Cape was left as a separate region in the party's preferred nine-region scheme but linked with the south-west Cape in the seven-region scheme. It seems likely that the NP had hopes (which subsequently proved unrealistic) of winning control of all these areas, whether as two regions or three, banking among other things on the relative conservatism of coloured and black voters in the Orange Free State. The NP's preference for the nine-region map could also have been related, *inter alia*, to the potential for greater representation in the Senate.

The proposals of the delimitation commission were first released in August 1993 and subsequently confirmed with only minor changes after a second round of enquiry and many new submissions (Figure 4.7). Compromise between the National Party and the ANC was evident in the division of the western Cape and the unity of the eastern Cape. In the

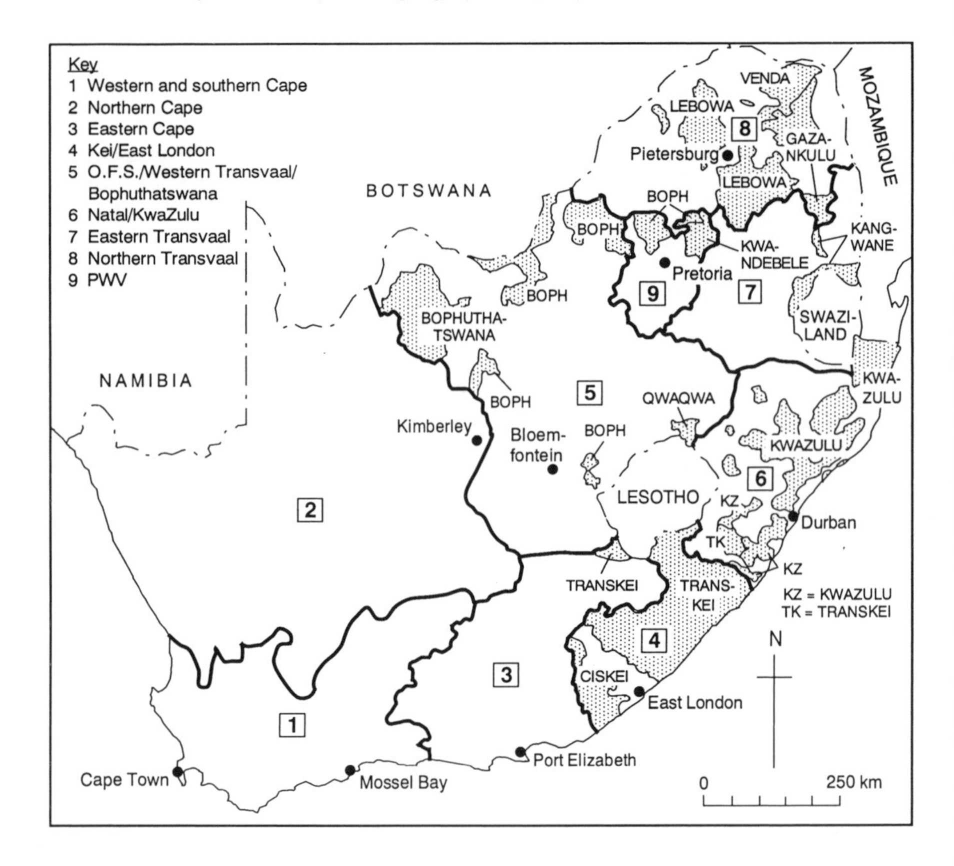

Figure 4.5 South Africa: the National Party's nine-region submission to the delimination commission in 1993

latter, the ethnic unity of the Xhosa population appears to have outweighed white economic concerns. The inclusion of East Griqualand in the eastern Cape also represented a triumph for ethnic over functional considerations, as the district's communication and trade links were with the main centres in Natal.

South Africa's ethnic geography is far too complicated for any of the proposed regions to be ethnically pure, but the relationship between the new regions and South Africa's ethnolinguistic geography is undeniably close in the Cape, the western Transvaal, Natal and the Orange Free State. The multi-ethnic character of the northern and eastern Transvaal, and of PWV economic heartland, reduced the significance of ethnicity in drawing regional boundaries in these areas.

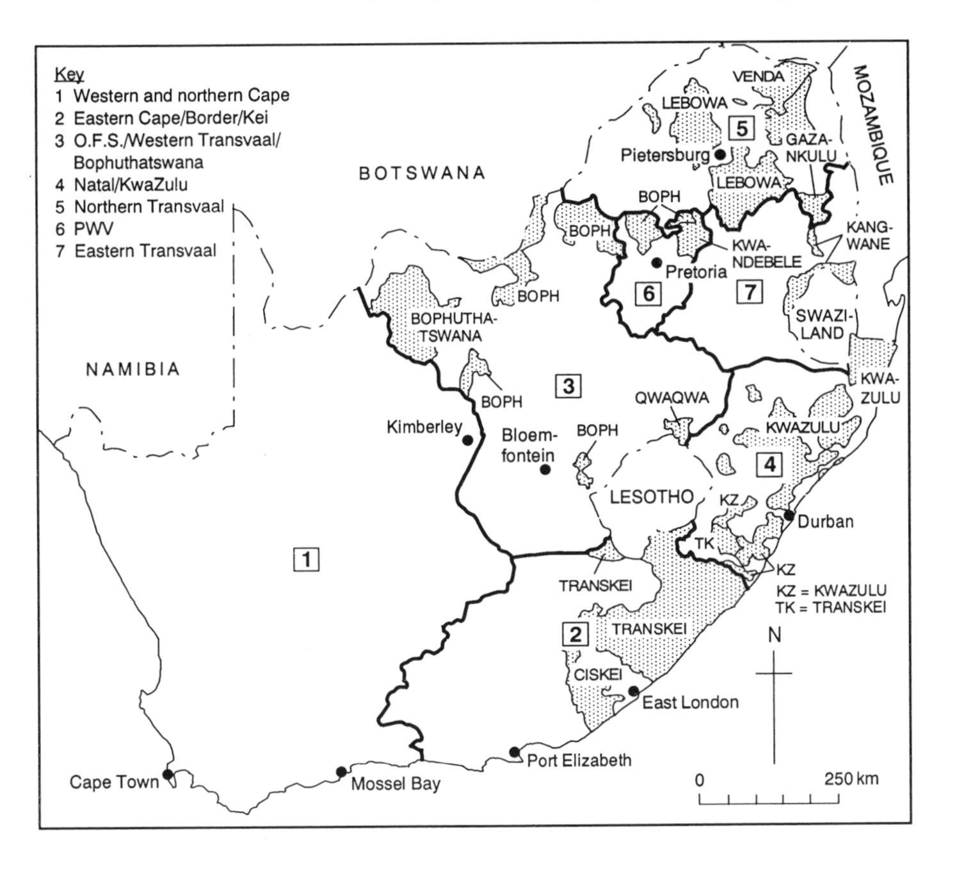

Figure 4.6 South Africa: the National Party's seven-region submission to the delimitation commission in 1993

The machinations of the two main protagonists in drawing boundaries clearly point to the perceived significance of coloured, Xhosa, Tswana and possibly Sotho voters, while Zulu dominance in Natal is assured. The NP's best change of regional control was by common consent in the western Cape (which it duly won). Its next best hope was to unite with Buthelezi and Inkatha to deny Natal/KwaZulu to the ANC, but this would undoubtedly have undermined the power-sharing relationship of the NP and the ANC in the central government.

Buthelezi, Inkatha and Zulu Nationalism

Ethnonationalism is more strongly present among the Zulu than any other group at the moment, and it is Chief Buthelezi and his Inkatha Freedom

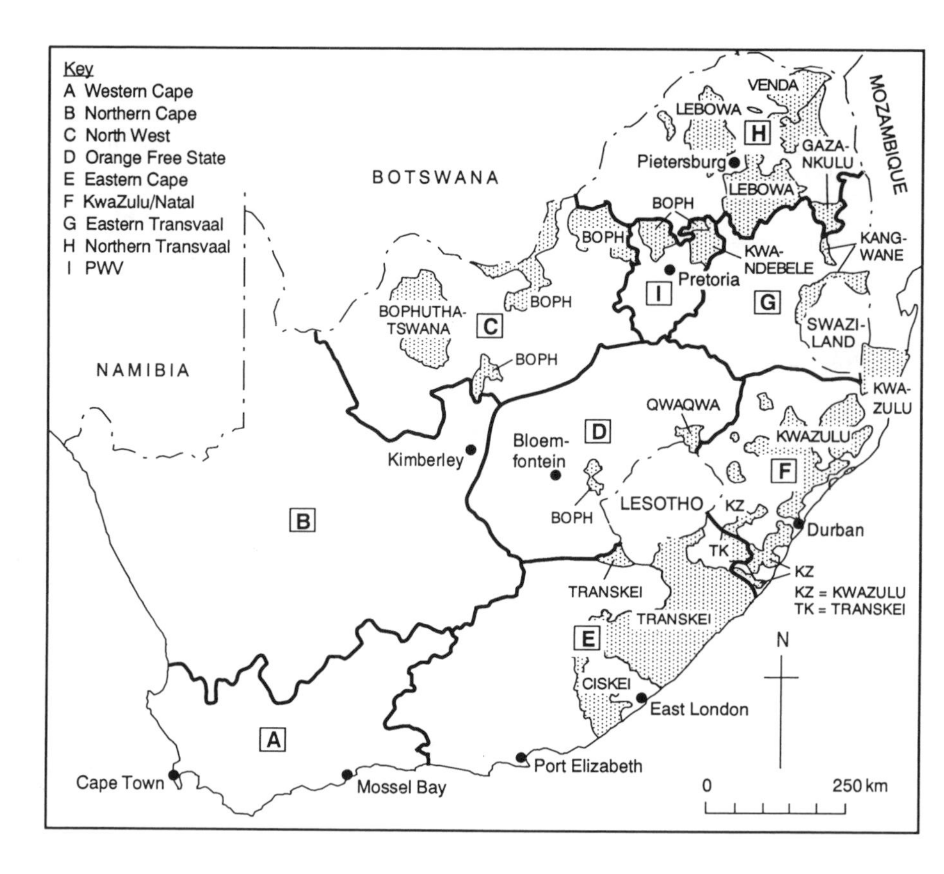

Figure 4.7 South Africa: the nine-regions confirmed by the delimitation commission in late 1993

Party who pose by far the greatest challenge to those who seek a non-ethnic political future for South Africa. Buthelezi once enjoyed strong support from the Ndebele, Swazi, Tswana and Venda peoples, and in the late 1970s he emerged in one important survey as the country's most popular leader (Hanf *et al.* 1981). His support has since contracted considerably and at the time of writing almost certainly includes less than half the country's 8.7 million Zulus. The prolonged violence in parts of Natal since the late 1980s, especially in the Pietermaritzburg region (Cornell 1990), underline the divided allegiance of the Zulus, although the divisions are far more complex than a simple ANC/Inkatha rivalry.

Buthelezi's ambitions have long been clear. Ideally he wanted a prominent place in national government, but this seemed unlikely in the early 1990s. This explains his vigorous advocacy of federalism, which would give him a strong chance of regional leadership in Natal; in earlier years he had expressed a preference for a unitary state but a willingness to consider a federal compromise. His association with the violence in which Inkatha has been involved has given Buthelezi a higher profile and greater political significance than is warranted by the much diminished numerical strength of his support. Thus the exclusion of Buthelezi from a negotiated settlement could accentuate violence in Natal/KwaZulu and destabilize a future South African government, damaging the country's economic prospects in the process. Buthelezi's behaviour is but one more indication of the unacceptability of political opposition in black Africa; he is, quite simply, determined not to be left out.

In explaining the potential strength of Zulu ethnonationalism, it is common to refer to 19th-century military history: the Zululand kingdom expanded dramatically through conquest and incorporation of other peoples, and was defeated by Europeans only in the last quarter of the 19th century. This sense of shared history, with a strong warrior element, certainly lends itself to military as well as political mobilization (Mare 1992). However other factors are also important, and in this instance one should not discount the strength of individual ambition and leadership qualities (Mare and Hamilton 1987). Attempts to end violence between Inkatha and ANC supporters, and to keep negotiations on track, have repeatedly revolved around the personal stance of Buthelezi. The Inkatha Freedom Party is very much Buthelezi's creation and a tool of his personal power and ambition. He has mobilized the past through Inkatha, 'telling a story which provides a plausible explanation of what exists', and through its governing role in KwaZulu ensured that allegiance to the 'Zulu nation', measured through membership of Inkatha, could determine access to resources (Mare 1992, p.67). From the late 1970s the drive for ethnic mobilization through Inkatha was reinforced using education (the introduction of the so-called 'Inkatha syllabus') and the newly formed KwaZulu police (ibid, pp.84–9).

Buthelezi is also helped by Zulu territoriality. Hennayake (1992) notes that there is a high degree of correlation between ethnic groups who possess a 'homeland' and those who develop counterhegemonic ethnonationalist politics. For the Zulu, territoriality is relatively strong because their 'homeland' of KwaZulu, while territorially more fragmented than any other, abuts several towns and cities which make 'frontier commuting' possible: Durban, Pietermaritzburg, Newcastle and Richards Bay are the most important. The Transkeian Xhosa, in contrast, have no significant commuting opportunities, and the Ciskeian Xhosa have only the depressed port city of East London to turn to for local employment. Many Zulu have, of course, gone further afield, but those living in migrant workers' hostels in the southern Transvaal are, in a sense, living in exclaves which maintain their Zulu territoriality. Zulu who live with their families in the townships of the Reef are much less likely to support Inkatha.

In the face of what amounted to a bilateral deal between the ANC and the government in February 1993, Buthelezi threatened secession if the political demands of the KwaZulu government and Inkatha were not met. It was clear that the territory involved would be the whole province of Natal, not merely KwaZulu, whose fragmentation rendered it an absurd political unit and had already led to the creation of a Joint Executive Authority with the Natal provincial authorities to carry out limited planning functions. The distinctive political history of Natal over two centuries lends some credibility to such a secession. Its 'Englishness' was the basis of Natal's unsuccessful claim for autonomy in a federal South Africa in the debates which led to Union in 1910. Subsequently there were sporadic revivals of federal proposals (Lemon 1980, pp.4-5) and even a threat to 'go it alone' at the time of the Republican referendum in 1960, when Natal was the only province to vote against the Republic. In the 1980s and early 1990s Natal whites showed considerable support for Buthelezi's 'moderate' views, and for the proposals of the KwaNatal Indaba in the late 1980s, which would have given the region a racially based constitution designed to bring about power-sharing. Subsequently, however, white support appears to have declined in the face of Inkatha's violent methods.

Christopher (1992, p.9) has gone so far as to suggest that 'South Africa might be able to achieve a more prosperous and peaceful future without the need to coerce a potentially hostile and disruptive population in Natal'. While they lack the power of the whites in 1948 to impose their solution, the Zulu – or those who support Buthelezi and Inkatha – have demonstrated their power to disrupt. Partition, Christopher suggests, is one means of eliminating disruption. In this he may be right, but such solution seems politically distant, if not impossible. It would be highly unpopular with those Natal Zulu – probably the majority – who do not support Inkatha. It would probably also be unwelcome to Natal's Indian community, who fear both the ANC (as was borne out by some two-thirds of Indians supporting the NP in the 1994 election) and Buthelezi, who reminded them of their victimization in the 1949 riots when he threatened them of the consequences of participating in the first Indian elections for the tricameral parliament in 1984. The ANC would vigorously oppose secession, just as it opposed the KwaNatal Indaba, because it wishes at all costs to avoid dismemberment of the country and the likely loss of control of an economically dynamic region which includes South Africa's leading port, Durban, on which the Reef depends. The ANC has nevertheless gone to considerable lengths to negotiate a compromise with both Buthelezi and the white right, with its demand for an Afrikaner-dominated Volkstaat.

During 1993 Buthelezi made common cause with President Mangope, who was also determined to secure the survival of a Tswana-dominated region but unable to pose the same disruptive threat (Drummond 1991), with Brigadier Gqozo of Ciskei and with the white right, itself strengthened during 1993 by the formation of the Afrikaner Volksfront. This strange alliance, which initially called itself the 'Concerned South Africans Group' (COSAG) and subsequently the 'Freedom Alliance', was united in its concern to maximize devolution along essentially ethnic lines in a post-apartheid South Africa. Its continued rejection of the constitution agreed by other parties, and of the authority of the Transitional Executive Council installed in December 1993, led to fears that the 'new South Africa' would be born in the teeth of the opposition of large elements of the country's two historically most powerful ethnic groups, the Zulus and the Afrikaners.

The Freedom Alliance was twice fractured in 1994, first by the withdrawal of Ciskei in January, and secondly by the overthrow of Mangope in March, following strikes by civil servants fearful of their jobs and pensions and desertion by the Bophuthatswana Defence Force. The South African 'ambassador' to Bophuthatswana then took over the administration of the territory. Shortly afterwards a major break occurred in right-wing Afrikaner ranks when General Viljoen, embarrassed by the abortive attempt of the Afrikaner Weerstandsbeweging (AWB) to defend Mangope, and frustrated by the refusal of his right-wing allies to participate in the election, registered his own party, the Freedom Front. Attempts to form a conservative Zulu–Tswana–Afrikaner alliance were thus shattered with the removal of the Tswana element, the further division of Afrikaners and the continuing division of Zulus between support for Buthelezi and the ANC.

Ethnic conflict and regional security in southern Africa

Hettne's discussion of ethnic conflict and regional security in south Asia in the opening chapter of this volume prompts some consideration of this issue in southern Africa. The existence of a common enemy, South Africa, has led to a degree of regional co-operation in the rest of the region which is lacking in south Asia, with the establishment in 1979 of the Southern African Development Co-ordination Conference (SADCC), recently renamed the Southern African Development Community (SADC). Its concerns have, however, been essentially economic, with SADCC pursuing a project-orientated approach and SADC apparently veering towards a more conventional regional economic integration which now embraces a post-apartheid South Africa (Gibb 1993).

The level of political homogeneity among the countries of the region is certainly increasing as Mozambique, Angola and Zimbabwe retreat from socialism and as South Africa sheds apartheid. There seems little likelihood, however, of SADC or any other regional body contemplating a regional approach to conflict resolution in the foreseeable future. The region's recent history is one of South African destabilization accentuating internal conflicts, one of which, in Angola, is far from resolved. Even economic co-operation is likely to produce considerable strains, given the overwhelming dominance of South Africa in the regional economy and its inability to afford largesse, given the expectations of its own people. Its military strength would inevitably make it an equally dominant partner in any regional security system which its neighbours would be unlikely to welcome so soon after the destabilizing activities of the apartheid regime. Nor is it likely, following Hettne's south Asian scenario, that a federal South Africa will significantly weaken Pretoria and diminish the fear of regional bullying; foreign policy and control of the reformed defence force will undoubtedly remain in the hands of the central government.

Conclusion

Ethnicity is far from a spent force in South Africa. The regional debate has brought its potential significance to the fore, as both the ANC and the NP appear to have been influenced by ethnic factors (among others) as they modified their regional proposals. The fluctuating significance of ethnicity in relation to political circumstances and its susceptibility to manipulation are well illustrated by the narrowing of Buthelezi's support base and his subsequent use of Inkatha to secure continuing prominence at the negotiating table. A critical problem for the negotiators has been, as Mare (1992, p.113) puts it, 'disentangling legitimate diversity from the structurally embedded, politicised ethnicity of Inkatha'. The potential disruptive power of Inkatha is undoubted and may be better contained within a federal structure.

If ethnicity has already influenced political development to this extent, it seems probable that it will assume a higher profile in the new South Africa, now that the common enemy of apartheid has finally been removed. It is important that those sharing power in the present government, and those charged with the formulation of a permanent constitution (to be implemented in 1999) do not deny the reality of ethnicity but seek to incorporate it positively, at Hettne has done at a theoretical level in this volume, as an integral part of the development process.

In the South African context, two specific factors will need very careful attention. One is the choice of electoral system which could perhaps go some way to containing the negative effects of ethnic political mobilization (Horowitz 1991). The party list system of proportional representation used in April 1994 is far from ideal in this respect. The second factor is the distribution of tax revenues among the new regions – which has still to be finalized at the time of writing: will this rest on the principle of derivation, thus accentuating current inequalities, or will redistribution from the centre reflect regional development needs? In terms of the interim constitution, the principle of redistribution seems assured, but its extent remains unclear. Competition for economic resources in an economy unable to meet black expectations is likely to be an important factor shaping the course of any ethnic political mobilization which does occur in a post-apartheid South Africa.

Postscript: the 1994 general election and beyond

After the downfall of Mangope in Bophuthatswana, attention in the closing weeks of the 1994 election campaign focused on two issues: Inkatha's threatened non-participation and the extent to which right-wing Afrikaners would support the Freedom Front rather than boycott the election altogether.

General Viljoen undoubtedly performed a service to the incoming government, and to the country's stability, by offering right-wing Afrikaners a constitutional channel to pursue their desire for some form of autonomy. The party secured notably more support in regional elections (572,000) than at national level (424,000), suggesting a degree of pragmatism on the part of many of its supporters, who recognized that only the NP would be in a position to share power with the ANC in the new government. Only a small minority of Afrikaners boycotted the election altogether, and no significant right-wing violence or resistance has materialized since the election, suggesting that this ethnic threat has been defused. President Mandela clearly recognizes the role of Viljoen in achieving this, and has activated the provisions of the interim constitution allowing for the establishment of a Volkstaat Council to investigate and advise on the possibility of establishing a Volkstaat. The likely outcome, if any, is not a territorial authority but some form of cultural autonomy.

By December 1993 Inkatha itself was showing signs of division over the policy of non-participation in the election (*Weekly Mail* 1993). This policy was reversed with just one week to spare after a series of public concessions, including international mediation on constitutional differences, constitutional entrenchment of the Zulu monarchy and a deal (kept secret from the ANC until after the election) whereby control over all land in KwaZulu was transferred from the 'homeland' government to the King. Inkatha's narrow overall majority of votes in KwaZulu–Natal (50.3 per cent) was effectively a negotiated outcome following substantial evidence of electoral malpractice in the region.

During most of the election campaign, many areas of KwaZulu–Natal had been effectively no-go areas for parties other than Inkatha, giving the party an obvious advantage when it decided to participate. Its control of traditional structures of authority was also used to advantage, particularly in rural areas where the party performed most strongly, especially in northern KwaZulu. Inkatha received few votes in those eastern areas in dispute between KwaZulu–Natal and the eastern Cape, or in those areas of the eastern Transvaal where Zulu speakers are numerically dominant. The ANC gained substantial majorities in Durban and Pietermaritzburg, Natal's major cities.

Even if the Inkatha's official majority is taken at face value, these results demonstrate the limited effectiveness of Chief Buthelezi's ethnic political mobilization of the Zulu population. In terms of the proportion of a given ethnic group mobilized behind a particular leader or party, Buthelezi falls far behind comparable movements in, for example, Northern Ireland, Cyprus or Bosnia. His success stems rather from the threat which he has been able to pose to political stability and hence to potential investment and economic growth at the birth of majority rule. This economic factor rather than the extent of his support is why the ANC leadership has been anxious to keep Buthelezi and Inkatha within the government and parliament.

Within both the national government and the regional government of KwaZulu–Natal the two parties have predictably been uncomfortable bedfellows. Buthelezi appears to have shown little interest in his Home Affairs portfolio, concentrating his energies mainly on the constitutional battle for maximum regional devolution. During 1995 Inkatha repeatedly used the threat of non-participation in parliament and the constitution-making process as a weapon, but the ANC claims that, with a new constitution-making process under way, there is no point in involving international mediators to resolve differences over the interim constitution.

Within KwaZulu–Natal Buthelezi's position has been weakened by a power struggle with King Goodwill Zwelithini, his uncle, whose traditional authority Buthelezi had previously used to bolster his own position. Since the election royal finances and the King's security have passed to the new government, thereby removing Buthelezi's direct hold over the monarch. In response Buthelezi has created a House of Traditional Leaders in KwaZulu–Natal which, in January 1995, elected him chairman of its executive committee, effectively sidelining the authority of King Goodwill, who has challenged the legitimacy of this new body.

The state of emergency imposed in KwaZulu–Natal in March 1995 was lifted in August, notwithstanding the continuing high level of political violence. Disagreement between the ANC and Inkatha even extends to the location of the region's capital, with the ANC and NP favouring Natal's capital, Pietermaritzburg, and Inkatha favouring the KwaZulu capital at Ulundi. The region thus remains a potential source of instability, based on a partially successful ethnic political mobilization leading to intra-ethnic violence, which threatens to undermine national government attempts to attract investment and create a climate for rapid economic growth.

This threat should not be exaggerated, however. The peaceful nature of the 1994 election confounded widespread fears. Although a large majority of blacks voted for the ANC, small numbers supported the PAC and even the NP, as well as Inkatha in KwaZulu–Natal. No community in South Africa voted purely on ethnic or racial lines, and in this should be seen signs of genuine hope for the new South Africa. A country which has so long been a negative symbol could, if it maintains the nonracial democracy which it has initiated, become an example to a world beset by ethnic strife.

References

Adam, H., and Giliomee, H. (1979) *Ethnic Power Mobilized: Can South Africa Change?*, Yale University Press, New Haven.

Anonymous (1989) 'Ethnicity and pseudo-ethnicity in the Ciskei' in L. Vail (ed.), 1989, 395–413.

Bernstein, A. and C. Simkins (1992) 'Ready to Govern? An Essay on the ANC Policy Document', *Development and Democracy*, 3, 47–61.

Breuilly, H. (1982) *Nationalism and the State*, Manchester University Press, Manchester.

Bundy, C. (1979) *The Rise and Fall of the South African Peasantry*, Heinemann, London.

Christopher, A.J. (1982), 'Partition and Population in South Africa', *Geographical Review*, 72, 127–38.

Christopher, A.J. (1988), '"Divide and Rule": the Impress of British Separation Policies', *Area*, 20, 233–40.

Christopher, A.J. (1989), 'Apartheid within Apartheid: an Assessment of Official Intra-black Segregation on the Witwatersrand, South Africa', *Professional Geographer*, 41, 328–36.

Christopher, A.J. (1992), 'Post-apartheid South African and the Nation State', paper presented at the Second Southern African Geographers' Symposium, School of Geography, Oxford University.

Cornell, M. (1990) 'Pietermaritzburg, the Capital of Unrest', *Urban Forum*, 1 (2), 105–10.

Crankshaw, O. (1993) 'Squatting, Apartheid and Urbanisation on the Southern Witwatersrand', *African Affairs*, 92, 31–51.

Drummond, J. (1991) 'Reincorporating the Bantustans in South Africa: the Question of Bophuthatswana', *Geography*, 76, 369–73.

Eastern Province Herald (1993) 'Rush to Fight Border Plans', 7 July.

Epstein, A.L. (1958) *Politics in an Urban African Community*, Manchester University Press, Manchester, cited by L. Vail, 1989, 4.

Fox, R. (1992) 'Regional Proposals: Their Constitutional and Geographical Significance', paper presented at the Second Southern African Geographers' Symposium, University of Oxford.

Gibb, R.A. (1993) 'A Common Market for Post-apartheid Southern Africa: Prospects and Problems', *South African Geographical Journal*, 75, 29–36.

Hanf, T., H. Weland and G. Verdag (1981) *South Africa: the Prospects for Peaceful Change*, Rex Collings, London; David Philip, Cape Town and Indiana University Press, Bloomington.

Harries, P. (1989) 'Exclusion, Classification and Internal Colonialism: the Emergence of Ethnicity among the Tsonga-speakers of South Africa' in L. Vail (ed.), 1989, 82–117.

Hennayake, S.K. (1992) 'Interactive Ethnonationalism: an Alternative Explanation of Minority Ethnonationalism', *Political Geography*, 11, 526–49.

Horowitz, D.L. (1991) *A Democratic South Africa? Constitutional Engineering in a Divided Society*, University of California Press, Berkeley.

Lemon, A. (1980) 'Federalism in Plural Societies: a Critique with Special Reference to South Africa', *Plural Societies*, 11 (2), 3–24.

Lemon, A. (1982) 'Migrant Labour and "Frontier Commuters": Reorganizing South Africa's Black Labour Supply' in D.M. Smith (ed.), *Living under Apartheid: Aspects of Urbanization and Social Change in South Africa*, Allen and Unwin, London, 64–89.

Lemon, A. (1987) *Apartheid in Transition*, Gower, Aldershot.

Lemon, A. (1994a) 'Education' in J. Brewer (ed.), *Restructuring South Africa*, Macmillan, London, 91–110.

Lemon, A. (1994b) 'Desegregation and Privatisation in White South African Schools, 1990–1992', *Journal of Contemporary African Studies*, 12 (2), 200–21.

Mare, G. (1992) *Brother Born of Warrior Blood: Politics and Ethnicity in South Africa*, Ravan, Johannesburg.

Mare, G. and Hamilton, G. (1987) *An Appetite for Power: Buthelezi's Inkatha and South Africa*, Ravan, Johannesburg; Indiana University Press, Bloomington and Indianapolis.

Marks, S. (1989) 'Patriotism, Patriarchy and Purity: Natal and the Politics of Zulu Ethnic Consciousness' in L. Vail (ed.) 1989, 215–40.

Mayer, P. (1961) *Townsmen or Tribesmen*, Oxford University Press, Cape Town.

Mikesell, M.W. and A.B. Murphy (1991) 'A framework for comparative study of minority group aspirations', *Annals of the Association of American Geographers*, 81, 581–604.

Mitchell, J.C. (1958) *The Kalela Dance*, Manchester University Press, cited by L. Vail, 1989, 4.

Moll, P., N, Nattrass and L. Loots (eds) (1991) *Redistribution: How Can it Work in South Africa?*, David Philip, Cape Town.

Pirie, G.H. (1984) 'Ethno-linguistic Zoning in South African Black Townships', *Area*, 16, 291–8.

Prescott, J.R.V. (1979) 'Africa's Boundary Problems', *Optima*, 28 (1), 2–21.

Slabbert, F. van Zyl and D. Welsh (1979) *South Africa's Options*, David Philip, Cape Town.

Smith, D.M. (1992) 'Redistribution After Apartheid: Who Gets What Where in the New South Africa', *Area*, 24, 350–8.

Stone, J. (1992) Review of D.L. Horowitz, 1991, *Ethnic and Racial Studies*, 15, 634–6.

Vail, L. (ed.) (1989) *The Creation of Tribalism in Southern Africa*, James Currey, London; University of California Press, Berkeley.

Weekly Mail (1993) 'IFP Moderates Plan Elections . . .', 12–18 November, 2.

Western, J. (1981) *Outcast Cape Town*, George Allen and Unwin, London.

Williams, C. (1979) 'Ethnic Resurgence in the Periphery', *Area*, 11, 279–83.

Williams, C. (1980) 'Ethnic Separatism in Western Europe', *Tijdschrift voor Economische en Sociale Geografie*, 71, 142–58.

5 Tribe or nation? Some lessons from the Kenyan multiparty elections

Anders Närman

Introduction

Tribalism has often been a convenient concept in preference to a multitude of African developmental problems. The mere word points back to some kind of primitive social organization, built on superstition and beliefs not related to the demands of our modern times. As long as the dominating development strategies, consciously or unconsciously are rooted in the modernization paradigm there is no place for tribal communities in many countries. In this context, therefore, a prerequisite to enter into a development process was to create a set of unitary national policies. At an early stage after independence many countries attempted to create a national identity, often expressed in the names chosen for the political parties that achieved the status of rulers. We can here mention TANU (Tanganyika African National Union), Zambia's UNIP (United National Independence Party), ZANU (Zimbabwe African National Union) and KANU (Kenya African National Union).

The national boundaries established, and declared more or less sancrosant by the OAU (Organization of African Unity) in 1963, were a colonial creation. So is also the concept of nation as it was adopted by the newly independent states. Davidson (1992 pp.19) challenged the way African leaders adopted the model of their oppressors instead of searching for alternatives in their own history.

Tribal social organization, in the historical sense, is an aspect of development well worth exploring as an expression of solidarity among people sharing a common regional area and culture. Contrary to common belief this emerges as a positive factor of development, creating a civil society dependant on laws and the rule of law (Davidson 1992, p.11). However, what we now know as tribalism is a destructive disorder invented by the

Ethnicity and Development: Geographical Perspectives. Edited by Denis Dwyer and David Drakakis-Smith.

colonial rulers. It has been argued by, for example Chazan *et al.* (1992, p.107), that the identification of African ethnic groups, such as the Kikuyu and Luhya of Kenya, is a recent phenomenon. Various diffuse entities were classified jointly as a tribe to make the administrative rule easier. Apart from living in the same area, classification was also based on certain cultural affinities.

In stark contrast to this we find the classic anthropological work on the Kikuyu tribe, carried out by Kenya's first president, Jomo Kenyatta, in the 1930s. He refers to the tribal legend about Gikuyu, the founder of his tribe, living at the time 'when mankind started to populate the earth' (Kenyatta 1971, p.1). The tribal organization that emerged among the Kikuyu was established on three pillars: the family group, the clan and the system of age-grading. The Kikuyu, as a 'distinct group' long before the colonial period, have also been described by Muriuki (1974, p.62). Similar historic accounts are available for the Kamba (Ndeti 1972, p.27), as well as other tribes. The issue might not be so much the very existence of tribes, as what has formed their image, either the traditional African perception or the version distorted by the needs of colonialism.

Mazrui (1978, p.155) has dwelt on the humanitarianism found in traditional indigenous African societies, 'which is not even comprehensible to the western mind'. According to him the voluntary services provided within tribal welfare systems were an expression of social fellowship. This is the very opposite of Western individualism, on which the modernization process is based. Therefore, tribalism, as an African ethnic form of social relations, can hardly be directly transformed to fit into mainstream development strategies (Cobbah, 1988, p.72).

Thus, what we see as negative expressions of tribalism is more part of what Mazrui has termed a gap between principles and practice found in the Euro–Christian relationship to Africa. The colonial legacy has been taken over by the rulers in many African countries. The concept of tribe is most often used by the most 'de-tribalized' modern elite to promote their own vested interests within an adopted Westernized society. It is in that context we are viewing the 'evils of tribalism' in today's Africa. To illustrate this point this chapter will given an over-view of Kenyan development from the colonial period up to the present, from an ethnic perspective. As a recent example of this, the 1992 multi-party elections, and their aftermath, will be discussed.

The basic ethnic structure of Kenya

Tribal affiliation has been used officially as one statistical element in the population censuses. However, the divisions among the various entities have not always been the same. For example, in 1979 the Kalenjin group

Table 5.1 Kenya: percentage importance of the eight larges tribal groups, 1989

Tribe	(%)
Kikuyu	21
Luhya	14
Luo	12
Kamba	11
Kalenjin	11
Kisii	6
Meru	5
Mijikenda	5
others	15
Total	100

Source: Republic of Kenya, 1994

was referred to as such, while the 1969 census gave a separate account for Kipsigis, Nandi, Elgeyo, Marakwet *et al.*, only indicating them as Kalenjin-speaking tribes. Similarly the Luos of 1969 were in 1979 separated into Luo and the smaller fraction of Basuba (Republic of Kenya 1970 and 1981). Conversely Luhya and Mijikenda are two groups which are regarded as distinctly heterogeneous, even if they have always been given one entity in the census. Some of the nomadic tribes has also been described as unitary groups, for example, Somalis and Galla, or broken down into more detailed subgroups.

In 1989 there were five larger tribes making up almost 70 per cent of the total population, with another three representing at least 5 per cent respectively (Table 5.1). Some 25 groups constituted the remaining 15 per cent of the total population, including the Asian, European and Arab minorities. To a certain extent Kenya, like the rest of east Africa, has experienced confrontation between the non-African population and indigenous Africans. After independence this friction has mostly been related to economic control, primarily in connection with the fairly numerous Asian community. However, our main concern here is with the ethnic problem among the Kenyan Africans, i.e. the tribal equation. Apart from an eventual redefining of the tribal groups, the data given in Table 5.1 has been relatively stable over time, except for the influx of people from the border regions of Ethiopia and Somalia during times of turmoil in those countries.

Administratively Kenya has been divided into eight provinces and 41 districts. During the last few years some of the more populous districts have been subdivided. Due to the availability of population data we will, however, use the older district division in this chapter (Figure 5.1). In all but seven out of the 41 districts, one of the tribes constitutes an absolute majority. Not fewer than 26 districts have 75 per cent or more of their population from only one tribe. Consequently, districts are to a large extent not only a spatial but also an ethnic division. This fact is clearly evident in Figure 5.2 which indicates the districts according to the share of population represented by a single majority tribe.

The three largest tribes, Kikuyu, Luhya and Luo, are all living on high-potential agricultural lands, with a comparatively high population density. Still there are certain differences in basic economic conditions between the Kikuyu on the one hand and Luhya/Luo on the other. The Central province (comprising the districts of Kiambu, Kirinyaga, Muranga, Nyandarua and Nyeri) is the traditional home of the Kikuyu. Many of them belong to a smallholder farming community, with coffee as an important cash crop.

Compared to the Kikuyu, the Luhya in Western province (Busia, Bungoma and Kakamega) are much more dependent on subsistence agricultural production on relatively small plots. The same is the case with the Luo, living in Kisumu, Siaya and South Nyanza. The fourth district (Kisii) in what makes up Nyanza province is an important centre for small-scale tea production. Directly across the borders of Nairobi and Central province good agricultural lands are found in neighbouring Machakos, Kitui, Embu and Meru districts. However, in these areas Kamba, Embu and Meru peasants are trying to eke out a living under conditions which become gradually harsher with increasing distance from the fertile regions around Mt Kenya (Ominde 1979, p.51–60).

Since independence a substantial migration has taken place to the coastal areas by people belonging to the Kamba, Luo and Luhya communities. At the same time many Kikuyu and Luhya have settled on parts of the former so-called 'White Highlands' in Rift Valley province districts of Uasin Gishu, Nandi, Trans Nzoia, Kericho, Nakuru and Laikipia which used to be dominated by large-scale commercial agriculture (Mbithi and Barnes 1975, p.83). Apart from this, the central Rift Valley province has been the home of the Kalenjin tribe. In many of the areas presently shared between Kalenjin and other ethnic groups there have been scenes of fierce tribal clashes during the last few years (Republic of Kenya 1992). Often these occurrences have been attributed to powerful Kalenjin individuals in the KANU party, unwilling to relinguish their positions (see below).

In the vast arid and semi-arid areas in the north of the country the districts of Turkana, Samburu, Marsabit, Isiolo, Mandera, Wajir, Garissa and Tana River are the home of many pastoralist groups, living in a marginal existence within the modern state. Among them we find Turkana, Samburu, Somalis and Galla. Further to the south the Masai people inhabit Kajiado and Narok districts (Ominde 1979, pp.61–3). The integra-

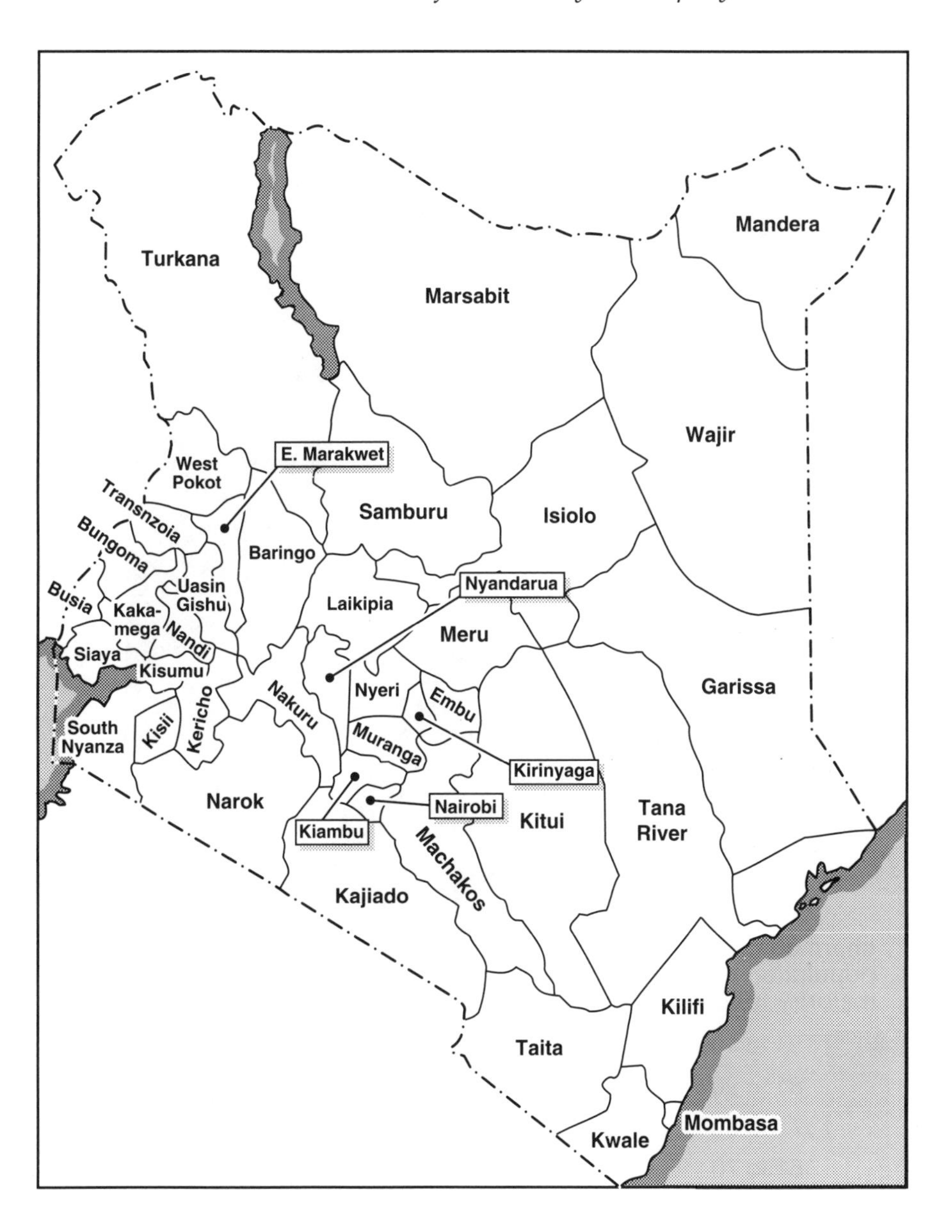

Figure 5.1 Kenya: administrative districts

tion of the Somalis into a Kenyan nation has been a difficult task. Due to alleged interference from neighbouring Somalia, the North-Eastern province has for long periods been under a state of emergency; the so-called *'Shifta'* (bandit) conflict. The Somalian civil war that has escalated

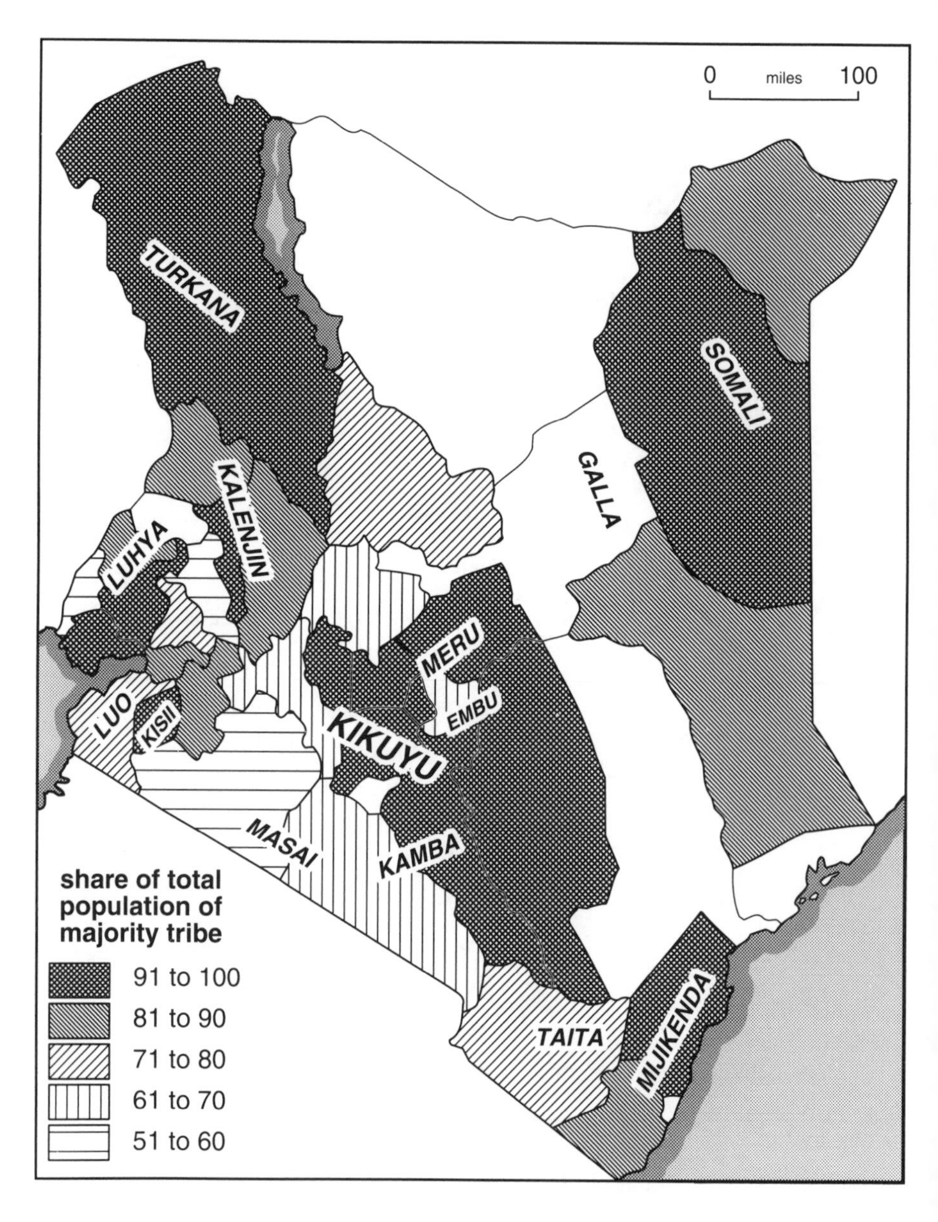

Figure 5.2 Kenya: the majority tribe dominance and principal region for the larger tribal groups

during the 1990s has also had serious consequences across the border into Kenya.

The colonial background

The official policy during the colonial period was to separate the various tribal entities as much as possible. Outside the commercial agricultural lands owned by white settlers, the 'White Highlands', Africans were expected to eke out a living within so-called 'tribal reserves'. To a certain extent they were also needed as farm labourers on the huge plantations (Kitching 1980; van Zwanenberg 1975; Leys 1975). Thereby, some tribes, notably Kikuyu, but also Luo, Luhya and the Kamba, came to be involved early in a monetary economy. Apart from agricultural work there was also some service employment available, such as domestic servants, or work at the Mombasa harbour.

Not only were some tribal segments of the population involved earlier than others in the monetary economy, they were also gaining from the process of modernization in terms of education and health services. Traditional social organizations were broken down and adjusted to fit in with the needs of colonial rule (Mutiso 1975). Among the Kamba, for example, a tribal system of joint work (*Mwethya*) was utilized to extract communal labour (Hill 1991). Most of the Africans were secluded in their own home areas. Migration was efficiently restricted, though the *kipande* system. People were made to wear a compulsory identification document in a metal container kept on a string around the neck. With this it was an easy task for the colonial authorities to control movements from one place to another (wa Kinyatti 1991).

Early expressions of nationalism were largely identified with particular ethnic organizations, such as the Kikuyu Central Association, the Kavirondo Taxpayers' Welfare Association (Luo), the Ukamba Members' Association and the Taita Hills Association. Still the common anti-colonial struggle brought them together in a more or less loose alliance. After the middle of the 1940s much of the political work was to be incorporated within the Kenya African Union (KAU). At the same time a radical trade unionism had been established, mostly within the Asian community. A couple of young Kikuyu, Fred Kubai and Bildad Kaggia, were also involved in this activity (wa Kinyatti 1991). Both of them were later part of the armed struggle for liberation, which for the outside world became famous under the derogatory term 'Mau Mau'.

This liberation movement, which was called KLFA (Kenya Land Freedom Army) by its own officials, basically found its support among the Kikuyu people. They had lost their land to the colonial settlers and demanded its return. Tribes with a strong affinity to the Kikuyu, such as

Meru, Embu and partly the Kamba, were also recruited to the struggle. There is a feeling among these groups that, since they delivered independence to Kenya, their claim for a greater share in the subsequent reward was justified.

The issue of Mau Mau/KLFA, as a tribal or nationalistic struggle for independence, has resulted in an intensive debate among Kenyan historians. During the initial stages of the Mau Mau war of liberation, the KAU had been banned. Thereafter, up till the end of the 1950s, the only political parties allowed by the colonial government were those based on a distinct tribal or regional affinity. A similar consideration was also found in the first independence constitution. According to this, Kenya was supposed to be a federative (*Majimbo*) state, with substantial power delegated to seven regional assemblies (*Weekly Review*, 17 December 1993).

The *Majimbo* structure was opposed by one of the main political parties at the time, KANU, which was seen as something of a Kikuyu/Luo alliance. At independence it was led by Jomo Kenyatta, a Kikuyu and also the first president, together with two prominent Luo politicians, Oginga Odinga and Tom Mboya. Against this, the Kenya African Democratic Union (KADU) was formed in an attempt to safeguard the rights of smaller tribes, thereby favouring the federative government. Among the early leaders in this configuration we find Daniel arap Moi (Kalenjin), Joseph Muliro (Luhya) and Ronald Ngala (from the coast).

After an election victory for KANU the regional constitution was replaced by a strong central government. This also led to the dissolution of KADU, its members being integrated into KANU (Walker 1987). As will be seen below the so-called '*Majimbo* issue' has once again resurfaced, in connection with the multiparty debate. To a certain extent the proponents of this system are former members of KADU.

The Kenya left by British colonalists was a country largely based on spatial and tribal inequalities. At the same time a strong identification with region and tribe had been a deliberate colonial policy. In spite of calls for a national development, it became a fertile ground for exploitation by the already advantaged tribal communities. Thus the notion of tribe became even more alientated from its indigenous meaning to an instrument for promoting a local elite thriving on a Western modernization strategy. For a lengthy period Kenya could hid away glaring inequalities within a comparatively positive aggregate national 'development'.

Tribal politics under Kenyatta and Moi

With the demise of KADU Kenya was turned into a more or less *de facto* one-party state which, with a few exceptions, has been the situation up to the early 1990s. The most serious opposition came from the formation of the Kenya People's Union (KPU) by the former vice-president, Oginga Odinga. This party had a distinctly more radical approach to politics compared to KANU. Odinga noted in his own book that Kenya had not achieved *uhuru* (independence), as it was still dominated economically by external forces (Odinga 1967).

The main reason for the formation of the KPU, apart from ideological differences, was that Odinga had lost out in the internal power struggle. Mboya, who was widely regarded as a national figure, had been able to out-manoeuvre his more traditional tribesman. With Odinga at the helm KPU was viewed as a more or less Luo affair, with a few Kikuyu also joining. After a few years the KPU was banned and its leadership, including Odinga, detained. That marked an end to any kind of formal opposition party for more than two decades. A strong tension between the Luo, and mainly Kikuyu on the other side, built up in relation to the KPU affair. Mboya was killed in a Nairobi street by a Kikuyu, and Kenyatta's motorcade was stoned in Kisumu, the 'capital' of the Luo. In the latter incident a few people were killed as the security personnel opened fire into the crowds. This was also the last time that Kenyatta ever visited Kisumu (Walker 1987).

Even after their release from detention many prominent Luo were not allowed to re-enter elective politics as long as Kenyatta lived which contributed to an increasing polarization between Kikuyu and Luo. Moreover, that there was also a clear failure to provide for smaller tribes in the development strategy of modernization was also obvious.

In choosing a new vice-president after Odinga, it had been important to select a non-Kikuyu to keep up any kind of national image. His immediate successor resigned after a short period, leaving the post to a Kalenjin, Daniel arap Moi. Even with these vice-presidential appointments, the mere thought of a future non-Kikuyu president seemed to be unrealistic. These feelings were coming out into the open during the so-called 'change the constitution' move just before the death of Kenyatta. Some leading Kikuyu politicians made an attempt to block the vice-president from automatically taking over as president. However, this attempt was aborted by the then Attorney-General, Charles Njonjo, himself a Kikuyu (Karimi and Ochieng 1980). Whether this was done out of personal ambition or due to a belief in the constitution is not clear. In any case his own fall from political power a few years later was certainly dramatic.

In spite of this opposition Daniel arap Moi was able to secure the presidency in a rather smooth transition after the death of Kenyatta 1978 (Karimi and Ochieng 1980, P3). After an early period of populism the Moi regime has transformed itself into a rule characterized by repression and irrationality. This erupted less than three years after his assumption of power in an attempted coup. Detention soon became the principal method of dealing with various expressions of opposition. During the middle of the 1980s numerous people were arrested for an alleged connection to the illegal organization Mwakenya. Among those affected were many belonging to the Kikuyu and also the Luo tribes.

Without the backing of a majority tribe, a situation enjoyed by Kenyatta, Moi had to use other tactics to stay in power. The most important instrument in this was the party machinery, especially so by making KANU constitutionally the only legal party. Through a system of party expulsions followed by reinstatements of the 'reformed' politicians, the new president managed to build up a core of devoted supporters, based more on fear than any kind of ideological conviction. Support from previously neglected tribes was gained by bringing some of their members into the government or to top administrative posts elsewhere. For example, a Somali was appointed as a minister of state, while his brother was given the post of commander of the armed forces. In retrospect this seemed to give a clear advantage to Moi and the KANU party among minority groups in the 1992 multiparty election (see below).

Initially it seems that Moi wanted to stay with a tribal balance of power, as evidenced by the appointment of Mwai Kibaki, a Kikuyu, as vice-president. After the election in 1988 Kibaki was replaced by another Kikuyu Josephat Karanja (now deceased), a former vice-chancellor of the university of Nairobi. An unofficial reason for Kibaki's demotion seems to have been his inability to support the president over a series of contentious issues. However, it might also have been part of a scheme to limit further the power held by the Kikuyu. Karanja was soon attacked bitterly by a number of loyalist KANU Kikuyu and was forced to resign. With the selection of George Saitoti, a Masai according to his own claims, as vice-president, Kenya was for the first time without any Kikuyu among the two top political positions.

Patterns of development under Kenyatta and Moi

Already, before formal independence, the Kikuyu had taken a favourable position from a socio-economic point of view. This was to be accentuated further under 'their' president, Kenyatta. The way the Kikuyu came to dominate the higher echelon of the administration and politics has been described convincingly by Nellis (1974). With political clout followed strong economic power for the Kikuyu. In the name of modernization, the same individual could establish himself politically or in the civil service and combine this with his own business. Multinational companies were lining up to enrol leading Kikuyu personalities on their local boards, preferably someone with close connection to the 'royal' (Kenyatta) family.

Economic strength among the Kikuyu is rooted in an early involvement in cash crop production which has been maintained throughout the first three decades after independence. The Central province dominates coffee production and has a fairly large share of the tea output. These two crops have been the backbone of the Kenyan export market. Grains, on the other hand, are primarily grown in Rift Valley province, but once again in districts with a high proportion of Kikuyu settlers such as Nakuru, Uasin Gishu and Trans Nzoia. Industrially the Central province gained from employment opportunities in the manufacturing sector, located in the capital Nairobi, and also from those in the main industrial town, Thika, in Kiambu district. Other important industrial towns are Nakuru and Eldoret, both with a high number of Kikuyu inhabitants.

Even if 'the fruits of *uhuru*' were not trickling down to the entire Kikuyu community, comparative advantages in fields such as education were tremendous. While secondary education was something of a rare privilege to most Kenyan children, it was not so special for the Kikuyu. Not only were the Kikuyu prominent in the community development programmes (*harambee*), they were also gaining disproportionate access to national catchment schools, as well as dominating other good governmental schools, located in the Central province (Kinyanjui 1974).

Through their educational standards, it was possible for the Kikuyu to legitimate a recruitment into top administrative jobs. During these years many Kikuyu experienced a positive trend within the Kenyan society and formed a high proportion of the national wage-earning population. Educationally some other larger tribes were also gradually finding an avenue into the newly emerging elites. This path was still to a large extent closed to most of the smaller groups, especially the pastoralists in the north (Närman 1990).

However, within the Kikuyu society there was also a radical opposition to the kind of modernization strategy followed and the subsequent inequalities. This was to a large extent centred around the outspoken parliamenatrian J.M. Kariuki, whose name became even more legendary as a symbol of resistance after his assassination in 1975. Culturally a radical movement of protest emerged through literature and drama in the Kikuyu language. This is largely connected to the author Ngugi wa Thiong'o, plus the Kamiriithu theatre group (wa Thiong'o 1981). The ideological diversity among the Kikuyu group under Kenyatta was a reaction to the way an elite used the ethnic factor to promote their own sectional interests. While some members of the Kikuyu tribe had been amassing enormous wealth, the widest economic gap was also to be found within this group (Karimi and Ochieng 1980, p.8).

With Moi in power the Kikuyu supremacy in business, to some extent, and public civil service, in a more substantial way, gradually dwindled. This was obvious not least in local administration. The main beneficiaries in this move were members of the president's own tribe, the Kalenjin. Compared to the Kikuyu these were not only fewer in number but had a substantially more limited educational background. Consequently considerable experience and skills were lost in vital sectors of the Kenyan society. Another dilemma was that while the Kikuyu held a supreme economic position, this was largely built on directly productive activities which was not the case for the Kalenjin.

Economically, Moi soon overtook his predecessor in personal wealth accumulation. At the same time other leading Kalenjin, primarily the obscure Nicholas Biwott, quickly managed to establish themselves as major economic figures. When Biwott was later mentioned as a prime suspect in the murder of the minister for foreign affairs, Robert Ouku, he lost some of his political clout but remained an economic force. Lately he has been accused of using his considerable wealth to promote the intense tribal clashes in the build-up for the elections.

During Kenyatta's regime various tribal 'welfare' organizations were turned into virtual business empires. The most significant of these was GEMA (Gikuyu, Embu, Meru Association), established among the Kikuyu and the two closely related tribes. Sports were also sometimes divided along tribal lines. During the 1970s some of the best football clubs were known as Abaluhya, Luo Union or the like. This kind of tribal identification within social and economic activities was banned by Moi. Despite this, the notion of tribe was probably more openly used in the political debate than ever before at the end of the 1980s. The settlement of Kikuyu ('foreigners') outside their own tribal area was referred to by cabinet ministers. In an (in)famous speech the Masai minister William ole Ntimama told the Kikuyu in Narok district to 'lie low like envelopes'. Federalism (Majimboism) once again resurfaced, a reminiscence of the old KADU politics. It is in the wake of this that tribal clashes began escalating. Even within churches a trend emerged with various congregations asking for sub-division so as to get a bishop, representing certain tribes or by blocking the appointment of a 'foreign' bishop. It was in this atmosphere that the surge for multipartyism gained momentum. From an early stage this was supported by the international community, in an effort to promote Western-style democracy.

Back to multiparty politics

A repeal of the law making KANU the sole legal party was a topic gaining momentum at the end of the 1980s, initially among representatives from the churches and the Kenya Law Society. In both cases many of the most vocal statements came from members of either the Kikuyu or Luo tribes. One outstanding exception was the Kalenjin bishop Alexander Muge, who was killed in a car accident under very suspicious circumstances. Something of a political alliance for multiparty democracy seemed to be formed by two former Kikuyu ministers, both expelled from KANU, Kenneth Matiba and Charles Rubia, in conjunction with veteran politician Oginga Odinga. After a number of press conferences Matiba and Rubia suddenly found themselves in detention, together with Odinga's son Raila. From the very start Moi defended his one-party stance with the argument that Kenya was still not mature enough for a multiparty system. According to him the only basis for parties outside KANU could be tribally motivated. After an unsuccessful attempt to get a political party registered, Odinga formed FORD (Forum for the Restoration of Democracy) as a pressure group.

When at the end of 1991 donors interupted most development assistance to Kenya, officially on account of its human rights record, Moi accepted a new multiparty constitution for the country. Of course, these two factors had nothing to do with each other, according to a statement made by Vice-President Saitoti. As FORD was already in existence, it was soon a leading force. Initially it enjoyed a broad popular support among many groups in the country. It seemed like the chairman Odinga, at the age of almost 80, was on his way to challenge Moi in a man-to-man encounter for the presidency.

FORD was a very heterogenous party, consisting of various multiparty proponents, KANU political rejects and the radical 'young turks'. The latter group was made up of young opponents to the Moi human rights record, and was led by the then Kenya Law Society chairman Paul Muite. The litmus test for FORD was the home-coming of Matiba from hospital in London, where he had been treated for a stroke, suffered while in detention. Suddenly FORD found itself with no less than five official presidential candidates. Besides the two front-runners Odinga and Matiba, there were two Luhya, Martin Shikuku and Joseph Muliro (now deceased), and Muite (a Kikuyu). Eventually FORD was split into two major groupings, FORD Asili (the real FORD), and FORD Kenya. Within this division the tribal identification was rather obvious. FORD Asili, under Matiba, was to be a basically Kikuyu party; with Shikuku, as his vice-presidential candidate, some Luhya support was also forthcoming.

The FORD Kenya power base was initially more unclear, but with Odinga as the leader, a strong Luo support was obvious. However, at the same time Odinga chose to select Muite as his candidate for the vice-presidency and relied on the backing from a few young radicals in the society. This is to a large extent in accordance with Odinga's traditional left-leaning politics. In addition, an informal alliance was struck with a coastal Muslim party which was not allowed to stand on its own.

Apart from the two FORD factions, there was also the new Democratic Party (DP) which the minister of health, and former vice president, Kibaki had formed together with some Kikuyu ministers from Kiambu and a nominated MP John Keen (a Masai). The DP was to a large extent just another Kikuyu party in addition to FORD Asili, although it also gained some backers among neighbouring tribes such as Embu, Meru, Kamba and also from the Kisii.

A smaller FORD splinter group, mainly Kikuyu, then broke away from what was to become FORD Asili. This was the KNC (Kenya National Congress). Although it contained many former parliamentarians, and even former cabinet ministers, it never made much impact. Among smaller parties to stand during the elections, there were two led by former political detainees: KSC with George Anyona and KENDA under Mukaru Nganga. In addition, a Nairobi businessman, John Harun, formed a loose organization for independent candidates, PICK. All three were also to stand as presidential candidates. At the end Moi found himself challenged by no less than seven opposition candidates, of which three (Odinga, Matiba and Kibaki) could be considered as serious. In tribal terms Moi was to build his support primarily on the Kalenjin group but also on various smaller ethnic entities.

The election and its consequences

The election, in December 1992, was preceded by tough in-fighting. As an established party, and also constituting the government, KANU had a clear organizational, but also economic, advantage, which was utilized to a large extent. However, the opposition parties also assisted KANU by a fierce battle among themselves. All of them made a major effort to create some kind of a tribal balance within their ranks. This was given a higher priority than the establishment of an ideological foundation. Personalities within important tribes were poached by the parties to increase their support. The free movement from one party to another indicated the lack of ideological conviction in affiliation. Someone rejected in the preliminaries by one party could turn up the next day as a candidate for another one. It has been claimed that in the exercise to get the strongest team possible a great deal of money was used to lure the 'right' parliamentary candidates. Such a practice would have favoured KANU, whose spending during the election time is said to have increased an already substantial inflation rate even further. (*New African*, May 1993).

In the parliamentary election KANU was able to secure an absolute majority, with 100 MPs out of 188. With the presidential right to nominate another 12 MPs, KANU domination has turned out to be even stronger. However, it is useful to know that the British-style electoral system opens considerable advantages to the largest party because it is able to field more candidates and is able to avoid over-concentration of voting support. Even if we include a substantial majority for the unchallenged candidates (see Table 5.2), KANU total support hardly reached 35 per

Table 5.2 Kenya: Tribal distribution of MPs by party

Tribe	KANU	FORD K	FORD A	DP
Kikuyu	0	1	21	12
Luhya	7	5	9	0
Luo	0	29	0	0
Kamba	12	0	1	4
Kalenjin	22	0	0	0
Kisii	6	2	0	1
Meru	2	1	0	4
Mijikenda	6	2	0	0
Other	45	1	0	2
Total	100	31	31	23

Source: *The Weekly Review* 8 January 1993

cent of the electorate, with the three main opposition parties sharing some 60–65 per cent in a fairly equal manner.

From the results for the four main parties a number of conclusions can be drawn with regard to ethnic significance. In this analysis we are not taking note of the allegations of rigging, a record number of election petitions or two almost immediate changes of party alliances as the parliament sat down to business. Table 5.2 and Figure 5.3 clearly show the role of the ethnic factor in the elections. Among the five major tribes it is only the Luhya that divided its sympathies. This might be closely linked to the fact that, apart from the FORD Asili vice-presidential candidate Shikuku, the tribe lacked any candidate for any of the top offices. Before the elections leading Luhya politicians complained bitterly about this. Since the election many Luhya have expressed dissatisfaction with the development in their home region, resulting in defections by many Luhya FORD Asili MPs. Most of these have been re-elected to parliament on a KANU ticket which in turn has meant that Shikuku's role has been seriously undermined.

One disturbing factor for KANU must be that it does not include any Kikuyu or Luo MPs. In fact to compose a cabinet built on some kind of credibility the president had to nominate one election loser from the Kikuyu and Luo communities respectively in order to include them in the government. The Kikuyu themselves are divided between FORD Asili and the DP, each with its own districts of dominance. Especially among the FORD Asili many previously unknown candidates won fairly easily. The only FORD Kenya Kikuyu to be elected was the party vice-chairman, Muite. He has, however, subsequently stepped down from all his official positions in FORD Kenya, while still technically remaining MP for the party. This is the present situation (1995), even if Muite was one of the main forces behind the formation of a new opposition party (Safina).

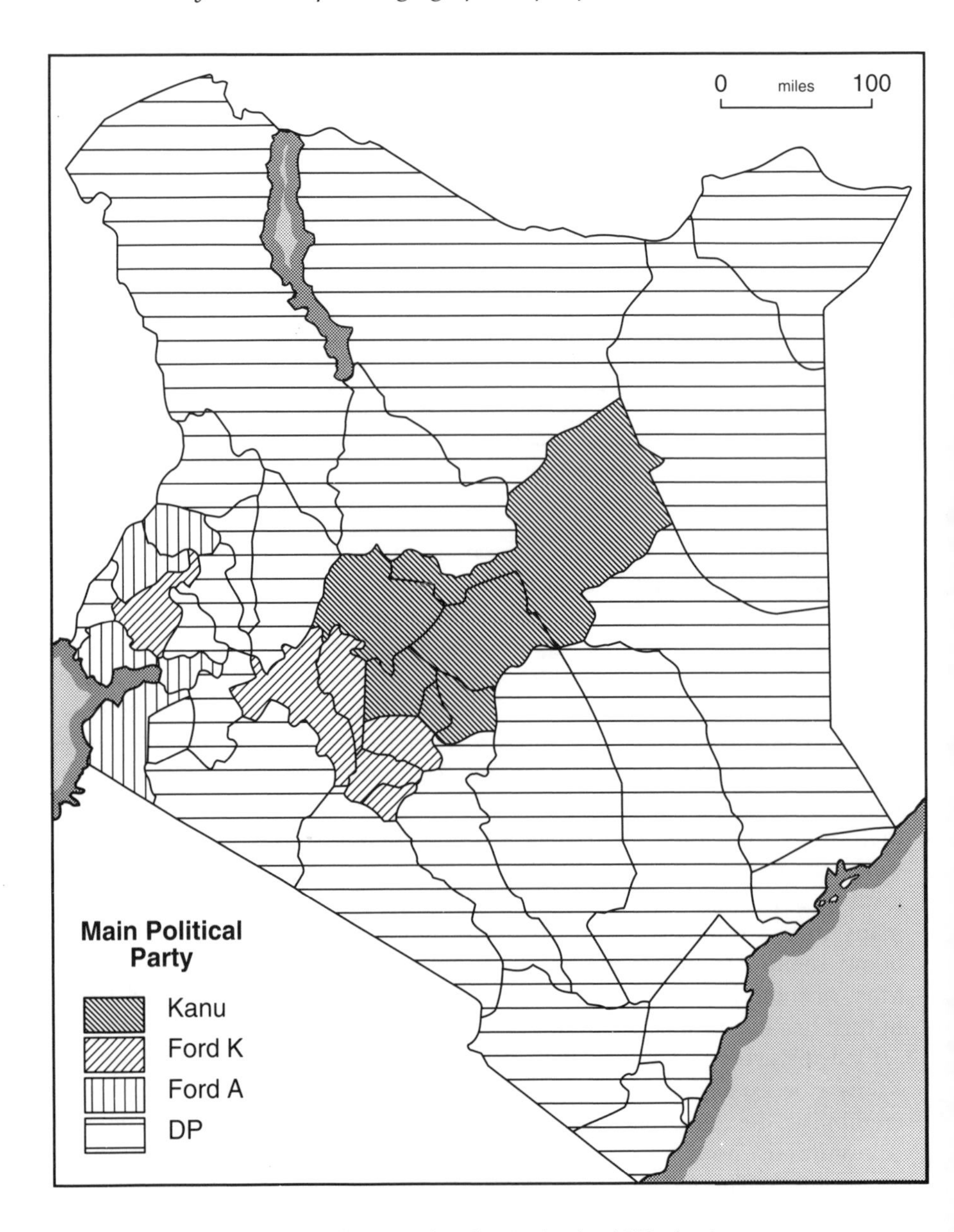

Figure 5.3 Kenya: principal parties by district in the 1992 elections

The Kamba support for KANU might not be as substantial as would appear. In many cases the KANU candidates won with a rather small margin. Only among the Kalenjin does KANU totally dominate. It is noticeable that as many as 15 of the Kalenjin MPs were unopposed, a fact that has been challenged in numerous petitions. Among the five major tribes it is only the Kalenjin that has a share of elected MPs comparable to its national share of population. Of course, it can be argued that a higher share for minority tribes is necessary to secure their interests. On the other hand this seems to be the very factor which has given KANU its present parliamentary supremacy.

Out of the 188 MPs, 49 (26 per cent) were from an ethnic group other than the eight largest. The percentage share of the total population for these minority tribes is in total 15 per cent (Table 5.1). If we average the total population in Central (Kikuyu) and Nyanza (Luo) provinces per constituency, it is approximately 120 000. In the Kalenjin heartland of Baringo and Elgeyo/Marakwet each MP, of which all are Kalenjin, represents some 60 000 people. Somali, Samburu, Turkana, Galla, Pokomo and Taita MPs represent in the range of 30 000 to 60 000 people. Here, 22 out of the 24 MPs belong to KANU. The KANU vote in these areas, with their largely uneducated population can be related to a lack of knowledge about the opposition. The government (i.e. KANU) machinery has had a clear advantage in projecting itself as the only real option.

It has been suggested that a joint opposition could have won the election. On this point it is noticeable that KANU might have lost 18 seats, if it had been faced with a combined opposition party. What is important in this case is that two Luhya, six Kamba, three Kisii and two Meru seats were won against a higher vote aggregate for the opposition. Consequently, the only major tribes firmly behind KANU seem to be Kalenjin and Mijikenda, and following a number of by-elections probably also the Luhya. This situation poses some problems for KANU, with such limited support from the Kikuyu and Luo and especially in the national capital of Nairobi. This kind of a result might be attributed to the ethnic differences in Kenya, but it might equally reflect the fact that an earlier elite has lost many of its privileges and economic supremacy. The reaction against KANU rule might not have so much to do with a total rejection by the Kikuyu and Luo tribes as to dwindling fortunes among the so-called Wabenzi (i.e. rich people) tribe.

The presidential election to a large extent followed the same pattern as the parliamentary one. As indicated in Figure 5.4a Moi enjoys massive support in most parts of the arid and semi-arid lands, as well as the Kalenjin heartlands of the Rift Valley province. This is echoed by the presidential picture on display in all official buildings, shops and often even homes. It can be observed in many of these areas Moi, as president, received a substantially higher share of the vote than KANU, as a party. On the other hand, he managed to gather a meagre 2 per cent of the votes in Central province. This is a much lower share than that achieved by his party. In Kisumu and Siaya, the situation is not much better where only 4 per cent of the votes were for Moi. South Nyanza would be fairly

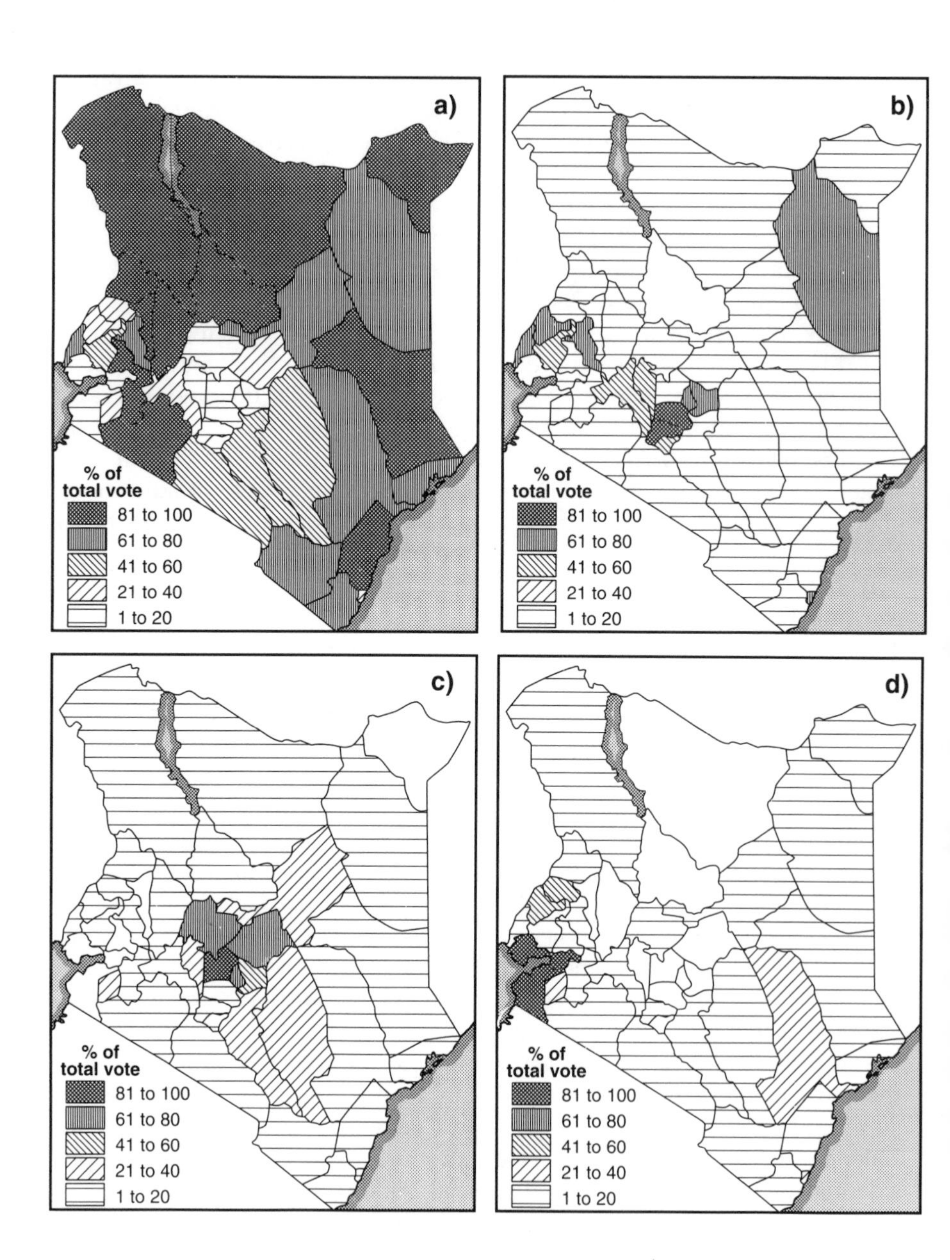

Figure 5.4 Kenya: percentage vote for each presidential candidate in the 1992 elections: (a) Moi; (b) Matiba; (c) Kibaki; (d) Odinga

similar were it not for a substantial non-Luo population, mainly made up of Kuria. The support of only 17 per cent of the Nairobi voters will also be a complicated factor for the president during the next few years.

If Moi has difficulties in projecting himself as a truly national president, the image of a national leader fails to fit any of the other candidates for the post (Figure 5.4). Second place was attained by the FORD Asili candidate Matiba, with Shikuku as his vice-presidential choice. However, Matiba was not even the chosen candidate for the whole Kikuyu community. In four Kikuyu-dominated districts he obtained above 50 per cent of the votes: Muranga, Kiambu, Nyandarua and Nakuru. The assistance of Shikuku brought the Kakamega figure up to 53 per cent. Apart from these five districts, only the capital Nairobi gave Matiba more than 30 per cent. In Luoland (Kisumu, Siaya and South Nyanza) the Matiba share of the vote was lower than that for President Moi.

In the presidential election the Kikuyu vote was obviously split, by district, between Matiba and Kibaki. In the 'DP' regions, within Kikuyuland (Kirinyaga, Laikipia and Nyeri), Matiba had a rather poor performance. Apart from strong support in these three districts, Kibaki seems to have many followers in Embu and Meru districts. In both cases the confidence in Kibaki as a person was higher than that for the DP party. Like Matiba, Kibaki was totally without support in Kisumu, Siaya and South Nyanza, with less than one per cent in any of these districts. A couple of years after the election the status previously held by Matiba and Kibaki in their respective parties has been challenged from within. This, in addition to the fact that the present FORD Kenya chairman, Wamalwa, is accepted only by some of his party executives, leaves the opposition without a serious candidate to opposed Moi for the presidency, more than two years after the 1992 election. Clearly this says more about the inability among the opposition to unit, not least across tribal lines, than on any strength being credited to the incumbent president.

It was obvious from the presidential results that Odinga, who died in early 1994, was still an important leader in Luoland. This was a position held by the veteran politician since the KPU days at least, since despite the fact that the main street in Kisumu town has been named after him, he had been banned from standing for any kind of national or local election until 1992. Odinga, like all the other presidential candidates, was far from being a national figure. Only in Bungoma and Trans Nzoia, both districts with a strong FORD Kenya support, did Odinga seem to make any real impact outside his own home area. In Mombasa, his alliance with the Muslim party, and the presence of a substantial number of Luo voters, increased his support. It is also probable that much of his fairly high Nairobi vote was due to the large Luo community in the capital. In Kikuyuland (Central province), Odinga gained more than one per cent only in Kiambu, with the assistance of Muite as a vice-presidential candidate.

The only clear conclusion from this analysis of the presidential vote is that none of the candidates has any kind of semblance of being a national figure. All of them have been able to get a substantial number of votes in their own 'back-yards', regionally and tribally, but none has any following at all outside his specific power base. From that point of view Kenya is much more a number of tribal communities than a nation.

After the elections

The first years after the elections were filled with many dramatic events but hardly anything in the name of a positive national development, thus pointing to a rather gloomy future. KANU has to a large extent assumed that 'winner takes all'. With a new lease of power the priority in resource allocation seem to be favouring KANU regions. In recent by-election campaigns, following party defections, this bias has continued with some ministers promising potential development if the constituency makes the 'right' choice. Even if some opposition MPs have defected back to KANU, no Kikuyu or Luo have so far been voted back on that party ticket. However, KANU has won a few additional seats among other tribes.

Among both the Luo and the Luhya there have been discussions on the future tribal leadership. One suggestion for a potential successor to Odinga, even before his actual demise, was Dalmas Otieno, a nominated MP and thereby the only Luo to represent KANU in parliament. With him as a Luo leader some were starting to count on a larger slice of the development cake in the future for the Luo community. For the Luhya the confirmation of one of their own, Kijana Wamalwa, as the new FORD Kenya chairman, after Odinga could at first have been a factor for changing the struggle for tribal supremacy within that party. However, as Wamalwa has not been able to swing the Luhya support in the direction of FORD Kenya in any of the by-elections taking place in Western province, his position has been dwindling gradually. This has also led to a new split within FORD Kenya, which was coming to the surface in mid-1995, with the suspension of Raila Odinga.

As a repayment for the way certain minority groups have voted in the elections, they have been granted district status for their particular home regions. For example, the Sabaot (a Kalenjin subgroup) and the Kuria, both groups with an expressed sympathy for KANU, were separated from existing districts with a clear opposition majority (*Economic Review* 23–9 August 1993).

With the election results following clear tribal lines, politics have also followed similar tendencies. Among the Kikuyu in both FORD Asili and the DP, the revival of GEMA has been a serious issue. At the same time the concept of Majimboism has been taken up by leading politicians, especially in Rift Valley and at the coast. In a somewhat confused debate, statements on minority rights have been intermingled with claims for ethnic cleansing. Two senior cabinet ministers, William ole Ntimama (a Masai) and Francis Lotodo (a Pokot), have, in separate statements, threatened 'foreigners' (primarily Kikuyu) if they were to remain in certain parts of Narok and West Pokot respectively. This in itself has contributed to increased intensity in the tribal clashes. Among Kikuyu leaders fears have been expressed that a Majimbo policy is a way of 'driving off the Kikuyu from areas where the community is not indigenous' (*Weekly Review* 17 December 1993).

Instead of bringing a functional democracy to Kenya, the first multiparty elections have rather accentuated the previous tribal animosity and tensions among the population. Under the present circumstances it will take a long time before we can expect any kind of positive development, irrespective of how we define this concept, to include the entire Kenyan nation. However, the suffering will not be exclusively felt by the Kikuyu, Luo, Luhya, Kalenjin, Masai or whichever tribe to which an individual belongs; it will be the poor sections of the population that will feel the pinch under a continuous process of underdevelopment. For the elite, tribal identity is but one of the factors at play in an elaborate power struggle far away from the immediate perils of poverty.

Concluding remarks

African tribalism, as we have come to know it, is largely a colonial creation. In the attempt to control the dependant territories, traditional social structures were transformed to suit a policy of domination. The Kenyan experience since independence illustrates some of the difficulties in trying to bring about some kind of national development strategy. Tribal affinities have to a large extent influenced the outcome and implementation of development planning. This has been so in the ethnic rivalries during the Kenyatta as well as the Moi regimes. You are what you are in society – not because of your abilities – but due to your relationship to those in power. Belonging to the same tribal group, or one favoured in an ethnic power game, is the key to success. Even the multiparty elections have nothing to do with actual democracy but are only a perpetuation of an alien nation-state system. Looked upon from the point of view of a modernization paradigm of development, tribalism can be nothing but a negative factor. It can be fitted into the context of corruption, nepotism and so on. Against this we have a traditional social organization that might be more geared to an original African way of thinking about development.

For the African the tribe, clan, extended family and home area are still very much alive. To use these concepts as a means to gain favours in the modernization process is an easy way out but is at the same time contrary to the traditional understanding of collective responsibility for the community. As a distributive function within an indigenous culture, rather than a way to take as much of the cake as possible, such organizations might very well be strong contributers to an internal development process. Often we all find ourselves trapped by Eurocentric perceptions when talking about the ethnic dimension. To get out of this we have to admit that cultural diversity and identity in itself is something that is part of development (Verhelst 1992).

It has to be pointed out that this call to review basic African traditions and concepts in the name of alternative development is not to bask in the glory of African primitivism. Nor is it an 'anti-development' conspiracy to deny the Africans their fair share of the material standards that have been reached in the North. These standards have been refused by all the mainstream development strategies so far formulated. Their benefits have only been obtained by a minute national elite.

It is well known that African peasants had developed ways and means to counteract most calamities during the pre-colonial period (Richards 1985; Rau 1991). The problem was the difficulty of fitting these into a modern cash-crop farming system. Attempts to find a development strategy based on an African ideology have been assessed from an Eurocentric value system. Neither the Tanzanian *ujamaa* or the Zambian humanism were ever given a fair chance to 'develop' because of conditions set within a global economic structure. Cultural expressions in the vernacular, such as the literature by Okot p'Bitek in Acholi and Ngugi wa Thiongo in Kikuyu, are not a picturesque oddity but a way to rediscover the roots of the people. Similarly, it is surely time to improve our understanding of traditional social organization, of which the tribal system is one component. It is clearly necessary to move away from the distorted perception of tribe with which we have come to be familiar in the North.

References

Chazan, N., R. Mortimer, J. Ravenhill and D. Rothchild (1992) *Politics and Society in Contemporary Africa*, Lynne Rienner Publishers, Boulder.

Cobbah, J. (1988) 'Toward a Geography of Peace in Africa: Redefining Sub-state Self-determination of Rights' in R.J. Johnston, D. Knight and E. Kofman (eds), *Nationalism Self-Determination and Political Geography*, Croom Helm, London, 70–86.

Davidson, B. (1992) *The Black Man's Burden – Africa and the Curse of the Nation-State*, James Currey, London.

Hill, M.J.D. (1991) *The Harambee Movement in Kenya: Self-Help, Development and Education among the Kamba of Kitui District*, The Athlone Press, London and Atlantic Highlands, NJ.

Karimi, J. and Ochieng Ph (1980) *The Kenyatta Succession*, Transafrica, Nairobi.
Kenyatta, J. (1971) *Facing Mount Kenya*, Heinemann, Nairobi.
Kinyanjui, K. (1974) *The Distribution of Educational Resources and Opportunities in Kenya*, Discussion Paper No. 208, Institute for Development Studies, University of Nairobi, Nairobi.
Kitching, G. (1980) *Class and Economic Change in Kenya – the Making of an African Petite-Bourgeoisie*, Yale University Press, New Haven.
Leys, C. (1975) *Underdevelopment in Kenya, the Political Economy of Neo-Colonialism*, Heinemann, London.
Mazrui, A. (1978) *Political Values and the Educated Class in Africa*, Heinemann, London.
Mbithi, P. and C. Barnes (1975) *Spontaneous Settlement Problem in Kenya*, East African Literature Bureau, Nairobi.
Muriuki, G. (1974) *A History of the Kikuyu 1500 – 1900*, Oxford University Press, Nairobi.
Mutiso, G.C. (1975) *Kenya: Politics Policy and Society*, East African Literature Bureau, Nairobi.
Nellis, J.R. (1974) *The Ethnic Composition of Leading Kenyan Government Positions*, Research Report No. 24, Scandinavian Institute of African Studies, Uppsala.
Ndeti, K. (1972) *Elements of Akamba Life*, East African Publishing House, Nairobi.
Närman, A. (1990) 'Pastoral Peoples and the Provision of Educational Facilities. A Case Study from Kenya', *Nomadic Peoples*, 25–27, Uppsala, 108–121.
Odinga, O. (1967) *Not Yet Uhuru – An Autobiography*, Heinemann, London.
Ominde, S.H. (1979) 'Regional Disparities and the Employment Problem in Kenya' in R.A. Obudho and D.R.F. Taylor (eds), *The Spatial Structure of Development: A Study of Kenya*, Westview Press, Boulder, 46–73.
Rau, B. (1991) *From Feast to Famine: Official Cures and Grassroots Remedies to Africa's Food Crisis*, Zed, London.
Republic of Kenya (1970) *Kenya Population Census, 1969, Volume I*, Statistics Department, Ministry of Finance and Economic Planning, Nairobi.
Republic of Kenya (1981) *Kenya Population Census, 1979, Volume I*. Central Bureau of Statistics, Ministry of Economic Planning and Development, Nairobi.
Republic of Kenya (1992) *Report of the Parliamentary Select Committee to investigate Ethnic Clashes in Western and Other Parts of Kenya 1992*, The National Assembly, Nairobi.
Republic of Kenya (1994) *Kenya Population Census, 1989, Volume 1*, Central Bureau of Statistics, Nairobi.
Richards, P. (1985) *Indigenous Agricultural Revolution*, Hutchinson, London.
van Zwanenberg, R.M.A. (1975) *Colonial Capitalism and Labour in Kenya 1919–1939*, East African Literature Bureau, Nairobi.
Verhelst, T.G. (1992) *No Life without Roots: Culture and Development*. Zed, London.
wa Kinyatti (1991) *Mau Mau: A Revolution Betrayed*, Mau Mau Research Center, New York.
wa Thiong'o N. (1981) *Detained. A Writer's Prison Diary*. Heinemann, London.
Walker, R. (1987) 'Kenya Recent History' (based on an earlier article by J. Lonsdale) in *Africa South of the Sahara 1987*, Europa Publications, London, 549–55.

6 Nationalism, democracy and development in Ethiopia

Abebe Zegeye and Dawit Abate

Introduction

Ethiopia is the third largest and most populous country in Africa. Lying at the western and southern tip of the Red Sea, which divides Africa and Asia, its history and culture reflect diverse influences. Noted for its long history of independence unparalleled by any other African country, Ethiopia has presented an enigma for foreign scholars (in the search for 'Prester John of the Indies', for instance) for many centuries. The country began to open up to foreigners from the 15th century onwards but closed its doors again between the 17th and 19th centuries. Ethiopian modernization began and moved steadily onwards from the mid-19th century but owes its present shape largely to the period of Emperor Haile Sellasie (1930–74).

The recent history of Ethiopia both under Haile Selassie and the Dergue (the military government which replaced imperial rule) has been characterized by the absence of democratic institutions. Although both regimes had written constitutions, they governed in an authoritarian manner, power essentially being invested in one man. Both regimes were intolerant of opposition, which they did not hesitate to quell by arrest and execution. Both instituted strong censorship of the press and were opposed to free assembly. In neither case was there an effective judiciary able to control the action of the executive and popularly elected officials played a small part.

The attitudes of both governments towards the aspiration of national or ethnic groups for forms of self-rule and a share in the development process have not been remarkably different. The response to expressions of discontent among the nationalities has been a growing enforced centralization of the state, a declaration of war on various oppositional 'national liberation fronts' and the imposition of plans and policies of economic construction which failed to take account of local needs or wishes.

Ethnicity and Development: Geographical Perspectives. Edited by Denis Dwyer and David Drakakis-Smith.

It remains to be seen if the new government, elected in 1995 despite the boycotting of the election by nearly all opposition parties, will be able to overcome these deeply entrenched policies and anti-democratic practices. The declaration of the right of nationalities for self-determination at the 1991 national conference represented a distinct departure from all past experiences. However, only time will tell if its implementation will satisfy the demands for autonomy or even 'independence' of the nationalities in accordance with their expressed desires made public long before the conference.

The Ethiopian People's Revolutionary Democratic Front (EPRDF) has control over the Council of People's Representatives and of the seven regional state councils so far elected which will return members to the Federal Council. Elections were postponed in three of the ten regions. Harer, Somali Region and Afar Region; the latter two are likely to field genuine opposition candidates to the government.

A principal problem that the government faces is how to modernize an economy not only ravaged by war and famine but still predominantly peasant based. This task is similar to that confronted by Haile Selassie and the Dergue in that economic resources are limited, and the immediate temptation might be to over-exploit the peasantry rather than develop long-term economic strategies. However, the emergence of demands by national groups for equal access to resources and to any benefits that the pursuit of development produces makes the task of the present or any future government extremely arduous.

Above all, it is important that the peasantry (who comprise the majority of the nationalities) should feel secure in their drive to maximize their productive capacities without being subject to punitive demands or 'national oppression'. When this happened in the past, they inevitably reduced production to the minimum subsistence level (thereby suppressing the market and further weakening the country's economy) and became fertile ground for the launch of oppositional 'liberation movements'.

In addition, pressure for privatization of land by foreign sponsors must be squared with ensuring security of land use; otherwise the problems of peasants displaced from the land but having no other employment prospects will arise.

First we will explore how attempts at 'nation building' failed and counter-movements gathered momentum, leading to the downfall of the Dergue. Then we will examine the approach adopted afterwards to resolve the 'nationalities question', as it is usually referred to among Ethiopians. After this we will take up the problems underlying the quest for democracy and its limits and prospects in Ethiopia, followed by a consideration of the impending influence of nationality or ethnic issues on development. Finally, we conclude by pointing out that the lack of a stable balance among (and incomplete formation of) class forces, especially the weaknesses of the emerging middle class, is at the root of the severely limited nature and fragility of the democratic process recently launched by the Transitional Government (TG).

The failure of 'nation-building' and the rise of nationalism

Unlike most other African countries, the formation of present-day Ethiopia was due largely to the interaction of indigenous social and political forces spanning many centuries. While the greater portion of the current territorial expanse had been incorporated into a single state by the time of the Berlin Conference of 1884–5, which divided up Africa among the European powers, the rest was integrated soon after in an attempt to preempt European colonial ambitions in the area. A direct outcome has been the co-existence of over 80 disparate groups, tribes and nationalities within a state dominated by the Christian highlanders (the Amhara and Tigreans).

The consolidation of the various peoples into a single Ethiopian state involved the removal from power of local kings or chiefs (such as Tona of the Wollaita) or systems of self-rule (the Gada system of the Oromo or the Gurdina system of the Soddo). Others who did not resist the series of conquests were assimilated to the Amhara and Tigrean nobles and military chiefs. From early on, the upper echelons of the ruling classes consisting of general and high officials included Oromos, Guraghes and others as well. In a sense, therefore, there did not develop any formal or permanent split between 'ruling' or 'subject' nationalities. Certain sections of the conquered nationalities were able to raise themselves into the ruling classes (through marriage or on the basis of proven loyalty). A few of the sovereigns also acknowledge Amhara or non-Tegrean ancestors.

Assimilation of the conquered peoples to the dominant nationalities proceeded through conversion to Orthodox Christianity, the state religion until very recently, and the espousal of Amhara cultural traits. Under Emperor Haile Sellasie, the modern school system came to play a significant role in bringing up an elite of multinational character which was loyal to the established state, in particular to the Crown and to the objective of arriving at 'one culture and one nation'. The extent to which this effort of 'nation-building' (as it was dubbed) succeeded or failed under Haile Sellasie and the Dergue (or military government) might be an interesting question to pursue, but here we seek to explore the sequence of events that let to the current situation in Ethiopia.

It is possible to discern several strands in the development of nationalist struggles. Overall disenchantment with the policies and practices of the imperial regime formed the major background for such movements. These will be discussed before specific causes and forms are addressed.

Disillusionment with the regime

The policy of national assimilation pursued by the Haile Sellasie government managed to entice leading elements of the subordinate or conquered nationalities into organs of power. Besides the traditional chieftains, the nobility and their retinue who were co-opted to head regional or local administrations, their newly educated descendants were raised to positions of privilege and power. The expansion of the educational system, the proselytizing activities of the Orthodox Church and the use of Amharic as the principal language in administration and the courts led to increased influence of the Amhara–Tigrean culture over wider sections. The Western missionaries who were allowed to operate mainly the the south helped achieve the same end. The bureaucracy and military accepted increasingly broader sections who went through these processes so that by the time of the 1974 revolution even major organs of power and other influential posts were filled by Oromos, Guraghes, Somalis and the rest; by Muslims as well as Christians.

Nevertheless, the expected smooth integration of the various nationalities into an 'Ethiopian Nation' has failed to materialize. On the one hand, the attempt to reproduce, through the educational system, Western values and beliefs to the exclusion or neglect of indigenous ones proved to be counter-productive to the imperial system in the long run. Not only did this induce alienation of the emerging educated elite from the concrete problems and the needs of the country (something that would grow over the years), it prompted the rejection of the autocratic rule of Haile Sellasie.

The educated elite as a whole increasingly perceived the landed gentry around Haile Sellasie as the main source of backwardness, the cause for the lack of liberty and loss of land property rights. (After the series of expansionist victories by Menilik in the 1880s, virtually all the peasants in the south were reduced to serfdom under the conquering northern soldiers and chiefs.) Study of the history and experiences of Western countries revealed that a leap into the 20th century would only be possible through transformation of the inequitable situation regarding access to land and power in the country. The first articulate writings on these issues date from early this century and were produced by elements from the Amhara–Tigrean as well as other nationalities. The advocates of change swayed Haile Sellasie to institute certain reforms (of land taxes, the 1931 constitution and other laws) at various stages in his reign; but the insufficiency of these reforms was laid bare by the Italian invasion in 1936.

The call for change became even greater with the expulsion of the Italians and the return of Haile Sellasie to power. The Patriots (who put up resistance to the Italians) pushed for a greater say in the affairs of the country, while the Exiles, led by the Emperor allied with the 'Quislings' (called *Banda*) attempted to suppress and neutralize them. A series of plots were to ensue in an attempt to overthrow Haile Sellasie.

The birth of the student movement soon after most of the Patriots had been disposed of by Haile Sellasie and his co-exiles, and the defeat of the first major *coup d'etat* in 1960, introduced a new element into the political scene. Reflecting the inherently contradictory foundations of the educational system and drawing upon the experiences of Western countries, students went on to question the basis of the *ancien régime*: the land system, the sacrosanct role of the Crown and gradually also the 'oppression of nationalities'.

Through the apt slogan of 'land to the tiller', the Ethiopian Student Movement (1960–75) exposed the infamy surrounding the expropriation of much of the land that many of the southern nationalities had owned before their defeat during the years of conquest or re-conquest in the last century by the northern warlords. The virtual vassalization of the defeated ruling classes in the south went hand in hand with the reduction of the southern peasantry to serfs of northern warlords. This meant that the proceeds from the sale of Ethiopian coffee or produce obtained from the rich lands went towards the upkeep of those warlords (and their armed detachments) who ruled over the south on behalf of the Emperors sitting at Addis Ababa. Tax systems also made sure that the central treasury would benefit. The fact that the southern peasantry was not only supporting the Amhara–Tigrean aristocracy and the up-and-coming bureaucrats but subsidizing a regime which did not relent from squeezing them whenever necessary for more taxes was bound to lead to revolts.

Centralization of power in Showa

Another major feature of the times was the process of centralization of power around the Showa nobility that ensued from about the beginning of this century. This proved to be detrimental to the loyal non-Showan chiefs and kings, including the Tigreans. While the resentment against the loss of power to the 'Showans' felt by the Gojjam and Gondar royal houses lingered for a long time (and still permeates popular attitudes in those provinces to everything Showa), it did not lead to any persistent confrontation on the battlefield. The only events of consequence against the centralization of power in Showa were the defiance of Ras Gugsa Wole (ex-husband of the Empress Zawditu) to Ras Tafari (later Haile Sellasie) in Gondar in 1930 and the alignment of the descendant of the last Gojjame king (Tekle Haimanot) with the Italian invaders.

An event having wider repercussions appears to be the ousting of the Tigrean chiefs and kings by the Showan Amahara ruling circles from ultimate decision making in major questions of the state. The Tigrean rulers who were reduced to kingship over Tigray attempted to make up for this loss by resorting to external support (mainly the Italians who had meanwhile occupied the north and christened it 'Eritrea') as leverage (decried by the Showans as 'treachery') against 'Showa' in their attempt to regain previous positions. Even when foreign influence may not have been a major factor, the urge 'to regain lost positions' has been a central element in all movements that were initiated among the Tigreans whether in 1943 as the Woyane rebellion, in 1961 as the 'Eritrean Liberation Front' (and others such as the EPLF from 1969 on) or from 1975 in the form of competing liberation fronts in Tigray (the strongest of them being the Tigray Peoples Liberation Front).

The centralization of power in the Showa nobility and around Haile Sellasie did not appear to have perturbed what remained of the chiefs and nobles in the south, who had been forced to acquiesce to Emperor Menelik early on. Indeed, the share of power allowed to local chiefs, in terms of local administration including descendants of the Afar, Somali, Wollega and Jimma Oromo ruling circles, served to appease any opposition that these groups might have had. Whether or not their involvement in the central state continued to have local chiefs, *balabats, koros, garadas* and sultans as the basic unit in certain areas until the 1974 revolution.

The process of centralization of power and the modernization of the state entered a new phase upon the expulsion of the Italians in 1941. The shock of defeat and subjugation by a technologically superior European power made modernization not only desirable but an urgent necessity. Whatever was begun in the past (education, a regular army and a bureaucracy, more institutions and infrastructure) was recommenced with added zeal.

But the pursuit of modernization was problematic from the start. Internal resources had to be found to finance any expansion of the bureaucracy, the military and for vital projects. The gradual integration of the Ethiopian economy from the end of the last century into the world economy had to be speeded up to pay for imports. The unchanging state of agriculture and the low level of revenue it yielded necessitated, on the one hand, the resort to foreign aid as a long-term policy and, on the other, government moves to introduce more rigorous methods of exacting levies from peasant households. This provoked two provinces (Bale and Gojjam) and parts of Wollo to rise up in rebellion against what they perceived to be an unbearable burden.

The Bale rebellion (1963–70) assumed an added aspect since the province is comprised of Oromos and Somalis. Yet, apart from being an expression of dissatisfaction with the specific actions of the central government in Addis Ababa, it did not seem to have reflected any larger political ideals such as independence or even an assertion of national identity among the Oromos. The Somalis, however, were instigated and assisted by the government established in 1960 in Mogadisho to further irredentist aims. Nevertheless, the defeat of the Bale movement by the Ethiopian army did not prevent the Oromos from instigating another rebellion (led by ex-leader of the Balle rebellion, Wako Gutu) upon the collapse of the Dergue in 1991.

The conflict over Eritrea

The muddled (not to say annexationist) manner in which the Haile Sellasie government treated the 'return of Eritrea to its motherland' revived the feeling of shame that Showan supremacy within the Ethiopian state had left behind among the Tigreans. Having had no accurate assessment of the implications of the 'return' and of the forces that were against or for unity, the regime resorted to its well-worn policy of dictating everything from Addis Ababa and of providing no solutions to those sectors that might have been alienated by its eagerness to unite the country.

First, the regime steamrolled through the idea of unity against existing opposition, irrespective of its divisions and weaknesses. Second, it relied on foreign (rather than internal), particularly US, support to push through its federal plan in the UN. Third, having won its case against formidable opposition, it did not continue to work against that opposition. Indeed, it did not even concern itself with consolidating the support it had obtained among the so-called 'unity' forces. Some prominent personages were forced to undergo the indignity of the Showan practice of *dejtenat* – that is making themselves available at the Emperor's court day in and day out without having any specific task other than to greet him and await any orders. This practice was applied indiscriminately as a means of disciplining persons considered independent-minded and, perhaps, of doubtful loyalty.

An underlying cause for the disenchantment of the Eritrean 'elite', former translators and clerks of the Italian colonial regime educated to no more than grade four level (the equivalent in Ethiopia of mid-primary school stage), seemed to be the impending decline of their relatively well-off position by the incorporation of Eritrea into Ethiopia. This might have been contrasted with the better prospects that they had though independence would have brought.

In addition, the prevalent view among the opponents of unity seemed to be that colonial states would be given independent status, as had already been initiated in the British colonies. Although the British (ruling over Eritrea as a protectorate from 1941 to 1952) attempted to cut off the western lowlands, or at any rate to influence the disintegration of the former Italian colony, in favour of the Sudan, no account exists of why the Tigreans in Eritrea should have preferred to detach themselves from their kinsmen across the river Mereb to the south (in Ethiopia) and become independent. Indeed, Wolde-ab Woldemariam conceived a united Tigrean national state (called 'Tigray-Tigrigny') as the core of the Eritrean independent state he sought to see established. But this is a line of inquiry that has been blocked since, after the intensification of the struggle, it was considered treasonable to talk of a part of Eritrea as being identical with anything in Ethiopia. Instead, an ideological device was created that promoted an 'Eritrean nation' whose defining feature was argued to be the common characteristics formed by the Italian rule and the struggle for freedom from such colonialism and the 'colonialism' of the Ethiopians.

The Eritrean Fronts gained from the support afforded by the Ethiopian student movement to national struggles. This support was, however, based on the assumption that the struggle of the Eritreans would facilitate the overthrow of the Addis Ababa regime and the introduction of democracy throughout the entire country. That the leadership of the Eritrean People's Liberation Front (EPLF) in particular had been drawn from past activists in the student movement in Addis Ababa University gave further credence to the belief in a 'common struggle'. Yet doubts persisted in connection with the alleged 'Arabic' or 'Panislamic' connections of the fronts as well as their ultimate aims.

The overthrow of the Solomonic Dynasty in 1974 brought into sharp focus several of the major problems: economic mismanagement, political oppression and inequality in the land-tenure system. Curiously, the 'nationalities question' did not figure as important in itself. At first it seemed that the Provisional Military Government (PMG) that took over power in September 1974 would opt for a negotiated settlement with the Eritrean 'brothers' (very soon changed to the old label 'bandits'). But internal power struggles within the PMG resulted in the decision that the Eritrean fronts should be eliminated unless they consented to disarm in return for some measure of autonomy, the contents of which varied with the success or failure of the PMG in its military campaigns. This was to be the approach of the PMG until it was overthrown in May 1991.

The rise of other liberation movements

The collapse of the old regime in 1974 and the establishment of the Dergue was seen by many of the constituent nationalities of Ethiopia as an opportunity to assert their identity in order to gain some form of autonomy. Such expectations were, however, soon dashed as the new government seemed even more bent on centralization than the former one. It is in light of heightened expectations and then disappointment that one can understand the vigour with which ethnic-based liberation fronts of various complexion sprang up throughout much of Ethiopia.

The origins of the Oromo nationalist movement are not very clear. However, there is a consensus that the Metcha Tulama Association, established on an official basis to channel development efforts, was the harbinger of latter-day political forms. The scepticism of the Haile Sellasie government concerning the aims of that organization gave rise to the imprisonment of its leading officials (major functionaries of the state) and the banning of the organization. The Oromo Liberation Front (OLF) reportedly followed in its footsteps around 1972. By the time of the 1974 military coup, therefore, the OLF was just setting up its bases in the Harar area.

The thinking behind the formation of the OLF has not been sufficiently clearly expressed with the result that, to this day, arguments are still heard about its real aims. It is a present mainly directed from abroad, and its opponent, the OPDO, has become increasingly entrenched in Oromia. Nevertheless, it should not be forgotten that the notion of liberation was widespread in the 1960s. Thus, besides the influence of national independence moves in African countries, the Vietnamese struggle was reported daily and found a sympathetic audience among Ethiopian students. In the domestic sphere, the Eritrean struggle inspired those who sought to challenge 'Showan domination', the '*naftagna*' (colonial settlers) or 'Abyssinian colonialists', depending on the perception of the proponents of the struggle. The Somali state established in 1960 (Mogadishu) had also sponsored movements of various shapes and names to promote its claims over the Ogaden region of Ethiopia. This was to engage the two countries in several conflicts and two major wars.

In effect, the ideology of nationalism, the need to establish liberation fronts (LFs) was something that readily came to mind for those of the 'oppressed nationalities' who sought to change the status quo and establish newly independent states. It never occurred to many to enquire whether this was a rational thing to do or whether they could succeed. The only thing that mattered was a name, a flag and sponsorship from neighbouring states to set up an office and channel foreign assistance (not only from China and Russia but also Syria, Iraq and other interested parties).

During the imperial period, the Afar were largely left to their own devices under their traditional ruler. The Dergue, however, attempted to introduce land reforms which led to the Sultan fleeing abroad and his setting up of the Afar Liberation Front (ALF). The aim of the ALF has been to maintain their traditional society within an Ethiopian framework. In forthcoming elections it is quite likely to defeat the pro-government Afar People Democratic Organization but is probably not seen as a great threat as it has no secessionist policy.

Unlike most liberation movements, the Western Somali Liberation Front (WSLF) was formed in Mogadishu as a result of irredentist claims on the part of Somalia to territories it believed were wrongly ceded to Ethiopia by European colonial powers. The movement was thus essentially based outside Ethiopia and was the result of conflict between two nation states. This led to war between them, and following the defeat of Somalia in 1978 claims to the Ogaden were abandoned. Somalia itself has since disintegrated to a state of civil war, and the Ogaden can be seen as a sad example of the destructive effects of liberation movements arising not from internal considerations but from state rivalries. The Ogaden National Liberation Front, which supports secession, has recently split with the leadership favouring an election boycott being dismissed. As now constituted, ONLF maintains its willingness to participate in elections.

Inspired by the Eritrean movements and inflamed by the tributary status to which 'Showan domination' had reduced their region, the Tigreans of Tigray established various movements opting variously for secession or autonomy. Working in close alliance with the Eritrean fronts, they managed to obtain a foothold in the west of Tigray and in the Sudan and to progress throughout the whole of Tigray.

The ambivalence of the Dergue towards the Tigray People's Liberation Front (TPLF) especially, while deriding their pursuit of 'independence', delayed the Dergue from waging a full-scale war and ended with it relinquishing Tigray altogether. Whatever the merits or demerits of the strategy of the Dergue, the loss of Tigray only added to its predicaments in Eritrea, first in the north, then at Massawa and finally in Asmara. The cumulative effect led to the collapse of its hold on Addis Ababa by May 1991. The United States had meanwhile replaced the Soviet Union as the power behind the various political equations, persuading Mengistu Haile Mariam to step down in return for a deal for a peaceful outcome in which the Devane government would be represented, and talking the EPLF into participation in a transitional government until the fate of Eritrea was decided through a referendum.

A new approach to resolve the nationalities question

After the defeat of the Dergue in May 1991, hidden moves and countermoved related to power sharing in the formation of the transitional government. The refusal of the EPLF to be part of the Ethiopian Transitional Government opened a gap that left the rest of the participating movements uneasily poised against a powerful Ethiopian People's Revolutionary Democratic Front (EPRDF). Even the OLF, which purported to have charted, along with the United States and the EPRDF, the future of the political process, seemed uncomfortable. On the one hand, it had sought to make its presence felt in the political process, but it refrained from participating fully in a state it saw as a continuation of the *naftegna.*

Nevertheless, the basic principle of national self-determination had found official confirmation in the Charter of the Transitional Period adopted by the July Conference (of 1991) in which most groups opposed to Dergue rule were represented. There was no single opposition from within the country to this departure from previous state policies and practice in Ethiopia. The Charter expressed in no uncertain terms that the will of the nationalities was paramount regarding their decision to be part of the political future of Ethiopia.

The Constitutive Assembly elected in 1994 and boycotted by opposition parties ratified the EPRDF draft constitution, as a result of which each regional council will return members to a Federal Council. Although the constitution recognizes the rights of secession of a region in theory, the fact that only parties allied to EPRDF have participated in elections ensures that this option will not in fact be on the agenda.

Before the 1995 election, the number of regions was reduced from 14 to 10 as a result of merging Gurage/Hadiya/Kembata, Sidama, Wolaita, Omo and Keffa to form a Southern Ethiopia People's Administration.

Accusations soon emerged of a 'hideous plan to dismember Ethiopia' agreed on between the EPLF and the TPLF, the latter being seen as a stooge for the EPLF and an instrument for realizing the separation of Eritrea. Finding ready support in popular perceptions of having been let down by the EPRDF, this sentiment has been steadily increasing. The EPRDF viewed this as being caused at the instigation of 'chauvinist elements' and responded with harsh treatment of those opposing the solution of national self-determination adopted in the Charter. The violent suppression of a student demonstration on 4 January 1993 and the consequent sacking of 42 academics from the Addis Ababa University illustrate this.

While the outcome of the impending referendum on Eritrea agreed at the July Conference was a foregone conclusion (later proved by the 24 May 1993 declaration of independence), the 'Eritrean question' seems destined to remain as hotly debated among Ethiopians as ever. Indeed, the fury against the developments in Eritrea and the perceived support of Israel and the United States for the 'dismemberment of Ethiopia' may yet grow and assume violent forms. The existence in Ethiopia (and in a vague sort of alliance with the TPLF) of Eritrean groups that are opposed to the politics of the EPLF may contribute to this. Moreover, the increasing pressure brought to bear on the EPRDF by popular dissatisfaction over this and other policies (especially the crises induced by the adoption of IMF/World Bank economic reforms) may precipitate unexpected changes.

The relations of the EPRDF with the other national movements have been characterized by official submission to its policies and proposals in the Council of Representatives set up by the Charter and to which some 25 movements had been admitted. Owing to the imbalance of their forces as compared to that of the ERDF, and reflecting their distrust of the declared 'democracy', the other national movements have sought to contain the penetration of the EPRDF into their separate 'domains', i.e. the nationalities they claim to represent.

The OLF was most vociferous in its denunciation of an Oromo wing of the EPRDF, the Oromo People's Democratic Organization (OPDO), which is now well established in power. Deriding it as a 'quisling' in the likeness of an Oromo chief, Ras Gobena, who later became a general of Menelik, the OLF denies the OPDO is an Oromo organization. On the other hand, the OPDO claims to be the sole representative of the oppressed Oromo, while presenting the OLF as instrument of Oromo landlords and the rich, now organized from abroad.

The existence of competing groups (five among the Oromo and the Ghurage, nine among the Somali in Ethiopia and a minimum of two elsewhere) claiming to be the sole representatives of their respective nationalities is a characteristic feature of the new period. No doubt, the EPRDF has helped form at least one group in each nationality committed to its perception of how the country should be run, and these are now well established as a result of opposition groups repeatedly boycotting various elections.

Under these circumstances, therefore, the practical outcome of the declaration for self-determination of the nationalities could be the entrenchment of the EPRDF in all parts of the country. Local and regional elections confirmed that the EPRDF did not act everywhere as an usher for other national groups to take power in the localities and determine the fate of the nationalities. Indeed, the illusions that had spread far and wide about the opportune moment for nationalists to assume power in their 'natural territories' gave way, on their defeat at the elections or shortly before then (upon withdrawal in case of the OLF and a few others), to accusations of 'treachery', even 'new slavery'.

Not only have the anti-ERPDF nationalists 'lost' in elections throughout the length and breadth of the country but blueprints for mapping out the national territories and the institutionalization of new self-governing bodies, as well as the writing of the constitution (already determined by the EPRDF to uphold federalism as the structure of the state) have been driven forward without their participation. The manipulation of the Council of Representatives by the EPRDF, in order to push through all manner of measures and solutions no matter what the support or opposition of the rest of the country, seems set to alienate increasing sections of the public and other nationalist movements not represented in the government. The random armed conflicts reported in certain areas bode ill for a smooth transformation, even on the basis of the plans of the EPRDF.

Meanwhile, the opponents of the regime are trying to convince the US government that its choice of the EPRDF as a partner in Ethiopia was wrongly conceived and deserves to be overturned. It is impossible to speculate what the United States will do as regards Ethiopia and its current rulers but, as things stand, the fragmented state of the non-EPRDF political forces will leave it with very little to choose from.

The nationality factor in development

At one state, the Dergue had expressed some concern that development should benefit 'national minorities'. This seemed to target those groups inhabiting remote areas in the country and 'neglected' by the imperial regime. However, it did not spell out the conditions under which any of the numerous small nationalities could qualify. In practice, very few benefited from this gesture. And when they did so, it was managed within the context of their strategic importance to the Dergue. Thus the building of the Baro river bridge (a major project), the opening up of a modern airport and the establishment of a number of new tourist facilities in the Gambella area pointed more to military objectives in connection with the southern Sudan problem than the satisfaction of needs of the local peoples, who undoubtedly had been 'neglected' for decades.

A further concern of the Dergue for the resettlement of over-populated areas (the Tigreans, the Hadya and Kembata, the Wollo people, among others) in fertile or under-populated zones of the country was conducted in such an ill-prepared manner that it was branded at the time as a violation of human rights. The Dergue, however, had additional motives for carrying this out. Both the prospective settlers and the recipients (the Beni-shangul in Gojjam, the Oromo in Diddessa) were hosts to rebel movements, and the Dergue was keen to eliminate these. Far worse than this was the fact that the recipient nationalities were forced to accept for settlement groups who were often armed to protect themselves, thus sowing the seeds of antagonism from the start. The intolerable situation therefore, in which the settled people were installed, and the subjugation to which the indigenous peoples saw themselves to be destined, proved in the long run the undoing of plans executed on military lines and at enormous cost. At the collapse of the Dergue, most of the 'resettled' groups returned unassisted to their old homeland; some died on the way.

Apart from such attempts of the state to impose schemes it deemed to be in the interest of 'national minorities', there was no clear statement of the need to take account of the national aspirations of the diverse peoples in the country, particularly in the matter of resource use or allocation. The economic plans laid down or projects set up discounted such factors. The state seemed to operate under the illusion that it was an Ethiopian nation populating the whole country. Consequently, as far as it was concerned, giving any concession to any section of the population under the signboard of 'nationality' would amount to accepting the failure of the policy of national integration.

The nearest the state came to recognizing minority aspirations was in the decision to set up radio stations and newspapers which used some of the local vernaculars. The literacy campaign launched in the early 1980s gradually accepted the use of 15 languages of the relatively larger nationalities for purposes of rudimentary education at village level only. The campaign was conducted in such a way as not to give the impression that there was distinctiveness or that the state was giving in to local demands.

Under these circumstances, the claims for sharing in the development pursuits of the state, for safeguarding national identity or for setting up independent states that some of the LFs made could not be understood, least of all accepted, by the Ethiopian state. As far as the traditional elites in power were concerned, such calls were a reflection of instigation by Ethiopia's sworn enemies: Arab governments and the Somali state. The belief in this line of thinking has been around for centuries and permeates even the educated section of the elite to such an extent that any expression of dissent was considered treasonable.

The fanaticism that sprang from such a perception was amply demonstrated in the drive of successive Ethiopian governments to mount a virtual genocide on the Eritrean people. The calm statement of a chief administrator of Gojjam in 1975, which was neither opposed or censured by the Dergue, to the effect that if all Eritreans should be wiped out or thrown into the Red Sea to save Eritrea from being detached from Ethiopia so be it, was a perfect embodiment of such fanaticism. The effect has been the mass slaughter or exodus of the people of Eritrea and the ruin of the already weak economy of Ethiopia.

Until the overthrow of the Dergue and the setting up of the TG, therefore, nationality considerations in developing the economy or in transforming the society were practically non-existent. Reflecting the subordinate status of most of the nationalities and the elite's scorn for them, each was left to its own devices and the combination of fortuitous circumstances. For instance, building up an infrastructure in the south or west of the country, which proved to be much more successful than elsewhere, arose from the state's need to export coffee and other agrarian produce from those areas. The tax concessions given to Eritrea for many years and the incomparable level of subsidies for its schools and administration were based more on political calculations than on an assessment of what it deserved.

Indeed, if the national economy was to informed by the principle of equitable access by the nationalities to their own resources, the deficit in most parts of the country would be evident. Such a thought has fired the imagination of Oromo nationalists who resent the use of 'their' resources for the benefit of an 'occupying colonial power' and to their own detriment. This feeling has been fuelled by an awareness that the Oromo probably constitute the largest ethnic group in Ethiopia and occupy one of the most fertile and mineral-rich lands in the country.

The situation since the establishment of the TG in 1991 has not been any different so far. Although the urge to reconstruct the war-damaged economy seems paramount in the country as a whole, and to that extent the TG has not been required to set out plans that cater to the needs of nationalities for development, the manner in which the reconstruction has been conducted has been a subject of dispute inside Ethiopia. The claims for priority by the Eritreans and Tigreans over the rest for resources, in view of the devastation that the past governments have wrought on them, has not been unanimously accepted. There are those who argue that the Dergue wrecked the entire economy; others oppose the idea that only those two should benefit when all of the northern provinces had suffered.

All sides seem oblivious to the undercurrents in the debate: the questionable nature of any rationale for skimming off national resources or the use of international assistance to help the recovery of the northern region; the basis on which such a decision seems to have been made – the presumed inauguration of democracy implies that those concerned, the other nationalities or regions, should have had a say; the implications for the future of the TG's introduction of such a scheme.

Since the majority of LFs are still intent on winning their battles and establishing their own nation states the question of sharing their resources with other national groups does not, strictly speaking, arise. In so far as most of them now perceive the goal of their struggle to have been unattained by virtue of the fall of the Dergue, their neglect of this issue is only natural. Only those who deem the struggle for political power to have been generally decided in their favour (the EPRDF and allied groups) might possibly consider how to resolve such an issue.

In the heated public controversy that arose between the OLF and the EPRDF in March–April 1992, the charge of stealing from the pubic purse and the grain warehouses was thrown at the latter, while pilfering Ethiopia's chief export commodity, coffee, across the various unprotected borders, was a charge against the former. These charges point to the ultimate question that will surface when the 'nationalities problem' is taken to its logical consequence. The grouping of diverse nationalities, whether in a democratic or authoritarian framework, is bound to raise the issue of resource allocation and use for the betterment of each nationality.

Ethiopian regimes in the past have tried but failed to suppress the existence of the problem of self-determination and national awakening. The devastation that the conflict over Eritrea and in the north of Ethiopia in general brought to the people and their environment is too fresh to warrant any renewed attempt to suppress national revival and independence. On the other hand, the means of channelling the collective energies and resources of 'the mosaic of nationalities' cannot be simple and ready to hand. If democracy is to be allowed to flourish at all in Ethiopia, then the best evidence for such an experiment would be the creation of avenues for a voluntary combination of efforts and resources by the various nationalities or ethnic groups. The ongoing efforts of drawing up a new constitution will be expected to address this crucial issue. The consequence for Ethiopia as a whole of any neglect of, or irresolute approach towards, it would not be difficult to predict or imagine.

Conclusion

The 'nationalities question' in Ethiopia has emerged as a reaction against the centralization of political and economic power by the Showan ruling classes, essentially dominated by the Amhara but including Tigreans and open to loyal nobles of the south and their educated offspring. Tigrean opposition has been directed towards regaining positions lost to Showa without requiring that national unity of the Tigreans be a precondition at any stage. While nationalism by definition places the differentiation of one nation from another as a principle of the first order, no Tigrean movement (whether south of the Mereb river in Tigray or in the north in Eritrea) has ever adopted this as its standpoint.

Consequently, any expression of discontent in Tigray or Eritrea that fails to embrace this central principle is certainly not a Tigrean national movement. Indeed, movements north or south of the border have a tacit recognition of each other's territorial basis and refrain from 'encroaching' on the other's territory. Consequently, any reference to nationalism that the movements may make has only an ideological significance. Lacking the political form in which such a nationalism may be expressed, it resorts to spurious claims of 'national oppression – even 'colonial domination – whereas in fact, the issue is something else.

This is not to say that Tigreans have not had any cause for rebellion against Showa but rather than the form of their current opposition remains within the framework of old rivalries between the royal houses that used to represent the various Amhara–Tigrean regions in Ethiopia. That the champions of Tigrean opposition to Showa today are typically sections of the educated elite does not alter the basis of the claims. The gradual shifts in the claims for independence of Tigray that the TPLF originally proposed but has now virtually scrapped can only prove this point. Indeed, the referendum sanctioned for Eritrea by the TPLF and accepted by the Tigreans in the EPLF without any qualms with regard to its implications for the (future) formation of a Tigrean nation (within or outside Ethiopia) highlights the low level of national consciousness hidden behind the rhetoric of nationalism and 'self-determination'.

The situation in the rest of the country is not dramatically different, although in the south the feeling of national exclusiveness is more evident. The emerging national movements do not yet have a solid basis on which to challenge the Showan or *naftagna* state. The embryonic state in which the middle class is found among all the nationalities (arguably many of the 'subject' ones have none) has reduced any aspiration for national independence to being the exclusive vocation of the still unformed intelligentsia of the various small nationalities. This may help explain the limited appeal of the call for national independence by these sections and the willingness to support PDO, which supports the EPRDF. Certainly, the peasants and nomads to whom this appeal is advanced might gradually but slowly embrace it and provide an army that would fight for and gain national 'independence' Yet, the difficulties of this path have been adequately demonstrated by the Somali tragedy across the border. That rival groups, each claiming to be the sole national 'representative', have emerged and operated (with or without arms) in much of the south (including among the Oromo) delineates a grim picture of might happen in Ethiopia, too, unless ways are found for transforming the genuine aspirations for national self-governance into reality. It remains to be seen what part the Federal Council will play. Viewed against the large number of these nationalities (estimated at above 40 in the south-west corner of the country alone), creating a healthy climate for collaboration among the political forces seems an imperative for any positive outcome in this matter.

Top of the list, in the creation of a sound basis for transforming past conflictual relations among the various nationalities, is the democratization of the country. A constitution has now been approved and elections taken place accordingly, yet in the almost complete absence of participation by opposition parties, this is more democratic on paper than in reality. Providing the possibility for national groups to operate freely among their respective peoples and to gain or lose the latter's trust seems to be the only way forward. Nevertheless, the lack of a stable balance among the political forces in the country, with the EPRDF exercising a dominant role in all spheres, does not appear to encourage a movement in this direction.

Indeed, the fragility of the democratic process launched by the Charter of the Transitional Period and continued in the constitution has been proved on many occasions. Despite the pretensions of the TG and the present government for 'full democracy', evidence points to the curtailment of democracy occasioned by pragmatic considerations for the consolidation of political power interspersed with excesses that will obliterate it from time to time.

Therefore, whether or not the fledgling 'democratic' processes that have emerged in Ethiopia will weather the tests that the combatants put them through might depend on three factors. One is an appreciation by the EPRDF of the bleak alternatives that might be the lot of all combatants if a return to the old days, dictatorship and no dissent, is allowed through short-sighted and pragmatic policies that aim to consolidate its power. Second is the continuity of the power that the EPRDF has, and the existence of external forces prodding it to maintain the situation. The third factor may be the development of a responsible opposition (including the media) which knows how to play its role within the context of regional and international forces that have a bearing on events in Ethiopia. But this last is disturbingly absent.

The influence of the changes that have taken place throughout the world recently might also contribute towards improvement of the status quo. On the most basic level financial and military resources are no longer available following the resolution of the East–West conflict. Aid is therefore likely to continue to be tied to the maintenance of at least nominal democratic forms. So far this has not resulted in them being put into practice, and the USA has put less pressure on the government than might have been possible. The nature of Ethiopian internal problems and the historical experience during the last century are such that one can hope that the various factions will see the advantage of stability even at the cost of abrogating some of their own power and diffusing it throughout the population at large. Only then might it be possible for national groups to feel confident that past practices in which their concerns for development have been little heeded will be abandoned for good and that a collective drive for development will benefit them all.

References

Baykadagn, Gebrahiwot (1992) *The Political Economy of Ethiopia c1910: Government and Public Administration* (translated by Tenker Bonger), Haddis, London.

Dillebo, Lapisso G. (1983) *Ve Ethiopia Vegebar Seratna Jimmir Capitalism 1900–1966* (2 vols.), Vol.I, Commercial Printing Press, Addis Ababa.

Hassen, Mohammed (1989) 'The Oromo Struggle in the Context of the Battle for Social Justice in the Horn', *Focus on the Horn*, April.

Negash, Tekeste (1986) *No Medicine for the Bite of a White Snake: Notes on Nationalism and Resistance in Eritrea, 1890–1940*, University of Uppsala, Uppsala.

Negash, Tekeste (1987) *Italian Colonialism in Eritrea, 1882–1941: Policies, Praxis and Impact*, Studia Historica Upsaliensia 148, Uppsala.

Rouaud, Alain (1991) *Afä-Wärq 1868–1947: un intellectuel éthiopien témoin de son temps*, Editions du Centre National de la Recherche Scientifique, Paris.

Tareke, Gebru (1991) *Ethiopia: Power and Protest – Peasant Revolts in the Twentieth Century*, Cambridge University Press, Cambridge.

Transitional Government of Ethiopia (1991) *Transitional Charter of Ethiopia*, Addis Ababa.

Trevaskis, G.K.N. (1960) *ERITREA: A Colony in Transition 1941–52*, Oxford University Press, Oxford.

PART IV

The economic context

7 Cultural pluralism and economic development: perspectives from 20th-century Mexico and the Caribbean

Colin Clarke

Mexico and the Caribbean form adjacent but distinctive mainland/island regions. However, they possess some partially overlapping detailed characteristics – the Spanish language and Roman Catholicism, and have several key features in common – political economies determined by colonialism, social and economic organizations based on the large landed estate and histories of force labour affecting their non-white populations.

Mexican cultural pluralism is now expressed in 'islands' of 'indigenous' non-Spanish speakers who number less than 10 per cent of the national population of about 85 million. In the Caribbean, plural features are particularly marked, not in the Hispanic islands, where slavery was never the dominant feature of the plantation mode of production, but in the former British, French and Dutch colonies, with fewer than 15 million inhabitants *in toto*, where black slaves and later (East) Indian indentured workers filled the void in the labour market, created after the genocide of the entire Amerindian population. Here majority populations now live by cultures that are substantially, and often differentially, at variance with European norms.

Pluralism as policy and pluralism as analysis

This chapter compares and contrasts the conceptions of pluralism developed, respectively, in Mexico and the Commonwealth Caribbean. *Indigenismo* used the 'Indian', as distinct from the European-colonial, past to provide the foundations for a sense of Mexican identity, while incorporating the indigenous population into the nation – linguistically, education-

Ethnicity and Development: Geographical Perspectives. Edited by Denis Dwyer and David Drakakis-Smith.

ally and economically. This was a state project, generated and administered by archaeologist–anthropologists, and adhered to by successive political administrations, with slightly varying emphases, down to the present day.

In the Commonwealth Caribbean, three interlocking analytical models of pluralism – cultural, social and structural – were developed by M.G. Smith, a Jamaican-born anthropologist, who drew on the writing of J.S. Furnivall, a British administrator with extensive experience in the Far East. Mexican *indigenismo* was developed in the post-revolutionary 1920s, a decade characterized by educational experimentation, land reform, the re-creation of a peasantry and the projection of the country as 'a nation of bronze', that is *mestizo*, in defiance of the scientific racism then current throughout the world. In contrast, Smith's earliest writings about cultural pluralism coincided with the post-Second World War years of progressive decolonization, international racial equality and the anticipation of black governments controlling autonomous democratic states and economically developing capitalist economies.

Mexican *indigenismo*, like the Revolution itself, emerged out of a reaction to the *laissez-faire* positivism of the decades-long dictatorship of Porfirio Diaz (the *Porfiriato*), which had increased land-holding monopolies and the impoverishment – even *de facto* enslavement (Turner 1910; 1969) – of many rural Mexicans; but it was subservient (in practice even more than in theory) to a state policy preoccupied with capital accumulation, a concern which was to become paramount after the Second World War. Thus, Ricardo and Isabel Pozas (1978) were to characterize Mexican society as economically driven and class stratified but with an 'Indian' enclave, or *intraestructura*. In contrast, Smith's characterization of pluralism in the Commonwealth Caribbean focused exclusively, in its first phase of elaboration, on anthropological issues, notably culture, played down the significance of class and neglected to address the relationship between pluralism and economic development in theoretical terms. However, Smith became deeply involved in the practical side of anthropology in Jamaica, where he was eventually a cabinet-rank adviser to the Manley government in the 1970s.

Neglect of the theoretical implications of cultural pluralism for economic development has been mirrored in government policy throughout the Commonwealth Caribbean, though Jamaica, since independence, has supported the local arts – music, dance, drama, poetry and painting – as a counter-culture to the banal provincialism of Jamaican whites in the last decades of the colony. It must also be added that both Trinidad and Tobago and Guyana have been acutely aware of their segmentation along (largely) brown-black Creole versus Indian lines because of the pervasiveness of race in politics and because urban–rural segregation means that government-inspired development strategies have differential communal implications. In short, the developmental consequences of pluralism have been neglected in culture–class stratified societies, such as Jamaica, Barbados, and the Windwards and Leewards, but have been used 'negatively' in the vertically segmented societies, such as Trinidad and Guyana, to ensure that government supporters (racially determined) are the gainers.

This chapter is divided into four parts. The first two examine, in greater detail, the parallel but separate development of ideas about cultural pluralism in Mexico and the Caribbean. The third looks at the work of Furnivall and explores the linkage he made between pluralism, economic dualism and capitalist exploitation under colonialism. It then examines the way in which Mexican scholars have related pluralism to development, since the 1960s, through the elaboration of ideas about internal colonialism, thus incorporating class and spatial dimensions, and linking pluralism to dependency. The fourth and last section explores the ways in which pluralism might be used more effectively to inform economic development policy and practice in the Commonwealth Caribbean.

This is a particularly appropriate moment to delve into the association between pluralism and development. The decade of the 1990s is clearly going to be dominated by the process of structural adjustment imposed on Third World countries from the outside by the World Bank and the IMF, in a potentially neocolonial way. Neither institution, nor development theory more generally, is particularly sensitive to local conditions, perhaps least of all to those features that pertain to cultural pluralism (see Hettne in Chapter 2).

Pluralism in Mexico

While Europeanized late 19th-century Mexican liberals 'dismissed the Aztecs as mere Barbarians and viewed contemporary Indians as a hindrance to their country's modernization' (Brading 1988, p.75), the Mexican Revolution of 1911–17 destroyed the obstacles to the creation of a *mestizo* national identity. At the same time, in his book *Forjando Patria*, Manuel Gamio (1916), the founder of Mexican archaeology and anthropology, insisted on the enduring contribution of Indian civilizations – Aztec and other – to the evolution of modern Mexico.

Rejecting neoclassical cannons of aesthetic judgement, Gamio demanded a revaluation of native art forms. He called for land distribution on a collective basis, thereby reversing the process of positivistic modernization introduced by the late 19th-century *Reforma*, and advocated the revival of village handicrafts. However, the official *indigenismo* of Gamio and his associates had, as its principal objective, the incorporation of the Indian communities into the national society. A secular liberal,

Gamio opposed both the Catholic Church and the folk Catholicism of the masses (and the Indian population). Although, as Brading remarks, 'modernising nationalism of the brand advocated by Gamio certainly found consolation in past glories', its goal was 'to transform a backward country into a modern nation able to defend itself from foreign hegemony' (Brading 1988, p.77).

By training, Gamio was an archaeologist. In 1909–10, while in his late 20s, he had studied at Columbia University with Franz Boas, the doyen of American anthropology, who had also played a key role in the establishment of the International School of Archaeology and Ethnology in Mexico City. In 1912, under Boas's direction, Gamio undertook excavations at Azcapotzalco, the first time that stratigraphical analysis was used anywhere in the Americas. Gamio's career was made: he succeeded Boas as Director of the School of Archaeology; became Director General of Archaeological Monuments; and from 1917 to 1924 was Director of the newly established Department of Anthropology. It was during this period that he undertook the work for which he is remembered – the reconstruction and sample excavation of Teotihuacan, the details of which were set out in a two-volume study, *La Población del Valle de Teotihuacan* (1922).

Additionally, Gamio then set out 'to analyse and reform the present' (Brading 1988, p.78) by organizing an ethnographic survey of the district of Teotihuacan in tandem with the excavations. These findings were discussed in the second volume of his book and dealt with a variety of contemporary problems ranging from agriculture, land tenure and diet to religious practice, folklore and medicine, with colonial history used as the bridge between the archaeological past and the post-Revolutionary situation. Drawing on the concept of culture, which Boas had argued had greater explanatary value than that of race (Boas concluded there were no superior or inferior races), Gamio escaped from scientific racism and proceeded to explain Indian backwardness by poor diet, lack of education, material poverty and isolation from the mainstream of Mexican life. In short, Gamio embraced Boas's conception of culture – namely, the natural and intellectual manifestations of any human group – as the underpinning for social variability.

Gamio's professional career of archaeologist–restorer–anthropologist was followed by younger Mexican intellectuals, notably Alfonso Caso, the excavator of Monte Alban and the discoverer of the Mixtec jewels of Tomb 7. 'In all this', according to Brading, 'Gamio thus inaugurated what was to become a distinctively Mexican industry, the reconstruction of ancient monuments – a craft industry financed by the Mexican state and justified by the joint aim of recuperating national glory and attracting mass tourism' (1987, p.78). All this effort, however, was to be of little benefit to the culturally defined Indians who survived – speaking pre-Columbian languages, wearing *huaraches* (sandals) or going barefoot and cleaving to traditional dress – notably, woven and embroidered *huipiles* for women. For *indigenismo* was first and foremost a *mestizo* project.

The *indigenista* movement was opposed by those who considered themselves 'Indianists': some urban extremists advocated the extirpation of all Spanish and foreign influences; other argued for the autonomous development of the Indian communities. In contrast, there were those who adopted a 'leftist Westernism' approach and identified Indians as peasants, merely suffering the common oppression of their class. The mainstream *indigenista* current, running from the Revolution to the present day, however, adheres to the principle of enlightened, planned, non-coercive integration and rejects all other approaches, including 'Indianism' as heresies. The principal tool of *indigenista* integrationism was education; when rural and Indian schools were set up throughout the 1920s and 1930s, one of their main tasks was the preparation of a new generation of bilingual Indian teachers. These rural schools became the centre not only of education in the narrow sense but of technological diffusion, agrarian reform, political mobilization and nationalist propaganda (Knight 1990, p.82).

> Indian customs, music, dance and rituals were rehabilitated and woven into a new tapestry of folkloric nationalism; revolutionary martyrs, like Zapata, were claimed for the *indigenista* cause; and reformers like Carillo Puerto in Yucatan subtly blended radical discourse with traditional Maya symbols. The *ejido*, the village land grant sanctioned by the agrarian reform program, was somewhat misleadingly equated with the old Aztec *calpullalli* (Knight 1990, p.82).

With the active involvement of two Mexicans of a younger generation than Gamio, Julio de la Fuente and Gonzalo Aguirre Beltrán, both of whom had anthropological training in the USA, an Instituto Nacional Indigena (INI) was inaugurated in 1948. Three years later, the first co-ordinating centre opened in San Cristobal de las Casas to serve the Tzeltal–Tzotzil people. Subsequently, parallel centres have been inaugurated wherever Indians, namely those speaking a pre-Columbian language, are concentrated. Changes have certainly been effected but often not the ones intended.

A major dispute running across the decades has been the language in which Indians should be taught to be literate (Bravo Ahuja 1976). Given the shortage of materials in the pre-Columbian languages, their sheer number and the variety of dialects-cum-separate languages spoken, plus the ultimate aim of integration, it is perhaps not surprising that Spanish has been the main medium of instruction and the language through which literacy has been achieved (Heath 1972). Indeed, it has become the lingua franca, even in the most culturally Indian areas, to the extent that bilingualism is now virtually the norm among those who still retain a facility in the pre-Columbian languages.

Other problems have focused on the role of the bilingual promotors. Many, over the years, have used their facility in Spanish to move into the *mestizo* population – the boundary is remarkably permeable if language shift is accompanied by the wearing of Western clothing (*revestido*) and out-migration from the parental village. Others have stayed at their posts but used their language and literacy, essential in local government, as a means to acquire power and wealth, especially as capital penetration of the rural communities began to be marked in the 1930s and 1940s. Some even emerged as local bosses – *caciques* – dominating the local Indian peasants, especially in the coffee-rich mountains, in ways that the more optimistic reformers never anticipated (Heath 1972).

A more careful appraisal of the relationship between economic development and *indigenismo* will be attempted in a later section of this chapter. For the moment, it is sufficient to conclude that the programme of *indigenismo* has gradually equipped the Indian populations with Spanish and some literacy (and the land reform has validated their traditional holdings of communal land); but it has also eroded the Indian population, many of whom have been the direct or indirect victims of Mexico's spectacular economic development in the period 1940–80. Indian areas were arguably among the poorest regions of Mexico at the end of the Revolution: they remain the most backward parts of late 20th-century Mexico.

Pluralism in the Caribbean

M.G. Smith was similar to Gamio in that he, too, was an anthropologist and nationalist, and, in his case, also a poet. However, his preoccupation with pluralism was as a framework for analysis rather than as a programme for national identity construction or for the incorporation of 'the other' – although it does have implications for each. Born in Jamaica in 1921, Smith was educated at McGill University in Canada and University College, London. Returning to Jamaica in 1952, he was for almost a decade a Research Fellow of the Institute of Social and Economic Research at the then colonial University College of the West Indies. Smith carried out a number of research and government-commissioned projects in Jamaica, writing *A Report on Labour Supply in Rural Jamaica* (1956) and, with Roy Augier and Rex Nettleford, *The Ras Tafari Movement in Kingston, Jamaica* (1960). He also spent a very productive year in Grenada and Carriacou. The major fruits of his scholarly endeavours were published soon after he moved to a chair at the University of California at Los Angeles: *Kinship and Community in Carriacou* and *West Indian Family Structure* in 1962, and *Stratification in Grenada* and *The Plural Society in the British West Indies* in 1965. The burden of these books was to show that Commonwealth Caribbean societies were not differentiated solely by colour–class, as Henriques (1953) and Braithwaite (1953) had insisted, but by more pervasive and significant distinctions associated with culture.

In *The Plural Society in the British West Indies*, which was mostly a collection of previously published papers, and in subsequent books, Smith set out to refine and amplify the concept of the plural society first advanced by Furnivall and to explore racial and cultural domination under colonialism. Describing conditions in Burma and Java, Furnivall noted:

> the first thing that strikes the visitor is the medley of peoples – European, Chinese, Indian and native. It is in the strict sense a medley, for they mix but do not combine. Each group holds by its own ideas and ways. As individuals they meet, but only in the market place, in buying and selling. There is a plural society with different sections of the community living side by side, but separately, within the same political unit . . . Few recognise that, in fact, all members of all sections have material interests in common, but most see that on many points their material interests are opposed (Furnivall 1948, pp.304, 308).

Furnivall identified additional features of the plural society that have provided lines for theoretical elaboration by Smith: 'the union is not voluntary but is imposed by the colonial power and by the force of economic circumstances'; 'each section is an aggregate of individuals rather than a corporate or organic whole'; 'in a homogeneous society the tension is alleviated by their common citizenship, but in a plural society there is a corresponding cleavage along racial lines' (Furnivall 1948, pp.306, 307, and 311).

Institutional analysis is the key feature of Smith's early work on pluralism. 'I hold', he wrote, 'that the core of a culture is its institutional system. Each institution involves set forms of activity, grouping, rules, ideas and values' (Smith 1965, p.79). Smith cogently argued that 'the institutions of a people's culture form the matrix of their social structure, simply because the institutional system defines and sanctions the persistent forms of social life' (Smith 1965, p.80).

What does Smith mean by institutions? The principal institutional systems that are involved in defining a population's culture and social relations are family, kinship, education, religion, property, economy and recreation. Language, so significant in Mexico, is not mentioned. People who practise the same institutions, and for whom they have the same values and significance, form a cultural section (horizontally layered) or segment (vertically differentiated) in the society. Smith concluded that societies, either colonial or independent polities, typified by minor features of differentiation but with common forms of organization are culturally heterogeneous. The term 'homogeneous' is reserved for small non-differentiated societies, whereas societies that express institutional cleavage are viewed as culturally pluralistic.

Critics of Smith's early work on cultural pluralism claimed that it emphasizes institutional differences and neglects the importance of shared values (Rubin 1960, pp.780–5). Another critic, referring to the issue of institutional analysis, has enquired 'at what point variations within an institutional sub-system become great enough to warrant our identification of two separate sub-systems?' (R.T. Smith 1961). However M.G. Smith had already remarked that 'when identical statuses and roles are defined differently we have a plurality of structural systems' (Smith 1960, p.764). Notwithstanding these debates, empirical work employing a culturally plural framework has been used by Despres (1967) to examine the relationship between race, culture and politics in Guyana; by Clarke (1975, 1986b) to explore the economic development and socio-spatial structure of Kingston, Jamaica throughout the colonial period and to study segmental pluralism in San Fernando, Trinidad; and by Lowenthal (1972) in his comprehensive survey of the West Indies.

Subsequent to his work on cultural pluralism, Smith (1966, 1969, and 1974) developed the idea of structural pluralism. This occurs when population aggregates are differentially incorporated into society on a legal or political basis. For example, in the Caribbean there has been a crucial distinction, historically, between slaves, freemen and citizens. Smith (1969, p.435) contrasted differential incorporation with uniform or universalistic incorporation, when each individual adult has full voting rights and equality before the law; and also with equivalent or segmental incorporation, where a consociation is established, as in Switzerland, and the separately incorporated segments have formal parity. Differentially incorporated sections that lack group organization are called 'corporate categories' by Smith (1966); they include assemblages of individuals such as castes, serfs, and slaves. Corporate categories that develop their own internal organization thereby become corporate groups – rather like 'classes for themselves'; in hierarchical plural societies they are usually the superordinate strata (Clarke 1991).

With structural pluralism defined in this way, Smith (1969, p.440) was then able to identify three variants of pluralism: cultural, structural and social. Cultural pluralism involves institutional differences which, of themselves, do not generate corporate social differences. Provided they are restricted to the private domain through universalistic incorporation, they are of personal importance but do not have structural implications for society as a whole. Structural pluralism requires differential incorporation of the cultural sections. Where it occurs, either *de facto* or *de jure*, it creates social pluralism through the projection of institutional differentiation from the private into the pubic domain. Under conditions of structural pluralism it is therefore possible to predict an individual's socio-legal status from his or her cultural characteristics.

Structural pluralism is either based upon or, as in the Caribbean, creates cultural pluralism through differential treatment of the various sections in the society. Smith (1969, p.440) concludes that 'uniform or universalistic incorporation proscribes social pluralism, though it is equally consistent with cultural uniformities or cultural pluralism among its citizens'. Hence, structural pluralism in this formulation always involves social and cultural pluralism, and social pluralism always involves cultural pluralism; except that social pluralism may occur apart from structural pluralism when culturally distinct segments are or claim to be equal in rank and form a consociation, either *de facto* or *de jure*. This latter case occurs *de facto* in the Caribbean in Trinidad and Tobago, Guyana and Suriname, where (East) Indian–Creole contraposition gives rise to segmental pluralism.

Where cultural distinctions do generate corporate social differences, Smith distinguishes between the social sections and segements formed in this way and social classes. In his opinion, classes are 'differentiated culturally with respect to non-institutionalised behaviors, such as etiquette, standards of living, associational habits and value system which may co-exist as alternatives on the basis of common values basic to the class continuum' (Smith 1965b, p.53). In contrast, social sections and segments possess their own value systems. They may be ranked hierarchically (sections) or may occupy parallel positions (segments) in the social order. Moreover, each section or segment may be internally stratified by class. Those sections in the Caribbean practising Creole cultures developed within the framework of plantation slavery, are not ethnic groups with memories of parent lands or cultures extending back over centuries – although these characteristics apply to the many language groups of Mexico to whom the term *etnia* is often attached.

In the Caribbean there is a major problem in distinguishing between ranked sections and classes, since the historic mode of production, plantation slavery, was simultaneously a mode of incorporation; both, of course, were installed by British, Dutch or French colonialism. It is clear, however that the stratification has involved more than class and that in most societies there has evolved a hierarchy of cultural and politico-legal sections, shadowed by class (Clarke 1991). As those societies have developed historically (through popular protest and colonial liberalization), so slaves have become freemen and, finally, in most Commonwealth Caribbean societies between 1944 and 1953, enfranchised citizens, uniform incorporation has been extended down the social order as a prelude to, and precondition for, independence. This sequence of incorporation has, as yet, to expunge the consequences of social pluralism, but the process is under way, and it carries the most fundamental implications of pluralism for development. For there can be no true development in complex societies without uniform incorporation and democracy – a warning to Mexico's one-party state, headed by the Partido Revolucionario Institucional (PRI).

It is a warning which requires attention also in the segmented Caribbean societies, Trinidad and Tobago, Guyana and Suriname, where post-slavery Indian indenture has created large racial groups – in Guyana the majority – which stand outside the Creole segment and are differentiated from it by religion, family structure, caste (for Hindus) and race. In each country, decolonization has been accompanied by political alignments and conflicts which have followed closely the vertical segmentation of the society. In the case of Guyana this has led to a quarter of a century (now ended) of Creole domination by non-democratic means.

The major achievement of plural analysis, however, has not been the development of a specific policy but the construction of an analytical framework through which to understand complex societies. For as Smith has more recently commented, 'pluralism itself is a multi-dimensional condition which varies in its structure, division, and intensities in different societies and in different sections and segments in the same society' (1984, p.153). The differentiating variables of pluralism themselves have been 'relaxed' by Smith since his early insistence on culturally incompatible institutions. They now include race as well as culture – race is often the major basis for differential incorporation *de jure* or *de facto*, language and differences of sect within a single universal religion; and 'secular ideologies of racism, nazism and various kinds of communism' which 'operate as primary bases for divisive incorporation of population segments in various social contexts' (Smith 1984, p.153). In the Caribbean and Mexico, race, historically, was the basis for differential incorporation, and much of the culture of the lower section and the indigenous population was a construct of the colonial period.

It is clear that by the early 1980s Smith's framework had become global and more flexible and less geared to explaining the complexities solely of Caribbean societies. Using his revised formulation it is possible to interpret Mexican 'Indians' as a cultural section within the rural peasantry (witness the Pozases *intraestructura*), a linguistically complex minority within a class-differentiated stratification awaiting *de facto* incorporation and development – despite more than 70 years of *indigenismo*. Before examining the recent Mexican ethnic scene in greater detail, dominated as it has been by ideas about internal colonialsm and dependency, it seems appropriate to consider what Furnivall thought about the relations between pluralism and development in the colonial Far East.

Furnivall, the dual economy and internal colonialism

Furnivall characterized the plural society as having

> a dual economy, comprising two distinct economic systems, capitalist and pre-capitalist, with a Western superstructure of business and administration

> rising above the native world in which people, so far as they are left alone, lead their own life in their own way according to a traditional scale of values in which economic values rank so low as to be negligible . . . But everywhere experience has shown that the desire of gain can easily be stimulated or, rather, liberated from the control of custom (1948, p.304).

But liberation from custom occurs only under circumstances which allow 'the economic process of natural selection by the survival of the cheapest to prevail (p.310).

The consequence is that, in plural societies,

> the working of economic forces makes for tension between groups with competing and conflicting interests; between town and country, industry and agriculture, capital and labour . . . the foreign elements live in the towns, the natives in rural areas; commerce and industry are in foreign hands and the natives are mainly occupied in agriculture; foreign capital employs native labour or imported coolies. The various peoples meet only in the market, as competitors or opponents, as buyers and sellers (1948, p.311).

Furnivall was greatly exercised by the lack of 'common standards beyond those prescribed by law'. (1948, p.311).

> In a homogeneous society the desire of profit is controlled to some extent by social will, and if anyone makes profits by sharp practice he will offend the social conscience and incur moral, and perhaps legal, penalties. If, for example, he employs sweated labour, the social conscience, if sufficiently alert and powerful, may penalize him because aware, either instinctively or by rational conviction, that such conduct cuts at the root of common social life (1948, p.11).

Invoking Boeke, Furnivall concluded that in plural societies 'there is materialism, rationalism, individualism, and a concentration on economic ends far more complete and absolute than in homogeneous western lands' (1948, p.312).

These ideas, written for a decolonizing world after the Second World War, found resonance in the work of the Mexican school of internal colonialism in the early 1960s. However, both major proponents, Pablo González-Casanova and Rodolfo Stavenhagen, have developed their ideas independently of the work of Furnivall (and Smith) and markedly in opposition to the 'non-exploitative' conventional wisdom of *indigenismo*. A break with *indigenismo* is, however, detectable in the writings of Aguirre Beltran, the first director (1951) of the San Cristobal de las Casas INI centre. In *Regiones de Refugio*, published in 1967, he wrote about isolated Indian-language enclaves persisting at high altitude in the fastnesses of Mexico; he also drew attention to their domination by regional service centres, such as San Cristobal, pointing out that the relationship of superordination–subordination involved culture as well as class.

By the time Aguirre Beltran's book was out, Stavenhagen (1963 reissued 1970) and González-Casanova (1965 reissued 1969), both of them Mexican sociologists, had already published counterblasts to official *indigenismo*,

Stavenhagen deploying the term 'colonialism' and González-Casanova 'internal colonialism'. Their main concern was 'to shift from the sphere of the Indian community to that of the intercultural region where Indians and mestizos co-exist' (Stavehagen 1970, p.239). To González-Casanova, the pattern of dominance seemed age-old: 'the exploitation of the Indians continues, having *the same characteristics* it had before independence' (italics in original) (1969, p.119).

A coherent brief statement of the essentials of the internal colonialism model is given by González-Casanova.

> Internal colonialism corresponds to a structure of social relations based on domination and exploitation among culturally heterogeneous, distinct groups. If it has a specific difference with respect to other relations based on superordination, it inheres in the culture heterogeneity which the conquest of some peoples by others historically produces. It is such conquests which permit us to talk not only about cultural differences (which exist between urban and rural populations and between social classes) but also about differences between civilizations (1969, pp.130–1).

In language reminiscent of Furnivall, González-Casanova concludes:

> the colonial structure and internal colonialism are distinguished from class structure since colonialism is not only a relation of exploitation of the workers by the owners of raw materials or of production and their collaborators, but also a relation of domination and exploitation of a total population (with its distinct classes, proprietors, workers) by another population which also has distinct classes (proprietors and workers) (1969, pp.131–2).

This emphasis on dominating and dominated blocks that are culturally different is also highly reminiscent of Smith's cultural and structural pluralism.

In the appendix to his paper, González-Casanova sets out a check-list of the forms of internal colonialism: (a) monopoly and dependence, which examines unequal exchange via trade and credit, and the use of the internal colony as a labour reserve; (b) relations of production and social control, which provides an inventory of different types of exploitation – such as linguistic – in trade, at law and through wages; (c) culture and living standards, in which the impoverishment of the Indians is highlighted.

Internal colonialism has been criticized on many grounds: that it overemphasizes culture; that economic exploitation of Indians at the market-place is not inevitable; that it stresses opposition of *mestizos* to Indian-language speakers in situations that are increasingly fluid, given both bilingualism and capitalist economic development in Mexico; that indigenous language-speakers are ever more self-confident, partly through migration experiences which have enabled them to transcend the isolation of their original communities; and that it does not take into account regional differences in social structure or by language group (Kay 1989). Colby and van den Berghe (1961), for example, have drawn attention to the relaxation in *mestizo* (*ladino*)–Indian relations as one moves northwards from Guatemala into neighbouring Chiapas and then into Oaxaca and the rest of Mexico.

The case of Oaxaca state merits greater attention (Clarke 1986a). Oaxaca City (300 000 population) could be interpreted as a *mestizo*-controlled *centro rector* for the entire state, surrounded by a Hispanized aureole in the Central Valleys and an Indian-language-speaking hinterland at high altitude, from which surplus value is being extracted by the market mechanism. But the peasant market (Beals 1975) fails to operate in this way (though there is substantial monopolization of coffee exports and imported consumer durables by Oaxaca's urban commercial elite), and the language boundary between Spanish and non-Spanish speakers is highly permeable, especially in the Central Valley, and particularly so in Oaxaca City itself, where three-quarters of household heads are migrants (Murphy and Stepick 1991). Where exploitation occurs in Oaxaca it concentrates in the production and distribution of woven and embroidered goods (Cook 1990) and *mezcal* (alcohol) (Sánchez López 1989). All of these commodities have regional, national and international markets; involve huge mark-ups that benefit out-putters and merchants; and give rise to class structures at the community level. But this exploitation is a product- and place-specific phenomenon that epitomizes parts of the Central Valleys but rarely the Indian-occupied sierras.

The class model fits Mexico as a whole and reminds us that, while there is a problem of Indian subordination, it is not on the scale of Guatemala – where the Indian population (by culture) is arguably the majority – or some of the highly segmented societies of the Caribbean (notably Guyana), though in Oaxaca the Indian segment accounts for almost 40 per cent of the population. Pluralism helps us to separate the cultural from the class dimension and to see that it my be of greater significance than class in certain situations at the appropriate scale. Yet internal colonialism reminds us of the historical and geographic underpinning for (ethnic) linguistic inequality.

I conclude that Oaxaca state is characterized by social division into two ranked sections, the superordinate *mestizo*, the subordinate Indian. *Mestizos* are stratified by class and live in urban settlements, where they have privileged access to many of the material benefits of modern life. They disparage Indian culture and values, rurality and poverty. In comparison, Indians are essentially classless and emphasize the corporateness of their life at the municipal level. Indians, however, are divided linguistically in complex ways not only into, but between, 15 major language groups. So they rarely take action as entire groups (though their capacity for doing so is increasing) and never collectively as Indians. Hence their enduring subordination as a collectivity, from which individuals can escape at will into the *mestizo* section of society, but only by running the risk of proletarianization and impoverishment.

Although not organically linked to dependency theory, internal colonialism can be readily assimilated to the First World–Third World, metropolis–satellite, surplus extraction model of Frank and others. Indeed Frank's *Capitalism and Underdevelopment in Latin America* (1967) contains a chapter on 'The "Indian Problem" in Latin America' that is highly reminiscent of internal colonialism and cites Stavenhagen's 1963 paper. This model, and variants on it (Kay 1989), dominated thinking about Latin American and Caribbean development in the 1970s but has been increasingly marginalized in theory and in practice by the geopolitical hegemony of the USA, (re)-established first throughout the Caribbean Basin (witness the invasion of Grenada in 1983) and then at global scale with the demise of the Cold War and the dissolution of the USSR since 1990.

While not wishing to advocate a 'trapped' dependency approach, according to which all transactions are locked for ever and at all scales into cascading systems of economic dominance–subordination (or exploitation), it does seem useful to reiterate that capitalist development is always uneven in time and space; it is accumulative and competitive. One has only to contemplate the globe to appreciate that development and underdevelopment are functions or positions in an international system of production and development: thus, 'economic development and underdevelopment are the opposite faces of the same coin. Both are the necessary result and contemporary manifestation of the world capitalist system' (Frank 1967, p.9).

Furnivall saw capitalism in Europe as tamed but in the colonies as invariably exploitative, especially where inter-racial relations were involved; the internal-colonialists emphasize the same issue at a subnational scale. Smith, however, pays little attention to the economic environment surrounding pluralism, accepting the colonial-capitalist (dependency?) context of the 1950s Caribbean, which by this time was producing modest economic diversification and social welfare provision. Both of these developments were encouraged by the increasingly self-governing colonies and the British government. It is clear that pluralism in the Caribbean has been nested, historically, within dependent colonialism but that the economic framework of dependency has shifted over time from mercantilism in the 17th and 18th centuries via free trade in the mid-19th to a 'trade-and-aid' position since the 1930s, as I have shown in the context of Kingston (Clarke 1985).

In Jamaica, on the eve of independence, achieved in 1962, the traditional export crops of sugar and bananas were grown (for a sheltered UK market) on plantations and peasant plots, while bauxite, tourism and incentive industrialization were transforming the GDP, even though open (12 per cent) and disguised unemployment was a problem. Here, then, dependency had been mitigated by the imperial conscience and local political and economic energies released by partial de-colonization. Any

Jamaican in 1962 with the clairvoyance to see today's decrepit scene with measured unemployment at about 15 per cent; the sugar and banana industries in possible terminal decline; manufacturing industry either wiped out by the socialism of the 1970s and US retaliation, or existing in sweat-shop portside enclaves; bauxite surviving, largely in nationalized form; and only tourism (de-nationalized in 1989) with any elasticity – would have despaired at this antithesis of Rostow's take-off into sustained economic growth.

That the economy faltered (Jamaican GDP per capita declined year after year between the mid-1970s and 1980s) has not been due to the compex-ities of pluralism but to a combination of Jamaican mismanagement and anti-dependency, British withdrawal and US hostility. What can be stated quite categorically, however, is that development plans, whether capitalis-tic or geared to welfare, have rarely taken the socio-cultural characteristics of the population into account; they have been too aggregate (national as opposed to regional planning); and frequently they have involved borrow-ings from other countries.

Pluralism and Caribbean development

Socio-economic *malaise* in the Commonwealth Caribbean is reflected in IMF involvement in the three largest countries, Jamaica (2.3 million popu-lation), Trinidad and Tobago (1.2 million) and Guyana (0.8 million). CARIFTA, inaugurated in 1968, and CARICOM, established in 1972, are in disarray, and larger trade blocks in Europe (the EC post-1992) and North America (NAFTA) involve all the Commonwealth Caribbean's tra-ditional trading partners and may eventually affect the Caribbean adversely. Although the Windward Islands have held up quite well in the circumstances, they are still so dependent on banana exports that their exclusion by the EC from the benefits of Lomé would plunge them into a deep crisis (Ramsaran 1989). Under these circumstances, the Heads of Government Conference of CARICOM set up a West Indian Commission in 1989. Its report, *A Time for Action*, based on extensive consultations with Caribbean peoples both in the region and overseas, was published in 1992. Chapter 6 is especially interesting because it discusses 'human resource development', while Chapter 7 deals with 'the cultural dimen-sion' and Chapter 9 treats 'social concerns'. Admirable though they are, for they focus on education, language, religion, polyethnicity, gender, housing, health and 'our original peoples', no detailed connection is made between pluralism and development. What might those connections be?

The best starting place is a focused consideration of the plural nature of Caribbean societies (Clarke 1974 and 1975). For reasons of manageability I shall consider only the plural stratified societies, of which Jamaica is the prime example, though, as we have seen, the larger Leewards and Windards are analogous (Clarke 1991). In 1800, towards the end of slavery, Jamaican society consisted of three legally defined strata or estates – white freemen, black slaves and an interstitial group of (mostly) mixed descent who were no longer bondsmen but possessed only limited civil rights. The culture of each subordinate stratum reflected the legal differences: blacks adopted a plantation culture; browns syncretized the behaviour of masters and slaves but emphasised white norms, which were substantially, but not entirely, European.

Since emancipation in 1834, Jamaica has experienced no legal colour bar. By the middle of the 19th century political power in the colony was being shared by whites, Jews and the brown elite; blacks were emerging from, but were still impeded by, the restricted property franchise. In 1865, after the Morant Bay Rebellion, the Assembly abdicated in favour of Crown Colony government. Whites regained control over the destiny of the island; the rapid advance to power of the browns was stemmed; and the latent influence of the burgeoning group of black peasant freeholders was swept aside.

While each stratum became more multiracial with the subsequent arrival of East Indians, Chinese and Syrians, the ranked cultural sections remained intact. Differential incorporation (structural pluralism: *the* plural society) persisted until adult suffrage in 1944, so that cultural pluralism was projected as social pluralism. Members of the upper section married before having sex, and household headship was invested in males. They were nominal members of the denominational churches, and the highest-ranking ones were usually Anglican. Secondary education, often obtained overseas, was the hallmark of this group. In the middle section, marriage and extra-residential unions co-existed, though illigitimacy was despised. Fundamentalism prevailed, but educational standards were moderate to high. In the lower section, illigitimacy was the norm, and the household headship was invested in males or females depending on the composition of the household. Sexual relations depended neither on marriage or co-residence, and there was little correlation between family and household. The consensual, or commonlaw, union was typical of this section. Most members were non-denominational Christians belonging either to sects or Afro-Christian cults. Access to secondary education was negligible, and absenteeism and illiteracy were commonplace.

Occupational and linguistic characteristics underwrote these differences. The upper section spoke standard English with a Jamaican accent and controlled the plantations, commerce, industry and the professions; members of the middle section spoke standard English and Creole, dominated the bureaucracy and filled subordinate white-collar positions in the private business houses; the lower section spoke Creole and remained tied to manual, service and agricultural pursuits.

Clearly, Jamaican – and Caribbean – society has changed a great deal since independence 30 years ago. The urban white population has largely emigrated; government scholarships have produced some social mobility through education; out-migration, first to the UK, and more recently to the USA and Canada, has provided an escape route of a more traditional kind. The society has become blacker, more Creole, but more polarized by competitive politics, drugs, gangs and, at times of political tension, gang warfare. The cultural characteristics of the lower section, now less denigrated and better understood, remain different (but no longer deviant!).

How might a knowledge of Creole pluralism, notably the cultural characteristics of the Jamaican lower section, better inform economic development? We need look no further than M.G. Smith and G.J. Kruijer's book, long out of print, *A Sociological Manual for Extension Workers in the Caribbean* (1957). Published by the Extra-Mural Department of the University College of the West Indies, it deals with 'man and society in rural Jamaica', 'fact-finding and analysis', 'communication' and 'working with people'. 'Man and society in rural Jamaica' is most relevant to this chapter, particularly the sections which discuss the main characteristics of family organization, wider kinship groupings, religion, magic, healing, death rituals, illiteracy and land tenure. The characteristics of each set of institutions is neither discussed in terms of plural theory, nor are their developmental implications drawn out. But the book contains many words of sociological wisdom: the extension worker (likely to be from the middle section), 'should certainly avoid simple moralisation about field facts' (p.54); and he 'cannot afford to be a cultural missionary, he has to accept the cultural make-up of the people and to work with them through their institutions' (p.73).

Let me set out a few situations, by no means exhaustive, in which it seems to me that knowledge of Jamaican folk culture might have been (might be) relevant to development at the grass-roots level. I turn first to sexual relations and then to family land and language. Jamaican lower section men and women begin to have sex extra-residentially; later they will enter co-resident consensual unions and, later still, marriage. This sequence may be interrupted, involve many partners (serial polygamy) and may not end with marriage. Young women are expected to prove their fertility, men their virility, and bearing a child for a man is taken to be proof of love. The implications of this for family planning are profound. Yet the founder-figures of family planning in Jamaica urged:

> our women must be firm, however hard it may be, so that our men will realise that their women are determined to have a full family life. If a man wants a woman enough, he will see it her way and will marry her and begin the foundation of a stable family. Only then can our women be at

> peace with themselves, with a serenity that comes not from indifference but from a sustained standard of values (Len and Beth Jacobs 1967, p.15).

The discrepancy between this ideal and folk reality in Jamaica hardly needs emphasizing. I have cited the passage because it illustrates both Smith and Kruijer's point and exposes a major developmental problem in a society characterized not only by class but also by cultural stratification.

Family land is an unknown category at law in Jamaica, though it has been studied in considerable detail by Besson (1987). This is untitled land which came into the ownership of ex-slaves and was to be passed to their descendants, without subdivision, in perpetuity. Descendants share usufruct and rights to building and grave plots; its economic significance, with population growth, has declined in recent decades, though it has always had a special significance for the security it has provided to family lineages – as the ex-slave ancestors intended. This land is unquantifed, unsurveyed and effectively outside the law. But it does help to explain why country people may not be able to get collateral for loans; and it underpins the overall economic strategy of rural folk, which is to minimize losses, avoid the expense of fertilizers and opt for occupational multiplicity – involving urban and tourism employment – rather than to place too much emphasis on small farming.

The language question in Jamaica is even more a 'national' issue than the other two. Should young people, who normally speak Creole English, be educated in Creole or standard English, and to what level (Nettleford 1989)? This debate is highly reminiscent of the language-literacy controversy in Mexico to which allusion has already been made. An 'A' grade in English in the CX examination (roughly equivalent to GCE 'O' level in the UK) is often used as the basic credential for entry to the Jamaican civil service; but many people argue that it is effectively a foreign language to children from the folk. A Lecturer in English at the University of the West Indies (it ceased to be a College of London University in the early 1960s) has pleaded for the entire register from standard to Creole to be recognized – but in what context (Cooper 1993)? Creole in its various registers is widely used on the radio, on panels, in call-ins and in chat shows. Even if a degree of credentialism remains, there seems a good case for using Creole in general education among the younger age groups and progressively introducing and using standard English in the secondary schools.

It would be unfair to conclude this section without reference to the recognition given in official circles to some of the peculiar features of Creole pluralism. In particular, it is appropriate to highlight the Status of Children Act, for which legislation was passed in 1976. This outlawed the category of bastardy and ensured inheritance rights for the three-fifths of live births in Jamaica, up to that date categorized as illigitimate. Here, I believe, we see the hand of M.G. Smith at his cabinet post.

Conclusion

In neither the 'regions of refuge' in Mexico, nor in the recently de-colonized states of the Commonwealth Caribbean has economic development occurred on a sufficient scale in recent years for the archaic structures of pluralism to be dissolved. In Mexico, the oil boom of the period 1979–83 was followed by a debt crisis from which the economy recovered only briefly. It may well be that the neo-liberal policies of the Salinas administration, which include not only the ratification of NAFTA but the provision for individual property titles on land reform units and the possibility for their subsequent sale, will transform the socio-economic scene. Yet the very backwardness and corporate land-holding tradition of the 'regions of refuge' will give them some protection from these changes.

Pluralism in the form of *indigenismo* provided the basis for a state policy of incorporation into the national society and economy that has led to social subordination with bilingualism, if not to outright exploitation. If exploitation has been less than the model of internal colonialism foretold, it has probably been due to the absence of easily exploitable resources in the indigenous-language areas. Where those resources do exist, exploitation is the norm in Mexico and it affects all peasants irrespective of language (*pace* internal colonialism). There has, however, been a tendency in recent years for peasants and Indians to take back control over their resources and to emphasize ethnodevelopment – the management of their immediate physical environment along lines consistent with their household economy (Blauert 1990). In this way, forest resources together with soil and water conservation are being increasingly managed by communities, often with NGO support. Needless to say, these circumstances are essentially confined to resource deficient or depleted areas or areas that are inaccessible.

Cultural pluralism in the Caribbean fits in with no national project, though Robotham has argued, unconvincingly that 'the theory was in every way a scientific abstraction and elaboration of the socio-political views of the social stratum to which Smith belonged, namely, the nationalist middle class' (1980, p.86; see also Smith 1983). It has been a bone of contention among social theorists and, except through historical analysis, has never been linked theoretically to development; and it has never been recognized by the independent states of the Commonwealth Caribbean as significant for national development plans, so anxious have they been to copy models created elsewhere. In my view, however, pluralism, when used in conjunction with colour-class analysis, provides a vital insight into Caribbean social complexity and, consequently, a crucial entrée into the strategy for development (capitalist, socialist or welfare) most likely to be appropriate in various field conditions. I have confined myself to circumstances of Creole pluralism, but attention to Hinduism or Islam, for example, in the development of small farming in Trinidad or Guyana would pay dividends; and extension work in rural Mexico would benefit greatly from a similarly grass-roots and culture-orientated approach.

Given the evidence of the last half century in both Mexico and the Caribbean, however, and the continued domination of the subordinate cultural sections, only self-empowerment *within the framework of universal incorporation,* that is, by driving social pluralism out of the pubic domain, is going to set a new agenda for rural development. Empowerment, in turn, is increasingly placed in peril by progressive urbanization (with its attendant forms of marginality) and, in many countries, rural decay. This process is especially well advanced in some of the Commonwealth Caribbean states, where agriculture is no longer an attractive basis for life, and multi-occupations and periods of migration or emigration are highly attractive. In Mexico, too, similar socio-economic processes are ancient, but transparent democracy is currently prioritized by radicals, and a national project of universal incorporation (as distinct from regional empowerment) has been advocated by the indigenous guerillas of the Zapatista National Liberation Army that briefly occupied four cities in Chiapas in January 1994.

I conclude that pluralism in Mexico has been used naively, or cynically, and has left the indigenous population in positions of subordination *vis-à-vis* the national society and economy. Caribbean pluralism has served as a valuable analytical model, but there has been a disjunction between Smith's theoretical work and the use (non-use) to which pluralism has been put in practice. This has been due to the dominance by economists of thinking about development in the Caribbean (including those in Grenada who flirted with challenging dependency). This very same criticism could be levelled at recent Mexican administrations. Indeed, it is a global phenomenon but particularly applicable in countries like Mexico and the states of the Commonwealth Caribbean, where structural adjustment provides the overall context for national decision-making. With another bout of dependent development likely in the near future, Mexico's indigenous-language speakers may have to make ever more difficult decisions about remaining or ceasing to be 'Indian'; and cultural pluralism among the Creole lower section may be set, even in the rural areas, as it already is in Kingston, Jamaica, in a sea of informal activities that emphasize individualism and illegality.

References

Aguirre Beltran, Gonzalo (1967) , *Regiones de Refugio,* Instituto Nacional Indigenista, Mexico DF.

Besson, Jean (1987) 'A Paradox in Caribbean Attitudes to Land' in Jean Besson and Janet Momsen (eds), *Land and Development in the Caribbean,* Macmillan Caribbean and Warwick University Caribbean Series, London, 13–45.

Beals, Ralph (1975) *The Peasant Marketing System of Oaxaca, Mexico,* University of California Press, Berkeley and Los Angeles.

Blauert, Jutta K. (1990) Authochthonous Approaches to Rural Environmental Problems: the Mixteca Alta, Oaxaca, Mexico, unpublished Ph.D. thesis, Wye College, London University.
Brading, David (1988) 'Manuel Gamio and Official Indigenismo in Mexico', *Bulletin of Latin American Research*, v 7(1), 75–89.
Braithurite, L. (1953) 'Social Statification in Trinidad', *Social and Economic Studies*, 2(2–3), 5–175.
Bravo Ahuja, Gloria (1976) *Los Materiales Didácticos para la Enseñanza del Espanol a los Indígenas Méxicanos*, SepSetentas, México DF.
Clarke, Colin (1974) *Jamaica in Maps*, University of London Press, London.
Clarke, Colin (1975) *Kingston, Jamaica: Urban Development and Social Change, 1692–1962*, University of California Press, Berkeley and Los Angeles.
Clarke, Colin (1985) 'A Caribbean Creole Capital; Kingston, Jamaica (1692–1938)' in Robert J. Ross and Gerard J. Telkamp (eds), *Colonial Cities*, Martinus Nijhof, Dordrecht, 153–70.
Clarke, Colin (1986a) 'Livelihood Systems, Settlements and Levels of Living in "Los Valles Centrales de Oaxaca", Mexico', Research Paper 37, School of Geography, University of Oxford.
Clarke, Colin (1986b) *East Indians in a West Indian Town: San Fernando, Trinidad, 1930–70*, Allen and Unwin, London.
Clarke, Colin (1991) 'Introduction: Caribbean Decolonization – New States and Old Societies' in Colin Clarke (ed.), *Society and Politics in the Caribbean*, St Antony's–Macmillan, London, 1–27.
Colby, Benjamin and Pierre van den Berghe (1961) 'Ethnic Relations in SouthEast Mexico', *American Anthropologist*, 63, 779–92.
Cook, Scott (1990) *Obliging Need: Rural Petty Commodity Industry in Mexican Capitalism*, University of Texas Press, Austin.
Cooper, Carolyn (1993) *Noises in the Blood: Orality, Gender and the Vulgar Body of Jamaican Popular Culture*, Warwick University Caribbean Studies–Macmillan, London.
Despres, Leo (1967) *Cultural Pluralism and National Politics in British Guiana*, Rand McNally, Chicago.
Frank, Andre Gunder (1969) *Capitalism and Underdevelopment in Latin America; Historical Studies of Chile and Brazil*, Monthly Review Press, New York and London.
Furnivall, J.S. (1948) *Colonial Policy and Practice: a Comparative Study of Burma and Netherlands India*, Cambridge University Press, Cambridge.
Gamio, Manuel (1916) *Forjando Patria*, México DF.
Gamio, Manuel (1922) *La Población del Valle de Teotihuacan*, México DF.
González-Casanova, Pablo (1965; reissued 1969) 'Internal Colonialism and National Development', *Studies in Comparative International Development*, 1(4), reprinted in Irving L. Horowtiz, J. de Castro and John Gerassi (eds), *Latin American Radicalism*, Jonathan Cape, London, 118–39.
Heath, Shirley Brice (1972) *La Política del Lenguaje en México*, Instituto Nacional Indigenista, México DF.
Henriques, F. (1953) *Family and Colour in Jamaica*, Eyre and Spottiswood, London.
Jacobs, Len and Beth (1967) *The Family and Family Planning in the West Indies*, Allen and Unwin, London.
Kay, Cristobal (1989) *Latin American Theories of Development and Underdevelopment*, Routledge, London and New York.
Knight, Alan (1990) 'Racism, Revolution and *Indigenismo*: Mexico 1910–1940' in Richard Graham (ed.), *The Idea of Race in Latin America, 1870–1940*, University of Texas Press, Austin, 71–113.
Lowenthal, D. (1972) *West Indian Societies*, Oxford University Press, London.

Murphy, Art and Alex Stepick (1991) *Social Inequality in Oaxaca: a History of Resistance and Change*, Temple University Press, Philadelphia.

Nettleford, Rex (1989) *Jamaica in Independence: Essays on the Early Years*, Heinemann Caribbean and James Currey, Kingston and London.

Pozas, Ricardo and Isabel H. de Pozas (1978) *Los Indios en las Clases Sociales de México*, Siglo Veintiuno, México DF.

Ramsaran, Ramesh (1989) *The Commonwealth Caribbean in the World Economy*, Macmillan Caribbean and Warwick University Caribbean Series, London.

Robotham, Don (1980) 'Pluralism as Ideology', *Social and Economic Studies*, 29(1), 69–89.

Rubin, Vera (ed.) (1960) *Social and Cultural Pluralism in the Caribbean, Annals New York Academy of Sciences*, 83, New York Academy of Sciences, New York.

Sánchez López, Alberto (1989) *Oaxaca Tierra de Maguey y Mezcal*, Instituto Technológico de Oaxaca, Oaxaca.

Smith, M.G. (1956) *A Report on Labour Supply in Rural Jamaica*, Government Printing Office, Kingston.

Smith, M.G. (1962) *Kinship and Community in Carriacou*, Yale University Press, New Haven and London.

Smith, M.G. (1962) *West Indian Family Structure*, University of Wasington Press, Seattle.

Smith, M.G. (1965a) *Stratification in Grenada*, University of California Press, Berkeley and Los Angeles.

Smith, M.G. (1965b) *The Plural Society in the British West Indies*, University of California Press, Berkely and Los Angeles.

Smith, M.G. (1966) 'A Structural Approach to Comparative Politics' in David Easton (ed.), *Varieties of Political Theory*, Prentice Hall, Englewood Cliffs, 113–28.

Smith, M.G. (1969) 'Some Developments in the Analytical Framework of Pluralism' in Leo Kuper and M.G. Smith (eds), *Pluralism in Africa*, University of California Press, Berkeley and Los Angeles, 415–58.

Smith, M.G. (1974) *Corporations and Society*, Duckworth, London.

Smith, M.G. (1983) 'Robotham's Ideology and Pluralism: a Reply', *Social and Economic Studies*, 32(2), 103–39.

Smith, M.G. (1984) *Culture, Class and Race in the Caribbean*, Department of Extra-Mural Studies, University of the West Indies, Kingston.

Smith, M.G. and G.J. Kruijer (1957) *A Sociological Manual for Extension Workers in the Caribbean*, Extra-Mural Department, University College of the West Indies, Kingston.

Smith, M.G., Roy Augier and Rex Nettleford (1960) *The Ras Tafari Movement in Kingston, Jamaica*, Institute of Social and Economic Research, University College of the West Indies, Kingston.

Smith, R.T. (1961) Review of *Social and Cultural Pluralism in the Caribbean*, Vera Rubin (ed.), in *American Anthropologist*, 64, 165.

Stavenhagen, Rodolfo (1963; reissued 1970) 'Clases, colonialismo y aculturación: ensayo sobre un sistema de relaciones interétnicas en Mesoamérica', *America Latina*, 6(4); reprinted as 'Classes, Colonialism and Acculturation: a System of Inter-ethnic Relations in Mesoamerica' in Irving Horowitz (ed), *Masses in Latin America*, Oxford University Press, London, 235–88.

Turner, John Kenneth (1910; reissued 1960) *Barbarous Mexico*, University of Texas Press, Austin and London.

West Indian Commission (1992) *A Time for Action*, Black Rock, Barbados.

8 Ethnicity and industrial development in Penang, Malaysia

Jill Eyre and Denis Dwyer

One of the most conspicuous phenomena in the world during the last two decades has been the increase in the number and intensity of ethnic conflicts (Dwyer in press); but in what is now Malaysia, the experience of dealing with ethnic tensions, and on occasion conflict, has been much longer, since large-scale immigration of Chinese and Indians into the Malay peninsula during the 19th century produced a classical plural society. Ultimately, a situation arose in which the Malays came to be dominated economically not only by foreign (colonial) capital but also by the immigrants, particularly the Chinese. In these circumstances, the Constitution of 1957, which was the basis for Malayan independence, was essentially an exercise in ethnic balancing. The Malays were to be politically dominant, and the political leaders of the Chinese and the Indians accepted this, for in return the immigrant races were granted citizenship and freedom to follow their own cultures and religions. The economic problem remained unresolved, however.

By 1969, a situation had arisen in which it appeared that Malay political dominance, through their principal political party, the United Malays National Organization (UMNO), was in process of being threatened (Slimming 1969). The results of the 1969 general election, which seriously weakened UMNO, precipitated rioting in Kuala Lumpur; a national state of emergency was declared and parliamentary government was suspended between May 1969 and February 1971. During this interim period, two significant changes took place. The first was political in that a group of younger Malay politicians advocating more interventionist and ethnically assertive policies ousted the 'old guard' within UMNO which consisted of the group of leaders that had been largely responsible for brining Malaya to independence. The second was socio-economic in that the changed political leadership embarked upon a fundamental reap-

Ethnicity and Development: Geographical Perspectives. Edited by Denis Dwyer and David Drakakis-Smith.

praisal of the goals of national development policy and recast them in ethnic terms.

Although there had been steady improvement in the nation's economic prospects since independence, the overall course of development planning was perceived by the new leadership as not to have been sufficiently beneficial to the Malays. It was claimed that there had been too little attention paid to the problems of rural poverty, which were very largely Malay problems, while the urban sector remained dominated by Chinese enterprise. The overall thrust of development policy served, according to Dr Mohamed Mahathir (who has been Prime Minister since 1981), only to open up for Chinese businessmen 'more and better opportunities for the acquisition of unlimited wealth' (Mahathir 1970, p.42).

Government policies to assist Malays – or the *bumiputera* (literally: 'sons of the soil') as they have now become known – were substantially strengthened by the introduction of the New Economic Policy in March 1970, and in 1973 the framework was extended into a 20-year plan to run from 1970 to 1990 (see Faaland *et al.* 1990). Although the attainment of national unity was repeatedly stressed as the overall objective of the New Economic Policy, as was the expectation that gains for the Malays would come only from a steadily increasing national income and not from the extraction of wealth from other ethnic groups, in reality overwhelming emphasis was placed upon Malay participation in the attainment of two major national development goals. These goals were the eradication of poverty and the elimination of the identification of race with economic function. In the industrial sector, this involved a major thrust of policy directed towards increasing Malay employment and management to the point at which it would reflect the ethnic composition of the national population – which in 1970 was Malay (and other *bumiputera*) 54 per cent, Chinese 35 per cent, Indians 10 per cent and 'others' 1 per cent – and attaining a target of Malay ownership of at least 30 per cent of total commercial and industrial activities at all scales of operation. In the modern urban sector as a whole, Malay employment stood at 27 per cent of the total in 1967 (Faaland *et al.* 1990, p.41), while in 1970 Malay corporate equity ownership was only 2.4 per cent of the total, compared with a foreign ownership level of 63.3 per cent and that of 'other interests' (largely Chinese) of 32.2 per cent (Government of Malaysia 1991, p.49).

Although the numerical goals for Malay participation in the industrial sector were not fully achieved during the course of the New Economic Policy, substantial changes were made with the *bumiputera* accounting for 49 per cent of manufacturing employment in 1990 and their ownership of share capital increasing to 20 per cent of the total (Government of Malaysia 1991, pp.47–8). In addition, the government claimed a substantial decrease in the overall incidence of poverty. On the face of it, such large-scale changes point towards greater equity in economy and society.

However, they have generated considerable controversy both within Malaysia and internationally, and a critique of the New Economic Policy has been mounted from many directions. From this critique (see, for example, Salih and Zainal 1989; Cho 1990; Jomo 1990 and Wangel 1991), it has emerged that it would be most unwise to take the Malaysian government's claims of general poverty eradication at face value. As far as restructuring is concerned, there has been little in the way of multi-stream restructuring – a positive commitment to increasing Chinese participation in the Malay-dominated civil service, armed forces and the police, for example – and while the *bumiputera* proportion in the universities has been substantially increased, it has been claimed that this has been at the risk of institutionalizing mediocrity, especially in professional courses which have become very heavily Malay-dominated, not to mention the generation of a substantial stream of non-Malay students going abroad (Salih and Zainal 1989, p.44). Further, within the general climate of lengthy political dominance by the Malay UMNO party, a significant list of cases of large-scale official corruption and financial mismanagement has built up in recent years (for details see Cho 1990, pp.251–2), and there can be no doubt that, in contrast to the situation in colonial times and in the early years of independence, substantial corruption now exists even at the highest levels of government. According to the semi-official 'think tank', the Malaysian Institute of Economic Research, the effect of restructuring under the New Economic Policy has been to produce a *rentier* class among the middle and upper-class Malays rather than to foster true Malay entrepreneurship at a variety of levels (Seaward 1988, p.103). As a result the national trend is one of growing income disparities, with income inequality being associated much more with differences within ethnic groups than between them. Overall, it is difficult not to agree with Lubeck (1992, p.183) when he observes in respect of Malaysia that

> Undoubtedly, when state expenditure represents more than half of GDP . . . the propensity for patronage and *rentier* capitalism expands accordingly . . . The scale of these expenditures, together with detailed studies of political party holding companies, non-competitive public sector contracting, abuses of loan schemes, and banking scandals, simply contradict the requirement that a NIC-developmentalist state be dirigiste, relatively autonomous and technocratic.

In industrial policy, Malaysia has placed heavy reliance since the mid-1960s on the attraction of foreign investment into a low value-added branch plant system based upon the international division of labour, and growth in the manufacturing sector during the period of the New Economic Policy was heavily dependent upon a few export-orientated industries, principally electronics, textiles and clothing. By 1987, for example, the electronics industry alone contributed 18 per cent of the country's manufacturing output, employed 21 per cent of the manufacturing workforce and produced 44 per cent of Malaysia's exports of manufactured goods (Young 1987, p.15).

In 1971 a Free-Trade Zone Act was passed which provided for the creation of free-trade zones and export-processing zones within the country. With an Investment Incentives Act, passed the same year, which provided for a system of tax exemptions related to the number of workers employed by each firm, a strong legislative framework of attraction for internationally footloose industries was created. The state of Penang benefited substantially from these developments, and it is therefore to that state that attention will now be turned in terms of examining the industrial effects of the New Economic Policy in greater local detail.

Economic development in Penang State

Penang is one of the smallest of the Malaysian states. It consists of two separate areas Penang Island (Pulau Pinang) and Seberang Perai, a strip of the mainland (Figure 8.1). By the beginning of the present century, Georgetown, the principal settlement on the Island, had become the largest town in peninsular Malaya, having developed as a port for the export of primary resources and as the general commercial centre for the north of the country. In the period after independence, Georgetown was soon overtaken in growth and economic development by the national capital, Kuala Lumpur; today its population, including suburbs, is somewhat over 400 000. Georgetown's declining fortunes in the immediate post-independence period, in particular the removal of its free port status by the Federal government in 1969, mirrored those of Penang State as a whole which between 1957 and 1970 became a major out-migration state.

The evolving national ethnic situation was to change Penang's fortunes dramatically, however. In 1969, at least in part because of its declining economy, the state had been captured at the polls by a Chinese-led opposition party, the Gerakan Party. After parliamentary government resumed in 1971, the Gerakan Party was incorporated at national level into the ruling Malay-dominated coalition but only at the price of greater attention being devoted by the central government to the state's problems, despite the preponderance of Chinese in its population mix. Penang remains ruled by the Gerakan Party to the present day and benefits have continued to flow from the centre to the state. The first free trade zone in the country was established in Bayan Lepas to the south of Georgetown in 1971. By the end of the 1980s there were eight industrial estates in Penang state, four being free-trade zones, of which two are among the largest in Malaysia (Figure 8.1). The one at Bayan Lepas is adjacent to the airport and thus has proved particularly attractive to the electronics industry, while the second major free trade zone in the state, at Perai, is intended

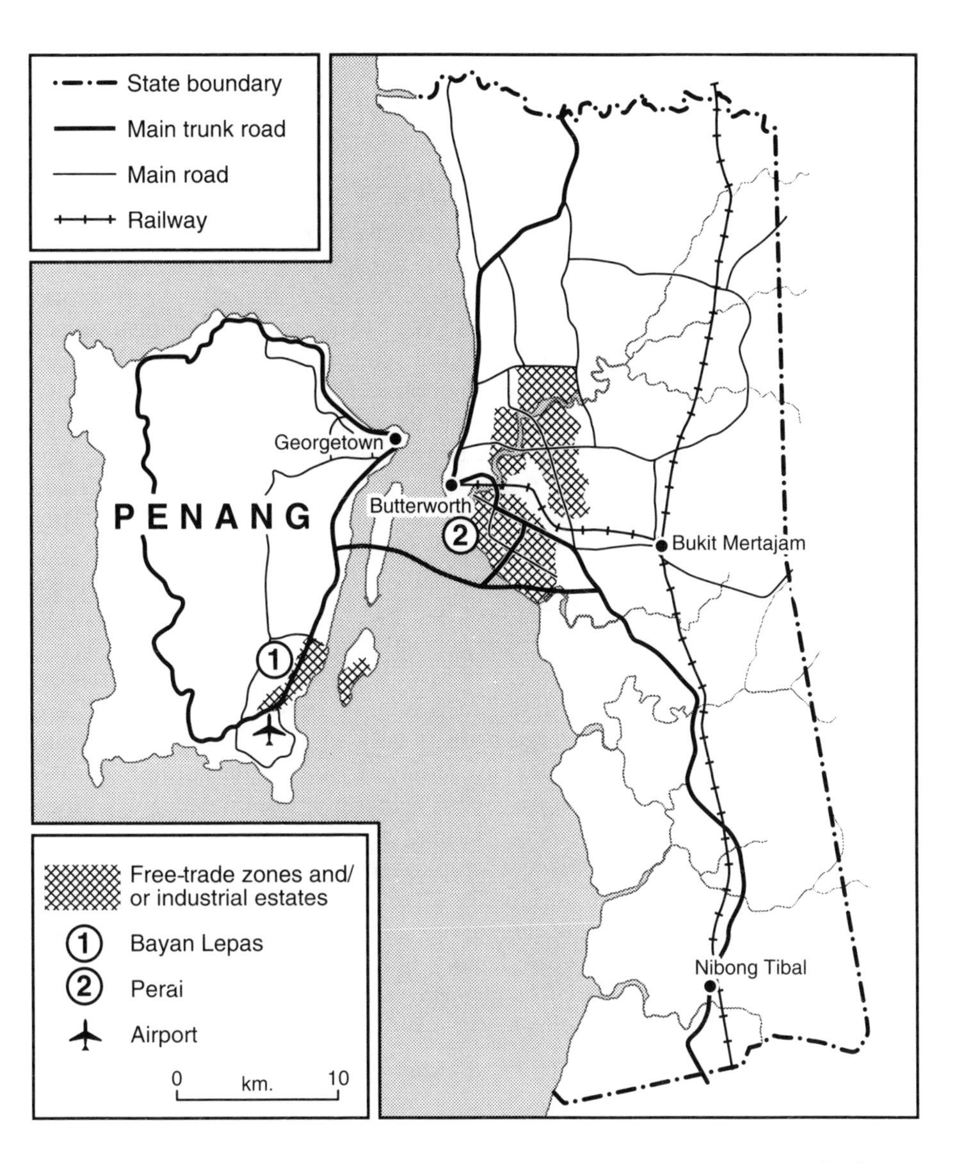

Figure 8.1 Penang: free-trade zones, industrial estates, communications and urban centres

more for companies needing port facilities. By the end of the 1980s, Penang had become second only to Selangor state in terms of state manufacturing contribution to the national GDP.

Given that under the New Economic Policy the major source of the workforce in the new factories on the industrial estates had become the *bumiputera*, particularly in Penang's case young females arriving as in-migrants from the neighbouring states of Kedah and Perak, a previous paper by the present writers (Eyre and Dwyer, in press) focused on *bumiputera* advancement as workers in these factories and also on the issue of *bumiputera* industrial ownership and control.

In 1991, at the time of field survey (Eyre, in preparation), Penang Island had 49 manufacturing firms employing over 200 workers. All were located in the free-trade zone or industrial estate areas to the south of Georgetown and 40 had majority foreign ownership. Most of the latter were branch plants of international companies. No firm was *bumiputera*-owned, although four had some Malaysian public-sector financial participation. As for employment, while the New Economic Policy established a general target that employment should come to reflect the national population composition by 1990 (when *bumiputera* comprised 59 per cent), the local situation was complicated by the fact that Penang state traditionally had a preponderant Chinese population, with the comparable *bumiputera* proportion being only 35 per cent. The survey showed that one-half of the large firms surveyed had reached the national-level target in respect of *bumiputera* employment and that 85 per cent had met the more local criterion.

These basic employment figures conceal a marked lack of progress in terms of subsequent advancement of *bumiputera* into management responsibility and the occupation of skilled positions, however. The presence of foreign management in the large firms is very small. Virtually all the companies are managed day-to-day by Malaysians, but the survey revealed that management positions are overwhelmingly dominated by Chinese and, to a lesser extent, Indians. Further, none of the firms reached the national criterion for *bumiputera* employment even in skilled positions below management level and fewer than a quarter of them the much lower local criterion. Overall, the survey gave good grounds for the assertion that, in terms of large-scale factory industry, at the end of the period of the New Economic Policy *bumiputera* were still very far from playing their planned role in the modern sector of the Penang, and by implication the Malaysian, economy.

The new industrial policies

During the period 1970–90, Penang's GDP more than quadrupled; and within the state's GDP manufacturing increased in proportion from 12.7 to 46.0 per cent (Penang Development Corporation 1992, p.19). This rapid development parallels a high level of economic performance by Malaysia as a whole over the same period, one in which manufacturing had come to contribute 30 per cent to national GDP by 1992. However, the industrial base had remained quite fragile as the recession the country experienced during the period 1984 to 1986 revealed. Manufacturing was proportionately the worst sector affected in terms of lay-offs. In the electronics industry, about 30 000 persons lost their jobs. Many of them were in Penang and they were overwhelmingly women, especially Malay women.

The other major problem with the industrial base is its narrowness. The official reaction to this from the early 1980s onwards has been to seek to complement light export-orientated manufacturing based upon foreign capital with the development of heavy industry financed internally, in part, by using contributions to the compulsory national Employees Provident Fund, a kind of forced saving (Noland 1990, p.58). Two petroleum refineries, a petrochemical complex, a methanol plant, a urea ammonia plant, two cement plants, two sponge iron plants, a cold steel rolling mill, a paper pulp plant and a factory to produce the Malaysian Proton Saga car (based upon Mitsubishi technology and technical support) have been established, but the general record has been one of poor performance and, on occasion, financial disaster. The steel plant, for example, which was established in partnership with a Japanese consortium, was never able to produce steel according to specifications and eventually the Japanese consortium had to be bought out and compensated by the Malaysian government. By 1990, the urea ammonia plant had generated in excess of US$ 50 million foreign-exchange losses (Noland 1990, p.59).

In response, industrial policy in its most recent phase has been reorientated somewhat. In one direction, this reorientation has been extended towards the greater exploitation of natural resources. Wood products – with controversial environmental implications – cocoa butter and frozen prawns are typical items that have been added to a list of desired products. At the same time, the limitations of heavy reliance upon foreign investment as a principal industrial strategy have received greater recognition. As Lubeck (1992, p.182) has put it,

> Despite the boom in direct foreign investment in the EOI [export-orientated industries] sector, value added is comparatively low; linkages to domestic suppliers are weak; and efficiency spin-offs that might raise productivity in the domestic ISU [import substitution industries] sector are absent. The rapidly expanding consumer electronics and appliance industries, to take a glaring example, use electronic chips and components, but there is no strong supplier linkage to Malaysia's components sector. Nor . . . are Malaysian firms prominent in existing domestic linkages.

In these circumstances, the need both to promote linkages and to stimulate all levels of industrial activities, including particularly the smaller-scale levels, has become both increasingly apparent and increasingly acknowledged. A central problem is, however, that such goals imply potential conflict with the deeply entrenched ethnically oriented attitudes that were articulated in the New Economic Policy and still provide the framework for the economic expression of the ethnic structure of the country. As Lubeck (1992, p.184) states

> Rather than aligning with the domestic bourgeoisie, the Malay-dominated state elite have, until now, aligned themselves with foreign capital in exchange for directorships, joint ventures, and other passive, essentially *rentier* rewards, gained at the expense of Malaysian-controlled accumulation. Virtually all analysts stress that ethnic competition and cultural differences are the root causes of these structural weaknesses in the Malaysian economy.

Recently, increased official attention has been directed towards the developmental potentialities of small-scale industry – a sector heavily dominated by the Chinese – though broadly within a political framework that has remained consistent in terms of promoting the economic interests of the *bumiputera*. Previously, industrial promotion policies had tended to neglect the small-scale sector, for example the 1968 Investment Incentives Act allocated financial incentives such as tax-free holidays in accordance with the size of capital investment; and the infrastructure of the industrial estates and free-trade zones was designed to benefit large establishments much more than small ones (Fong 1990, p.157). Further, the Industrial Coordination Act, which was introduced in 1975 and required all new and existing manufacturing enterprises with equity above M$ 250 000 or employing more than 24 persons to apply for licences in order to commence or continue operation, was seen by smaller entrepreneurs in particular as an official attempt to impose on them ethnic quotas in respect of investment and employment. As a result, as the World Bank observed, the Act 'affected the willingness of local businessmen to invest or reinvest' (Young *et al.* 1980, p.185).

However, in 1980 Malaysia negotiated a World Bank loan of US$100 million specifically for financing *bumiputera* small enterprises. By 1986, the distribution of the loan had achieved less than 10 per cent of its target and it started to be made available to non-*bumiputera* businesses (Fong 1990, p.158). In 1985 the operational ceiling for the Industrial Co-ordination Act was increased to equity of M$1 million or above and a workforce of 49 persons; and in 1986 these limits were further relaxed to M$2.5 millions or 74 workers, thus freeing a wider range of enterprises from compliance with ethnic policies. In the 1989 budget, pioneer incentives were accorded automatically to all small industries producing certain designated products, while a sum of M$890 million from the ASEAN–Japan Development Fund was assigned for financial assistance to smaller industries. This was supplemented in 1990 by a M$50 million Technical Assistance Fund established by the government to assist small industries. By then, a national climate of much more positive assistance towards small-scale industries in general had been created.

Small scale industry in Penang

Although there has been no recent comprehensive survey of small-scale industry in Penang, official work carried out in the early 1980s in connection with the preparation of a structure plan for Penang Island gives a picture that is still relevant it its essentials today. As might be expected, small-scale industries predominate in terms of numbers. Out of a total of 1285 industrial enterprises identified on Penang Island in 1983, 1220 employed fewer than 50 persons. Of the latter 745 were tiny enterprises employing fewer than five persons. Enterprises employing fewer than 50 persons accounted for 16 per cent of the industrial workforce (Majlis Perbandaran Pulau Pinang 1985, pp.56–7). The survey also confirmed what was already well known: that ownership of small-scale manufacturing was very largely in Chinese hands. Out of the 1285 manufacturing establishments, 1163 were Chinese-owned. *Bumiputera,* in contrast, were identified as owning only 27 establishments. These would be small, since large-scale manufacturing was dominated by foreign firms in the electrical and textile sub-sectors, and very largely associated with the development of the Bayan Lepas free-trade zone and industrial estate. As for employment, the *Report of Survey* for the structure plan stated that 67 per cent of Malay industrial employment was in the electrical sub-sector and 11 per cent in the textile sub-sector (Majlis Perbandaran Pulau Pinang 1985, p.55–6) and, further, that 84 per cent of Malay industrial employment was in the Bayan Lepas estates. The corollorary of this was that small-scale industry was almost exclusively a Chinese preserve as far as employment was concerned.

The survey also showed that 93 per cent of the small-scale industries on the Island were located within the boundaries of the city of Georgetown, particularly within and in the vicinity of the central business district and in the Brick Kiln Road, Perak Road and Jelutong Road areas. Two thirds of the owners were tenants of the premises occupied and in general such premises were both very restricted – with only 18 per cent of such factories occupying more than 2000 square feet – and makeshift in the sense that less than one-third were purpose-built factories or workshops. The traditional shophouses of Georgetown's urban core were a highly favoured location for such small enterprises, as to a lesser extent were more recent terrace houses and to some extent more peripheral village-type houses.

A field survey conducted by one of the present writers has updated and extended this picture in certain respects (Eyre, in preparation). After consultation with the official list of small firms used for the structure plan survey in 1983, discussions with officials from the Municipal Council and preliminary field reconnaissance, a block of streets located between the

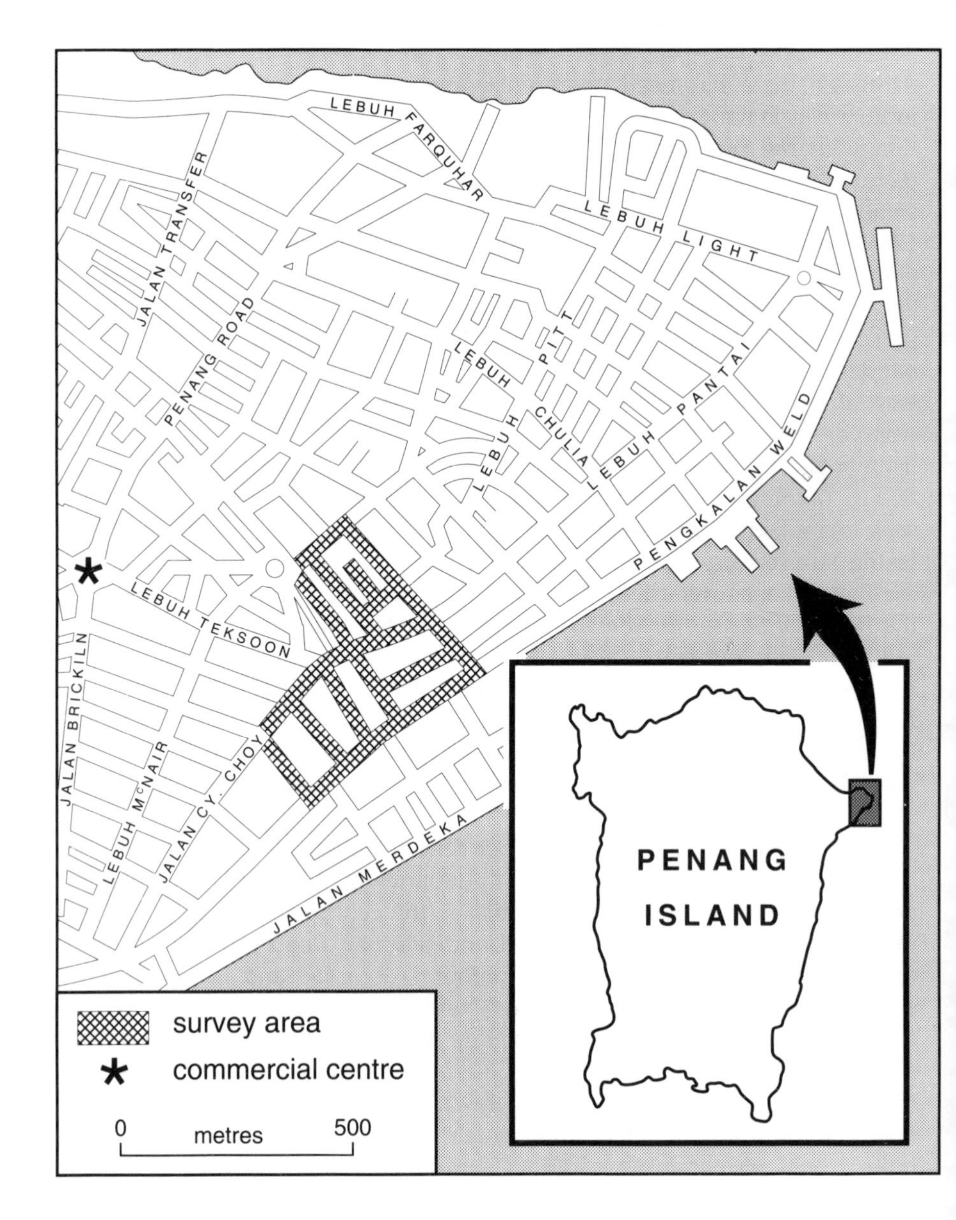

Figure 8.2 Georgetown, Penang: the survey area

business centre of Georgetown and the jetty area (Figure 8.2) was selected for survey as it contained a relatively large number of small firms. Detailed field work revealed a total of 59 firms within the area. Five firms were covered in a pilot survey and, after the questionnaire had been adjusted as a result of the pilot survey, a random sample survey of the remainder were carried out, the total population having been stratified according to type of industrial product as defined by the International Standard Industrial Classification. In all, 29 questionnaires were satisfactorily completed, a number of adjustments to the original selection having been made because of non-response. The survey broadly confirmed the findings of the 1983 survey regarding ownership and workforce. All the firms surveyed were owned by Chinese Malaysians on an individual basis. As for employment, the survey revealed very little *bumiputera* presence in the small firms; indeed 22 of the 29 firms surveyed employed only ethnic Chinese, a significant indication of the continued intractability of the problem of *bumiputera* participation in Penang's myriad of small-scale economic activities.

Given that the creation of a viable *bumiputera* commercial and industrial community was an important objective of the New Economic Policy, the wider research work of which the present results are a part (Eyre, in preparation) also examined the learning of transferable skills as opposed to the ability to perform relatively simple repetitive tasks as part of a factory discipline. The survey revealed that no small firms participated in formal training schemes external to the workplace. Half of them offered no training at all, while the remainder gave some internal training. The prevailing attitude was that training was expensive and investment in training for workers would simply make them more likely to be poached by larger firms. Further, there was always the possibility that newly trained workers might leave and set themselves up as rival small firms in the same business. Such training as was provided tended to be much more 'on the job' and specifically task-oriented than the inculcation of transferable skills. Less than 7 per cent of the firms surveyed employed persons who had received any technical or managerial training elsewhere.

Attitudes towards training supported an overall impression of introversion and isolation from external official agencies given by the firms responding to the survey, and the responses to other questions demonstrated additional aspects of this. None of the firms surveyed had ever received official financial, technical, training or marketing assistance, and only two envisaged any future application for such assistance. As far as capitalization was concerned, only 23 per cent of the firms had gone beyond individual or family financial resources in their financing, with 10 per cent of the total using banks for this purpose. Although many official agencies exist in Malaysia to direct and assist industrial development, small firms in the survey showed not only a striking lack of contact with the principal agencies operating in Penang but also a high level of unawareness even of their existence. The impression given was that small firms strive to limit contact with government organizations. The principal reason for this emerging from supplementary questioning was the overriding distrust small Chinese entrepreneurs feel for a national government whose prime aim appears to them to be the promotion of *bumiputera* interests. A fear – rational or not – that repeatedly stressed was that of ultimately being forced to take on a *bumiputera* partner or to employ a given number of *bumiputera* workers. The general feeling seemed to be that in the prevailing circumstances it would be better for the firm to struggle on alone, relying only on individual or family resources, or if necessary those of the local Chinese community. For a variety of reasons, only 5 per cent of the firms surveyed claimed to be generally satisfied with government attitudes towards small-scale firms. Such attitudes did not necessarily imply a lack of confidence in the business future, however, Sixty per cent of the firms expected still to be in business in five years time and 17 per cent that their business would be expanding. Many such firms are viable enterprises at their present level and within their own organizational context of working. What needs to be examined is whether such an organizational context is satisfactory both in terms of Malaysia's perceived future development and in terms of national goals in respect of ethnicity.

Ethnicity and the economic future

The changed national perception of the role of small-scale industries could be significant for Malaysia, especially in terms of the limitations of the type of foreign branch factory investment that has been a major propellant in its development over the period since 1970. Nationally, the volume of foreign direct investment has been markedly erratic, exceeding US$1 billion annually during the period 1981–3, for example, and then falling to a trough of only US$423 million in 1987 (Noland 1990, p.59). Since 1991, after a period of some recovery, foreign direct investment has continuously declined, with Japanese investment falling by no less than 73 per cent (*South China Morning Post* 13 April 1994). The recent decline in foreign direct investment reflects in part the pressure investment in the South East Asian countries as a whole is now experiencing from investment opportunities in China.

Problems of foreign investment are exacerbated by other structural problems of the industrial economy. Despite the apparent sophistication of some of the electronics factories, Malaysia is very far from a state of autonomous high-technology development. At the same time, its labour costs are rising relatively rapidly; and in terms of the total assemblage of industrial skills there is real fear that relatively soon electronics factories may become much more completely automated and thus much more demanding in terms of skills. Should the response either to rising labour costs or to a skills shortage be an out-migration of factories, there would be very little left since very few of the inputs used in the foreign-owned factories have been manufactured locally. As late as the mid-1980s, for example, only 5 per cent of the inputs used in the electronics factories were produced locally (Noland 1990, p.61).

In Penang, the response of the state government, largely through its highly active Penang Development Corporation, has been directed towards the encouragement of higher technology, greater skills and the small-scale industrial sector as a whole. A 60-hectare site consisting of reclaimed waterfront land adjacent to the airport has been designated as a projected Penang Technoplex, with new technology firms and research and development groups as target tenants. This development will include a Technocentre designed to provide industrial resource support and technical consultancy, including research and test laboratories that smaller technological firms can rent. In 1989 Penang's larger firms responded to the shortage of skills and the generally low level of the country's higher education system by establishing the Penang Skills Development Centre. There are now 51 participating companies (but only one or two are locally owned), and over 8000 shop-floor workers have been trained as technicians and engineers. An International College, partly privately funded and partly financed by the Penang Development Corporation, is also in course of completion. It will emphasize technological education and be based on a twinning relationship with the University of Sydney (Penang Development Corporation 1993, p.3).

In 1993 Penang became the first state in the country to set up a resource centre to encourage the growth of small and medium-sized industries with the establishment of the Penang Small and Medium Scale Industries Centre. The Centre, headed by the deputy chief minister of Penang, has advisory, information and research functions. In addition, the Penang Development Corporation has embarked upon a programme of factory building for smaller local manufacturers which will eventually include premises for small workshops.

Clearly, in a vigorous response to the new perceptions of its current economic situation and future prospects, the Penang state government in partnership with private enterprise has created a realistic and viable framework of official support for the desired directions of new development. The economic future of Penang, as of that of Malaysia's other states, rests not only upon the actions of the state governments to complement those of local and international entrepreneurs, however, but also upon those of the national government. It remains to be seen whether the entrenched ethnic attitudes of both the present prime minister, Dr Mahathir Mohamed, and his heir apparent can accommodate changes necessary in certain specifics, for example to the national education system, to make best use of Malaysia's human capital, and especially its non-*bumiputera* capital. There is also a need for change in the whole ethos of development policy of recent decades, for the ethnic aspects of this ethos have produced a wide gap in trust between the government and some of the potential participants crucial for further and broader-based industrial development. These latter include not only some of the larger of the indigenous Chinese capitalists but in particular the mass of smaller entrepreneurs who, even now, remain overwhelmingly Chinese.

References

Cho, George (1990) *The Malaysian Economy: Spatial Perspectives*, Routledge, London.

Dwyer, Denis (in press) 'Ethnicity, Self-Determination, and Development in South East Asia', in B.J. Craige, Clifton W. Pannell and S. Elliott-Gower (eds), *Ethnicity and Nationalism in the Pacific Rim*, University of Georgia Press, Athens, Georgia.

Eyre, Jill (in preparation) *Industrialisation in Penang, Malaysia: the Impact of the New Economic Policy*, Ph.D. thesis, Department of Geography, University of Keele, UK.

Eyre, Jill and Denis Dwyer (in press) 'Ethnicity and the New Economic Policy in Malaysia: A Penang Case Study' in Yeung Yue Man (ed.), *Global Change and the British Commonwealth*, Chinese University Press, Hong Kong.

Faaland, Just, J.R. Parkinson and R. Saniman (1990) *Growth and Ethnic Inequality: Malaysia's New Economic Policy*, St. Martins Press, New York.

Fong Chan Onn (1990) 'Small and Medium Industries in Malaysia: Economic Efficiency and Entrepreneurship', *The Developing Economies*, 28, 152–79.

Government of Malaysia (1991) *Second Outline Perspective Plan 1991–2000*, Government Printer, Kuala Lumpur.

Jomo, K.S. (1990) *Beyond the New Economic Policy: Malaysia in the Nineties*, Sixth James C. Jackson Memorial Lecture, Asian Studies Association of Australia, Cairns.

Lubeck, Paul. M. (1992) 'Malaysian Industrialisation, Ethnic Divisions and the NIC Model' in Richard P. Appelbaum and Jeffrey Henderson (eds), *States and Development in the Asian Pacific Rim*, Sage Publications, London.

Majlis Perbandaran Pulau Pinang (1985) *Report of Survey: Penang Island Structure Plan*, Penang.

Mahathir Mohamed bin (1970) *The Malay Dilemma*, Donald Moore, Singapore.

Noland, Marcus (1990) *Pacific Basin Developing Countries: Prospects for the Future*, Institute for International Economics, Washington, DC.

Penang Development Corporation (1992) *Penang: into the 21st Century*, Penang.

Penang Development Corporation (1993) *Penang Development News*, Oct–Dec, 3.

Salih, Kamal and Aznam Yusof Zainal (1989) 'Overview of the NEP and Framework for a post-1990 Economic Policy', *Malaysian Management Review*, 24, 13–68.

Seaward, Nick (1988) 'Debating the NEP', *Far Eastern Economic Review*, 15 December, 102–3.

Slimming, John (1969) *Malaysia: Death of a Democracy*, John Murray, London.

South China Morning Post (1994), Hong Kong 13 April.

Wangel, Arne (1991) 'Beyond 1990: New Development Policy in Malaysia', paper presented at the eighth annual conference of the Nordic Association for South East Asian Studies, Gran pa Hadeland, Norway.

Young, K., W.C.F. Bussink and P. Hasan (1980) *Malaysia: Growth and Equity in a Multi-racial Society*, World Bank, Johns Hopkins University Press, Baltimore.

Young, Mei Ling (1987) 'Industrialisation and its Impact on Labour Migration', *MIER Discussion Papers*, Kuala Lumpur.

9 The Ibans of Sarawak, Malaysia: ethnicity, marginalisation and development

Victor T. King and Jayum A. Jawan

Introduction

The Federation of Malaysia provides an excellent example of the crucial importance of the relationships between ethnicity and economic development in a developing economy, but these relations must be seen in the context of the Malaysian political process, particularly in regard to the distribution of power among ethnic groupings and between the federal authorities and the constituent states. Much has been written about these issues in Peninsular or West Malaysia since the Federation of Malaya was granted independence from Britain in 1957 (King and Parnwell 1990). Unfortunately we know much less about ethnic politics and problems of economic development in the two East Malaysian or Bornean states of Sarawak and Sabah; from 1946 to 1963 these territories had been separately administered British Crown Colonies until they gained their independence and were incorporated, along with Malaya, into the wider Federation of Malaysia in 1963 (see Figure 9.1).

Peninsular Malaysian politics has been dominated by the ethnic distinction between the indigenous Muslim Malays (or *bumiputera*: lit 'sons of the soil') whose leaders and party representatives are politically dominant, the Chinese who generally occupy a strategic position in the economy, and the Indians who are found in a range of economic activities from wage-labouring in rubber plantations to running successful businesses in towns and cities. Unfortunately a common assumption in studies of Malaysian politics is that the peninsular model of politicized ethnicity also applies to the structure and content of politics in the two Bornean states (Horiwitz 1989; cf. Jayum 1991a). There is some truth in this assumption

Ethnicity and Development: Geographical Perspectives. Edited by Denis Dwyer and David Drakakis-Smith.

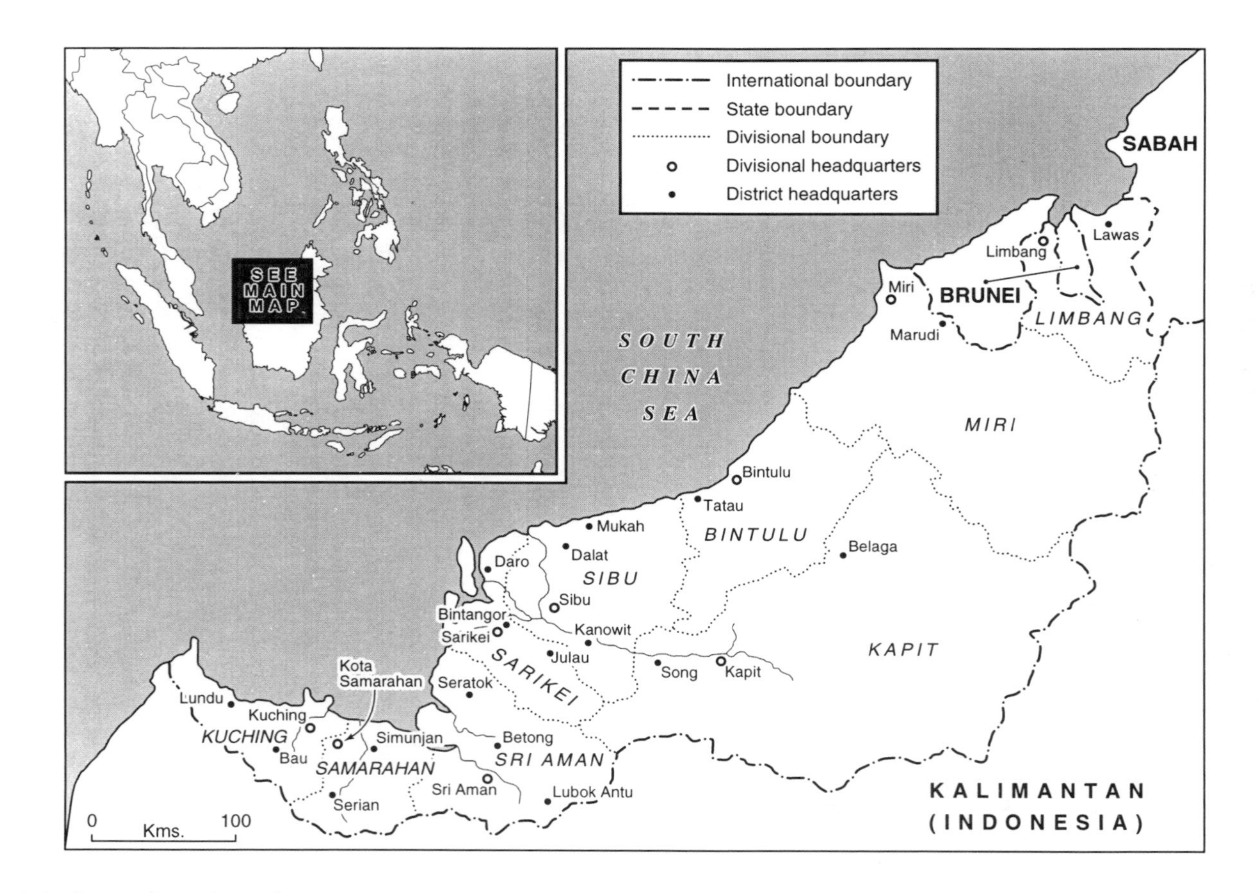

Figure 9.1 Sarawak: main settlements

because ethnicity has indeed been an increasingly crucial dimension in Sarawak's and Sabah's political development since 1963. However, there are two further considerations which need to be borne in mind in any study of East Malaysia. First, the ethnic composition of these states is more complex than in the peninsula, particularly because the indigenous population comprises several non-Muslim, non-Malay groups, collectively known as Dayaks[1], and Muslim natives are in a minority in Sarawak and Sabah. In the case of Sarawak, for example, Leigh has remarked on the relatively fluid nature of the alignments between ethnic-based political parties because no one ethnic grouping has a clear legislative majority and there has to be considerable manoeuvring to secure the support of constituencies from other ethnic groupings (Leigh 1974). In West Malaysia, the main division is Malay/non-Malay, while in Sarawak there are three broad ethnic categories – Malayo-Muslim/Dayak/Non-native – which are themselves internally subdivided (King 1990a).

Second, and most important, the Malaysian Borneo territories were brought into the Federation as less economically and politically developed states, subordinate to the more advanced peninsula, which had achieved its independence some six years previously (King 1988; 1990a). It is this marginality and its persistence, and the dominance of the federal authorities in Kuala Lumpur, largely comprising peninsular Malays, which has constantly to be referred to in any attempt to understand the political and economic fortunes of Malaysian Borneo and their relationship to ethnic affiliations.

In this chapter, we are specifically concerned with the state of Sarawak and within this, the most important non-Malay indigenous group, the Ibans. It is noticeable that, although there is a substantial literature on native cultures, religions, social organization and traditional economies in Sarawak (e.g. King 1993), there is not much available on modern politics and its relevance to economic development since independence in 1963 (see Jayum, 1991b, p.51ff.; 1994). We shall be examining in some detail the issue of Iban political and economic marginality in the context of ethnic-based politics and government development policies.

The Iban dilemma

Iban marginality is, in part, a product of Sarawak's peripheral position within Malaysia (King 1990a). Sarawak's marginality is also the product of two main sets of internal factors: environmental and historical. First, the inhospitable Bornean environment, characterized by dense tropical rainforests and a terrain dominated by coastal swamps and deeply dissected interior hilly and mountainous regions, poor soils and high rainfall, has presented problems for economic development (King 1993, p.19ff).

There are few suitable sites for intensive, settled agriculture so that population densities are low and settlements are dispersed, apart from some concentration in a few favoured coastal locations. This small and scattered population with densities in parts of the interior of 1 person per square kilometre or less, and on average 17 persons per square kilometre, also helps explain the existence of considerable ethnic diversity in Borneo as populations in relative isolation from one another gradually developed social and cultural differences over a long period of time. The traditional economies comprised forest hunting and gathering, shifting cultivation, horticulture focused on such crops as sago, taro, bananas and sugarcane, and inland and coastal fishing.

Second, given these environmental constraints, the period of European colonialism was characterized by general neglect and a slow pace of development in Borneo. The northern areas of the island were incorporated into the British Empire from the 1840s by indirect means. Britain had consistently shown a reluctance to become directly involved in the affairs of the northern coasts, and it was left to the Brooke family – the White Rajahs – in Sarawak and the Chartered Company in North Borneo (Sabah) to administer the territories. Though Britain established a residential system in the neighbouring Sultanate of Brunei, which was eventually surrounded on all landward sides by the state of Sarawak, the numbers of European personnel there were always small. In fact, Britain's position was secured by the convenient arrangements of protectorates from 1888 over the three northern Borneo territories. Only in 1946 did Sarawak and North Borneo become Crown Colonies, but from then on they were gradually prepared for independence.

Specifically, the Brooke Raj, which administered Sarawak for about one hundred years, had neither the resources nor the desire and temperament to 'develop' Sarawak or to equip the native population for eventual independence. Nor during the 17 years of post-war colonial rule was much done, especially in the desperately needed area of rural development. Britain looked for ways of divesting itself of its commitments in northern Borneo as painlessly as possible, and the proposed Federation of Malaysia offered the best prospects.

Thus, on the eve of independence in 1963, Sarawak was poorly equipped economically and politically to survive and cope within a Malaysia dominated by the numerically larger and more politically conscious populations of the peninsula. To make this arranged marriage at all workable, both Sarawak and Sabah were given special constitutional protection. Yet the constitutional provisions are relatively weak and, to a significant degree, the federal authorities have often overruled state wishes and interests (King 1990a, p.119ff.) Although Malaysia is a federation, the constitution and governance of the country is remarkably centralized or unitary, at the expense of the position of its constituent states (Jemuri

1986, pp.114–15). One of the main means of federal political control is the authority to declare a state of emergency during which time the federal government can assume exclusive legislative and executive competence in the country or it can pass an Act extending beyond its constitutionally accepted central powers 'in order to deal with a threat of subversion' (Jemuri, p.127).

Aside from the constitutional powers enjoyed by Kuala Lumpur, the federal authorities have considerable control over the nation's financial and economic affairs. This ensures that such a state as Sarawak, already marginal in a number of respects, has little political and economic leverage, and finds it difficult to resist the direction of federally generated policies and programmes. This status is not absolute; Sabah, in contrast to Sarawak, has managed to secure some room for manoeuvre, and in the 1980s non-Muslim Dayaks, particularly the Kadazans, fully entered, and controlled for a considerable time, the arena of state-level decision-making. Therefore, in the case of the Ibans of Sarawak, there are both particular external forces and certain internal factors and processes which have acted and continue to act to perpetuate their subordinate position, and we shall refer to these in our subsequent discussion.

The Iban and politics

The Iban issue in Sarawak politics is complex and contentious. Although the Ibans comprise the single largest ethnic group in Sarawak (Table 9.1), they have been unable to exert their majority demographic status to secure political control within the state during the past 25 years; nor have they exercised any significant role in the dominant political coalition formed since 1970. This Iban political predicament prompted Searle to ask 'why the Ibans were unable to marshal either their superior numbers or their constitutional *bumiputera* status to advantage?' (Searle 1983, p.3). The reasons are relatively straightforward and we have already touched on some of these.

First, the federal government has used emergency powers to deal with difficult chief ministers at the state level. The first Chief Minister of Sarawak, Stephen Kalong Ningkan (1963–6), was an Iban, who attempted to champion the rights and prerogatives of the state and specifically the native Dayaks over the federation. He was ousted from his post in 1966, following the federal government's declaration of a state of emergency in Sarawak. In 1969 another state of emergency was declared by Kuala Lumpur, this time throughout Malaysia, as a result of the Malay–Chinese race riots in the capital on 13 May 1969. A range of emergency laws was passed affecting various administrative procedures with which the constituent states had to comply. In Sarawak, this

Table 9.1 Population and its distribution by ethnicity in Sarawak

Ethnic group	*Numbers ('000)*		*Percentage*	
	1970	1990	1970	1990
Iban	303	493	31.1	29.5
Bidayuh	84	140	8.5	8.4
Malay	181	348	18.6	20.8
Melanau	53	96	5.5	5.8
Other Indigenous	51	91	5.2	5.5
Chinese	294	483	30.1	28.9
Others	10	19	1.0	1.1
	976	1670	100.0	100.0

Source: *Annual Statistical Bulletin, Sarawak* (ASBS), 1993, p.9

enabled the federal government to bypass the Chief Minister, Penghulu Tawi Sli, another Iban and successor to Kalong Ningkan. Tawi Sli, although a much weaker and more vacillating minister than Kalong Ningkan, was beginning to prove himself difficult in regard to such federally generated initiatives as the national language policy (Roff 1974, pp.141–2, 161–2; Leigh 1980: p.241). After Tawi Sli's downfall Muslim politicians stepped into the political vacuum and have controlled Sarawak's state government ever since.

Nevertheless, this shift in power must also be placed in the context of the broader changes in the perceptions and organization of politics in Sarawak. The political pattern that emerged in the state after independence was, to a large extent, influenced by its incorporation within the Federation of Malaysia. While there were no clear political preferences and alignments along ethnic lines prior to 1963, the formulation of the Federation gradually imposed on the peoples of Sarawak a structure based on ethnic divisions that had characterized and which continues to dominate political and socio-economic relations between the Malays, Chinese and Indians in peninsular Malaysia (Jayum 1991b). The direct effect, among others, was the assertion of a Malayo–Muslim dominance, although in Sarawak the Malays and the Muslim Melanaus comprised only about 26 per cent of the total state population in 1990. As in the peninsula the dominant Muslim party in Sarawak is supported in government by a subordinate Chinese party. Clearly federal politicians are more comfortable dealing with state governments led by like-minded Malay or Muslim counterparts.

A second major reason for Muslim superiority in Sarawak must also be, in part, the result of the skills and acumen of certain local politicians.

The Malayo-Muslim constituencies have been fortunate in finding leadership in two astute politicians, the Chief Minister of Sarawak from 1970 to 1980, Tun Abdul Rahman Ya'kub, and his nephew, and successor, and current Chief Minister, Tan Sri Abdul Taib Mahmud. Both leaders saw it as essential to unify the Muslim vote as far as was possible and to build support through the state apparatus by dispensing political and economic patronage. In this enterprise they were aided by Muslim politicians from the powerful peninsula-based United Malays National Organization (UMNO). Once in power these Muslim leaders ensured that their advantages in controlling the state bureaucracy and the considerable revenues from the timber industry in particular, with the addition of smaller funds from the petroleum sector and from land, would not be easily lost.

The third factor in explaining over two decades of Muslim political dominance is the persistence of deep divisions within the non-Muslim native or Dayak communities. These divisions arise from real social, cultural, economic and historical differences among and within the various Dayak ethnic groupings, but they have also been perpetuated by the skilful exploitation of these differences by the ruling Muslim party. The Dayaks are especially prone to political cleavages; and although the Ibans comprise the majority of Dayaks, there are also significant numbers of socio-culturally different Bidayuhs and smaller numbers of Kayans, Kenyahs, Kajangs, Penans, Kelabits and others. The Dayak category is therefore defined more by what it is not, rather than by any positive characteristics; in other words, Dayaks are natives who are not Muslims.

Traditionally, different Dayak groups were enemies and they engaged in raiding and feuding against each other. Even the Ibans, who share a broadly similar language and culture, have been divided internally by different historical experiences during the Brooke rule. For example, Ibans of the Skrang and Saribas regions were early on subject to modernizing influences such as Christian mission activities and education and to a money economy, while the more physically remote Ibans of the upper Rejang river retained more of their traditional culture and held out longer against Brooke rule. Interestingly, in the period of independence these two subgroups generally gave their allegiance to different political parties (Searle 1983, pp.20–33, 48–68).

What is more, most of the Dayak populations are in rural areas, in scattered longhouse and village communities; some of them are still quite remote from urban centres. This physical fragmentation and social distance, in addition to cultural variations and traditional enmities, have made it especially difficult for political parties representing Dayak constituencies to forge unity and a common sense of purpose and identity.

The Iban and economic development

It is a fact that the Iban, in general, have been left behind in economic terms. This is partly a consequence of the politically and economically marginal position of the state of Sarawak in the Federation but also rather more importantly because of the politically peripheral position of the Ibans in relation to the Chinese and Malays within Sarawak itself. The fact is that the economic problems of the Ibans have persisted even though the Malaysian government introduced an economic programme which was specifically designed to improve the lot of the indigenous people or *bumiputera*. The New Economic Policy (NEP) was introduced in 1970 and was implemented from the commencement of the Second Malaysia Plan in 1971. It was the government's response to the Malay–Chinese race riots in Kuala Lumpur in May 1969 which were, in turn, partly generated by general Malay dissatisfaction with their continued economic backwardness in comparison with the Chinese.

There are two main aims of the NEP: first, to eradicate poverty irrespective of race, and second, to restructure Malaysian society so that different economic functions, statuses and opportunities are no longer identified with racial or ethnic differences (King and Nazaruddin 1992). The policy therefore sought by direct government intervention to distribute the country's wealth among the various ethnic groups broadly in proportion to their respective demographic size. Originally the NEP was planned for a 20-year period up to 1990. In modified form, it has been continued, although the government's current strategy, embodied in the Sixth Malaysia Plan (1991–5), is to reduce state participation in the economy. The NEP resulted in a dramatic increase in public-sector involvement in economic affairs in order to sustain economic growth but also to engineer the redistribution of its fruits in favour of the native populations. This policy was only made possible because indigenes, or rather their representatives, held political power in the form of the dominant Malay party, UMNO.

However, in Sarawak one problem in relation to the NEP is the very definition and concept of *bumiputera*.[2] In the West Malaysian states, where the principal *bumiputera* population comprises the Malays, the target group to receive benefits is clear; but with regard to Sarawak, as well as Sabah, with its majority population of Dayaks and smaller numbers of Malays and other native Muslims, the interpretation of the term *bumiputera* has always been used deliberately to embrace all the indigenous groups. The development planners and policy-makers have not addressed the fact that the Muslim and the non-Muslim *bumiputera* of Sarawak are not one and the same and that they have potentially different political and economic interests. Obviously there is a need to identify the different ethnic groups within the *bumiputera* category to establish their relative economic success or failure within the government's New Economic Policy. However, government statistical material after 1980 does not permit us to do this because native ethnic groups are not differentiated. Nevertheless, we shall try to give some indication of Iban circumstances in this regard.

There are four broad areas of the economy and economic development which we shall examine to try to assess the achievements or otherwise of the Ibans in particular: rural development; the commercial timber industry; occupational distribution and education; and poverty.

Rural development

The Sarawak state authorities, within the framework of the various Malaysian plans have adopted two strategies to promote rural development in the post-independence period. One, which is commonly referred to as the 'improvement' approach, is mainly administered by the State Department of Agriculture. This strategy concentrates especially on subsidies to improve crop quality and management and to diversify farming operations, material assistance in the form of minor rural infrastructure projects and on extension services to assist farmers in upgrading their methods and techniques of cultivation. There has been some success in these programmes, although the government is planning to reduce subsidies because of their expense and the fact that they create a dependence syndrome; and it has acknowledged the need to upgrade its extension services (King 1986). The second strategy is concerned with land development; Sarawak has established various statutory bodies to introduce large-scale, centralized forms of cash-cropping in either designated development areas or in areas with serious problems of poverty and economic backwardness. There are two kinds of land development scheme: one comprises *in situ* development, and the other is directed to the opening of new land and resettlement (Masing 1988, p.57ff.). These schemes are given a high priority in government attempts to 'modernize' the countryside and alleviate rural poverty (Table 9.2) (King 1990b, pp.168–9).

It is clear that, in general, Sarawak takes its models of rural development from peninsular Malaysia. In particular, the federal government, by political patronage and financial pressures, is concerned to promote national integration by ensuring that, as far as is possible, the outlying states conform to federally generated development models. However, though planning policies and programmes are formulated in Kuala Lumpur, they have been largely instituted in Sarawak by state-managed bodies controlled by an urban-based, mainly non-Dayak elite.

An especially influential rural development model in Malaysia has been that of the Federal Land Development Authority (FELDA). The Majids

Table 9.2 Land schemes in Sarawak, 1987 and 1992

	1987		1992	
	Number of Schemes	Planted Area (has.)	Number of Schemes	Planted Area (has.)
Rubber	8	6,524	7	5,415
Oil Palm	17	20,548	34	39,735
Cocoa	9	4,265	12	4,740
Tea	1	200	1	220
Total	35	31,537	54	50,110

Source: ASBS 1993, pp.51, 53, 54

state that 'rural development in Malaysia is often taken to be synonymous with the Federal Land Development Authority' (Majid and Majid 1983, p.66). FELDA provided a blueprint for early experiments in land development in Sarawak, under the auspices of the Sarawak Development Finance Corporation (SDFC) which, in 1968, became responsible for various resettlement schemes cultivating rubber. More recently FELDA has become directly involved in land development in the state.

The other federal organization which has acted as a model for Sarawak rural development is the Federal Land Consolidation and Rehabilitation Authority (FELCRA). Initially this agency was responsible for rehabilitating land in failed state land schemes which were in close proximity to existing villages to increase the farm size of smallholders *in situ*. FELCRA subsequently became involved in new planting of land to such crops as rubber and oil palm near to established communities, frequently in concert with the rehabilitation of already cultivated land (Majid and Majid 1983, p.87). FELCRA has already had some limited involvement in land schemes in Sarawak, but its state counterpart, the Sarawak Land Consolidation and Rehabilitation Authority (SALCRA), has been the most active agent for *in situ* land development in the state.

Sarawak's adoption of federal models did not entail a slavish imitation of peninsula schemes, but they were adhered to in broad terms (King 1988). Unfortunately the directives in the Five-Year Plans have been largely unsuitable in Sarawak, given that the state is more ethnically complex and culturally diverse than the peninsula. Sarawak is relatively economically backward in terms of infrastructure and plantation development: it still has a large number of natives involved in the shifting cultivation of subsistence crops; it has large areas of land under unregistered native customary tenure; and there is a scarcity of expertise for the implementation and management of large-scale estate forms of cultivation (King 1990b). What is more, development thinking in Malaysia, as it is expressed in national planning documents, tends to conceive of rural society in too simplistic terms. In attempting to transform 'traditional' rural communities into 'modern' ones, the tendency is to evaluate negatively Dayak shifting cultivation and smallholding agriculture and to favour so-called 'modern', large-scale centralized, capital-intensive plantation enterprises, even when these may be locally inappropriate.

Let us briefly examine the various kinds of land development scheme with a view to assessing in general terms the effects on the Iban population (King 1986, 1988). The first seven government-sponsored schemes were set in motion after independence from the mid-1960s and came under the managerial and financial authority of the SDFC soon after they were established by the Department of Agriculture. Many Iban households were resettled on these schemes and given a plot of land each, most of it planted to high-yielding rubber with sufficient land for a house and garden plot. Purpose-built centralized processing factories were established to which settlers had to deliver their latex. A proportion of the proceeds was then deducted by the SDFC to help cover some of the development costs of the schemes.

In 1972 the SDFC was reorganized into two statutory bodies and one of these – the Sarawak Land Development Board (SLDB) – took over the responsibility for the land schemes as well as launching a large-scale programme of estate development in the Miri-Bintulu region of Sarawak. Originally envisaged as a resettlement project, again moving poor farmers such as the Ibans on to large estates and providing them with economic-sized holdings, the SLDB then decided to develop publicly owned estates, mainly based on oil palm, using wage labour. By 1985 there were 12 schemes, employing 2500 people, some of them Ibans, on nearly 16000 hectares of land.

Overall the schemes have been singularly unsuccessful in terms of one of their main aims, which has been to 'modernize' rural dwellers and solve problems of rural poverty. Local farmers had little or no say in the formulation, implementation and administration of the schemes. The top-down, urban-based planning initiatives, with little consideration of local circumstances, led to considerable problems of adjustment on the schemes, especially for Iban shifting cultivators. The move from a mixed economy of subsistence and commercial agriculture to a concentration on cash-cropping proved too difficult to make for many Iban farmers. On the earlier schemes, the low market prices for rubber meant that the settlers could not even meet their subsistence needs let alone cover some of the development costs of the scheme. Furthermore, the Board suffered from a lack of financial, managerial and administrative expertise and rapidly moved into deficit. The SLDB also found it difficult to recruit local labourers among the Iban and other Dayak groups because of their dislike of the low paid, routine work on plantations, and it has had increasingly to resort to recruiting immigrant Indonesian labour. These problems resulted in the state government calling in management consultants from a private plantation company to restructure the SLDB and set it on a firm financial footing; the Board also abandoned its interest in the earlier rubber estates. Therefore, overall, its activities have done little to improve the economic position of small-scale farmers such as the Ibans.

The state government established the Sarawak Land Consolidation and Rehabilitation Authority in 1976 to accelerate the development of estate agriculture, particularly as a response to some of the problems being experienced by the SLDB. The Authority was charged with the responsibility of developing, consolidating and rehabilitating land, especially native customary land, for agricultural purposes on behalf of poor farmers. Importantly the Authority temporarily takes charge of the land to develop it, but the land rights remain with the local farmers, and ultimately they are granted official title to it. The participants in the scheme can also continue their other agricultural activities outside of the estate project because they only release some land for development. Thus, this is also a gradualist approach in that the local farmers can deploy their resources to both new and established economic activities. SALCRA has established schemes in low-income areas, particularly among the Ibans and Bidayuhs, planting rubber, oil palm, tea and cocoa.

Despite this more appropriate form of agricultural development in relation to the realities of Sarawak's land tenure systems, SALCRA schemes have also met with problems. Yet again, as with the SDFC and SLDB programmes, they have suffered from major shortcomings – the lack of managerial expertise and personnel skilled in establishing and running estates; and the difficulty of securing a regular, committed labour supply from the local communities to support the estates. The nature of estate work and the discipline associated with it still present difficulties for SALCRA in its attempt to win over local farmers. What is more, when shifting cultivators have been used to cultivating various cash crops, and emphasizing one or another activity depending on market price movements, while generally maintaining subsistence farming and retreating back into this when circumstances demand it, then it is difficult to incorporate them into monocrop estate schemes. This is especially so if they are uncertain about the long-term benefits of the projects; the farmers are anxious that market prices for the crops may not be sustained so that loan repayments can be met and an adequate livelihood secured; they also often feel that they are not receiving sufficient returns on their labour in relation to the other activities in which they are involved. Even SALCRA is experiencing difficulties, and it has been decided that the Authority should slow the pace of its agricultural development because of operational and financial problems. Furthermore, it has had very serious difficulties in implementing a major farm scheme among resettled Iban farmers in the Batang Ai region of Sarawak which has preoccupied the Authority and caused a particular drain on personnel and funds (King and Jayum 1992, p.145ff.).

These considerable problems in land development, particularly in resettlement schemes, have led to the state authorities inviting the large federal development agencies into Sarawak. Yet it is by no means clear that these agencies, generally effective as they have been in peninsular Malaysia, will be much more successful than the state bodies. There still seems to be a contradiction between the strategy of estate development, ostensibly for the benefit of native farmers, and certain prevailing cultural, social and economic conditions among shifting cultivators and smallholders in Sarawak.

Recent attempts in Sarawak to introduce private enterprise into land development by establishing another statutory body – the Land Custody and Development Authority (LCDA) – have been similarly unsuccessful. The LCDA has tried to bring the capital of private estate companies into relation with native land and labour to develop plantation enterprises. The major problem has been that local farmers are suspicious of schemes which might lead to the loss of their rights in land. Despite assurances to the contrary, the opinion of Iban farmers on the involvement of private companies in the development of their land is that the companies must be in it for profit. On the other hand, from the perspective of private capital there has been a reluctance to become embroiled in protracted negotiations over native customary land.

Some of the land schemes have obviously made some differences locally, in bringing in resources and infrastructure to poor areas. However, benefits have been limited and have not made much impact on poverty and inequality among Iban farmers. The Ibans have had little influence on the direction and nature of rural development. Policies have been mainly formulated by non-Dayak urban elites with little knowledge of local-level circumstances. The stark nature of this urban–rural and non-Dayak–Dayak divide is seen very clearly in the issue of logging and forest clearance.

Logging and the timber industry

The commercial timber industry in Sarawak has expanded dramatically in the last 20 years. Malaysian forests are under state rather than federal control and therefore provide a vital source of finance for state politicians to achieve their political and economic goals. These resources are also used for personal enrichment.

In 1972 Sarawak exported over M$600 million worth of goods, of which just over 20 per cent comprised timber (ASBS 1993, p.119). To generate the level of earnings just under 15 million cubic metres of saw logs and 900 000 cubic metres of sawn timber were exported. In the first half of the 1960s the clearance rate in Sarawak was a manageable 45 000 hectares per annum approximately. Recent figures suggest a rate of over 300 000 hectares per annum (Hong 1987, p.128). It is clear that in the near future most of the commercially viable forests will have been exploited.

The scale of logging activities in the state has had adverse effects on such rural, forest-based populations as the Ibans (King 1993). Rapid forest clearance has resulted in serious soil damage and erosion, long-term forest degeneration and water pollution. Recent studies undertaken in the Bintulu region of Sarawak in 1992–3 (King n.d.; Parnwell n.d.) suggest that one of the major problems facing the Ibans there is lack of clean water supplies, this appears to be having an impact on the incidence of disease and is certainly having an effect on the availability of freshwater fish stocks. The decline in fish supplies and the loss of protein in the diet as a result is also paralleled in a decline in the availability of meat from hunting forest animals such as deer and wild pig, in the decrease in important forest products such as rattan for handicrafts and timber for construction, as well as for firewood.

Increasingly, Ibans have to rely on paid work, including in logging camps, to meet their immediate needs because rice farming cannot be sustained, and many of the food and other products secured from the surrounding forests and streams can no longer be found in sufficient quantities, if at all. Given the clearing of forests, shifting agriculture has declined because it is dependent on sufficient vegetation for producing ash-fertilizer after clearing and burning. Permanent cultivation is replacing it.

Apart from turning to the market-place to earn money and to buy goods which are no longer available in the rainforest, Ibans have also begun to cultivate certain plants such as rattan, bamboo and ferns in house gardens, as well as relying on government assistance to switch to new cash crops.

In concluding his survey of the effects of environmental pressures on a sample of 13 Iban longhouses in the Bintulu region, Parnwell states that

> the communities have demonstrated a characteristically high degree of resilience in responding to the quite fundamental changes which have taken place in the forest ecosystem from which they have traditionally derived their most important source of livelihood. But in the vast majority of cases these responses have taken the form of 'coping strategies'–means of sustaining their existence, but often at a considerable cost to their self-reliance, self-identity and social cohesiveness (n.d.:20).

Many Ibans are therefore rapidly being either proletarianized and transformed into low-paid migrant labourers and estate workers or becoming small-scale peasant cultivators with a precarious dependence on the world market.

Occupational structure and education

While appropriate rural development must be a key element in any attempts to improve the economic position of the indigenous population, another vital focus must be the encouragement of native participation in the industrial, or more broadly, the modern sector. Indeed, the government has devoted increasing attention to training and education. Since the inception of the NEP from the 1970s onwards there has been a rapid expansion in tertiary education, with the creation of new universities, colleges and training centres.

To assist in native entrepreneurial development, institutional support has been made available to the *bumiputera* by means of banks and other agencies, some of them specifically established to provide facilities for small business loans to potential *bumiputera* businesspeople.

Some indication of government performance in this regard can be gleaned from an examination of the occupational structure and educational data. Unfortunately statistical material for Sarawak on these matters categorized according to ethnic group is not available for recent years. But we can get some indication of Iban employment patterns, the incidence of poverty and the level of education achievement up to 1980.

In 1960, out of a total Iban labour force of 122 700, 98 per cent or about 120 000 were engaged in the primary sector of the economy, largely dominated by low-income agriculture, with only 2 per cent in the tertiary sector. Of the total labour force in the primary sector, the Ibans comprised 50 per cent, the Chinese 14 per cent and the Malays 13 per cent (ASBS, 1970:41).

In 1970 the Iban labour force in this sector had increased to 53 per cent of the total or 130 000 of the state total of 246 000; the Malays and Chinese recorded a slight decrease (ASBS 1980, pp.18–19). In the secondary and tertiary sectors the Ibans still formed only 8 per cent (4000) and 10 per cent (3000) respectively of the workforce in each case.

Ten years later, after the introduction of the NEP in 1970, there was no discernible change in the pattern of Iban labour deployment. Ibans continued to dominate the low-income, agricultural sector. In the primary sector in 1980 Iban numbers had increased to 142 000 or 56 per cent of the total work force of 255 000 in that sector. In the secondary and tertiary sectors there were only 11 000 (12 per cent) and 8000 (14 per cent) Ibans respectively out of totals of 90 000 and 56 000. Therefore, 88 per cent of the total Iban labour force was still engaged in the primary sector in 1980 (ASBS 1984, pp.37–8). In contrast, both the Malays and Chinese recorded decreases in the absolute numbers and percentages of their labour forces in the primary sector.

Unfortunately more recent statistics no longer divide employment figures according to ethnic group. Now all indigenous groups are lumped together as *bumiputera*, but indications from field observations and interviews with government officers and representatives of different ethnic communities tend to suggest that the 1980 situation has not changed that much over the past decade. Ibans are still overwhelmingly rural- and agricultural-based.

The statistics on educational attainment are similarly unenlightening for the post-1980 period. From 1970 to 1980 there has been an increase in the numbers of Iban children attending school at all levels, particularly at the primary and lower secondary levels. However, of the approximately 33 000 children completing their upper secondary education in 1980, only 9 per cent (or 3000) were Ibans compared with 59 per cent of Chinese and 19 per cent of Malays (Jayum 1991a, p.66). The achievements at the primary level have been much more impressive with 29 000 Ibans attending school (or 18 per cent of total numbers), up from 8400 in 1970. However, these figures do not indicate completion rates. When we look at numbers who obtained the Higher School Certificate in 1980, only 200 Ibans (6 per cent of the total) were successful, compared to 500 Malays (16 per cent) and 2200 Chinese (70 per cent). In 1980, of the 3878 Sarawakians who had higher education degrees only 11 were Ibans (0.3 per cent), compared to 393 Malays (10 per cent) and 2183 Chinese (56.3 per cent) (Jayum 1991b, p.453). As a supporting piece of evidence of low Iban educational attainment in higher education, Jayum surveyed the Sarawak civil service lists in 1984 and discovered that very few Ibans had high-level positions in important state government or statutory bodies (1991b, p.456). Furthermore, in 1980 only 35 per cent of Ibans were literate compared to 62 per cent of Malays and 74 per cent of Chinese (p.458).

Figures of the labour force by educational level in 1990 show that over 60 per cent of the *bumiputera* labour force either had only primary level education or no formal education at all. The equivalent figure for the Chinese was 37 per cent. The *bumiputera* figure presumably includes a very significant number of Ibans, based on the data on educational attainment by ethnic group which we have for 1980.

Poverty

There is a real problem in operationalizing and conceptualizing poverty and deciding how to measure it. In Malaysia, and in Sarawak in particular, the study of poverty is made even more difficult because of the sheer lack of reliable data (King 1986, pp.73–4). Until the mid-1970s, statistics on poverty rates for Sarawak were not available. The first data on poverty are for 1976 when out of a total of about 207 100 households in Sarawak, 107 100 (or 51.7 per cent) were considered to be poor. The absolute poverty level was between M$150 and M$180 per household per month in the mid-1970s. Of these 107 100 poor households, 94 per cent were rural dwellers. What is more, 48 500 of the 107 100 households were Ibans and of these 47 600 were located in rural areas. In 1982, still nearly half of all rural Iban households were designated as poor (King 1986, pp.73–8).

We also have several case studies which provide anecdotal evidence of Iban poverty. It was found, for example, in case studies of Ibans in the Batang Ai, Engkilili, Lubok Antu, Nanga Spak and Julau areas in the late 1970s, that the majority of households suffered regularly from acute rice shortages, sometimes up to 80 per cent in a given sample (King 1986, pp.74–6).

As of 1984 the Fifth Malaysia Plan estimated that out of 282 000 households in Sarawak, 90 100, or 31.9 per cent, were below the poverty line (see King 1990b, p.165). This is a clear improvement from 1976, but the majority of these households still comprised Ibans (King 1988, pp.275–6). In the mid-1980s King suggests that probably about 40 per cent of Sarawak's total population of 1.2 million was below the poverty line or at least considered to require some assistance from government to raise incomes. Again the main groups concerned were shifting agriculturalists and small-scale rubber, sago and coconut cultivators, many of whom were Ibans.

In 1990 the number of poor households was calculated at 70 900 (or 21 per cent), and in 1989 we have a figure for *bumiputera* households of a mean monthly gross income of M$932 in comparison with Chinese households of M$1754 (at current prices) (ASBS 1992, pp.159–60). Again many of the *bumiputera* households are Ibans, and one would assume that they comprise many of the 70 000 or so poor households.

Conclusions

From 1970 the Sarawak state government has been dominated by a group of Muslim politicians supported by a dependent Chinese political party. The Muslim political party has been committed to creating a wealthy class of *bumiputeras*, predominantly Malayo-Muslim, who could then sponsor native political activities. In the course of achieving this objective, the state administrative apparatus has intervened in the economy to redirect resources to the leaders and supporters of the dominant political party. Sources of wealth have come mainly from timber and from the control of state agencies and bodies. Aside from a few client Ibans who have allied themselves with these powerful Muslim patrons, most Ibans have been marginalized; they have little political influence, and they are subject to centralized planning directives and the implementation of projects which demonstrate little understanding of their plight.

Despite the introduction of the NEP the Ibans have not benefited much from the general economic growth of Malaysia in general and Sarawak in particular. Although it has been a clear national policy to restructure Malaysian society in accordance with various ethnic prerogratives, Sarawak is far from meeting these goals. Iban underdevelopment is part of Malaysian inter-ethnic relations and politics. It stems largely from the relative political isolation of the Ibans from the centres of power which is, in turn, a product both of factors and processes external to Sarawak in the context of federal–state relations and those internal to the state. These latter are especially to do with those divisions in Iban society arising from the socio-economic conditions of scattered, rural-based shifting agricultural communities, the consolidation and exacerbation of these divisions during the Brooke and colonial periods and the post-independence marginalization of Ibans by astute and skilful Malayo-Muslim political manoeuvring supported by the federal authorities.

In a more recent detailed analysis of the parliamentary general election of 1990 and the Sarawak state election of 1991, Jayum concludes that they did not result in 'any overall status change in Iban politics and socioeconomic underdevelopment' (1994, p.241). One cannot be too optimistic about the future developmental prospects of the Iban, at least in the short to medium term.

Overall one cannot understand the dilemma of the Ibans without examining the ethnic dimension of development. The Malaysian population is divided into well-defined ethnic blocs of competing interests, and Sarawak has been drawn increasingly into this system since the involvement of the federal authorities in Sarawak politics and the inception of the New Economic Policy. Ethnicity and marginality then are the twin axes around which much of the political and economic activity of Sarawak revolves. Unless and until the Ibans begin to co-ordinate their political representation at the state level and overcome their internal divisions, it is likely that they will continue to lag behind other ethnic groups and that, in general, their economic backwardness will persist.

Notes

1. Strictly the term 'Dayak' comprises the so-called 'Sea Dayaks' (Ibans) and 'Land Dayaks' (Bidayuhs) (Federal Constitution of Malaysia, Article 161 (A) [7]); however, since 1987 it has become increasingly common to refer to the Ibans, Bidayuhs and Orang Ulu (the various smaller non-Muslim indigenous groups) as Dayaks. These native populations are also classified, along with the Malays, as *bumiputera*.

2. The term *bumiputera* is a post-Malaysia concept and it arose from the need to reclassify indigenous populations so as to include the non-Malay and non-Muslim native populations of Sarawak and Sabah.

References

Hong, E. (1987) *Natives of Sarawak. Survival in Borneo's Vanishing Forests*, Institut Masyarakat, Pulau Pinang.

Horiwitz, D.L. (1989) 'Incentives and Behaviour in Ethnic Politics of Sri Lanka and Malaysia'. *Third World Quarterly*, 11, 18–35.

Jayum, A.J. (1991a) *The Ethnic Factor in Modern Politics: the Case of Sarawak, East Malaysia*. Occasional Paper No 20, Centre for South-East Asian Studies, University of Hull.

Jayum, A.J. (1991b) *Political Change and Economic Development among the Ibans of Sarawak, East Malaysia*. Unpublished Ph.D. thesis, University of Hull.

Jayum, A.J. (1994) *Iban Politics and Economic Development. Their Patterns and Change*, Penerbit Universiti Kebangsaan Malaysia, Bangi.

Jemuri bin Serjan and Datuk Haji Mohamed (1986) 'The Constitutional Position of Sarawak' in F.A. Trindade and H.P. Lee (eds), *The Constitution of Malaysia: Further Developments and Perspectives, Essays in Honour of Tun Mohamed Suffian*, Oxford University Press, Singapore, 114–34.

King, V.T. (1986) 'Land Settlement Schemes and the Alleviation of Rural Poverty in Sarawak, East Malaysia: a Critical Commentary', *Southeast Asian Journal of Social Science*, 14, 71–99.

King, V.T. (1988) 'Models and Realities: Malaysian National Planning and East Malaysian Development Problems', *Modern Asian Studies*, 22, 363–98.

King, V.T. (1990a) 'Why is Sarawak Peripheral?' in V.T. King and M.J.G. Parnwell (eds), *Margins and Minorities: The Peripheral Areas and Peoples of Malaysia*, Hull University Press, Hull, 110–29.

King, V.T. (1990b) 'Land Settlement Programmes in Sarawak: a Mistaken Strategy?' in V.T. King and M.J.G. Parnwell (eds), *Margins and Minorities: The Peripheral Areas and Peoples of Malaysia*, Hull University Press, Hull, 163–83.

King, V.T. (1993) *The Peoples of Borneo*, Blackwell, Oxford.

King, V.T. (n.d.) The Bintulu Region of Sarawak, East Malaysia: the Historical and Socio-economic Context, Hull, Unpublished ms.

King, V.T. and M.J.G. Parnwell (eds) (1990) *Margins and Minorities: The Peripheral Areas and Peoples of Malaysia*, Hull University Press, Hull.

King, V.T. and Nazaruddin, M.J. (eds) (1992) *Issues in Rural Development in Malaysia*, Dewan Bahasa dan Pustaka, Kuala Lumpur.

King, V.T. and Jayum, A.J. (1992) 'Resettlement in Sarawak' in V.T. King and M.J. Nazaruddin, M.J. (eds) *Issues in Rural Development in Malaysia*, Dewan Bahasa dan Pustaka, Kuala Lumpur, 145–170.

Leigh, M.B. (1974) *The Rising Moon: Political Change in Sarawak*, Sydney University Press, Sydney.

Leigh, M.B. (1980) 'Sarawak at the Polls' in H. Crouch, K.H. Lee and M. Ong (eds) *Malaysian Politics and the 1978 Election*, Oxford University Press, Kuala Lumpur, 240–54.

Majid, S. and A. Majid (1983) 'Public Sector Land Settlement: Rural Development in West Malaysia' in D.A.M. Lea and D.P. Chaudhri (eds) *Rural Development and the State*, Methuen, London, 66–99.

Masing, J. (1988) 'The Role of Resettlement in Rural Development' in R.A. Cramb and R.H.W. Reece (eds) *Development in Sarawak*, Centre of Southeast Asian Studies, Monash University, 57–64.

Parnwell, M.J.G. (n.d.) Environmental Change and Iban Communities in Sarawak, East Malaysia: Impact and Response, Hull, Unpublished ms.

Roff, M.C. (1974) *The Politics of Belonging: Political Change in Sabah and Sarawak*, Oxford University Press, Kuala Lumpur.

Sarawak Government (1970–93) *Annual Statistical Bulletin Sarawak*, Department of Statistics, Kuching.

Searle, P. (1983) *Politics in Sarawak 1970–1976: the Iban Perspective*, Oxford University Press, Singapore.

10 The people of Isan, Thailand: missing out on the economic boom?

Michael Parnwell and Jonathan Rigg

Introduction

Thailand's strong economic performance over the last eight to ten years has been accompanied by a plethora of enthusiastic appellations: she has become a 'second-generation NIC', an 'A-rated near-NIC' (EIU 1992, p.7), a 'remarkable success story' and, at least until the clock strikes twelve, the 'Cinderella of Asia' (*Far Eastern Economic Review*, 1 May 1990). Even if we accept the validity of these hyped-up images on the basis of macro-level economic performance, their appropriateness becomes highly questionable when this performance is analysed at the subnational level. The spoils of the country's love affair with the Prince Charming of world capitalism have been far from evenly distributed (Parnwell 1996). One region in particular, the north-east, has largely missed out on the economic boom. Here we find few factories of any note, little tourism and only limited pockets of international investment – three of the principal factors which have underpinned the country's overall economic success story. Meanwhile, the north-east continues to make a significant contribution to the economic boom through labour migration, providing the economic heartland with a plentiful supply of relatively cheap labour.

The aim of this chapter is to explore the ethnic dimension of uneven development in Thailand, particularly in seeking at least a partial explanation for the peripherality and marginality of the north-east, the region of Isan, in terms of national economic development. Superficially, this is a rather difficult task because the key players on this particular stage belong to the same broad T'ai ethnic group. Nor can the people of Isan easily be called, in quantitative terms, an 'ethnic minority', in that they constitute roughly one-third of the country's population. However, we will argue

Ethnicity and Development: Geographical Perspectives. Edited by Denis Dwyer and David Drakakis-Smith.

that there are a number of rather more subtle factors which explain the relative disadvantage of the Isan people, many of which have 'ethnicity', 'ethnic identity' or 'ethnic differential' at their heart.

A secondary objective is to move away from the economistic perspective which tends to dominate views of development in the 'Third World'. Thus this chapter will also emphasize the political, cultural, ethnic, representational, social and spatial dimensions of development in Thailand.

The chapter will be divided into three unequal parts. The first will seek to identify some of the factors which underpin the 'differentness' of the Isan people from the Central Plains Thai (for the purpose of this discussion the focus will be on the north-east–central region axis – see Figure 10.1), particularly in relation to ethnicity and identity. The second section will examine how differences so identified may be linked to the process of uneven development, which has seen the people of Isan largely bypassed by the country's phenomenal economic transformations of the last decade. As such, this represents little more than a continuation of a trend, the origins of which can be traced back at least to the mid-19th century. The discussion of 'development' in this section will attempt to move away from the economistic viewpoint to include discussion of political and other considerations. It will also look at factors associated with the process of change over the last two decades which have served to blur the distinctiveness of ethnic divisions and identities in Thailand. Finally, the last section, by way of a conclusion, will address the use of the question mark at the end of the title of this chapter, showing how the process of migration in particular has enabled the *khon isan* (the people of Isan) to claim for themselves a greater slice of the development 'cake' than might otherwise have been the case had they been obliged to rely exclusively on *in situ* development within the north–east region.

The basis of Isan 'differentness': ethnicity and identity

Our first task is to justify the inclusion of the *khon isan* in a volume on 'ethnodevelopment'. This is made difficult by the fact that they are typically included under the catch-all heading of T'ai, which includes all the T'ai-speaking peoples of modern Thailand (excluding the Thai-Malays of the far south), parts of Myanmar (Burma), Cambodia, Laos, northern Vietnam, and Yunnan in southern China (Keyes 1989, p.213). Wijeyewardene (1990, p.4) differentiates within this group between the Thai (the Ta'i people of the modern nation state of Thailand) and the Lao Lum (the 'lowland Lao', principally of present-day Laos), but again this is of little value to us because the *khon isan* remain lumped together with other

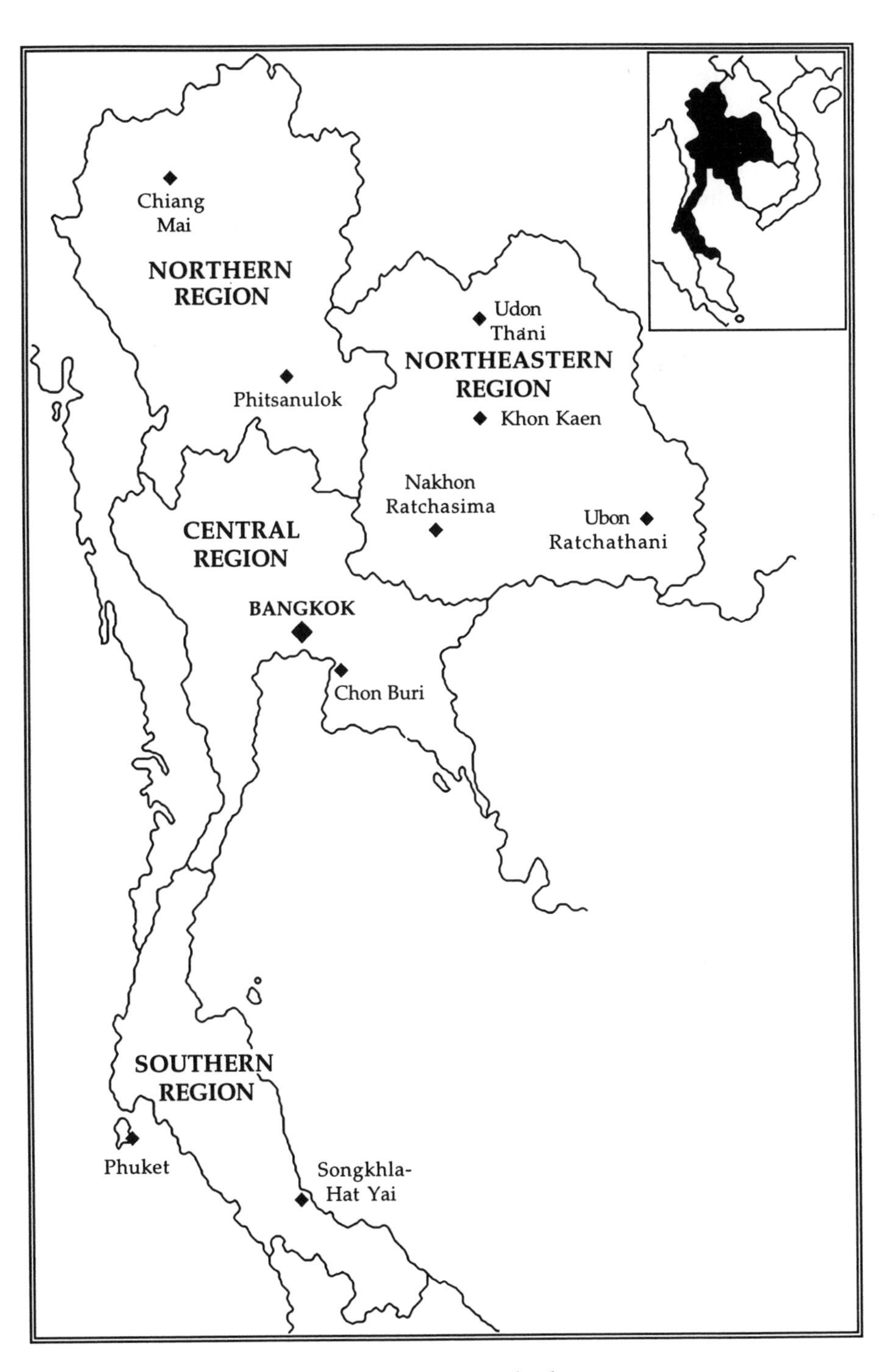

Figure 10.1 Thailand: regions and main regional urban centres

groups in Thailand under the banner heading 'Thai', even though, in reality, they effectively straddle the two categories. None the less, both Wijeyewardene and Keyes draw attention to the shortcomings of this classification and introduce terms such as 'Thai-Lao', to denote the people of Isan, who are then differentiated from the 'Siamese' or 'Central Thai' (Keyes 1989, p.213; Wijeyewardene 1990, p.4). This is more useful for our purposes because there are quite subtle linguistic and cultural differences between the two 'groups', which have underpinned differences in identity, history and, more recently, development experience. In terms of language and culture, the *khon isan* have more in common with the Lao who inhabit the left bank of the Mekong River. The Isan dialect which is widely spoken in the region is almost identical to the Lao language and, although similar to Central Thai in structure, differs quite substantially in terms of tones, pronunciation and vocabulary. The cultural preference for glutinous rice and other aspects of diet, their music, dance, drama and material culture serve further to distinguish the *khon isan* from the *khon thai* or *khon klaang*.

The Thai-Lao, or *khon isan*, therefore represent a subgroup of both the T'ai and Thai ethnic categories, and yet to describe them as an 'ethnic minority' would be somewhat misleading, since, in purely quantitative or demographic terms, there is little which would identify the *khon isan* as a minority. The population of the north-east constitutes approximately one-third (35 per cent) of the country's total, roughly equal to the proportion of Central Plains Thai (32 per cent – the 'majority' group in this discussion). In addition, at least 5 per cent of the population of Bangkok and the central region is, at any one time, made up of people who have migrated from the north-east, either on a long-term or short-term basis – a point which is of central relevance to the discussion in the later part of this chapter.

Within the north-east itself, the *khon isan* have been far and away the predominant ethnic group, constituting approximately 95 per cent of the region's population according to the 1960 Census, which was the last time that the population of Thailand was classified on the basis of ethnicity. The remaining five per cent was made up of six much smaller ethnic groups (see Figure 10.2: it should be pointed out, however, that the various peoples of the north-east show a greater level of cultural similarity with one another than is the case with the tribal groups of northern Thailand, for example: see Keyes 1967). The Kui (*c*150 000, according to Peter Kunstadter's (1967) analysis of the 1960 Census), who are described by LeBar *et al.* (1964) as a former tribal people who have become either 'Thai-ised' or 'Khmer-ised' (for example through inter-marriage); the Khmer (*c*300 000 in total, although only around 100 000 reside in the north-east), are located mostly in the provinces of Surin and Srisaket, and are virtually indistinguishable from the Khmer of Cambodia in terms of

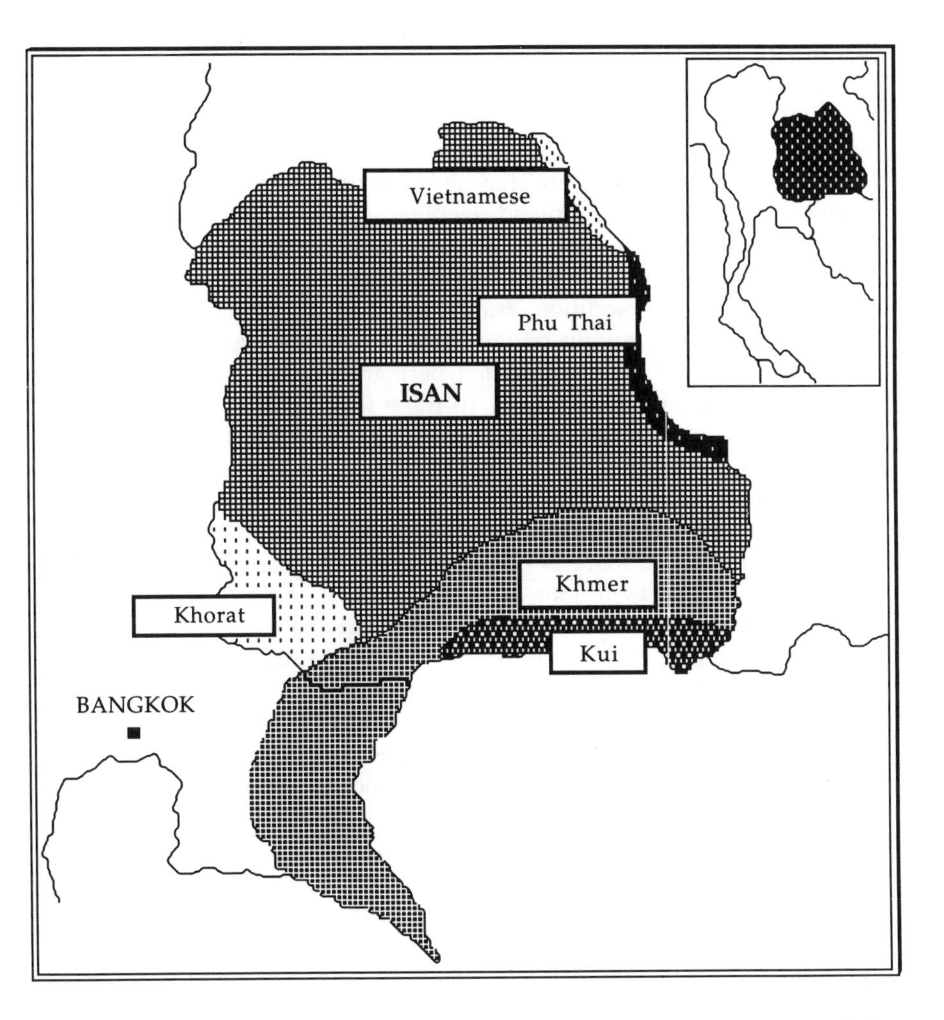

Figure 10.2 North-east Thailand: approximate location and distribution of the region's main ethnic groups

language, material culture and so on (they are the only sizeable non-T'ai community in the region); the Khorat group are T'ai-speakers found in Nakhon Ratchasima (otherwise known as Khorat) but who have a dialect which is quite distinct from either Central Thai or Isan and, for that matter, Khmer. They are said to be the descendants of Siamese soldiers and Khmer women. In essence, the Kui, Khmer and Khorat groups are very similar.

The Phu Thai (*c.*100 000) originated in the mountainous regions of north-eastern Laos, many of whom were 'encouraged' (under military pressure) by the Siamese state to settle in the Khorat Plateau during the mid- to late 18th and early 19th centuries as a way of forestalling possible influence in the region from Vientiane, the present-day Lao capital. The Phu Thai are now found on the fringes of the Khorat Plateau near the Mekong River, especially in the provinces of Nakhon Phanom, Sakhon Nakhon and Mukdahan. 'Phu Thai' was the name used by the Lao of the lowlands to refer to the upland-dwelling T'ai groups. The Vietnamese community in the north-east, one of two main concentrations in Thailand (the second being mainly Roman Catholics who settled in central Thailand to avoid religious persecution during the mid-19th century), consists of immigrants who also sought refuge (on a 'temporary' basis) from persecution and warfare. Many have settled permanently, although their precise nationality is still rather uncertain. To these five non-Isan minority groups in the regional setting, we should also add a sizeable number of ethnic Chinese who are fairly widespread throughout the north-east, principally in urban areas.

In spite of the many facets which distinguish them from the Central Plains Thai, however, there is clearly little in the quantitative field which would suggest the *khon isan* as a minority in either the national or regional contexts. How then might we support the view of the *khon isan* as a 'disadvantaged ethnic minority'? Wherein lies their differentness and distinctiveness? To answer these questions, we need first to consider some of the criteria which might be used in identifying a 'minority'. As we shall see in the context of the *khon isan*, it is not their numerical strength *per se* so much as their position relative to, and nature of their relationship with, other groups in society which provides the basis of their identification as a 'minority'. This point will become clearer as we delve briefly into the recent history of the north-east region of Thailand in an attempt to trace the emergence of a sense of 'differentness', in terms of ethnic and cultural identity, and 'disadvantage', in terms of development experience.

In simple terms, a minority is a 'group of people resident in a country but different from the majority of the inhabitants by reasons of race, religion, language, social customs and national sympathies' (Goodall 1987, p.307). But the numbers game – which this and most definitions stress – is not always very helpful. It has been observed, for example, that the Sinhala of Sri Lanka, the country's majority ethnic group, often perceive themselves to be a minority because of the millions of Tamils in the Indian state of Tamil Nadu, just a few kilometres distant across the Palk Strait. In fact, they feel themselves to be a double minority for they also feel swamped and to an extent threatened by the hundreds of millions of Hindus in India (the Sinhala are Theravada Buddhists). The key point is that minority status is often more a state of mind than a numerical state. In the case of the Lao of north-eastern Thailand, they perceive themselves to be a minority and are usually perceived as such by the non-Lao Thai.

Whether they constitute 25 per cent or 35 per cent of the total Thai population is, in a sense, neither here nor there.

With the above in mind, we use two main criteria to justify the identification of the *khon isan* as an ethnic minority: their peripherality and their self-identity. In outlining these two facets, it is hoped that we can also begin to identify some of the factors which have underpinned the relative backwardness or subordination of the people of the north-east or, in other words, their 'uneven development'.

Peripherality

We might expect a two-way link between peripherality and a group's 'minority' status. First, peripherality may be a consequence of an ethnic group's minority position: the relatively weak position of a small, dispersed and politically subordinate group of people may determine that they can continue to exist only on the margins of larger, more advanced and politically more powerful group(s). Alternatively, we might find that the minority status of a particular group is due in no small measure to their peripheral location: their distance or isolation from the main centres of economic activity and/or political decision-making may do little to enhance their position *vis-à-vis* the group(s) which control, and draw strength from, economic and political power. In this sense, 'minority groups are not, they become': their minority status represents the culmination of a process of change which has seen their subordination and subjugation at the hands of a more powerful, pervasive and advanced majority society. However, it should also be borne in mind that, for several ethnic groups in South-east Asia, their peripheralization resulted in no small measure from the somewhat arbitrary process whereby political boundaries were drawn up between nation states, especially under the auspices of colonial rule. Whether they were based on natural geographical features or the spheres of influence of competing European powers, it seems that seldom were national boundaries determined with reference to the peoples who inhabited what are now the border regions. True, subsequent migrations of people across these boundaries (either voluntarily or to escape persecution and hardship elsewhere) has served only to confuse the pattern and position of ethnic minorities in these peripheral areas.

In the case of the *khon isan*, it is the latter interpretation which is the more appropriate. It would be tempting to argue that the Khorat Plateau (the physiographic entity which broadly coincides with the administrative region in the north-east, and to which we shall refer when discussing the period before the 'full' incorporation of the Khorat Plateau into the Thai state in the 18th century) has always represented a peripheral, economically backward part of 'Thailand'. However, there is growing archaeological evidence to suggest that parts of the region may have constituted an important and, at the time, quite advanced nucleus of early settlement during the 2nd and 1st millennia BC (Higham and Kijngam 1982). Only with the region's incorporation into the great Khmer Empire centred on Angkor did its fortunes change quite dramatically and its peripherality begin (Keyes 1967). Thereafter, the region acted principally as a 'buffer zone' between the Khmer and Siamese and, later, the Siamese and Lao kingdoms (Lan Chang). Only with the decline of Lan Chang in the late 17th century and the growing strength of Ayutthaya were moves made to incorporate the north-east into the Thai state, with a short abatement following the Burmese siege of Ayutthaya in 1767 (Hall 1970). Thereafter, the region functioned as little more than a peripheral outpost of the Siamese kingdom. During the colonial era the presence of the French in Indo-China prevented the kingdom's spread further north-eastward, and led, ultimately, to the establishment of the present boundaries of the north-east. Only at the beginning of the 20th century did the north-east emerge as a distinct geo-political entity (Keyes 1967).

The north-east, and thus the people of Isan, has remained largely marginal and peripheral to developments in modern-day Thailand ever since. The considerable boost to the country's export economy which followed the signing of the Bowring Treaty in 1855, and the opening up of the country to world trade, largely passed the north-east by. The most significant initial impact was felt in the field of rice production, and it was the fertile Central Plains of the Menam Chao Phrya which were best suited and situated to capitalize on this. Even at the beginning of the present century, no more than two per cent of the country's rice exports emanated from outside the Central Region (Van der Heide 1906; referred to in Ingram 1971). The Central Plain had cheap and relatively easy transport access to the main seaport facilities of Bangkok, via a complex system of natural and person-made waterways which criss-crossed the flood plain of the Chao Phrya River. The flatness of terrain was also conducive to the development of irrigation facilities, and the region's close proximity to the financial institutions centred in Bangkok bestowed further locational advantages. The north-east, on the other hand, was faced with a variety of environmental, locational and even cultural barriers to its fuller involvement in the country's export trade and, more generally, economic development during the first half of the 20th century.

Although there is little doubt that the north-east is geographically marginal, the operative forces are not only geographical peripherality but also economic and political marginality. It is notable, for example, that north-easterners in Bangkok, arguably the primate city *par excellence*, still feel marginalized (and thus a minority) despite their location at the heart of the Thai world. It is therefore important to see in the north-east's case a coincidence of geographical peripherality and economic and political marginality allied to cultural/ethnic differentness (a point that is developed in the next section). A critical distinction here is that while the former condition is spatial, the latter two are structural. Admittedly there is an element of circular argument in the above: the region's peripherality promotes underdevelopment and this in turn accentuates peripherality. None the less, the roots of the explanation in each case are different and therefore the 'solutions' will probably be different too.

As we shall see in the next section, Thailand's recent economic boom has done little to change the geographical pattern of polarized growth which began to emerge during the late 19th century. Bangkok has become the pre-eminent focus of economic activity, political decision-making and both public and private investment (in this sense, every region of the country is marginal to Bangkok; it is just that the north-east is more marginal than any other). At the same time, the north-east has fallen further and further behind other parts of the country in terms of its contribution to GDP, average income levels and general standards of welfare and material well-being.

Thus the geographical peripherality, and associated economic disadvantage, of the *khon isan* may be used as a starting point in our attempt to define them as an 'ethnic minority'. It is the sense of *relative* deprivation and subordination which underpins their differentiation from the 'majority' group in Thai society, both historically and contemporaneously. According to Griessman (1975), subordination and relative deprivation are much more important in identifying the 'minority' status of a particular ethnic group than the numerical size of the group relative to another. In this sense the *khon isan* may constitute a fairly large peripheral ethnic minority in Thailand.

An interesting counterpoint to the above is the case of Malaysia. Here, the economically dominant Chinese, constituting 30 per cent of the population, are regarded by many, and by themselves, as a minority group. This is because of the feeling and the reality that ultimate political power lies, and will always lie, with the Malays (who make up 60 per cent of the population, although this figure also includes other *bumiputras* ('sons of the soil') such as the aboriginal Orang Asli of the Peninsula and the Dayaks of East Malaysia). Paradoxically, there is also some mileage in the argument that the Malays perceive themselves to be a 'minority' too, in the sense that they are economically disadvantaged *vis-à-vis* the Chinese. Thus, although the Malays in Malaysia may wield clear political power and be in numerical ascendancy, policies of positive discrimination have been introduced to narrow the gap between them and the economically dominant Chinese. The Malaysian example illustrates the complex manner in which minority status and perception may be manifested. It is also possible to take the line that in the Malaysian case, ethnic divisions are merely disguising far more important class-based distinction; the same might also be true, albeit to a lesser extent, in the case of Thailand.

To the spatial and economic perspective outlined above, we may now add a cultural dimension, which has served to emphasize the 'differentness' of the *khon isan* as manifested in their collective self-identity, which in turn has been moulded by myriad social and political processes and has been manifested, ultimately, in their development experience.

Identity

Having a collective identity is a further important factor in determining the 'differentness' of one group from another. This identity may, in turn, emerge from such factors as ethnicity, religion, language, skin colour, location, isolation, segregation and so on. It may either be endogenous, in that the strength and cohesiveness of a social group draws it together in a degree of perceived 'sameness' (intra-group identity); or it may be imposed on a society from outside, through such things as racism, discrimination, prejudice, attitudes and stereotypes (inter-group identity).

Whatever the precise nature and cause of a group's collective identity, it is seldom a static phenomenon. There are a number of processes which may operate either to strengthen a group's sense of identity (a process we will refer to as intra-group 'fusion', which may broadly parallel inter-group fission), in the process establishing significant barriers to inter-group interaction and integration; or, perhaps more typically, to weaken the foundations of a groups's identity (intra-group 'fission', inter-group fusion), in the process dismantling certain barriers to integration and assimilation. In the former sense, a minority group may come into being where a group identity develops which serves to highlight its 'differentness' from another group(s): '[a] minority group is not fully formed . . . . until it develops into a social unit, whose members are aware of their common identity and common interests' (Griessman 1975). This identity, and thus intra-group fusion, may result from the treatment of the group by the 'majority' or perhaps we should use the word 'dominant', society, which in turn may form a powerful barrier to inter-group fusion. This may be prevented by the majority society through such phenomena as ethnic and racial discrimination, creating a generally hostile environment which is not conducive to inter-group communication and integration. Occupational or educational discrimination may also prevent members of minority ethnic groups from having the opportunity to become socially mobile. The group's preference for intra- as opposed to inter-group social interaction may provide a further barrier to integration and may be influenced by such factors as religion, language, occupational specialization, spatial isolation or segregation and so on.

In the latter sense, the dismantling of group identity may relate to a group's need, willingness or opportunity to become a more fully integrated part of the wider society. There are a number of processes and phenomena which can serve to break down the rigidity of inter-group boundaries. For instance, in the interests of national security perhaps, governments may institute policies or programmes of national integration, perhaps involving the resettlement of minority groups; they may enact positive discrimination in their favour; development programmes may be targeted at economically depressed peripheral areas in order to reduce any sense of relative deprivation among the inhabitants; educational programmes may be introduced which aim at establishing a common language and common identity (typically, one which is built around that of the majority social group(s)) and so on. The passage of time is perhaps the most effective instrument in breaking down barriers between different ethnic groups: second, third and subsequent generations may more readily adopt an identity which is perhaps an amalgam of their own and that of the majority society; migration, as we will see, is an important process in bringing together and, over time, engendering a greater fusion (through assimilation and acculturation) of peoples of different ethnic and social backgrounds.

In almost all cases, though, it appears that the narrowing of the social distance which separates minority from majority inevitably necessitates the former adopting many of the cultural and behavioural traits of the latter, rather than *vice versa*. The speed of this transformation may be determined by such factors as the cultural distance which separates the two groups; the size and composition of the respective groups; and their spatial proximity and distribution: 'when a minority group is concentrated in one geographical area, assimilation is less likely to occur than when it is widely dispersed' (Keyes 1989).

The historical experience of the *khon isan* provides an appropriate illustration both of the historical process of inter-group fission (and thus intra-group fusion), wherein we can identify the origins and development of a distinctive common identity resulting largely from the attitudes and behaviour of the dominant groups in society towards the people from the north-east; and a more recent tendency towards fusion as a result of such processes as migration, development and modernization in Thailand today. In the discussion which follows, and in the next section, we shall argue that these respective processes of fission and fusion have been closely mirrored in the development experiences of the *khon isan*.

In the case of the *khon isan*, there are a number of events and processes which have taken place during their recent history which have served first to *create* and second to *strengthen* their sense of common identity. In the main this identity has been built around their own perception of discrimination, subordination and neglect at the hands of the dominant Central

Plains Thai: it is here that we can identify the emergence of a 'we–they' (or, if you like, minority:majority or subordinate:dominant) dichotomy which Keyes has argued, in the context of the north-east, is an important first step in the evolution of an ethnic and regional identity (Keyes 1967, p.vii).

The 'subordination' of the *khon isan* has principally resulted from the extension and consolidation of Central Thai control and influence in the region. As such, there is little point in going back any further than the late 19th century. As we have noted, before 1893, while constituting a part of the Siamese kingdom, the north-east existed as a fairly autonomous territory which was administered in the form of semi-autarchic principalities which were subject to the Siamese crown (Fallon 1983). Siamese influence was effectively channelled through the heads of important local families, who were more or less left to get on with things as they saw fit, provided they maintained a semblance of order in their domains and also supplied tribute (corvée labour or local products) to the Siamese crown. By constantly juggling these principalities, the Siamese were able to prevent any one centre from becoming too powerful and influential, and thus threatening the authority of the Siamese state.

In essence it was the expansion of French imperialism in Indo-China, and especially the growing French presence in Laos in the early 1880s, which precipitated moves by the Siamese to consolidate their control over the Khorat Plateau as a means of protecting the territorial integrity of the nation. In 1893, following the Paknam Incident (an example of French gunboat diplomacy, when two French Navy vessels sailed up the Chao Phrya River towards Bangkok), the Siamese ceded to French Indo-China all former tributary areas east of the Mekong and later some territory on the right bank of the river in 1904. The Mekong, as opposed to the Annamite Cordillera, became the line of demarcation between Siam and French Indo-China (Fallon 1983, p.199).

The administrative system which was then in place in the north-east made the region appear particularly vulnerable to further territorial concessions to the French. The Siamese responded by imposing direct authority over the region. Acting through Prince Damrong (the cousin of one of the great reforming monarchs, King Chulalongkorn), who headed the newly established Ministry of Interior, a series of new administrative units (*monthon*) was established, each headed by a governor appointed by, and answerable directly to, the Siamese crown. The word 'Isan' was used to describe one of these *monthon*. There is considerable significance in this in that 'Isan' is a Pali/Sanskrit word for 'north-east'. Thus not only do we find *isan* being used to describe (at least part of) the region, but we also find the region being referred to, largely for the first time, in geographical terms relative to the centre of the Siamese state (Fallon 1983, p.198). A sense of subordination emerges clearly from this situation, as does a feeling of peripherality in that, in spite of attempts being made to draw the region more fully into the national framework, these were being undertaken rather more for strategic reasons than as a sign of any altruistic concern to promote a wider degree of national integration and development.

The first evidence of resistance to this state of affairs (resistance perhaps being seen as a reaction to the sense of subjugation) came in the form of the *Phu Mii Bun* Rebellion of 1901–2. A handful of local 'holy men' (messianic leaders) were able to build upon a prevailing sense of discontent about the imposition of direct Siamese authority to organize what Edward Fallon has suggested might have represented a formal armed challenge to the legitimacy of the Siamese administration in the region. Following some early successes, including the capture of Khemmarat, an urban centre near Ubon Ratchathani, the rebellion, which involved a force several thousand strong, was quashed by the superior Siamese forces, the leaders executed and the movement disbanded. That was effectively that, as far as resistance was concerned, until the post-war period (there is a nice sense of irony in the fact that a latter-day reaction is also taking place in Thailand's peripheral regions, especially the north and the north-east, to a prevailing sense of disadvantage and the extertion of external (largely economic) influence, in which religious leaders in the form of 'development' and 'socially engaged' monks are playing a leading role).

While Siamese control in the region was consolidated, and the potential threat of French hegemony forestalled (although not necessarily by the actions of the Siamese), the north-east was viewed very much as an isolated backwater by the central administration. Generally, the weakest and most corrupt officials were posted to the region, principally as a form of punishment: Fallon has likened the north-east in this sense to a 'Thai Siberia'. The people of Isan clearly benefited little from such a state of affairs. The underlying aim of the extension of administrative control in the region was strategic rather than developmental. Government investment in the region was minimal; at the same time the development of taxation systems facilitated a significant drain of revenue from the region towards the centre. It was such phenomena which underpinned a growing sense of deprivation and exploitation at the hands of the Siamese administration and which may indeed have laid the foundation for the emergence of a 'common identity'. Also, while linkages with the central state were all the time being consolidated, the relative isolation and peripherality of the region from the Central Plain, together with, as we have described earlier, the common ethnic and cultural characteristics of the *khon isan*, may have strengthened the *regional* nature of this identity. Thus we begin to detect what Keyes and others have referred to as 'regionalism'.

It is important to ask at this point whether there was anything *qualitatively* different in the way that the central Thai government dealt with the north-east as opposed to the other regions of Thailand. In a sense, the north and the south have suffered in the same way as the Isan region, albeit to a lesser extent. Thus it is not just in the north-east that we find millenarian rebellions, the development of separatist movements and a growth in local 'identity'. But, the interesting thing about the case of the *khon isan* is that regionalism and ethnic identity are virtually synonymous. Certainly, in the period before the Second World War, there were few Thai-Lao living permanently outside the north-east as it was then defined (although there was some seasonal migration of *khon isan* to work on Central Plains farms (Johnston 1975), together with the traditional short-term 'going about' (*pay thiaw*) of Isan men which also took them quite far afield). Thus not only do we have a situation wherein intra-group interaction and communication have been relatively unrestricted, thus underpinning the development of a reasonably tight common identity, but because the level of communication with ethnic groups outside the region was, until quite recently, restricted by the isolation and peripherality of the north-east, there have not been in place the kinds of processes and opportunities which might have facilitated a greater level of inter-group interaction. Thus it would appear that the origins of a regional identity among the *khon isan* may have had a great deal to do with the peripherality of the Khorat Plateau to the main centre of political power and decision-making in the Siamese state.

Since the Second World War, a rather different set of processes has operated to bolster regionalism in the north-east. Both Charles Keyes and Edward Fallon have claimed that the process whereby the Isan region became more fully integrated within the Thai state, and at the same time linked with the central region, gave added momentum to the development of a regional identity. As a result of improvements in communications, both between Bangkok and the north-east and also within the region, a greater level of movement of population between the regions was facilitated. In general, this movement consisted of a small number of Central Thai government officials being posted to the 'Thai Siberia' and a considerable volume of migration of north-easterners towards the Central Plain. This latter movement was in part enforced by the growing taxation burden which was imposed on the region's population; but especially by the nature of the physical environment in the north-east – poor soils, unpredictable climate, periodic flooding and drought etc. The limited investment in infrastructure, particularly irrigation, meant that little had been done to offset such environmental influences on the regional (i.e. agricultural) economy. Migration to the central region thus became an important means of both supplementing meagre agricultural incomes and meeting taxation demands. Following the cessation of mass Chinese immigration to Thailand after the Second World War, migrants from the north-east were able to fill many of the lower-paid, unskilled positions which had previously been taken by newly arrived ethnic Chinese.

Inter-regional migration served to heighten the sense of regional identity in two important ways. First, north-easterners became more fully aware of the relative dynamism and wealth of the central region (linked to a post-war boom in the commercial agricultural economy in which the north-east had hardly shared at all: Keyes 1967, p.37), and this served only to heighten their sense of relative deprivation and neglect by central government. Second, migrant workers were very much treated as second, or even third-class citizens by the more affluent, sophisticated and better-educated Central Thai, who conjured up a number of stereotypical images of the *khon isan*, most of them negative and derogatory: backward, ignorant, rustic, inferior and so on. Francis Cripps, who worked as a school teacher in the north-eastern province of Mahasarakham in the early 1960s, writes of the response of some Bangkokians when they heard that he was venturing to the region to live and which illustrates the view from the 'centre': ' "Mahasarakham?" they asked. "Where is that? . . . . Oh! In the northeast?" They looked at me with pity. Communist infiltrators, drought, hard, unpalatable glutinous rice – these were the hazards of life on the neglected . . . . north-eastern plateau,' (Cripps 1965, p.15).

In relation to the processes of 'fusion' and 'fission' that we mentioned earlier, such attitudes and reactions had the effect of drawing the migrant north-easterners closer together: if you like, putting up a collective shield to protect themselves from abuse, discrimination and ridicule. Migration and spatial interaction thus served to heighten the sense of 'we–they' which is argued to be important in the development of a separate identity. Whereas the term *'khon isan'* had formerly been used by non-Isan people to describe these poor and unfortunate persons from the north-east, it very soon became used by the north-easterners to describe themselves. This, too, might be seen as evidence of an emerging common identity.

Not only did these 'external' forces have the effect of strengthening their collective identity but so too did various 'internal' factors – common language, common dietary preferences (which often led to migrant north-easterners eating at the same stalls selling Isan food), common tastes in music and drama (e.g. north-eastern folk drama, *mor ram*). Robert Textor's seminal work on northeastern migrant *samlor* drivers in Bangkok provides a very insightful account of the extent to which, and the means by which, the *khon isan* were drawn together by the circumstances of their migration to Bangkok (Textor 1961). A number of regional migrant associations (institutions) was established in Bangkok to help north-easterners to adapt to life in the alien, and often hostile, world of the capital city. These too served – and continue to serve – further to facilitate the strengthening of a common regional identity.

Several other factors have served to strengthen not only the sense of common identity but also the perception of subordination which is felt by the *knon isan* and which might be used to support the argument that they constitute a minority in Thailand. Perhaps the most significant of these was the assassination in 1949 of four Isan MPs amid growing concerns in central Thailand about the emergence of Isan separatism. The overthrow of the absolute monarchy in 1932, and the gradual development of a parliamentary 'democracy', provided for the first time a national platform from which representatives from the north-east could express their concern about the relative economic backwardness and neglect of the region. During the 1940s, Isan representatives created a lobby against alleged economic and political discrimination by the central government (Bell 1969).

In the main, northeastern MPs allied themselves with the civilian branch of the Thai political system and thus were usually placed in opposition to the more powerful and dominant military factions. Many north-eastern politicians had also been quite centrally involved in the Free Thai Movement, which developed in reaction to the Japanese occupation of Thailand during the war, and which therefore also stood in opposition to Phibun Songkhram's largely pro-Japanese government of the time. A number of north-eastern MPs also held important positions in the post-war government of Pridhi Phanomyang which had expressed support for the emerging nationalist movements in Indo-China (Fallon 1983, p.210). When Phibun Songkhram returned to power in 1947, Pridhi went into exile, and his north-eastern allies were branded for their alleged objective of Isan separatism and pan-Laoism (drawing together the Lao peoples in north-east Thailand and Laos), which also had communist overtones. Following an abortive coup in 1949 which was aimed at re-establishing Pridhi in power, four of the region's most prominent MPs, including two former cabinet ministers, were arrested and, in March 1949, subsequently killed by police on the outskirts of Bangkok (the so-called 'Kilometre 11 Incident') while being transferred between prisons, allegedly while trying to escape. Two other north-eastern MPs were later brought to trial for their separatist and communist tendencies but, possibly because of the public outcry which followed the Kilometre 11 Incident, they were found not guilty. One was later assassinated.

These events simply added to the prevailing feeling of subordination amongst north-easterners. Even the political process, whereby representatives from the north-east might have been able to influence government policy in the region's favour, had apparently been subverted in favour of the more powerful central regime. Political power had, it appeared to them, become the prerogative of the central Thai. These men had been killed because they were north-easterners. Thereafter, they became symbols of a growing resentment and sense of being discriminated against and this, in Charles Keyes's words (1967, p.17) 'provided a catalyst for the development of a regional political identity'.

The notion of separatism itself must also be viewed in terms of the prevailing sense of desperation in the north-east about the position of the region in the national political and economic set-up. An allegation which was levelled against the separatist MPs was that they wanted the north-east to join with Indo-China in a communist-dominated South-East Asia Union. There was certainly a close parallel between the growth of separatist sentiments and the expansion of the Communist Party of Thailand (CPT) in the north-east. It has been argued that three factors contributed to the attractiveness of the CPT to the region's disgruntled population: first, the repressive actions of the Phibun government against MPs from the north-east; second, the north-easteners' growing sense of alienation from the central Thai; and third, the generally depressed state of the regional economy. This is given added weight by Keyes's claim that support for the CPT in the north-east was motivated as much by ethnic as by class concerns (Keyes 1989, p.108). However, support for the CPT in the north-east was limited and rather diffuse. At its peak, the CPT may have had 12 000–14 000 armed insurgents in the country as a whole, and only some 5000 in the north-east, although there were some two million villagers who were subject to a certain degree of communist influence and as many as 200 000–300 000 people under the direct control of the CPT. Since then, the strength of the CPT has very quickly waned, to the extent that there are only very small and isolated pockets left today, mainly in southern Thailand.

With the above in mind, it is worth stressing that during the years of the 1970s when it appeared to some that Thailand was about to become the next 'domino' to fall in South-East Asia (an editorial in the *Journal of Contemporary Asia* in 1978 stated, quite plainly, that 'Thailand is in crisis. Momentum is gathering towards full-scale civil war. A level of class struggle unimaginable until a few years ago . . . . now pervades the greater part of the country' . . .), it was not just the government – through its policies of neglect – that was contributing to the growth of a regional identity. The CPT saw regionalism as fertile ground for fermenting revolution and played this card to considerable effect – as it also did in the north (among the hill peoples) and in the south (among the Thai Muslims). Interestingly, and rather paradoxically, the Thai government has also tried to institutionalize distinctiveness by supporting it. In the south for example, King Bhumibol gives prizes to contestants in Koran-reading competitions thus, it is hoped, castrating the forces of separatism.

The recognition of a regional identity can be used constructively if it promotes the perception that such identities are valued and respected as an integral part of – in this case – the Thai experience. But at the same time, superior and discriminatory policies towards groups such as the Isan are likely to give rise to a different tenor of identity, one that is separatist rather than integrationist. We should add that a debate of this type has been under way in Indonesia for some years with respect to the Chinese and the so-called *masalah Cina* or 'Chinese problem'. There are those who favour assimilation and those who see integration as the answer. The latter argue that the Chinese should be accorded the status of a *suku*, or ethnic group, and thus become an integral – but separate – part of Indonesian society. The assimilationists meanwhile maintain that only dissolving the Chinese within Indonesia's dominant Malay-Muslim group will solve the 'problem' (see Tan 1991).

There have of course been strong suggestions that the emergence of communist insurgency and calls for separatism resulted from considerable external influence in regional affairs of the north-east, either from Beijing or Hanoi or both. While there is little doubt that the various irredentist movements received considerable external support, Peter Bell has claimed that: 'Rather than a foreign-inspired and foreign dominated "peoples' war" the . . . . conflict in the northeast appears "a complex of lawlessness, political dissidence and popular disaffection led by a number of political and social figures" '(Bell 1968).

In general, separatism in the north-east appears to have been built around attempts to remove the region from the spectre of centra Thai control and domination, rather than to engender a greater degree of pan-Lao union. Charles Keyes claimed that: 'One of the present-day manifestations of Isan regionalism is an attempt to foster a sense of ethnic identity in the face of Central Thai pressures, without necessarily equating such a quest with the weak "national" destiny, both historically and currently, of the Lao' (Keyes 1967, p.13). In other words, although 'Lao-ness' provides an important basis for the development of such an identity, it represents a genuinely regional rather than transnational identity (it should also be borne in mind that the vast majority of ethnic Lao (some four-fifths) are found in Thailand, not Laos).

We leave the final word in this section to Charles Keyes

> . . . the role of the central Thai state, and the sense of relative neglect and deprivation has led many Isan people to see themselves as a disadvantaged regional minority . . . . Politicians from the region have played on the Isan peoples' feeling of living in a Thai-dominated world to promote the ethnoregional interests of the people of the North-East (1989, p.126).

Isan 'differentness' and uneven development today

The discussion thus far has emphasized how, through a series of historical processes and events, the people of Isan have become progressively subordinated, disadvantaged, marginalized and disenchanted. One consequence of such processes has been the emergence of a quite strong self-identity among the *khon isan* which has ethnicity and regionalism at its heart. It is clear also that the relative position of *khon isan* within the modern Thai state has underpinned their relative backwardness in a developmental sense. They have not enjoyed political representation and power which is commensurate with their numerical presence in Thailand. They have suffered from a sense of being discriminated against and looked down upon by their more 'sophisticated' and privileged Central Plains neighbours.

As will become clear in this section, the *khon isan* have not experienced to an adequate extent the opportunities and welfare benefits which have accrued to Thailand at the macro-level as a result of the country's growing involvement in the world economy, not least during the last decade or so. It should also become clear, however, that the ethnic dimension of this situation does not have the prominence that it may have had in the past; in any case, it is almost impossible to isolate the 'ethnic' from the social, economic, political and spatial dimensions of the more recent developmental experience of the north-east and the *khon isan*. That is to say, the people of Isan continue to endure, in much greater proportions than in many other parts of the country, the problems and difficulties associated with uneven development, but this may be attributable as much to the effects of the Thailand's strong commitment to capitalism and export-oriented industrialization, and the operation of the country's spatial economy in general, as to the influence of ethnicity *per se*. In other words, is the north-east merely a lagging region which just happens to be populated by an ethnic minority? Or do we have here an ethnic minority who have been subjected to discrimination which is reflected in lower than average incomes? A third possibility is that the poverty of the north-east is best explained not by regional backwardness *per se*, but by rural–urban inequalities (urban bias). The implications of this would be that a poor farmer in the north-east would have more in common with a poor farmer in the north, the south or Central Plains than with an urban resident in the north-east.

Although figures to support such a view are not easy to come by, a World Bank study conducted in the mid-1970s found that average urban household incomes in the north-east were 90 per cent of average urban household incomes for the kingdom as a whole (36 610 baht versus 40 730 baht). Taking into account lower costs of living in the Isan region, we might argue, therefore, that urban incomes are relatively consistent across the nation (World Bank, 1979, p.54). If we look at the progress of poverty reduction in Thailand (and the deficiencies in the data need to be stressed) over the last 13 years (see Table 10.1), while the incidence of poverty in urban areas nation-wide has more than halved from 12.5 per

Table 10.1 Thailand: poverty incidence and economic growth, 1975–6 to 1988

	1975/76	1981	1986	1988	1990
Poverty Lines (baht per capita per year, constant prices)					
Urban	2961	5151	5834	6203	
Rural	1981	3454	3823	4076	
Poverty Incidence (%)*					
By Community Type:					
All Municipal Areas	12.5	7.5	5.9	6.1	
All Sanitary Areas	14.8	13.5	18.6	12.2	
All Villages	36.2	27.3	35.8	26.3	
By Region:					
North	33.2	21.5	25.5	19.9	
North-east	44.9	35.9	48.2	34.6	
Central	13.0	13.6	15.6	12.9	
South	30.7	20.4	27.2	19.4	
Bangkok and vicinities	7.8	3.9	3.5	3.5	
Whole Kingdom	30.0	23.0	29.5	21.2	
Average Growth Rate of Real GDP Over Preceding Period (per cent annum)	5.9	7.5	5.2	11.5	16.0

*Poverty incidence was calculated by applying the rural poverty lines to sanitary areas

Source: Warr 1993.

cent (1975) to 6.1 per cent (1988), that in rural areas has declined more slowly, from 36.2 per cent to 26.3 per cent.

Thus ethnic identity is disguising more deep-seated class-based or rural/urban-based inequalities, and the people of the region are suffering from false ethnic consciousness (in the same way as noted above with respect to the Chinese and Malays in Malaysia).

Linked to this is the question of the unit of analysis. Regions, in a sense, cannot be deprived; people are deprived. It is just that in the case of the north-east a so-called 'lagging region' is inhabited by a distinct ethnic group. In addition, while regions are static spatial units, people are mobile and able to cross between regions and in and out of different sectors of the economy. Thus, there is a sense in which the poverty – ethnically defined – can, and does, shift from the north-east, to the Central Plains, to Bangkok and back again as poor Isan migrants search for work and a livelihood. Statistics tend to be derived from geographical units – villages, districts, provinces or regions – but the people who inhabit those spatial units rather annoyingly insist on moving in complex patterns embracing commuting, circulation, seasonal migration, temporary labour migration and so on. Indeed, most of these movements are not even acknowledged by the national census in Thailand.

The issue of 'rural' versus 'urban', and 'agriculture' versus 'industry', as it applies to Thailand's north-east, is an important one. T.G. McGee has argued that Thailand, and Asia in general, has a geographical characteristic which sets it apart from other parts of the world (see McGee 1989 and 1991): that is, the presence of high-density agricultural regions based on the intensive cultivation of wet rice. These regions have provided the basis for a process of *kotadesasi*. This term is taken from two Indonesian words – *kota* (town) and *desa* (village) – and is used to describe the urbanization of the countryside. McGee argues that Asia exhibits not city-based urbanization, but region-based urbanization where formerly agricultural populations are drawn into the processes of urbanization and industrialization, *in situ*. Although the north-east could not be equated with an Extended Metropolitan Region, there is a sense in which urban bias, and the much highlighted rural–urban dichotomy, is ersatz. As Koppel states:

> Linkages in the urban–rural relations debate are presented either as fundamentally derivative of urban or rural realities . . . . or as illusory misspecifications altogether . . . . There are good reasons now to argue . . . . for the reality of rural urban linkages not as derivations or reflections, but as representative and indicative of independent social facts (Koppel 1991, p.48).

This has important implications for how we measure wealth and poverty, how conditions in the north-east are assessed and what form a 'solution' might take.

In order to explore further the ethnic dimension of regional inequality in Thailand, this section will, first, outline very briefly the nature of uneven development as it presently manifests itself in Thailand and will offer some explanations as to why the north-east has continued to prop up the country's development 'league table' in spite of quite strenuous efforts on the part of the state to support development in the region. Second, it will explore the extent to which recent social and economic changes (i.e. over the last 25 years or so), and especially the process of migration, have influenced Isan identity, and the degree to which any such changes may have served to reduce the ethnic dimension in 'explaining' uneven development in Thailand today, at least as it concerns the north-east.

There is not space here to discuss in detail the ways in which the Thai government has sought to confront the phenomenon of uneven development in the country (Parnwell 1996). The main point, however, is that, since formal centralized development planning was introduced to the country in the early 1960s, policy statements have consistently emphasized the need to introduce regional development and poverty alleviation measures to support development in the north-east and in Thailand's other peripheral regions. There is in fact a close link between the kinds of problems which were outlined in the previous section and this apparent 'enthusiasm' for overcoming uneven development. The short interlude of communist-inspired insurgency, which was itself given added momentum by these difficulties, helped focus the minds of government planners and practitioners on finding solutions to the region's very pressing economic and social problems. A somewhat naive view expressed by the prime minister of the time (Field Marshall Sarit Thanarat) was that 'if the people's stomachs are full they won't turn to Communism'.

The backwardness of the north-east has also provided the foundation for a number of political careers. For example, the dictatorial Field Marshall Sarit, when he came to power following a coup in 1957, drew considerable popular support from the north-east by promising to bring development to the region (he was also a *khon isan*, from what is now *Changwat* (province) Mukdahan). The north-east was given special priority in the national Accelerated Rural Development Programme, and infrastructural investment became the cornerstone of the programme for promoting regional development in the north-east. Sarit helped conceive the first North-East Development Plan in the late 1950s. Underpinning these seemingly altruistic objectives, of course, was Sarit's concern to eradicate communism in the region.

More recently, the former commander in chief of the Thai armed forces, General Chaovalit Yongchaiyuth, sought in the late 1980s to underpin his own political ambitions by championing the so-called *isan khiaw* (Green Isan) programme in the region. The aim was to use the armed forces to support a second 'green revolution' in the north-east, centred on a large-scale and controversial reafforestation programme, linked particularly to silviculture of fast-growing tree species such as eucalyptus in support of the region's pulp and paper manufacturing industry. It was suggested by some cynics at the time that the programme represented little more than a move by General Chaovalit to gain the eye and support of the Thai royal family (essential in the political process in Thailand), which has rural development issues very close to its heart.

Whatever the political agenda which may have underpinned these attempts at regional development, much progress has been made over the last three decades. In essence the region has been brought much more squarely into the national planning framework as a result, first, of considerable investment in physical and social infrastructure. This has certainly reduced the region's earlier peripherality and isolation from the main centres of economic activity and has underpinned agricultural development strategies and a modicum of industrial development in the region. Second, the government's growing commitment to poverty alleviation (the north-east has the highest proportion of people below the official poverty line), which has on occasions taken the form of quite high-profile development projects and schemes (e.g. the Rural Job-Creation Programme, designed to alleviate seasonal unemployment and reduce seasonal out-migration). Third, sustained efforts to diversify and improve the region's agricultural economy, and to overcome considerable environmental constraints in subregions such as the *tung kula ronghai* (the so-called 'Weeping Plains' around Roi-et, Yasothon, Mahasarakham, Surin and Sisaket which is environmentally the most disadvantaged part of this disadvantaged region, with the highest concentration of poor and destitute in the whole country: see CUSRI 1981).

In spite of the greater seriousness with which the government – at least on paper and in public announcements – has taken the development problems of the north-east, and thus also the *khon isan*, the record of achievement in terms of reducing wealth and development differentials between the north-east and other parts of the country has been rather disappointing. Indeed, such differentials appear to have widened as a result of the recent boom which Thailand's economy as a whole has enjoyed, a situation which the government openly recognizes and seems willing to confront:

> Admittedly, the country has not achieved . . . . complete success in economic development. Environmental pollution, erosion of the quality of life in the cities, the inability of people to adjust themselves in accordance with the change from rural, agricultural to urban, industrial society and the increasingly unequal opportunity of various groups to benefit from the nation's successful development are the challenges awaiting the government. (*Thailand Foreign Affairs Newsletter* 9 December 1992).

It is also worth noting that although successive government – particularly since the Third Five-Year National Economic and Social Development Plan (1971–6) – have stressed the importance of promoting development in the north-east, words have not always been translated into deeds. The World Bank in a report released in 1978 noted

> the frequency and extent to which development plans appear to be disregarded in the allocation of administrative and financial resources and in the introduction of new policies, programs and projects [adding that in] recent years it has become increasingly difficult to discern a sense of direction and purpose in public sector behaviour that is in any way comparable to its stated intentions and objectives (World Bank 1978, p.28; see also Demaine 1986; Rigg 1991).

It is notable for example that the centrepiece of the Fifth Five-Year Plan (1981–6), the poverty eradication programme which was focused on the north-east, received only 0.7 per cent of the total budget.

However, we should perhaps also be aware of how we measure 'success' in regional development. The increased attention paid to the north-east from the 1960s was in no small sense a product of ethnically based security fears (as noted above). As Vandenbosch and Butwell observed at the time, the administration was 'running scared in the wake of the known subversive threat in that part [the north-east] of the land (1966). Today, those security fears have vanished and the CPT is comprehensively vanquished. In this sense, the political 'problem' has been

Table 10.2 Regional economic disparities in Thailand, 1987–1989

	Per Capital Gross Regional Product at Current Prices (baht) 1987	1988	1989	% Growth 1987–9
Bangkok Metropolis	73 061	90 889	105 357	44.2
% of Bangkok Figure	100.0	100.0	100.0	
Bangkok and Vicinity	69 065	82 241	96 239	39.4
% of Bangkok Figure	94.5	90.5	91.4	
Central Region	21 359	26 032	30 587	43.2
% of Bangkok Figure	29.2	28.6	29.0	
Eastern Region	31 165	36 320	45 751	46.7
% of Bangkok Figure	42.7	40.0	43.4	
Western Region	21 333	23 513	28 434	33.3
% of Bangkok Figure	29.2	25.9	27.0	
Southern Figure	17 519	20 329	21 955	25.3
% of Bangkok Figure	24.0	22.4	20.8	
Northern Region	14 361	17 097	18 833	31.1
% of Bangkok Figure	19.7	18.8	17.9	
North-eastern Region	9 193	10 698	11 981	30.3
% of Bangkok Figure	12.6	11.8	11.4	

Source: Thailand: National Statistical Office, 1992, *Statistical Handbook of Thailand, 1992*, Office of the Prime Minister, NSO, Bangkok

solved, and the initial *raison d'être* for promoting regional development has vaporized. The fact that most Isan people remain – relatively – just as poor as they were in the 1960s is, at least in these terms, of little importance. Statements of intent *vis à vis* regional underdevelopment legitimize inequality – something that the former prime minister, Chuan Leekpai, has done with his statement to focus government efforts on rural development.

Table 10.2 provides a fairly crude indication of the extent of uneven economic development in Thailand on a regional basis, although it should be borne in mind that these aggregate figures mask a considerable degree of intra-regional variation, not least between rural and urban areas. The north-east lags considerably behind the central region and, most notably, Bangkok. Thus, the per capita Gross Regional Product for the north-east was one-third (37 per cent) of the national average in 1989, 18.4 per cent of the figure for the central region as a whole and only some 11.4 per cent of that for Bangkok. Furthermore, the differential between the central region and the north-east has risen steadily since 1987, as a result of the considerably faster rate of economic growth in and around Bangkok, and in the eastern region, where the government has been investing heavily in creating a corridor of industrialization from the capital city to the Eastern Seaboard Development Region.

Further, circumstantial, evidence of the differential pace of development in Thailand can be gleaned from other sources. It has been Thailand's manufacturing sector which has grown, and which is expected to continue to grow, at the most impressive rate over the last few years, as Table 10.3 clearly shows. If it is then considered that Greater Bangkok accounts for by far the largest share of industrial activity (76.7 per cent in 1985, for example, compared with approximately 5.7 per cent in the north-east), it is not difficult to see where the benefits of rapid industrialization have accrued most directly. The agricultural sector, which contributes more than one-third of Gross Regional Product in the north-east, has performed, and will continue to perform, far less impressively. Furthermore, given that a very high proportion of construction and investment is taking place in the Bangkok–central region, it is not difficult to see how differentials may be expected to widen further in the immediate future.

There are other facets of uneven development which might be introduced here. In terms of political representation, for example, the situation has improved considerably since the immediate post-war period. The inability of the *khon isan* to draw attention to their economic and welfare difficulties through the democratic political process because of their subjugation by, and weakness relative to, the central Thai polity provided an important source of grievance in the past and may have played an important role in underpinning intra-group 'fusion'. To a large extent this has been overcome by the current political system in Thailand which allocates constituencies, and thus a presence in the House of Representatives, according to fairly strict numerical criteria: in up-country areas, around one MP per 300 000 persons (many fewer in Bangkok). This means that constituencies in the north-east now contribute around one-quarter to one-third of the total number of MPs in the House.

Until the political turmoil in May 1992, and the subsequent instatement of the Chuan government, a significant proportion of MPs from the north-east sat on the 'opposition benches' and thus had little direct power in the political process. Furthermore, we have to call into question the fairness of an electoral system which, at least until the latest election (and even then, by some accounts) was built upon the phenomenon of vote-buying (widespread in the north-east), which clearly does little to underpin the democratic process. Few north-eastern MPs may therefore have been committed to putting the interests of the north-east ahead of their own pursuit of economic return on their political 'investment'. Vote-buying also means that outsiders can quite easily buy themselves into constituencies in the north-east – playing on rural constituents' poverty ahead of their sense of regionalism. Table 10.4 shows that the situation changed quite significantly following the election on 13 September 1992, which brought to power the former government, headed by the leader of the largest (Democrat) of the coalition of four so-called 'Angel' parties (Democrat,

Table 10.3 Economic performance and projected performance by sector (%)

	1990	1991	1992	1993*	1994*	1995*	1996*
Real GDP Growth[1]	11.5	7.7	6.9	8.1	8.5	8.3	8.3
Agriculture[1]	–3.7	3.8	3.6	3.4	3.4	3.3	3.5
Manufacturing[1]	15.9	9.5	7.7	8.4	9.2	9.2	8.5
Construction[2]	22.0	10.5	4.5	6.0	4.4	6.0	–
Investment[3]	28.4	9.7	1.2	8.5	13.6	13.1	11.4
Export Growth[1]	14.4	23.6	15.3	15.3	14.3	14.3	13.6
Import Growth[1]	28.9	15.5	8.4	16.1	17.4	16.5	15.7

*Projection
[1]Thai Development Research Institute and National Economic and Social Development Board figures
[2]Siam Commercial Bank figures
[3]Bank of Thailand and Thai Development Research Institute figures

Source: *Bangkok Bank Monthly Review* 1993

Table 10.4 1992 General election results by region and party

	Bangkok	North-East	North	South	Central	Total	22 March 1992
Democrat*	9	17	8	36	9	79	44
Chart Thai	–	21	18	–	38	77	74
Chart Pathana	–	27	21	–	12	60	–
New Aspiration*	–	31	8	6	6	51	72
Palang Tham*	23	9	6	3	6	47	41
Social Action	–	15	3	–	4	22	31
Solidarity*	–	2	–	–	6	8	6
Seritham	–	4	2	–	2	8	–
Muan Chon	1	2	1	–	–	4	1
Prachakorn Thai	2	–	1	–	–	4	7
Rassadorn	–	–	1	1	–	1	4
Samakkhi Tham							79
United Democrat							1
Total	35	128	69	46	83	360	360

*Denotes the current ruling coalition

Source: Economist Intelligence Unit, *Country Report: Thailand and Myanmar*, 1992, No. 3, p.11; No. 1, p.13

New Aspiration, Palang Tham and Solidarity), Chuan Leekphai. It also shows that, with 128 seats, the north-east had a degree of representation in the House which was more or less commensurate with its demographic and territorial importance in the country as a whole.

Whatever the finer points of the Thai political process, there is little doubt that the north-east does now have better political representation than in the past and that this representation has been quite successful in drawing attention to the region's considerable development difficulties. The north-east is being taken much more seriously in political and developmental terms, and this is gradually having the effect of removing some of the factors which Keyes and others have argued were in the past important in strengthening a sense of regional identity centred, broadly, on ethnicity. On the other hand, there have been occasional reminders that the national power structure continues to be heavily biased in favour of the elites of the Central Plain. A particularly illuminating example in this regard concerned protests in early to mid-1990 in the central north-eastern province of Mahasarakham over illegal salt-mining (*Far Eastern Economic Review*, 7 June 1990). Although there is not space here to go into detail about the episode, it centred on the role played by businesspeople from Bangkok, including three government ministers, in actively supporting the illegal, and environmentally very damaging, activity of extracting salt from the rock strata which underlie much of the north-east. One consequence of this activity was the severe pollution of the fields of a reputed 300 000 farmers in the north-east, many of whom suffered a significant decline in their already precarious livelihoods as a result. On the other hand, the government ministers and other businesspeople stood to gain considerable financial advantage from this illegal activity, and the industrial activities associated with it, to which the then-Chatichai administration was content to turn a blind eye.

The most significant part of this episode, as far as this chapter is concerned, was the reaction of the government to the protests which accompanied the pollution resulting from illegal rock-salt extraction. Far from bringing the full force of the law down on those who had transgressed the 1967 Mineral Resources Act, and a ban imposed by Prime Minister Prem Tinsulanonda in 1980 (and, ironically, reaffirmed by Prime Minister Chatichai Choonhavan in 1989), the interior minister (now Prime Minister), Banharn Silpa-archa (who had been indirectly linked to the salt-extraction activities) was allegedly responsible for ordering out a paramilitary police force from Mahasarakham to break up the demonstrations, as a result of which some 40 protesting farmers and students were arrested and several also injured. This was quite illustrative of where the sympathies of the state truly lay on this particular occasion. Many other examples of elite domination arise across the country, from hotel construction on national park land in Phuket, to land speculation in the north, to the alienation of farmers from their land in the west. In Phuket, the process would not be viewed as indicative of ethnic deprivation and powerlessness, just the powerlessness of the poor at the hands of the rich. So again, although the north-east may suffer more than most regions, to argue that government/

elite action in the region is *qualitatively* different from that in other parts of the kingdom, and that this is in part derived from the north-east's distinct ethnicity, is arguing – and claiming – too much.

None the less, better, more effective political representation may be contributing towards a declining sense of deprivation, discrimination and differentness among the *khon isan* and thus may be weakening their sense of self-identity as a disadvantaged ethnic group. More important than the political process in this regard may have been the medium of education and the process of migration. For quite some time now it has been government policy for Central or Standard Thai to be the sole medium of education in Thailand. Clearly, factors such as nation-building, national identity, security and logistics underpin such a policy, but this, and the fact that regional history and regional culture are also largely excluded from the curriculum, can also be seen as a means by which Central Thai domination continues to be extended to, and maintained at, the periphery. It is the younger generations who are perhaps losing their Isan distinctiveness and identity fastest through this process, although most continue to use the Isan language at home.

We might add here that other media, especially television and radio, are further bringing the 'outside world' into an increasing number of homes in the north-east and may also be causing younger people in particular to question the value of their strong sense of identification with a region which possesses little by way of sophistication, modernity and excitement. The trappings of modernity and urbanization, both of which are clearly much more closely associated with Bangkok than with the depressed north-east, have in many cases become of greater importance to young *khon isan* than their traditional socio-cultural and ethnic roots in the north-east. Charles Keyes, has claimed:

> Until quite recently there has been little allowance for a positive expression of distinctive regional and ethnic identities in national culture. In popular films and fiction, the Lao dialects spoken by the people of the North-East are still often stigmatised as uncouth. The Northern accent is also sometimes presented in a patronising way. In school curicula, regional history is almost totally ignored (Keyes 1989, p.203).

On the other hand, James Elliott, writing in the *Annals of Tourism Research*, has identified something of a change in attitude more recently, principally because of the growth of tourism in Thailand (Elliott 1983, pp.377–93): costumes, customs and crafts have suddenly been found worthy of positive official recognition, leading to the commercialization of people's ethnoregional identities (whether they like it or not, it should be said, and principally in the interest of entrepreneurial elites from the central region). Although the north-east does not have such striking forms of costume and material culture as, for example, are found among the montagnard peoples of the northern region, it has managed to capitalize on the demand for handicrafts emanating from tourism and more generally Thailand's burgeoning export trade in craft products, and has benefited also from the Thai government's emphasis on culture as a cornerstone of its tourism promotion strategy for the 1990s (see Parnwell 1992, pp.234–57).

A final factor which has had perhaps the most profound influence on Isan self-identity, and which clearly links it very closely with the unevenness of the development process, has been the large-scale and sustained movement of people from the north-east to find work in Bangkok and elsewhere in the central region. Unfortunately we do not have space to look in detail at how migration, at least in more recent times, has gradually been breaking down the strength of the Isan regional identity (by contrast, see Textor 1961, who shows how the migration of north-easterners to Bangkok was instrumental in strengthening identity by emphasizing a very pronounced sense of discrimination and relative deprivation). Put very briefly, the imperatives of adaptation and acculturation which, to a greater or lesser degree, accompany any form of migration between two quite strongly contrasting economic, social and cultural environments, determine that, over time, migrants begin to take on some of the 'cultural traits' of their host society and, again over time, tend to lose some of their own cultural traits (see Parnwell 1993). There are a great many factors which may determine that this process of socio-cultural change takes place more readily in some groups than others, but one might argue that the phenomenal rates of migration from the north-east to the Bangkok–Central Region which are taking place today, set against a situation where discrimination and job marginalization are much less prevalent than in the past, are having a perhaps quite significant effect on the nature of Isan identity among migrants (but also within the region more generally as a result of return-migration), in the process reducing the sharpness of the 'we–they' dichotomy which was argued earlier in the chapter to be important in shaping self-identity.

While processes of development and change over the last two decades or so have therefore served to reduce the strength of feeling among *khon isan* about their disadvantage relative to other groups in society (even though they are still, in the main, quite badly disadvantaged), in the process diminishing some of the factors which created a sense of regional ethnic identity in the past, this does not suggest that Isan self-identity has died out – it simply gains expression in slightly different ways and for different reasons. Indeed, Isan identity is still alive and kicking. The cultural elements which underpin this identity – music, folk culture, art, dialect, diet – still provide the nucleus for this identity and, in spite of the onslaught of popular music and other trappings of modernity, things like *mor ram* performances (musical folk drama) still attract huge numbers of followers who can recharge their 'Isanness' through such media. Furthermore, there are inhabitants in squatter settlements in Bangkok who, although they may have been Bangkok residents for 30 or 40 years or more, still consider themselves *khon isan* first and foremost, partly because they still hold on to the prospect of return, perhaps because, in spite of the passage of years, they have maintained a small stake in their home areas (land, family), or maybe because they maintain a close association with other *khon isan* in their neighbourhood.

What we have, then, is a multi-layered identity, which is born out of the different realms of association of the *khon isan*:

- At the most superficial level, say with north-eastern migrant workers in Bangkok, they may choose to mask their identity in order more readily to blend in with their broader socio-cultural surroundings.
- North-eastern migrants in the company of other migrants may be 'more Isan than the Isan', exaggerating their identity with the region either for reasons of self-reassurance or as a way of proving their Isan credential among their peers.
- The *khon isan* at home may, because a different set of imperatives are in operation, have a stronger sense of *local* as opposed to *regional* or *ethnic* identity.
- It is also possible to hypothesize that people of different ages, sex, educational background and income are likely to be affected by these forces of acculturation–deculturation, to various degrees and in different ways. A young woman working in one of the brothels of Bangkok serving a Western clientele will have a completely different formative experience from a girl working as a servant in a Thai household in Bangkok, or a young man working in a chicken slaughterhouse surrounded by fellow workers also from the north-east (and perhaps from the same village) or a household travelling to a sugar cane plantation in the Central Plains *en famille* to work harvesting the crop during the dry season.

Missing out

This chapter has sought to interfuse discussion of the development experience of the *khon isan* with an assessment of the role played by the ethnic identity of this underprivileged group. It has suggested that, at least in the past, less so today, there is a quite close, two-way association between ethnicity and development. Using a broader definition of development than the economistic one which is most commonly employed, it was found that the disadvantaged, dependent and subordinate position in which the *khon isan* have historically found themselves has been an important factor in drawing them together into a reasonably cohesive ethnically defined 'group'. It may also be – although the evidence presented above is far less conclusive – that 'ethnicity' may have represented a factor in the attitude of the dominant 'majority' society towards the *khon isan*, or *khon lao* as they were typically referred to by their central region neighbours.

Although there are clearly a large number of non-ethnic factors which have also played an important role (indeed, probably a far more important role, particularly more recently: e.g. environment, geography, infrastructure, international politics), it is clear that there has been a close correlation historically between ethnic divisions in Thailand and relative development experiences. In simple terms, the Central Plains Thai have done appreciably better than the *khon isan* (and also the *khon muang* of the northern region). It is impossible to say, however, just how important the 'ethnic dimension' has been, in relative terms, in explaining this situation. None the less, historically there has been a quite sharp division of power and influence along ethnic lines, and it is these factors which have played an important role in the unevenness of the development process in Thailand.

During the last quarter of a century, however, the sharpness of identities in Thailand along ethnic lines has tended in many cases (perhaps to a lesser extent in the case of the 'tribal' societies of the northern mountains) to become more blurred, not least as a result of such processes as educational improvement, political emancipation, government intervention and inter-regional migration. In place of ethnic divisions, we increasingly find that uneven development is leading to a much sharper polarization of Thai society on the basis of social and economic position (or 'class'). Thus there are poor *khon klaang* (Central Plains Thai) just as there are poor *khon isan*, there are also many well-to-do and influential *khon isan*.

It is thus rather misleading to state that the *khon isan* are missing out on the current economic boom because of their ethnicity. The *khon isan* may indeed be 'missing out' – macro-economic data on a regional basis suggest this, as do contemporary high levels of population movement away from the region – but we hope we have demonstrated that the ethnic dimension in Thailand's recent development experience is certainly not as important as it may have been during the immediate post-war period. Instead, we would suggest this has much more to do with the way that development is 'done', or 'happens', in Thailand today.

Furthermore, migration, and a whole host of recent *in situ* development policy initiatives, have enabled the *khon isan* to capitalize on recent developments in the Thai economy to a greater extent than might otherwise have been the case if the region had continued in a relatively dependent, subordinate position. Thus, conditions for *khon isan* have improved during the last decade or so, although it is fair to say that they have tended to improve at a generally slower pace than elsewhere. Ironically, it may have been the various expressions of regional identity and cohesiveness during the 1960s and 1970s, and the threat this posed to national security and integrity, which contributed to the present, slightly more optimistic, if not entirely egalitarian, situation.

This case study of the *knon isan* has, we believe, demonstrated an occasionally close association between ethnicity and development in Thailand. The most important point about this association is that it is two-way: the historical subordination of an ethnic 'group' has for a long time been manifest in its relative disadvantage in developmental terms, and yet this uneven development has itself been responsible for the strengthening of a regional ethnic identity. Over time, this situation has caused government planners to take this ethnic group much more seriously in its development policies or otherwise run the risk of severe social and political disruption in the modern Thai state. As a result of this process, and also a more general intermixing of Thai society, not least through migration and the media, ethnic divisions are becoming increasingly blurred and are being replaced by a much clearer social and economic stratification of society (itself a consequence of uneven development). In this sense, the model of 'ethnodevelopment' which was developed by Hettne in the first chapter of this volume, to a large extent holds true for the *khon isan*: migration has enabled the *khon isan* to participate in the country's economic growth to a greater extent than might otherwise have been the case, while at the same time the government has achieved a modicum of success in bringing development to the impoverished north-east. In the process, it has helped to release some of the potential inherent in the people of the north-east and, at the same time, has reduced the prospects of conflict born of discontentment and a sense of deprivation and neglect.

Looking to the future, it seems almost certain that, to capitalize on the current economic boom (should it continue), north-easterners will have to continue to move to where the work is. The prospects of bringing the work to where it is quite desperately needed, i.e. within the north-east, would appear, like the region itself, to be rather remote. However, a final twist of irony may be that, as the former states of Indo-China open up to the 'outside world' (Laos and Cambodia a lot more slowly than Viet Nam), so transportation routes which traverse the north-east may become increasingly important and the region's longer-term prospects increasingly brighter. It remains to be seen, should such a situation transpire, how the *khon isan* will treat their more backward and rather less sophisticated neighbours.

References

Bell, Peter (1969) 'Thailand's Northeast: Regional Underdevelopment, "Insurgency" and Official Response', *Pacific Affairs*, 42(1), 47–54.

Chulalongkorn University, Social Research Institute (CUSRI) (1981) *Kula Ronghai Project: Review for Implementation*, Report submitted to the National Economic and Social Development Board, CUSRI, Bangkok.
Cripps, Francis (1965) *The Far Province*, Hutchinson, London.
Demaine, Harvey (1986) '*Kanpatthana*: Thai views of development' in M. Hobart and R.H. Taylor (eds), *Context, Meaning and Power in Southeast Asia*, Cornell University Southeast Asia Program: Ithaca, 93–114.
Dixon, C.J. (1977) 'Development, Regional Disparity and Planning: The Experience of Northeast Thailand', *Journal of Southeast Asian Studies*, 8(2), 210–23.
Donner, Wolf (1978) *The Five Faces of Thailand: An Economic Geography*, Hurst, London.
Economist Intelligence Unit (1992) *Country Report: Thailand and Burma, 1992/2*, London.
Elliott, James (1983) 'Politics, Power and Tourism in Thailand', *Annals of Tourism Research*, 10(3), 377–93.
Far Eastern Economic Review, 3 May 1990.
Fallon, Edward Bernard (1983) The Peasants of Isan: Social and Economic Transitions in Northeast Thailand, unpublished Ph.D. thesis, University of Wisconsin, Madison.
Feeny, David (1990) 'The Political Economy of Regional Inequalities in Developing Economies: The Northeast of Thailand' *Proceedings of the 4th International Conference on Thai Studies*, Volume II, 81–114, Kunming.
Fry, Gerald W. (1990) 'The Other Thailand: Prospects and Problems Related to the Development of the Northeast' *Proceedings of the 4th International Conference on Thai Studies*, Volume II, 115–48, Kunming.
Goodall, Brian (1987) *Dictionary of Human Geography*, Penguin, Harmondsworth.
Griessman, B. Eugene (1975) *Minorities: A Text with Readings in Intergroup Relations*, Dryden, Minsdale, Ill.
Hall, D.G.E. (1970) *A History of South-East Asia*, 3rd edition, Macmillan, London.
Higham, Charles F.W. and Amphan Kijngam (1982) 'Irregular Earthworks in N.E. Thailand: New Insight', *Antiquity*, 61, 102–10.
Higham, Charles F.W., Amphan Kijngam and Payom Chantaratiyakarn (1984) *Prehistoric Investigations in Northeast Thailand*, British Archaeological Reports, International Series, No. 231, Oxford.
Ingram, J.C. (1971) *Economic Change in Thailand, 1850–1970*, Stanford University Press, Stanford.
Johnston, David Bruce (1975) Rural Society and the Rice Economy in Thailand, 1880–1930, unpublished Ph.D. thesis, Yale University, New Haven.
Journal of Contemporary Asia (1978) Volume 8, 3–4.
Keyes, Charles F. (1966) Peasant and Nation: A Thai-Lao Village in a Thai State, Unpublished Ph.D. thesis, Cornell University, Ithaca.
Keyes, Charles F. (1967) *Isan: Regionalism in North-East Thailand*, Cornell University Southeast Asia Program, Data Paper No. 65, Cornell University, Ithaca.
Keyes, Charles F. (1989) *Thailand: Buddhist Kingdom and Modern Nation State*, Editions Duang Kamol, Bangkok.
Koppel, Bruce (1991) 'The Rural–Urban Dichotomy Reexamined: beyond the Ersatz Debate?' in Norton Ginsburg, Bruce Koppel and T.G. McGee (eds) *The Extended Metropolis Settlement Transition in Aisa*, University of Hawaii Press, Honolulu, 47–70.
Krongkaew, Medhi, Apichat Chamratrithirong and Varai Woramotri (1983) *A Study of Low-Income Households in the Northeastern Region of Thailand*, Research Report No. 74, Mahidol University, Institute for Population and Social Research, Salaya.

Kunstadter, Peter (1967) *Southeast Asian Tribes, Minorities and Nations*, Princeton University Press, Princeton.

LeBar, Frank M., Gerald Cannon Hickey and John K. Musgrave (1964) *Ethnic Groups of Mainland Southeast Asia* Human Relations Area Files, New Haven.

McGee, T.G. (1989) 'Urbanisasi or kotadesasi? Evolving patterns of urbanization in Asia' JC. Ma and Allen G. Noble (eds), *Urbanization in Asia: Spatial Dimensions and Policy Issues*, University of Hawaii Press, Honolulu, 93–108.

McGee, T.G. (1991) 'The emergence of Desakota Regions in Asia: Expanding a Hypothesis' in Norton Ginsburg, Bruce Koppel and T.G. McGee (eds), *The Extended Metropolis: Settlement Transition in Asia*, University of Hawaii Press, Honolulu, 3–25.

Parnwell, Michael J.G. (1988) 'Rural Poverty, Development and the Environment: The Case of North-East Thailand', *Journal of Biogeography* 15(1), 199–208.

Parnwell, Michael J.G. (1991) 'Rural Industrialisation and Development Planning in Thailand', *Southeast Asian Journal of Social Science* 18(2), 1–28.

Parnwell, Michael J.G. (1991) 'Confronting Uneven Development in Thailand: The Potential Role of Rural Industries', *Malaysian Journal of Tropical Geography*, 22(1), 51–62.

Parnwell, Michael J.G. (1992) 'Tourism and Rural Handicrafts in Thailand' in Michael Hitchcock, Victor T. King and Michael J.G. Parnwell (eds), *Tourism in South-East Asia*, Routledge, London, 234–57.

Parnwell, Mike (1993) *Population Movements and the Third World*, Routledge Introductions to Development Series, Routledge, London.

Parnwell, Michael J.G. (1996) *Uneven Development in Thailand*, Avebury, Aldershot.

Rigg, Jonathan (1987) 'Forces and Influences Behind the Development of Upland Cash Cropping in North-East Thailand', *The Geographical Journal*, 153, (3), 370–82.

Rigg, Jonathan (1991) 'Grass-roots Development in Rural Thailand: A Lost Cause?', *World Development* 19(2–3), 199–211.

Tan, Mély G. (1991) 'The Social and Cultural Dimensions of the Role of Ethnic Chinese in Indonesian Society', *Indonesia*, 1991, 113–25.

Textor, Robert B. (1961) *From Peasant to Pedicab Driver: A Social Study of Northeastern Thai Farmers*, Southeast Asian Studies: Cultural Report No. 9. Yale University, New Haven.

Vandenbosch, A. and R. Butwell (1966) *The Changing Face of Southeast Asia* University of Kentucky Press, Lexington.

Warr, Peter G. (1993) *Thailand's Economic Miracle*, Thailand Information Papers no. 1, National Thai Studies Centre, Australian National University, Canberra.

Wijeyewardene, Gehan (ed.) (1990) *Ethnic Groups Across National Boundaries in Mainland Southeast Asia*, ISEAS, Singapore.

World Bank (1978) *Thailand: Towards a Development Strategy of Full Participation*, World Bank, Bangkok.

World Bank (1979) *Income, Consumption and Poverty in Thailand, 1962/63 and 1975/76*, World Bank Staff Working Paper no. 364, Washington DC.

11 Ethnic differences and public policy in Singapore

Peggy Teo and Ooi Geok Ling

Introduction

The Singapore of the 1990s is often cited as a 'success' story of development (Sandhu and Wheatley 1989). With a GNP per capita which grew from US$1216 in 1972 to US$10 450 in 1990 (World Bank 1991), this is not a surprise. Singapore is an exemplar of a country which has managed to marry ethnicity with development, thereby questioning the notion suggested by Hettne in Chapter 2 that development is concerned with ' "state" or "national economies" as basic units which precludes a serious treatment of the ethnic factor'.

The economic and social transformations which took place to bring Singapore from independence in 1965 to what it is today were a series of carefully planned events. The government had first to take into account the plural society it inherited. Made up of immigrants who saw themselves as sojourners rather than citizens, the People's Action Party (PAP), which has been in power since independence, had the daunting task of moulding a population so that individual as well as ethnic and communalistic interest were put aside for society's interests. Ethnic ideals were supplanted by the national ideal which was cogently the development of a national economy with a high level of economic growth. While the government did encourage each of the diverse cultural groups to preserve its own identity, it did not tolerate inter-ethnic conflict or prejudices. Instead, strict enforcement of racial harmony enabled the politically stable and economically thriving state to emerge today. Every ethnic group is permitted expression of its cultural values and codes of behaviour: e.g. the Religious Harmony Bill ensures that no one religion tries to impose itself on another; although English is the language medium used in businesses, Malay is the official national language; in schools, children can opt for two first language (English with Malay or English with Mandarin) so that

Ethnicity and Development: Geographical Perspectives. Edited by Denis Dwyer and David Drakakis-Smith.

they are proficient in both and therefore less likely to lose their cultural heritage.

While the government endeavoured to create a multiracial, multicultural, multireligious and multilinguistic society which is inherently equal in its treatment of the various ethnic groups, social and economic heterogeneity are difficult to manipulate and not all races can emerge equal in all measures of development or status (for examples within South-east Asia, see Evers 1980; Snodgrass 1980; Anand 1983; Robison *et al.* 1987; Dwyer 1990; King and Parnell 1990). What has happened in Singapore is that over the years, virtually the whole population, regardless of ethnicity, has improved its socio-economic condition. For instance, the literacy rate reached 90 per cent in 1990; home ownership 87.5 per cent in 1990; life expectancy 74 years; and infant mortality was 8/1000 live births in 1989. The GDP grew at an average annual growth rate of 6.1 per cent between 1980 and 1989 of which 74 per cent of GDP in 1989 was from services (Department of Statistics 1990; World Bank 1991).

However, certain patterns of inequalities between races still exist. This chapter traces the historical basis of the multiracial origins of the population to provide an understanding of how the inequalities came about. Current indices of ethnic stratification are also provided to underpin the logic which may have influenced government decision-making in policy formulation. Specifically, two areas of policy will be investigated in greater detail: population size and housing. These are selected because they constitute two critical issues in Singapore's economic progress. Population has always been integral to the nation's development as there are no natural resources in the country. Moreover, human resources are what power the economic engines in Singapore, thereby ensuring it a place in planning discourse. Housing policy is a complement to population policy and the largest component of the welfare programme. As Singapore grew, so her people needed to be sheltered. As early as the 1950s, the Singapore Improvement Trust (SIT), the precursor to the Housing and Development Board (HDB), was set up to deal with the housing of an expanding population. In the analysis of these two policies, it will be asked whether racial integration has been achieved and what the implications are arising from the policies. (For background reading see Ooi and Chiang 1969; Hassan 1976; Lee 1982; Chen 1983; Sandhu and Wheatley 1989; Quah *et al.* 1991; and Low and Toh 1992).

Ethnodevelopment in Singapore

The transition to Newly Industrializing Economy (NIE) status was for Singaporeans a consciously orientated and centrally planned drive with the goal of making Singapore into an economically viable, outward-looking society which is at the same time politically and socially cohesive. This was not an easy feat, as many South-east Asian countries discovered (see Evers 1980; Arief and Sundarum 1983; Hashim 1983; Hua 1983; Higgott and Robison 1985). As early as 1959, the government realized that the old infrastructure inherited from the British had to be improved especially in the areas of housing, public utilities, roads and community facilities. By the early 1970s, the policy of rapid economic development gained credence among the people. Singapore's viability was to be underwritten by attracting foreign capital, skills and enterprise from the international arena.

> Singapore's position has been that the major powers with world-wide economic, political and strategic interest will maintain their presence around the world. Consequently, it is prudent on the part of small states to devise policies that will seek to accommodate their presence . . . . Part of the explanation for Singapore's success is that the Republic has correctly set its priorities, *viz* that international relations must serve the goals of national development, with particular emphasis on economic growth Lau (as cited in Lee 1976, p.12).

These policies were propagated on the basis of public gain – the entire economic growth was directed at the people and the government deliberately distanced itself from subnational or ethnic groups. Such a tactic won the endorsement of the majority of the population and a whole generation of Chinese, Indians and Malays were persuaded to redirect their loyalty and identity toward Singapore rather than China, India or the Malay world respectively (Willmott 1989; Chua and Kuo 1991). By placing the emphasis on economic development first and delivering a strong infrastructure for business and the creation of jobs, Singapore can be said to be a practitioner of what Hettne terms as 'ethnodevelopment' in Chapter 1 of this volume. Each of the ethnic groups are self-deterministic but within a framework that delivers an economic surplus in which material welfare is accessible to all. Thus for Singapore, it is indeed a truism that a development strategy is also a strategy for nation-building.

The cultural ethos of Singapore is no longer composed of separate ethnic cultural interests but is made of economic rationality, productivity and meritocracy which encapsulate the local concept of a national culture or identity (Chan 1971; Quah 1990; Chua and Kuo 1991). However, these qualities which constitute the cornerstone of Singapore's development are unfortunately not universal and have not totally eradicated inter-ethnic differences. It is posited that because Singapore's ethnicity has overlapped with class consciousness, there has grown an increasing awareness of inter-ethnic differences. Such social differences between two main ethnic groups, Malays and Chinese, are not necessarily explosive but can undermine the progress that Singapore has made in developing her national identity of 'one people, one nation'. That Singaporeans are aware of these class differences is evidenced by the formation of self-help organizations such as Majlis Pendidikan Anak-anak Islam Singapura (MENDAKI), the Chinese Development Assistance Council (CDAC) and the Singapore Indian Development Association (SINDA). The main aim of each of these groups is to help the financially needy among them. That MENDAKI was the first to start up is telling. It records the realization that in terms of a socio-economic schism between the Malays and the Chinese, action had to be taken. Moreover, the entrepreneurial class of the Malays is being encouraged by Kongres Ekonomi Masyarakat Melayu-Islam Singapura (KEMAS or Singapore Malay Economic Association) in order to reduce the gap between the Malays and Chinese (*The Straits Times* 3 and 17 April 1993).

Before a full discussion of these issues can be developed, it would be appropriate at this point to examine first the historical background to Singapore's multiracialism.

Historical background of ethnic pluralism

Singapore has a short history of approximately 175 years which can be said to have started when Stamford Raffles representing the British East India Company bought the island from the Sultan of Johor in 1819. He saw in Singapore a strategic location for the growing trade between British India and China. With a sheltered harbour and deep waters, Singapore could also serve as a check to the northward advance of the Dutch in the East Indies. The free port proved to be a commercially sound investment and by 1823 exceeded Penang in the amount of trade.

When Raffles arrived, the indigenous people were 120 Malays and 30 Chinese. The population started to grow quickly. The free-port status attracted many Chinese from mainland China seeking fortune in the *Nanyang* (South Seas). It was in Singapore that they could hone their entrepreneurial skills and many became successful merchants. Immigrants also came from India, Britain and the Netherlands. Indians came mainly as labourers to work in the public-utilities system. Those more educated became civil servants. Forty years after Raffles set foot in Singapore, the Chinese outnumbered the Malays. Today the Chinese constitute 78 per cent, Malays 14 per cent, Indians 7 per cent and Others 1 per cent out of the total population of 2.7 million (Department of Statistics, 1992a).

The island's population therefore comprised largely immigrant people. Up to 1947, in-migration exceeded natural increase and was largely responsible for population growth. There was such an unequal sex ratio that the colonial government had to enact laws which allowed only wives and children of those already living in the colony to enter. Within each ethnic group, there was further diversity, which has remained today. The

Hokkiens, Teochews and Cantonese are the main dialect groups among the Chinese. Not only do they speak different dialects, other cultural traits like food preferences and preparation are also different. The Malays are similarly distinct from the Javanese and Boyanese, while the Indians are dominated by Tamils.

During the British tenure, the various ethnic groups were residentially segregated. Raffles stipulated that certain areas be set aside for the Europeans, Chinese, Bugis and Arabs. There was also segregation by occupation. Merchants could live near the central area as they had to trade. Artisans and labourers were given locations further away. Although the settlement pattern did not evolve exactly the way Raffles envisaged, there emerged a broad pattern similar to his ideas: the Chinese had their own geographical concentration in Chinatown in the central area, near the Singapore River where they could go on with their business of trade. Likewise the Indians congregated in Little India, not far from the central area. Many were employed to maintain public services. The Malays were much less distinct in their geographical distribution. They did not cluster near the town. Instead, they settled in peripheral areas near the sea, such as Changi, Geylang Serai and Pasir Panjang (Neville 1969). These ethnic enclaves did not pose many problems save for the three racial riots which occurred between 1964 and 1969 when Malays and Chinese clashed. Since then there have been no communal clashes.

Residential segregation of ethnic groups made it easier for the colonial government to govern the people. Not only were they geographically separated but within themselves there was so much diversity (as between the dialect groups or between caste in the case of the Indians) that they could not pose a serious challenge to the British (Lee 1991).

Furnivall (1980) defined a plural society as one comprising two or more social orders in one political unit. Here there is no 'common will' except when there is aggression from outside. Each culture retains its food, values, language and customs. Such differentiation is divisive as it represents ethnocentric forces that are centrifugal in nature. When such differences are underlaid by differences in the standard of living and economic activities, the chances for conflict increase, especially if the differences are conspicuous. The next section will outline these differences.

Ethnic differences after thirty years of development

By international standards, the Gini coefficient in Singapore is low at 0.432 (Department of Statistics 1992b), but it is a general statistic that hides many ethnic differences. Some studies have narrowed the measurement of social class in Singapore to three indices: educational attainment, occupational status and income (Chen 1973; Quah *et al.* 1991). We will explore

Table 11.1 Resident private households by monthly household income from work and ethnic group of head of household, 1990 (%)

Monthly Household Income (S$)	Ethnic Group of Head				
	Total	Chinese	Malay	Indian	Others
Below 1000	16.0	15.7	17.0	16.7	16.6
1000 – 1499	13.6	12.8	18.7	14.4	10.8
1500 – 1999	13.5	12.7	18.3	14.2	9.3
2000 – 2999	20.1	19.6	23.4	21.6	16.4
3000 – 3999	13.0	13.3	11.6	13.0	11.8
4000 – 4999	8.2	8.6	5.6	7.4	8.9
5000 & over	15.6	17.3	5.4	12.7	26.2
Average ($)	3076	3213	2246	2859	3885

Source: Department of Statistics, *Singapore Census of Population* 1990, Statistical Release No. 2, 1992, p.8

these with other indicators to show the extent of inequalities between ethnic groups which serve as impediments to development.

Relative poverty in South-east Asia tends to be associated with ethnic differentiation whereby one group with access to productive resources tends to multiply wealth faster and easier than other ethnic groups (Lee 1976; Evers 1980; Higgott and Robison 1985; Dwyer 1990). Income can be used as a measure of relative poverty, albeit not a very accurate one. The monthly household income from work is given in Table 11.1. It is evident that in 1990 Malays had the highest proportion of households earning less than S$1500 per month (35.7 per cent compared to 31.1 per cent Indians and 28.5 per cent Chinese). In contrast, those with over S$5000 were mainly the Others group (26.2 per cent), the Chinese (17.3 per cent), and the Indians (12.7 per cent). Only 5.4 per cent of Malays belonged to this income category. The average household income was S$3213 for the Chinese, S$2859 for the Indians and S$2246 for the Malays. Malays also had lower income per capita as their household size was on the average larger at 4.7 in comparison to 4.2 for the Chinese and Indians. Seventeen per cent of Malays had three or more generations in the same household compared to 13 per cent for Chinese and Indians (Department of Statistics 1992a; 1992b).

Home ownership is encouraged in Singapore, and 85 per cent of the population live in public-housing flats built by the Housing Development Board (HDB): 96 per cent of Malays live in HDB flats compared to 83 per cent of the Chinese and 83 per cent of the Indians (Table 11.2). The proportion of Chinese in private houses (7.7 per cent) or condominiums (4.6 per cent) is higher than Malay proportions (1.2 per cent for houses and 0.4 per cent for private flats) (Department of Statistics 1992a; 1992b). More

Table 11.2 Selective ethnic stratification indicators, 1990 (%)

Indicators	Chinese	Malay	Indian	Others	Total
DWELLING TYPE (Households)					
HDB Flats	83.2	96.6	83.7	57.7	84.6
1 & 2 room	8.0	7.1	12.6	4.8	8.1
3 room	33.7	49.7	31.5	19.1	35.4
4 room & above	40.8	39.7	38.6	33.0	40.4
Others	0.7	0.1	1.0	0.8	0.7
Private Houses	7.7	1.2	7.4	17.3	7.0
Condominiums and Private Flats	4.6	0.4	3.2	17.0	4.1
EDUCATION					
No Formal Education/ Incomplete Primary	32.0	30.7	27.8	15.6	31.4
Completed Primary/ Incomplete Secondary	27.7	38.5	34.7	28.9	29.6
Secondary	24.3	25.8	25.2	32.1	24.7
Upper Secondary (Including Polytechnic)	10.9	4.4	8.3	13.8	9.9
University	5.1	0.6	4.1	9.6	4.4
OCCUPATIONAL STATUS[1]					
Employers	4.5	0.4	3.7	5.0	
Own Account Workers	12.7	3.4	7.7	1.9	
Employees	79.7	95.7	87.7	93.0	
Unpaid Family Workers	3.1	0.5	0.9	0.1	
OCCUPATION[2]					
Professional and Technical Workers	17.6	10.0	12.0	9.2	15.6
Administrative and Managerial Workers	9.6	0.9	5.5	8.6	8.2
Clerical Workers	14.0	15.8	12.2	2.3	13.5
Sales and Service Workers	14.0	14.0	12.9	2.8	13.4
Agricultural Workers and Fishermen	0.4	0.3	–	–	0.3
Production Related Workers	38.4	56.0	51.3	75.2	43.5
Not Classifiable	6.0	3.0	6.1	1.9	5.5

[1]1980 figures, taken from Quah *et al.*, 1991, p.149
[2]The data were based on a 10% sample of census data

Source: Compiled from Department of Statistics, *Singapore Census of Population*, Advanced Data Release and Statistical Releases Nos 1–3, 1992–3

details of this aspect of inequalities will be outlined when housing policies are discussed.

Education is an important dimension of social mobility in Singapore. Meritocracy is the basis for socio-economic furtherance. Although one may be born economically and financially more disadvantaged, it has always been the philosophy of the government that all children must be given an equal opportunity to 'make good' through education. Education represents the key to better opportunities. Formal education credentials provide the means to the differential allocation of jobs and therefore income (Quah 1991). Hence, it is a good measure to use to gauge mobility. Unfortunately, educational differences tell the same story: 5 per cent of Chinese attained university education compared to only 0.6 per cent of Malays and 4.1 per cent of Indians (Table 11.2) (Department of Statistics 1993).

Class cleavages within ethnic groups are also evident by ownership of productive resources. In 1980, 96 per cent of Malays were employees and only 0.4 per cent employers. There were also more entrepreneurs and risk-takers among the Chinese (4.5 per cent) and the Indians (3.7 per cent) (Table 11.2); (Chiew 1991). By occupation, in 1990, 56 per cent of Malays were production and transport equipment operators and labourers; 15.8 per cent were clerical workers and 14 per cent sales and service workers. The Chinese and Indians had far more professionals, technicians, administrators, executives and managers.

These inequalities between the ethnic groups can become areas of contention. Hence, Prime Minister Goh Chok Tong has stated many times that Singaporeans must lift their sights to 'national' rather than ethnic issues (*The Straits Times*, 6 June 1993):

> Malay Singaporeans, like other Singaporeans, will have to worry about basic issues, like making a living, and how to sustain progress in the light of challenging regional and global developments. These issues will affect the well-being of your community. Your community's problems cannot be resolved in isolation. They can only be resolved in the context of the nation, and after overriding national interests have been resolved.

Singapore's population policy

One outcome of the successful story of Singapore's development policy is a declining birth rate which causes concern because of manpower needs. Since achieving nationhood, the Total Fertility Rate (TFR) has fallen from 4.66 in 1965 to 1.8 in 1988 (Department of Statistics 1990). For quite a while, Singapore has been the most developed country in the South-east Asian region. To maintain her competitive edge, she must regenerate herself or face the economic challenges posed by the larger populations and rich natural resources of her neighbours such as Indonesia and Malaysia which are growing rapidly themselves.

The population size of Singapore is 2.7 million (Singaporeans and Permanent Residents only) with an average annual growth rate of 1.7 per cent. The TFR began falling in the 1950s and went as low as 1.4 in 1986 before settling at 1.8 in 1989 (Department of Statistics 1990). The reasons for the decline are many: later age of first marriage for females, a higher female labour force participation rate, changing attitudes toward marriage and a family, a higher cost of living etc. These are socio-economic changes that cannot be reversed, therefore complicating efforts to change reproductive behaviour to the opposite pronatal trend.

Just like the inequalities addressed above, the population growth pattern of Singapore is also unequal. The TFR for the Chinese fell from 3.03 in 1970 to 1.88 in 1988. Malay TFR also fell from 3.5 to 2.31 and Indian from 3.19 to 2.19. While the Malays and Indians border close to replacement, the Chinese have fallen well below. While Malay mean age at first marriage of brides was 21 in 1990, Chinese mean age at first marriage was 23 and Indians 22 years. The later age will reduce the natural fertility period, thereby leading to lower reproduction. In combination with a higher labour force participation among Chinese women, the mean number of children born is not likely to go up (Department of Statistics 1990; 1992a).

The age pyramids of the various ethnic groups in Singapore are typical of LDCs with a characteristic pyramid-shape for the Malays but less so for the other races. The total age dependency ratio defined as total persons aged below 15 and 60 and above to total persons 15–59 dropped for the Chinese from 54 per 100 in 1980 to 46 per 100 in 1990 (Department of Statistics 1992a). The Malay ratio remained unchanged at 56 per 100 and the Indians increased from 46 to 50 per 100. While the burden of the Malays is with younger people, for the other races it is with older people. What the pyramids imply for the population is that the propensity to grow in numbers is higher for the Malays than for the other ethnic groups.

The differential fertility rates among the ethnic groups are in some respects the outcome of higher education. This point was first raised by the then Prime Minister Lee Kuan Yew in 1983. He noted an asymmetric procreation pattern in which secondary- and tertiary-educated women failed to reproduce themselves while those with less education reproduced two to three times more (Yap 1992). Moreover, better-educated women were less likely to marry down, allegedly leaving the pool of talented genes diminished. Ten years later in 1993, Prime Minister Goh Chok Tong noted a worsening of this trend. There has been a rise in the number of single women *and* men who are above 35 years of age. More marriages are also ending up in divorce and married women are having fewer children. Women with no formal education are producing 2.9 times more children than those women with tertiary education. While not denying that nurture plays a part in developing intelligent children, he did not eradicate the role played by nature (*The Straits Times* 14 June 1993).

The new population policy and its implications

The new population policy of 1987 was a package that consisted of new policies as well as a relaxation of the old ones. Its aim was to encourage more births, especially for those who can afford it. Called the 'Have three or more if you can afford it' policy, it was a departure from the previous 'Stop at two' policy. The new population policy reflected the government's concern for the negative replacement rate and the rapidly aging population. The highly controversial point raised in 1983 by the Prime Minister that a child's intelligence is inherited and is linked to the mother's educational attainment reflects the government's concern for the danger that population decline poses to manpower needs in the country, especially a *quality* pool of labour that can meet the Second Industrial Revolution (Rigg 1988). Thus, financial and other incentives given to the first two children were extended to a third and sometimes fourth child.

The changes included the following:

1. Enhanced child relief up to the fourth child but the mother must have at least three 'O' level passes; a S$20 000 tax rebate for a third child born after 1 January 1987; delivery and hospital expenses incurred for a fourth child can also be offset against the parent's earned income.
2. Priority for a place in primary schools was extended to include a third child.
3. A woman can take up to four years' unpaid leave to look after her child, regardless of birth order.
4. One week's unrecorded leave is given for every sterilization but only for those with no 'O' level passes; cash incentives are given to those lesser-educated, low-income parents who undergo sterilization after one or two children. A child will not lose his/her priority stage in placement into primary school if his/her parent who wants sterilization does it after the fourth or subsequent child. Compulsory pre-sterilization counselling must take place before it can be done.
5. Similarly pre- and post-abortion counselling must be given to women with fewer than three children and with some secondary-level education.
6. A childcare subsidy of S$130 a month to working mothers for each of their first three children in approved childcare centres.

7. Families with a third child born after 1 January 1987 and who apply for larger-sized HDB flats will have their applications backdated three years so that their waiting time to get the flat is significantly reduced. Those who wish to move to the private sector can sell their existing HDB flats in the open market even if they have not lived there for five years, the normal qualifying time.
8. Women officers in the civil service with a child under six can convert to part-time work for a period not exceeding three years.
9. Civil servants can have up to five days of unrecorded leave to look after sick children.

Implicit in the new population policy is the idea that lower-educated and poorer income groups should not have large families. This has ethnic overtones. In the 1990 census, it was mainly the Malays who did not complete their secondary education (38.5 per cent compared to 27.7 per cent for Chinese), and the Malay proportion with pre-university, polytechnic or tertiary education was far less than the other racial groups (Table 11.2). It was also the Malay households who comprised the bulk of those earning less than S$1500 a month. Together with the TFR trends examined earlier, the conclusion that can be drawn is that the Chinese are encouraged to have more children than the Malays.

This elitist viewpoint may not necessarily apply only to the Chinese, although the statistics suggest this to be a foregone conclusion. The elitism was given a rationale by the Prime Minister (*The Straits Times* 14 June 1993):

> If you don't have a balance (in the fertility between low and high educated women), those at the bottom will not have jobs created for them by those at the top of the society. In the 21st century, bear in mind that the lower skilled jobs will move to other countries like China, India and Indonesia. If you don't have the skills in the future, you will be left without jobs. So this is a big problem.

How successful has the new population policy been? This review uses some measures to answer this question (see also Drakakis-Smith *et al.* 1993). First, yearly vital statistics show signs of concern for the Chinese population. Births are favoured in certain zodiac years e.g. 1988, the dragon year and 1990, the horse year (Table 11.3). Other than that, Chinese are still producing below replacement rate. The figures also show that the Malays exceed the Chinese in third and fourth-order births, regardless of the education level of the mother (Table 11.4)

Despite the incentives available from the New Population Policy, there have been no changes because new social values and life-styles are difficult to reverse. Where once the government could persuade the people to accept policies for the common good of their country, with development it is now difficult for people to accept changes which may jeopardize their

Table 11.3 Crude birth rates for the three main ethnic groups, 1965–91

	Chinese	Malay	Indian
1965	27.3	39.7	32.6
1970	21.8	23.5	21.9
1975	17.7	16.9	15.6
1980	16.2	18.9	18.6
1985	15.0	21.3	19.9
1986	12.9	21.0	19.3
1987	14.8	23.7	19.2
1988	18.6	24.9	20.3
1989	15.5	25.9	20.0
1990	16.6	25.9	20.5
1991	15.4	25.1	19.2

Source: Compiled from various years of *Report on Registration of Birth and Deaths, Singapore*

Table 11.4 Live births by education qualification and ethnic group of mother and birth order, 1990

Education Qualification of Mother	Malay				
	First	Second	Third	Fourth	Fifth & above
No Qualification	24.6	27.2	28.0	12.9	7.3
Primary	30.9	31.1	25.5	9.1	3.4
Secondary	40.2	32.9	20.6	4.8	1.5
Upper Secondary	41.4	31.3	20.7	5.1	1.1
	Chinese				
No Qualification	31.9	36.7	23.8	6.1	1.5
Primary	39.1	38.5	18.6	3.2	1.2
Secondary	47.7	37.1	13.5	1.5	0.2
Upper Secondary	47.6	37.3	13.0	2.0	0.1
University	50.0	34.5	12.8	2.4	0.3

Source: National Registration Department, *Report on Registration of Births and Deaths, Singapore*, 1990, National Registration Board, Singapore, 1990, p.47

life-styles. Singaporeans do not see it as their national duty to reproduce as the cost of raising a child is expensive today. The policies themselves have been giving confusing signals: e.g. while women are encouraged to procreate, they are also encouraged to go out to work. These two roles are incompatible (for some debate see Wong 1979; Mason and Palan 1981; Standing 1983; Oppong 1983). When the foreign-worker levy was raised from S$200 to $300 a month in order to control the number of foreign maids in the country, mothers complained of the double standards of the government (*The Straits Times* 31 March 1991; 20 February 1992). The lack of childcare centres also made it difficult for women to continue working. In Singapore, the nuclear family has come to stay. Gone are the days when grandparents and other members of an extended household can help in child-raising. In the Malay community where communal ties are stronger than the Chinese, large-sized families are still feasible as extended households are more common among them. This is not so for the Chinese.

There is yet another implication of the New Population Policy regarding foreign labour. There are 200 000 guest workers in Singapore, many of them coming from Thailand, the Philippines, Malaysia, India and, to a lesser extent, Indonesia. They are mainly unskilled labour in the construction industry or those who work as domestic help. It is not uncommon to find the construction workers housed at the building sites or in rented houses in private housing estates, sometimes as many as 20 in a three-bedroom house. Complaints have been voiced against the foreign workers as being noisy and 'overtaking' the walkways and certain shopping centres on weekends. Residents of private estates have also complained about the cramped conditions under which the foreign workers live and the resulting untidiness which has been described as 'unaesthetic'.

While there may be prejudice against the foreigners by locals, the social cost of having so many foreign workers in Singapore is something of which the government is aware. There are strict laws regarding foreign workers. Foreign domestic workers are not permitted more than two contracts with the same employer, and each household is permitted only one domestic help (there are some case-by-case exceptions). In addition, all employers have to pay a bond to employ foreign workers, the minimum of which is S$5000. Illegal workers can be caned, fined and face imprisonment, and so can employers of such illegal workers.

Although there is a distinction between 'them and us', so long as the numbers of workers do not escalate beyond control, it is unlikely that serious negative consequences will follow. None the less, this is a situation that needs to be monitored as international relations are involved.

Public housing and ethnicity in Singapore

The massive scale of public housing in Singapore has ensured a wide-reaching effect of public-housing policy upon the majority of the population in the city state. Since the launching of the public-housing programme in 1960, an increasing proportion of the population has been accommodated in public housing and in 1990, 85 per cent of the households in Singapore were living in public-housing estates.

Apart from solving the housing crisis of the late 1950s and early 1960s, the public-housing programme in Singapore has been a major policy tool in integrating not only the different ethnic groups but also people of different income backgrounds. The success of the public-housing policy lies, according to Willmott (1989, p.589), in first, 'the integration of different ethnic groups by mixing families in high-rise blocks' and second, even more important than the integration of the different ethnic groups, 'the national housing policy provides for citizens of all income levels the opportunity of owning a flat and therefore of having a stake in the country'. On the other hand, likening public housing in Singapore to education, Lim considers that the former has also been a mechanism through which the government has fulfilled a multiplicity of goals – social, economic and political:

> in the early days, compulsory urban resettlement [to public housing estates] provided the PAP with the opportunity of breaking up established and potential opposition electoral communities by dividing up old ethnic, working-class communities for resettlement in dispersed locations. At the same time, the public housing estates, and the new towns of which they were a part, were expected to foster ethnic integration and national identity through the homogenization of life-style and experience in the same neighbourhoods, schools, stores, playgrounds, and so forth (1989, p.183).

To what extent are these favourable interpretations justified, and to what extent has ethnic integration been a guiding principle in the public-housing programme of Singapore? The following sections focuses on the definition of such integration by the HDB and the mechanisms employed to achieve its social and economic objectives.

In the decades since 1960, when it was established, the HDB has evolved from providing affordable homes for the city-state's squatters, slum dwellers and such low-income groups to becoming a major developer of profit-making housing for middle-income groups (Low 1985; Pugh 1989). While the types of housing provided by the HDB have increased in terms of their range, the emphasis of its policy has been a homeowning society. 'The fundamental aim of the present government from the inception of its public housing programme has been the creation of a nation whose people have homes they are proud to call their own. The underlying philosophy is that if one owns an asset in the country, one would stand to defend it' (Chong *et al.* 1985, p.231).

The encouragement of homeownership represented a change from the HDB's earlier provision of rental housing for low-income families. To promote homeownership, a series of schemes to help finance the purchase of public-housing homes was introduced. Housing loans with loan repayment periods of up to 20 years have been offered. Home-buyers have also been allowed to use part of their compulsory saving in the Central Provident Funds to purchase their homes. Furthermore, the Housing and Development Act also ensures that no homeowner loses his or her flat because of bankruptcy. Such assurance has been reinforced by an insurance scheme to protect the dependents of homeowners in the event of the inability to continue paying instalments on the purchase of their homes.

Equitability in the allocation of public housing has been emphasized in the public-housing programme. This has been ensured through a 'first come, first served' policy in the allocation of public housing flats. Applicants to buy or rent public-housing flats are given numbers which notify them of their turn in the queue or waiting list. Applicants also state their choice in the locations where they wish to buy public-housing flats.

HDB has aimed spatially to 'integrate' the different ethnic groups through its allocation policy. The ethnic mix in HDB estates is supposed to reflect that which characterizes the national population's mix of ethnic groups. While not an overt policy in public housing, the spatial integration of the different ethnic groups in Singapore was confirmed by the former minister of national development some years ago. According to the official statement,:

> The massive public housing effort gave us the opportunity to mix the population. We made sure that every HDB new town and estate had a balanced mix of racial groups. Community facilities were built in every housing estate to meet the diverse needs of the ethnic groups who were resettled from their traditional areas. Community organisations . . . . brought together local leaders of different racial and social backgrounds. These leaders were able to see the needs of the community as a whole and at the same time appreciate the specific concerns of each racial and social group in the community (*Parliamentary Debates*, Singapore, Official Report, Vol. 52, No. 9.)

Legal confirmation of the role of public housing in ethnic integration came with the introduction of HDB's ethnic integration policy in 1989. This was introduced to address the trend towards 'regrouping' of ethnic groups in specific new towns and public-housing estates to levels higher than the government was prepared to accept. Ethnic regrouping had occurred despite the HDB's allocation policy when the homeowners became eligible to sell their flats or apartments in order to upgrade either to larger apartments or to private housing. Unlike the initial sale of new apartments, which are regulated by HDB, the selling and buying of the so-called 'resale apartments' were less controlled.

Ethnic regrouping was therefore the outcome of locational preferences exercised by people buying resale rather than new public-housing apartments. The new legislation that was introduced and referred to by HDB as the ethnic integration policy was, therefore, intended to stop ethnic regrouping. With this new policy, HDB can disallow the resale of flats to people from ethnic groups which are over-represented in any of the high-rise blocks and neighbourhoods of public-housing estates. The new policy effectively sets quotas on the proportions of each ethnic group allowed in every block and neighbourhood. Ethnicity becomes an eligibility criteria in so far as it can constrain a person from buying or renting a public apartment in a specific location. This means that the home-buyer is obliged to buy an apartment in another location. The quotas on the proportions of different ethnic groups allowed in every block and neighbourhood in public-housing estates have been set using the ethnic composition of the country's population as guides. Some flexibility has, however, been allowed in the implementation of the ethnic quotas.

HDB has claimed that the policy is not discriminatory because all ethnic groups are subject to the quotas. According to HDB's rationale, these quotas have been introduced with the aim of maintaining good and harmonious inter-ethnic relations. Furthermore, public-housing residents who are unable to buy the homes they have selected because of the ethnic quotas have been given recourse to appeal to a committee that has been set up in HDB to give consideration to such cases. Basically, the HDB has not compromised its objective of ensuring equal access to public housing for all ethnic groups. What has been compromised is the exercise of choice by residents in selecting their flats and the locations in which they would like to live. Such a choice has, however, always been limited in the past by HDB's building programme, i.e. the locations where HDB is developing its estates, as well as the ethnic integration policy.

There is, nevertheless, the need for a review by HDB of the impact of its ethnic integration policy on the lower-income residents whose choice in housing would have been limited already by economic means. HDB needs to recognize that the exercise of locational choice by residents is influenced by the need for familial support in childcare and the care of the elderly particularly among lower-income residents. The greater proportion of the ethnic minority groups in these lower-income brackets makes it all the more important for HDB to assess the implications arising from the implementation of ethnic quotas.

Impact and implications

In the 1990 census, the comparison of the different ethnic groups in terms of types of dwelling shows that the largest group in public housing are Malays. The proportion of Malays in public housing exceeds the proportion of the Singaporean population in such types of dwellings. Similarly, there is also a higher proportion of ethnic minority groups, Malays and Indians, in the smaller public-housing apartments, i.e. the one-, two- and three-room apartments (Table 11.2). Other economic indicators can explain the difference in types of housing among the ethnic groups. Such indicators as income levels and education backgrounds account for the lag in economic well-being that is evident among the different ethnic groups. The gap in public housing is, however, less evident mainly because the proportions of Chinese, Malays and Indians in the larger apartments are more or less similar (Table 11.2).

Overall improvements in housing conditions are evident from a comparison of status in 1980 and 1990, the two census years. First, housing density has fallen. This is seen in the declining numbers of members in each household during the inter-censal period. Such improvement in housing density must be attributed to demographic changes: the small family sizes and the predominance of the nuclear family unit. The proportion of one-family households rose from 81 per cent in 1980 to 84 per cent in 1990. There was a corresponding fall in the proportion of two-or-more family households from 10.8 per cent to 6.7 per cent.

The mean household size decreased from 4.9 persons per household in 1980 to 4.2 persons per household in 1990. Among Chinese households alone, the decline in this inter-censal period was from 4.8 to 4.2 persons per household. Similarly, household sizes among the Malays fell from 5.5 to 4.7 persons per household in the same period. Among the Indians, there were 4.3 persons per household in 1980 compared to 4.2 persons in 1990. Homeownership levels also improved among the different ethnic groups. The greatest increase in level of homeownership has been among Malays.

Besides the increase in the levels of homeownership, there has also been upward movement or upgrading through shifts to larger public-housing apartments and from public to private housing. The growth in proportion of households living in public housing has been mirrored in all the different ethnic groups. Where 68.5 per cent of households were living in public housing in 1980, the proportion had increased to 84.6 per cent in 1990. Upgrading to larger apartments applied similarly to all of the ethnic groups.

The proportion of households in private housing has, however, increased only among the Chinese households. Among the other ethnic groups, the proportion of households living in private houses and apartments has declined between 1980 and 1990. While the increase in the proportion of private-housing dwellers among Chinese households has been marginal, from 11.4 per cent to 11.7 per cent, it is still significant that there has been a rise in the proportion compared to the other ethnic groups.

The changes in housing conditions between 1980 and 1990 show that public-housing provision has been reasonably equitable in terms of the accommodation of different ethnic groups. Emerging differences among the ethnic groups in the patterns of upgrading of housing, however, would be of concern to policy-makers. This would be particularly the case if the trends continued and differences among the different ethnic groups widened further in the future. Overall, however, housing policy has contributed towards stability in inter-ethnic relations over the last two decades or so. While the spatial integration of the different ethnic groups in public-housing estates has not, strictly speaking, promoted social integration among the different ethnic groups (Tai 1988), it has encouraged increasing levels of casual neighbouring activities among public-housing residents (Khoo 1981; Wong *et al.* 1985). In observing that closer relationships existed in the time before the public-housing programme was launched by HDB, there is nevertheless the concession that 'the children will play together in the void decks [ground floors of high-rise apartment blocks left void for throughways, breezeways and social gatherings] and develop friendships from childhood that will be reinforced in integrated schools' (Willmott 1989, p.589). The major implication is that HDB policy on inter-ethnic relations would at best, be expected to wield only limited influence, reinforcing broader social trends already underway.

Conclusion

The development achieved by Singapore in the past 30 years has been made possible by the subsuming of ethnic goals by national interests. In being non-assimilationist in its development programme, the government has been able to tide over possible inter-ethnic conflict. The population and housing policies indicate a proactive position on the part of the government to deal with new class inequalities in the more affluent society in which Singaporeans find themselves. In particular, there is an awareness that the larger-sized households of the Malays and their higher fertility would slow down their rise to a higher per capita income. This has implications for social mobility, such as upgrading to private houses and condominiums, even if many have already upgraded to larger-sized public-housing apartments.

Possible conflicts in the future may come not from ethnic diversity as such but from newly formed class inequalities that overlay ethnic differentiation. As these manifest themselves more and more, they will have to be addressed before the disparities become political issues. The growth of class cleavages is insidious. Housing is an area where the potential for class distinctions is possible. Although upgrading and home-ownership has gone up for all the ethnic groups in Singapore, the Malays still dominate the smaller one- two- and three-room public flats. In contrast, many Chinese have upgraded to private housing, especially two- or three-bedroom condominiums. This was made possible by the narrowing of the price gap between the upper end of public housing and the lower end of private housing over the last five years or so. This phenomena will serve to increase the correlation between class distinctions and ethnicity.

Also outlined above have been the occupational and educational differences between the Malays and Chinese. While the Chinese dominate white-collar and the upper levels of blue-collar jobs, the Malays still prevail in the lower echelons of industry and the service sector. The difference in wages is evidence of current class distinctions, but it will also serve to perpetuate these differences because, in the final outcome, the Malays' access to productive resources will always be lower (even upon retirement) because of their smaller contributions to the Central Provident Fund (CPF). This is important because the CPF can be used to purchase an array of things in Singapore: e.g. a house, shares in blue-chip companies and insurance. By itself, it therefore represents a means to multiply personal resources.

Some attempt is being made to overcome these differences. Self-help organizations such as MENDAKI, CDAC and SINDA try to reduce the gap between upper and lower incomes through programmes such as financial help or education. In particular, education is conceived as a means to escape the poverty trap. It is apparent that the approach adopted by the government is still very much non-assimilationist in nature. Organizations such as MENDAKI and CDAC are ethnic-based. The government does not influence the course of ethnic relations save for the maintenance of law and order and religious freedom. The efforts to reduce the income and class gaps are therefore largely based on the formula that has worked for the last 30 years. It has served well in establishing stability in ethnic relations and hopefully it will continue to do so for the future.

References

Anand, S. (1983) *Inequality and Poverty in Malaysia: Measurement and Decomposition*, Oxford University Press, New York.

Arief, S. and J.K. Sundaram (eds) (1983) *The Malaysian Economy and Finance*, Rosecons, East Balmain, NSW.

Chan, H.C. (1971) *The Politics of Survival, 1965–67*, Oxford University Press, Singapore.

Chen, P. (1973) *Social Stratification in Singapore*, Department of Sociology Working Paper No. 12, University of Singapore, Singapore.

Chen, P. (1983) *Singapore Development Policies and Trends*, Oxford University Press, Singapore.

Chiew, S.K. (1991) 'Ethnic Stratification' in S. Quah *et al.* (eds), *Social Class in Singapore*, Times Academic Press, Singapore, 138–82.

Chong, K.C., Y.F. Tham and S.K. Shium (1985) 'Housing Schemes: Policies and Procedures' in A.K. Wong and S.H.K. Yeh (eds) *Housing a Nation*, Maruzen, Singapore, 230–62.

Chua, B.H. and E.C.Y. Kuo (1991) *The Making of a New Nation: Cultural Construction and National Identity in Singapore*, Department of Sociology Working Paper No. 104, National University of Singapore, Singapore.

Department of Statistics, 1990, *Yearbook of Statistics*, Singapore.

Department of Statistics, 1991, *Census of Population 1990: Advanced Data Release*, Singapore.

Department of Statistics, 1992a, *Singapore Census of Population 1990*, Statistical Release No. 1, Singapore.

Department of Statistics, 1992b, *Singapore Census of Population 1990*, Statistical Release No. 2, Singapore.

Department of Statistics, 1993, *Singapore Census of Population 1990*, Statistical Release No. 3, Singapore.

Drakakis-Smith, D.W., E.F. Graham, P. Teo and G.L. Ooi (1993) 'Singapore: Reversing the Demographic Transition to Meet Labour Needs', *Scottish Geographical Magazine*, 109(3), 152–63.

Dwyer, D. (1990) *Southeast Asian Development: Geographical Perspectives*, Longman, Essex.

Evers, H.D. (ed.) (1980) *Sociology of Southeast Asia: Readings on Social Change and Development*, Oxford University Press, Kuala Lumpur.

Furnivall, J.S. (1980) 'Plural societies' in H.D. Evers (ed.), *Sociology of Southeast Asia: Readings on Social Change and Development*, Oxford University Press, Kuala Lumpur, 86–96.

Hashim, W. (1983) *Race Relations in Malaysia*, Heinemann, Kuala Lumpur.

Hassan, R. (ed.) (1976) *Singapore: Society in Transition*, Oxford University Press, Kuala Lumpur.

Higgott, R. and R. Robison (eds) (1985) *Southeast Asia: Essays in the Political Economy of Structural Change*, Routledge and Keagan Paul, London.

Hua, W.Y. (1983) *Class and Communalism in Malaysia: Politics in a Dependent Capitalist State*, Zed Books, London.

Khoo, C.K. (1981) *Census of Population 1980 Singapore*, Release No. 6, Department of Statistics, Singapore.

King, V.T. and M.J.G. Parnell (eds) (1990) *Margins and Minorities: The Peripheral Areas and Peoples of Malaysia*, Hull University Press, Hull.

Lee, E. (1991) *The British as Rulers: Governing Multiracial Singapore, 1867–1914*, Singapore University Press, Singapore.

Lee, S.A. (1976) 'The Economic System' in R. Hassan (ed.), *Singapore: Society in Transition*, Oxford University Press, Kuala Lumpur, 3–29.

Lee, Y.L. (1982) *Southeast Asia: Essays in Political Geography* Singapore University Press, Singapore.

Lim, K.P., H.P. Moey, K.T. Gran, K.H. Lim, S. Seow and G.C. Lee (1985) 'HDB and its residents', in A.K. Wong and S.H.K. Yeh, (eds), *Housing a Nation*, Maruzen, Singapore.

Lim, L.Y.C. (1989) 'Social welfare' in K.S. Sandhu and P. Wheatley (eds), *Management of Success: The Moulding of Modern Singapore*, Institute of Southeast Asian Studies, Singapore, 171–97.

Low, L. (1985) 'The Financing Sector in the Public Sector in Singapore,' *Bulletin for International Fiscal Documentation*, 39, 148–65.

Low, L. and M.H. Toh (eds) (1992) *Public Policies in Singapore: Changes in the 1980s and Future Signposts*, Times Academic Press, Singapore.

Mason, K. and V.T. Palan (1981) 'Female Employment and Fertility in Peninsular Malaysia: the Maternal Role Incompatibility Hypothesis Reconsidered', *Demography*, 18 (4), 549–75.

Neville, W. (1969) 'The Distribution of Population in the Post-war Period' in J.B. Ooi and H.D. Chaing (eds), *Modern Singapore*, University of Singapore, Singapore, 52–68.
Ooi, J.B. and H.D. Chiang (eds) (1969) *Modern Singapore*, University of Singapore, Singapore.
Oppong, C. (1983) 'Women's Roles, Opportunity Costs and Fertility' in R.A. Bulatao and R.D. Lee (eds), *Determinants of Fertility in Developing Countries*, Vol. 1, Academic Press, New York, 547–89.
Pugh, C. (1989) 'The Political Economy of Public Housing' in K.S. Sandhu and P. Wheatley (eds), *Management of Success: The Moulding of Modern Singapore*, Institute of Southeast Asian Studies, Singapore, 833–59.
Quah, J. (ed.) (1990) *In Search of Singapore's National Values*, Times Academic Press, Singapore.
Quah, S. (1991) 'Education and Social Class in Singapore' in S. Quah *et al.* (eds), *Social Class in Singapore*, Times Academic Press, Singapore, 38–73.
Quah, S., S.K. Chiew, Y.C. Ko and S.M. Lee (eds) (1991) *Social Class in Singapore*, Times Academic Press, Singapore.
Rigg, J. (1988) 'Singapore and the Recession of 1985', *Asian Survey*, 28 (3), 340–452.
Robison, R., K. Hewison and R. Higgott (1987) *Southeast Asia in the 1980s: The Politics of Economic Crisis*, Allen and Unwin, Sydney.
Sandhu, K.S. and P. Wheatley (eds) (1989) *Management of Success: The Moulding of Modern Singapore*, Institute of Southeast Asian Studies, Singapore.
Snodgrass, D.R. (1980) *Inequality and Economic Development in Malaysia*, Oxford University Press, Kuala Lumpur.
Standing, G. (1983) 'Women's Work Activity and Fertility' in R.A. Bulatao and R.D. Lee (eds), *Determinants of Fertility in Developing Countries*, Vol. 1, Academic Press, New York, 517–46.
Tai, C.L. (1988) *Housing Policy and High-Rise Living*, Chopmen, Singapore.
Willmott, W.E. (1989) 'Emergence of Nationalism' in K.S. Sandhu and P. Wheatley (eds), *Management of Success: The Moulding of Modern Singapore*, Institute of Southeast Asian Studies, Singapore, 578–98.
Wong, A.K. (1979) 'Women's Status and Changing Family Values: Implications of Maternal Employment and Educational Attainment' in E.C.Y. Kuo and A.K. Wong (eds), *The Contemporary Family in Singapore*, Singapore University Press, Singapore, 40–61.
Wong, A.K., G.L. Ooi, and R.S. Ponniah (1985) 'Dimensions of HDB Community' in A.K. Wong and S.H.K. Yeh (eds), *Housing a Nation*, Maruzen, Singapore, 455–95.
World Bank (1991) *World Development Report 1991*, Oxford University Press, New York.
Yap, M.T. (1992) 'Population Policy' in L. Low and M.H. Toh (eds), *Public Policies in Singapore: Changes in the 1980s and Future Signposts*, Times Academic Press, Singapore, 127–43.

Part V

Conclusion

12 Ethnicity, development and . . . geography

David Drakakis-Smith

Defining the concepts

One feature which has emerged in almost all the chapters in this volume is the centrality of space to the various discussions, whether written by geographers or not. This final chapter attempts to tease out a little more prominently the role of the spatial dimension in the analysis of ethnicity and development. But before we can discuss this relationship we need to discuss what we mean by these two terms. 'Development' initially meant evolution to some finished or complete state, but during the 18th century it became associated with change towards a better or more perfect condition (Estevez 1992). In terms of societal evolution it has become coincidental not only with an historical process but also with deliberate efforts aimed at progress towards specified goals (Thomas 1992). Until the 1950s, this contextual definition of development did not apply to what we now call 'the Third World' (Drakakis-Smith 1993). Indeed, the early incorporation of the term into the lexicon of global economic and social change was in a negative sense when President Truman in his inaugural address of 1949 popularized the term 'underdeveloped' as a description of the newly emerging group of independent nations. This was essentially an attempt to justify a role for the United states in the post-colonial, Cold-War era: to help the 'underdeveloped' countries to achieve the standards of the United States through capitalism rather than communism (Sachs 1992).

Development in the 1950s and 1960s, therefore, became associated with modernization towards the standards of the advanced capitalist nations by the same route (Forbes 1984; Thomas and Potter 1992). It was encapsulated by the 'non-communist' manifesto of Rostow and his 'stages of growth' model (Rostow 1960). Modernization implied technological, economic and social change from a traditional rural-based society to an urban industrial-based economy; and the undisputed measure of this tran-

Ethnicity and Development: Geographical Perspectives. Edited by Denis Dwyer and David Drakakis-Smith.

sition was, and still is for many, GNP per capita. The underlying assumption was that growth, once achieved, would diffuse within society bringing social and political change in its wake. As we know, however, modernization along Western lines has not transformed the Third World, and by the 1970s it became apparent that development ought to encompass more than just economic growth. Perhaps the embodiment of this approach was Dudley Seers (1969) whose human-needs-centred development focused on the following:

- low levels of poverty;
- low unemployment;
- relative equality;
- democratic participation in government;
- national independence in economic and political terms;
- adequate and accessible education.

Subsequent debates over the years have been structured around this conflict between growth and equity as the rationale behind development, although contemporary protagonists would argue that 'their' ideas target both. The World Bank in particular likes to cite the rapidly industrializing economies of Pacific Asia as examples of market-orientated growth with equity (World Bank 1993), although their evidence is less than convincing. Others would point to the structural adjustment programmes of the World Bank in Africa as evidence that economic growth still rides roughshod over social considerations (Riddell 1992; Gibbon *et al*. 1992).

Over the last 25 years, since Seers queried the meaning of development, relatively few additions have been made to his list of concerns (Thomas and Potter 1992). Two of the most notable additions have been the relationships between gender and development (Chant 1992; Momsen and Townsend 1987) and our responsibilities towards the environment, encapsulated by the phrase 'sustainable development' (WCED 1987; Elliott 1994, Adams 1990). As Hettne (Chapter 1) has remarked, however, ethnicity has not featured nearly so prominently, despite an awareness of the prominence of ethnic issues across the world (civil rights in the USA, native peoples, apartheid and the like) and the evidence that ignoring ethnic relations within the development process can tear apart even buoyant economies, such as Yugoslavia or Lebanon.

What do we mean by ethnicity? Hettne is surely correct to ascribe to it a fluidity and elusiveness; indeed, it is a concept often characterized more by its ability to be manipulated and distorted rather than used in more positive ways. Brown (1994, p.xii) thus defines ethnicity as 'one of several forms of association through which individuals pursue interests relating to economic and political advantage'. Within this context there are clearly two dimensions to ethnicity within the context of development. First, it can be seen as primordial, ascriptive and cultural in origin, making people naturally ethnocentric and giving rise to the concept of the plural state in which political stability can only be assured by an authoritarian approach. Second, ethnicity can be viewed as a more unconscious membership of a cultural group the identity of which becomes focused only in response to external threats from other social groups: Hettnes's 'interest group'. As in most instances, however, the situation in the real world is often represented by a combination of these two positions. This is clearly demonstrated in Malaysia (see Chapter 8) where the Malay elite has employed the '*bumiputera*' concept to give Malays an immutable identity with what is after all a colonial political construct. This tenuous position was then used to justify development bias towards the Malays in order to safeguard their 'natural' rights to economic and political power. The fact that such arguments and policies have been manipulated by and for a small Malay elite is another dimension to the *realpolitik* that often complicates theory. As Schlossstein (1991, pp.239–40) has observed, the consequence has been that 'interracial income inequality .... has been replaced by an even wider intra-ethnic inequality, particularly among Malays'. Moreover, as Bujra (1992) points out, ethnicity or tribalism is not fixed and immutable. Change and transformation are and always have been as common to 'traditional' societies as to 'modern' ones. Nevertheless, as Lemon (see Chapter 4) notes, in the pre-colonial world ethnicity was one of the principal foundations on which political entities were created. Unfortunately, colonialism paid little heed to such fundamental local forces when recasting the political map of the world in the 19th and 20th centuries. Physical and ethnic geographies were ignored in the face of the scramble for resources, routeways, markets or the desire simply to deny another colonial power some strategic territory. It is this spatial disjunction between politics and ethnicity which has caused so many problems in the post-colonial world.

And yet it would clearly be foolish to conclude that colonialism was ethnically neutral or unaware. Colonialism was founded on the perceived differences between ethnic or racial groups, not only between black and white but also among the various 'non-white' ethnicities. As Wallerstein (1989) has remarked, ethnicity and race are fluid social constructs that have been constantly redefined within the process of capitalist exploitation. This is clearly evident in the way in which the colonial powers in Asia and Africa encouraged non-indigenous, non-European peoples to take up much of the petty commerce of the colonial city. Despite their varied ethnic and cultural origins, such groups were categorized by deliberately insensitive blanket terminology. Thus, East African 'Asians' comprised a widely heterogenous group 'more culturally divided against itself than against anyone else' (Bujra 1992, p.352). Similarly, the 'Chinese' in South-east Asia were composed of many different linguistic and cultural groups, often keen rivals in the commercial field and also widely different in terms of their roles in the economy (Lubeck 1992). In Malaysia, for example, there was a clear class distinction within the Chinese community between the proletariat and the large-scale business proprietors. In the 1930s these two groups had contrasting ideas as to what they wanted in the context of the struggle for equal rights for immigrant communities. The tin-miners and factory hands wanted better working conditions and increased wages, their employers wanted none of this but were in favour of improved political representation and the rights to land ownership. Needless to say, these divergent positions soon became entrenched in quite different forms of political mobilization. In short, what appeared on the surface to be exclusively an ethnic issue, clearly had expressions of 'class relations of exploitation central to the overall functioning of the colonial economy' (Bujra 1992, p.354).

Such 'colonial' collapsing of ethnic identities into more 'convenient' categories continues today. In Singapore, for example, statistical publications refer simply to Chinese, Indians, Malays and others, despite the wide variety of linguistic, cultural and racial types contained within the first two. Since the 1970s Singapore's Chinese population has been encouraged to 'standardize' itself by, for example, learning and using Mandarin rather than regional dialects (Brown 1994). The very artificiality of these categories assists the government in its goal of relegating ethnic identification and loyalty into a subordinate role *vis-à-vis* the authority of the state (Drakakis-Smith and Graham 1994).

Ethnicity and development theory

Notwithstanding the presence which ethnicity has in the realities of the development process, as Hettne has correctly pointed out, it plays a minor role in most of the major theories of development, being implicitly rather than explicitly used as an explanatory concept, even in the world-system theory associated with Wallerstein (see Taylor 1985). Of course, most development theories and strategies are inherently based on an ethnocentric interpretation of what constitutes development, as discussed earlier. Underdeveloped nations, from their initial 'conceptualization' by President Truman, were expected to strive towards the standards that had been set for them by the developed nations, and by the United States in particular (Sachs 1992). Although development theorists have generally become more sympathetic to voices from the Third World over the years, with the notable exception of the new right (See Toye 1987), there is little indication that priorities have changed, despite Robert Chambers's (1993) encouragement to 'put the last first'. Eurocentrism is still as dominant as ever, whether in the form of the structural adjustment programmes imposed on debt-ridden and loan-desperate nations by the World Bank or the inflexible directives of the Holy See on birth control at the Cairo population conference.

However, in few of these development strategies or theories can ethnicity be said to have been designated a specific role, although in some it had more of an unstated presence. The place of ethnicity, therefore, often has to be clarified before the main conceptual building blocks can be seen to offer some sort of basis for further examination. Such is the case with mode of production analysis (see Forbes 1984; Hettne 1990; Peet 1980), an approach employed by neo-Marxists in the 1970s and 1980s to explain the interaction between pre-capitalist and capitalist systems. In this form of analysis the greatest emphasis is placed on the substructural components, particularly on the social relations of production, in accounting for the dominant–subordinate relationship between the two modes of production. Superstructural elements, including ethnicity and culture, are confined to relatively minor roles.

The superstructure is, however, given greater prominence in other explanations which seek to build on colonial analogies to explain continued exploitation of ethnic groups within individual states. This was, and is, most evident in theories on internal colonialism, many of which were based on the work of Michael Hechter (1975) and his eventual reworking of these ideas into an amended model of ethnic regionalism (Hecter and Levi 1979). Many of the subsequent investigations which purported to employ these concepts were extremely limited in their analysis (for a review see Drakakis-Smith and Williams 1982), restricting their investigations to the extraction of labour power by one mode of production or another. Valid as this is, it tends to mask other forms of exploitation which are more directly linked to culture and ethnicity. One such avenue is the voyeuristic exploitation of cultural values through tourism, for example of 'primitive' native peoples by the dominant mode of production/ethnic group. Almost inevitably this is associated with the specific territory that comprises the habitat of the exploited group, providing it with the spiritual as well as physical necessities of life. Thus, the tourist is invited to see Australian Aborigines in the context of Ayers Rock or Mount Olga, or the Yanomani in their rainforest. But the land has long been usurped by the dominant group which absorbs most, if not all, of the tourist receipts, and the indigenous groups are left with little more than their culture, language and history, most of which are being eroded by assimilationist policies and by contact with tourists (see also Young 1995).

What emerges from this brief review of the place of ethnicity within development theory is a suggestion that its role within the development process can usefully be structured within two perspectives: first within the context of the nation state; and second, as it relates to territoriality. Certainly in relation to the former, some of the attempts to elevate ethnicity above the level of the nation state have tended to become embroiled in rather exaggerated assertions of future global conflict being based on struggles between 'civilizations' (Huntington 1993), suggesting only a short step to star wars! In contrast, and in more realistic mode, territoriality features prominently, consciously or unconsciously, in many of the stronger analyses of the development process (Forbes and Rimmer 1984) and in turn has been identified as a crucial dimension in the emergence of the nation state. These arguments can certainly be seen in operation in Australia where land has been a key component both in the struggle for identity of its Aboriginal people, and in the way in which that ethnic group has been exploited within a system of internal colonialism (Drakakis-Smith 1984). It is to this link between ethnicity, territoriality and the state that the discussion now turns.

Nation, ethnicity and territoriality

There are clearly strong links between the concepts of nation state and ethnicity. Hettne (1993) identifies the 'nation-state project' as a primary goal in the development process and sees the creation of 'a certain degree of cultural homogeneity' as one of the five common objectives of this nation-building process. Indeed, he alleges that 'ethnic conflicts are usually difficult to understand unless put in [this] context' (Hettne 1993, p.127). In similar vein, Brown (1994, p.258) argues that 'ethnic consciousness constitutes an emotionally powerful ideological response to the pattern of insecurities generated by the power structure of the state and therefore that the character of the state constitutes the dominant influence on the character of ethnic politics', illustrating his argument clearly with reference to the wide variety of situations found in South-east Asia. This relationship is, moreover, underpinned by the importance of space or territoriality to both concepts. Brown places territory alongside race, language and religion as one of the principal cultural markers of ethnic identity, while Hettne structures all five of his basic nation-building objectives around the identification, control and development of 'territory'. As Brown (1994, p.20) consequently asserts, 'the community which possesses ethnic consciousness, a unique history and a specific homeland (territory) is deserving . . . . of political autonomy'. It follows, of course, that challenges to the legitimate nation state can be based on exactly the same criteria, as has happened in Eritrea and is happening in Kwa Zulu, for example.

The importance which the state attaches to territoriality varies enormously, as it does its attitude towards managing ethnic diversity. The latter can take the form of overt favouring of one ethnic group (usually but not always the majority), of seeking accommodation between ethnic groups or of attempting to subordinate ethnic identity into a synthetic national ethos, a common will. The last of these can best be accommodated either in a territory with very strong central controls, such as China, or in very constrained spatial circumstances, such as Singapore (note Teo and Ooi's earlier comment in this volume about how racial harmony in Singapore is 'strictly enforced'). Elsewhere neglect of the territorial dimension of ethnicity can give rise to a spatial unevenness in development that fuels ethnic resentment in neglected regions. This has occurred in north-east Thailand where Isan identification with growing poverty and neglect in comparison with the central area has undoubtedly increased political instability in the region (Dixon 1991). However, Isan resentment does not have as firm an ethnic focus since the 'centre' comprises both Thai and Chinese elements. In some circumstances, of course, ethnic and regional associations may be so deep-seated as to constitute an almost permanent challenge to the authority of the nation state, for example in Myanmar, where central control is Burman and where peripheral secessionist movements have distinct ethnic dimension.

The importance of territoriality in ethnic matters is, moreover, an issue which is likely to grow rather than to recede. The reasons for this are not difficult to discern for the world is becoming an increasingly smaller place as modes of transport and communications become more efficient and, more important, cheaper. For several decades, since independence came to the colonial world, populations have become much more mobile within their own countries. Not only has an extensive permanent shift from rural to urban areas occurred, but increasingly long-distance commuting or circulation has expanded, bringing people into the city for several months of the year and yet allowing them to retain a substantial rural, regional and ethnic identity (Prothero and Chapman 1985). The pressures on access to basic needs, which urbanization has intensified, can have adverse effects on ethnic politics. First, they further distract attention and investment which may be ethnically structured (Lowder 1991) from underdeveloped regions; and second, they increase the pressures from ethnic groups for favoured status and treatment in the city.

This situation has become even more intensified in recent years as populations have increasingly moved over international boundaries in search of work, often deliberately encouraged in this by host governments. A good example of this was the creation of the Central African Federation in which the former Southern Rhodesia sought to develop its industries by exploiting Northern Rhodesia's mineral resources and Nyasaland's labour (Drakakis-Smith 1986). As elsewhere, however, recession fuelled resentment and Malawians were soon being repatriated in order to reserve work for Zimbabweans. But ethnic labour movements can also create other types of resentment and the Singapore *Straits Times* has recently published letters from its more affluent citizens complaining that the domestic staff (usually Filipino or Indonesian) being brought by some employers into exclusive sports clubs do not practise the same level of hygiene as the members. Clearly there is an emerging class as well as racist dimension to such remarks. Ironically, a reverse form of resentment is also beginning to occur as professional, managerial and skilled technical labour also becomes more mobile as investment activity from regional multinationals intensifies. In the case of cities, such as Singapore or Kuala Lumpur, this has taken the form of complaints against Japanese salarymen who dominate membership of the burgeoning golf clubs around the major urban centres.

Clearly, increased mobility within and across international boundaries is creating an even more complex relationship between ethnicity and development, and suggests that even closer attention needs to be given to the question of territoriality in the future. Already there are ethnic clusters whose identity springs in part from their very failure to satisfy their territorial aspiration, not just in terms of independence but even in terms of spatial contiguity: both the Palestinians and the Nanyang Chinese in South-east Asia would fall into this category as would the adversaries in the Bosnian conflict.

Finally, although this chapter has stressed the importance of the spatial dimension of the relationship between ethnicity and development, it must be emphasized that it is difficult to separate ethnicity from other facets of the development process such as class, gender or the environment. The importance of the last of these is clearly evident in the continued difficulties facing many indigenous groups living in threatened, fragile environments such as rainforests or semi-desert regions. The recent embittered debate between the Malaysian prime minister and the Swiss activist Bruno Manser on the subject of the organized protests made by the Penan against Japanese logging in Sarawak illustrates a complex ethnocentrism interlaced with many other considerations. Ethnicity must be drawn more extensively into the debate on development but this must not be at the expense of other social, economic or political considerations with which it interacts, nor without considering the specific spatial dimensions of the whole process. It is hoped that this collection of essays has helped move the debate in the desired direction.

References

Adams, W. (1990) *Green Development: Environment and Sustainability in the Third World*, Routledge, London.

Allen, T. and A. Thomas (eds) (1992) *Poverty and Development in the 1990s*, OUP, London.

Brown, D. (1994) *The State and Ethnic Politics in Southeast Asia*, Routledge, London.

Bujra, J. (1992) 'Ethnicity and Class: the Case of East African "Asians" ' in T. Allen and A. Thomas, 1992, 347–61.
Chambers, R. (1983) *Rural Development: Putting the Last First*, Longman, London.
Chant, S. (ed.) (1992) *Gender and Migration in Developing Countries*, Belhaven, London.
Dixon, C.J. (1991) *Southeast Asia in the World Economy*, Blackwell, Oxford.
Drakakis-Smith, D.W. (1984) 'Internal Colonialism and the Geographical Transfer of Value: an Analysis of Aboriginal Australia' in D. Forbes and P.J. Rimmer (eds), 1994, 153–74.
Drakakis-Smith, D.W. (1986) 'Urbanization and Regional Development in Zimbabwe' in N. Thrift and D. Forbes (eds), *The Socialist Third World*, Croom Helm, London, 194–213.
Drakakis-Smith, D.W. (1993) 'Is There Still a Third World', *Chronos*, 1, Kulturgeografiska Inst., Gotheburg University.
Drakakis-Smith, D.W. and E. Graham (1994) 'Shaping the Nation-State: Ethnicity, Class and Population Policy in Singapore', paper presented to the British Society for Population Studies, University of Durham.
Drakakis-Smith, D.W. and S.W. Williams (1982) *Internal Colonialism: Explorations in Search of a Theory*, Monograph No. 2, Developing Areas Research Group, Institute of Bristol Geographers, London.
Elliott, J. (1994) *An Introduction to Sustainable Development*, Routledge, London.
Estevez, G. (1992) 'Development' in G. Sachs, 6–25.
Forbes, D. (1984) *The Geography of Underdevelopment*, Croom Helm, London.
Forbes, D. and Rimmer, P.T. (eds) (1984) *Uneven Development and the Geographical Transfer of Value*, Monograph HG 16, Research School of Pacific Studies, Australia National University, Canberra.
Gibbon, P., Y. Bangura and A. Ofstad (1992) *Authoritarianism, Democracy and Adjustment*, Seminar Proceedings No. 26, Scandinavian Institute for African Studies, Uppsala.
Hechter, M. (1975) *Internal Colonialism: the Celtic Fringe in British National Development 1536–1966*, Routledge and Kegan Paul, London.
Hechter, M. and M.C. Levi (1979) 'The comparative Analysis of Ethnoregional Movements', *Ethnic and Racial Studies*, 2, 260–74.
Hettne, B.C. (1990) *Development Theory and the Three Worlds*, Longman, London.
Hettne, B.C. (1993) 'Ethnicity and Development – an elusive relationship', *Contemporary South Asia*, 2(2), 123–49.
Huntington, S. (1993) 'The Clash of Civilizations', *Foreign Affairs* 73(3), 22–49
Lowder, S. (1991) 'The Context of Urban Planning in Secondary Cities', *Cities*, 8, 54–65.
Lubeck, P.M. (1992) 'Malaysia Industrialization, Ethnic Divisions and the NIC Model: the Limits to Replication' in R. Appelbaum and J. Henderson (eds), *States and Development in the Asian Pacific Rim*, Sage, Newbury Park, 176–98.
Momsen, J. and J. Townsend (eds) (1987) *Geography of Gender in the Third World*, Hutchinson, London.
Peet, R. (1980) *An Introduction to Marxist Theories of Underdevelopment*, Monograph HG14, Australian National University, Canberra.
Prothero, R.M. and M. Chapman (1985) *Circulation in Third World Countries*, Routledge and Kegan Paul, London.
Riddell, J.B. (1992) 'Things Fall Apart Again: Structural Readjustment Programmes in Sub-Saharan Africa', *Journal of Modern African Studies*, 30(1), 53–68.
Rostow, W.W. (1960) *The Stages of Economic Growth: a Non-Communist Manifesto*, Cambridge University Press, Cambridge.

Sachs, G. (ed.) (1992) *The Development Dictionary*, Zed Books, London.
Schlossstein, S. (1991) *Asias New Little Dragons*, Contemporary Books, Chicago.
Seers, D. (1969) 'The Meaning of Development' in D. Lehmann (ed.), *Development Theory: Four Critical Studies*, Cass, London.
Taylor, P. (1985) *Political Geography*, Longman, London.
Thomas, A. (1992) 'Introduction' in T. Allen and A. Thomas (eds), 1992, 116–41.
Thomas, A. and D. Potter (1992) 'Development, Capitalism and the Nation-State' in T. Allen and A. Thomas (eds), 1992, 116–41.
Toye, J. (1987) *Dilemmas of Development*, Blackwell, Oxford.
Wallerstein, E. (1989) 'The Myrdal Legacy: Racism and Underdevelopment as Dilemmas', *Cooperation and Conflict*, 24, 1–18.
WCED (1987) *Our Common Future*, Oxford University Press, Oxford.
World Bank (1993) *East Asian Miracle*, World Bank Research Report, Washington DC.
Young, E. (1995) *Third World in the First*, Routledge, London.

Index

DE PAUL UNIVERSITY LIBRARY
3 0511 00606 1386